POTTERY, POETRY, and PROPHECY

POTTERY, POETRY, and PROPHECY

Studies in Early Hebrew Poetry

DAVID NOEL FREEDMAN

WINONA LAKE, INDIANA
EISENBRAUNS

Library of Congress Catalog Card Number: 80-68378
International Standard Book Number: 0-931464-04-8

ACKNOWLEDGMENTS

Grateful acknowledgment is made to the publishers for permission to reprint the following articles:

"Pottery, Poetry, and Prophecy: An Essay on Biblical Poetry," *Journal of Biblical Literature* 96 (1977) 5-26. The Society of Biblical Literature.

"Prolegomenon" to G. B. Gray, *The Forms of Hebrew Poetry*, reprinted, New York: KTAV, 1972.

"Acrostics and Metrics in Hebrew Poetry," *Harvard Theological Review* 65 (1972) 367-92. The President and Fellows of Harvard College.

"Divine Names and Titles in Early Hebrew Poetry," *Magnalia Dei: The Mighty Acts of God*, ed. by F. M. Cross, et al., 55-107. New York: Doubleday & Co., 1976.

"Early Israelite History in the Light of Early Israelite Poetry," *Unity and Diversity*, ed. by Hans Goedicke and J. J. M. Roberts, 3-35. Baltimore: The Johns Hopkins University Press, 1975.

"Early Israelite Poetry and Historical Reconstructions," *Symposia Celebrating the Seventy-Fifth Anniversary of the Founding of the American Schools of Oriental Research (1900-1975)*, ed. by Frank Moore Cross. Cambridge, MA: American Schools of Oriental Research, 1979.

"Strophe and Meter in Exodus 15," *A Light Unto My Path*, ed. by Howard N. Bream, Ralph D. Heim, and Carey A. Moore. Philadelphia: Temple University Press, 1974.

"The Aaronic Benediction (Numbers 6:24-26)," *No Famine in the Land*, ed. by James Flanagan, et al. The Institute for Antiquity and Christianity, 1975.

"Psalm 113 and the Song of Hannah," *Eretz-Israel* (H. L. Ginsberg Volume), 14 (1975) 56-70.

"The Refrain in David's Lament over Saul and Jonathan," *Ex Orbe Religionum, Studia Geo Widengren Oblata*, 1, 115-26. Leiden: E. J. Brill, 1972.

"The Twenty-Third Psalm," *Michigan Oriental Studies in Honor of George G. Cameron*, ed. by Louis L. Orlin, et al., 139-66. Ann Arbor: Department of Near Eastern Studies, University of Michigan, 1976.

"The Structure of Psalm 137," *Near Eastern Studies in Honor of William Foxwell Albright*, ed. by Hans Goedicke. Baltimore: The John Hopkins University Press, 1971.

"The Structure of Job 3," *Biblica* 49 (1968) 503-8. The Pontifical Biblical Institute.

"Notes and Observations: The Elihu Speeches in the Book of Job," *Harvard Theological Review* 61 (1968) 51-59. The President and Fellows of Harvard College.

"The Broken Construct Chain," *Biblica* 53 (1972) 534-36. The Pontifical Biblical Institute.

"Critical Notes: II Samuel 23:4," *Journal of Biblical Literature* 90 (1971) 329-30. The Society of Biblical Literature.

"Isa 42,13," *Catholic Biblical Quarterly* 300 (1973) 225-26. The Catholic Biblical Association.

"God Almighty in Psalm 78,59," *Biblica* 54 (1973) 268. The Pontifical Biblical Institute.

FOREWORD

The invitation to write an introduction to Noel Freedman's collection of studies in Hebrew poetry has been the occasion for delight, for it is a task which I find most agreeable, and the occasion for temptation, indeed alternate temptations: to praise unreservedly a volume on Hebrew poetry unsurpassed in importance in this generation, or to seize opportunity to put onto paper my side of debates on issues of method and detail which have accumulated in discussion with Freedman over the past three decades.

The first temptation is the stronger. The papers which follow are pioneering studies, fresh and provocative, full of brilliant detail, together yielding major advances in the analysis of Hebrew poetry. Freedman's work shows the stimulus of his teacher W. F. Albright, and one detects on occasion the influence of colleagues, the joint studies with the undersigned, and common researches with Mitchell Dahood. The corpus, however, traces Noel Freedman's own independent development most vividly, and the whole exhibits the integrity of his mature scholarship.

Freedman is moved by symmetries in Hebrew poetry undetected by a previous generation of students, symmetries or rhythms at every level: phonetic, morphological, grammatical, structural in colon, verse, and strophe. He desires as well to provide a scholarly description and notation to Hebrew prosodic canons and techniques more refined and precise than alternate systems afford. He has a sure and instinctive literary feel for his material. His approach to the text may be described as conservative, but is not a mechanical or dogmatic allegiance to the received text. Without unambiguous textual evidence for alternate readings, he generally eschews manipulation or emendation. Similarly he adheres largely to the phonetic and grammatical stage of the language which had evolved when the text was fixed, and then later vocalized by the Massoretes. This procedure is followed despite Freedman's full awareness of the development of the archaic language, its special grammar, vocabulary, and orthography. He begins with Massoretic Hebrew as a methodological stance—to be abandoned if relunctantly—when essential to proper analysis. On the other hand in three of his most important papers, he moves without hesitation from tracing typological sequences in archaic poetry to very bold historical construction.

The second temptation is weaker but I am unable to overcome it entirely: to allude to our perennial debates. I have no doubt that Hebrew poetry, especially archaic poetry, reveals a level of symmetry and repetition inadequately represented by the usual stress or quantitative analyses. Syllable counting has proven a useful technique in isolating metrical structures. Yet this does not mean necessarily that the ancient poet counted syllables. Early

Hebrew poetry was formulaic, I believe, its symmetry in part "prefabricated." Assuming the oral composition of at least the more archaic poetry, I remain doubtful that the poet engaged in "long distance" syllable counting—my scepticism mounting as one moves from verses to strophes to complete poems—and have sought alternate modes of dealing with syllabic and structural symmetry. Similarily I am inclined to prefer more textual and grammatical reconstruction, using at least what data we possess for these tasks. Either approach builds in a percentage of error, to be sure, but I prefer one type of unavoidable error, Freedman another. These are lively issues between us, but they do not call into question the usefulness of the main lines of his investigation.

I am most grateful that these collected papers have been published now in one volume. It will be most useful and convenient to have them at hand in canonical form. As a matter of fact I have long since put them together in loose-leaf format, and can now put aside my dog-eared set of reprints and Xeroxes.

The collection is headed by general and historical studies of the discipline of Hebrew prosody, moves to typological analysis of the corpus of archaic poetry, to special studies, especially structural, of poems or psalms, early and late, and concludes with elegant single observations. It makes an admirable whole.

FRANK MOORE CROSS

Cambridge, Massachusetts
July 13, 1980

PREFACE

The current volume is a collection of articles and essays, practically all of which were published during the 1970's, and which have as their general theme the poetry of the Hebrew Bible. This subject has been a major interest of mine since graduate studies at the Oriental Seminary of The Johns Hopkins University. Early publications in the field, consisting of a series of studies of major poems embedded in the Torah and Former Prophets, were based upon one of two joint doctoral dissertations prepared in collaboration with Frank Moore Cross, now Professor at Harvard University. They belonged to a tradition firmly established by Paul Haupt, the founder of the first graduate department of Semitics in this country, and carried on in bravura style by his student and successor, W. F. Albright. In time the latter's students became teachers, and they and their students, and their students' students, have continued to explore and investigate, analyze and interpret the vast corpus of biblical poetry, and have published their findings and opinions extensively. It is clear that much progress has been made during recent decades, and much more is in sight.

Archaeological discoveries have played a major role in these developments, especially with the decipherment and publication of literary documents in a variety of Semitic languages, including such collecions as those of Nuzi, Mari, and Ebla, but especially the poetic texts of Ugarit from the latter part of the second millennium B.C.E. Equally important has been the intensive study of biblical poetry itself, in terms of structures and patterns, prosodic features, and rhetorical devices. While many basic issues concerning metrical principles and practices, strophic structures, evolutionary indications and directions (and the determination of relative and absolute chronologies), remain open and often highly controverted, it is fair to say that there is a growing consensus on important questions of the antiquity of the tradition and the integrity of the surviving texts, as well as their great value for the interpretation and reconstruction of the historical and spiritual experience of the people which produced and preserved them.

With a more substantial data base from which to evaluate the issues, and new and more effective techniques for examining the poems, we can expect greater gains in the near and more distant future. Perhaps the most important of these will prove to be computer-based research of a mechanical and statistical nature, whereby more ancient and more recent theories can be tested, and material information supplied in unlimited quantity on short notice. Far from displacing original scholarship, computer technology will provide powerful weapons in the scientific assault on the biblical bastion with its unsolved questions and inaccessible secrets, but only for creative and courageous thinkers.

The articles assembled in this book represent the efforts, on a time-available basis, of the past two decades. In this as in many other areas of biblical research, labor is long and arduous, and results often meager and questionable. Even so, it is often worthwhile to report both the process and the end product, if only to warn the unwary of what obstacles lie in the path. One reason for collecting the articles in book form is practical. A number of them have appeared in out-of-the-way places, especially those inevitable and inescapable *Festschriften*, which we all deplore and to which we all contribute, at least partly in the hope that we ourselves will be beneficiaries of the system, a sort of scholarly version of the notorious and delusive chain-letter scam, which seems never to lose its appeal. Another reason is the conviction that the articles in close association reinforce each other, and make up a sum with greater impact than the parts taken separately. There is an obvious danger here, since the arguments are interlocking and the more elaborate the superstructure the more resounding the crash should some serious defect be found in the substructure. But that is a risk we must run some time in our lives, and for me it can hardly be a question of waiting for a propitious moment. The third reason is that this book is intended to hold a place in the field until a more cohesive and comprehensive study of biblical poetry is completed for publication. Many of the ingredients will be found in the present collection: basic philosophy and approach, discussion of methodology and techniques, sequence dating and other chronological considerations, exemplary studies, and the like. A synthetic, carefully reasoned treatment should one day appear, and I hope to complete that within a reasonable period. That is also why it was decided to reprint the articles without revision or alteration (except for removing typographical errors which have been caught in the process of proofreading). Naturally, there are many things which I would now remove, or change; in fact, there are changes from one article to another on the same subject, including some dramatic reversals. Needless to say, some of these are embarrassing, and others are regrettable, but it would be even worse if there were no changes at all. On the one hand, the independent studies of these materials by other scholars, and their responses to proposals in my articles, have had a significant effect, and on the other hand, rethinking the issues and problems occasionally produces better or at least different analyses and evaluations. At least, I hope the changes are for the better.

DAVID NOEL FREEDMAN

Macquarie University
North Ryde, New South Wales
Australia
July 25, 1980

CONTENTS

ABBREVIATIONS

AB	Anchor Bible
*ALQ*²	*The Ancient Library of Qumrân*², Cross
ANET	*Ancient Near Eastern Texts*, Pritchard
ASTI	*Annual of the Swedish Theological Institute*
AYP and *SAYP*	*Studies in Ancient Yahwistic Poetry*, Cross
BA	*Biblical Archaeologist*
BH	*Biblia Hebraica*
CBQ	*Catholic Biblical Quarterly*
CMHE	*Canaanite Myth and Hebrew Epic*, Cross
HTR	*Harvard Theological Review*
HUCA	*Hebrew Union College Annual*
IB	*Interpreter's Bible*
ICC	International Critical Commentary
IDB	*Interpreter's Dictionary of the Bible*
JAOS	*Journal of the American Oriental Society*
JBL	*Journal of Biblical Literature*
JNES	*Journal of Near Eastern Studies*
JPOS	*Journal of the Palestine Oriental Society*
KJV	*King James Version*
LEDEHP	*Linguistic Evidence in Dating Early Hebrew Poetry*, Robertson
LXX	Septuagint
MT	Massoretic Text
RSV	*Revised Standard Version*
SITP	*The Settlement of the Israelite Tribes in Palestine*, Weippert
TWAT	*Theologisches Wörterbuch zum Alten Testament*
VT	*Vetus Testamentum*
YGC	*Yahweh and the Gods of Canaan*, Albright
ZAW	*Zeitschrift für die alttestamentliche Wissenschaft*

POTTERY, POETRY, AND PROPHECY: AN ESSAY ON BIBLICAL POETRY*

POETRY is not only central in the title, but for the study of the Hebrew Bible. There is no intention here of disvaluing the prose of the Bible, which constitutes the first major literary composition in that medium ever produced, so far as I am aware, whether we speak of the so-called Court History and the J source of the Pentateuch of the 10th century B.C., or the composite whole which we may call the Primary History (Genesis through Kings) of the 6th century.[1] The preponderance of prose is even greater in the NT, whether we speak of the narratives of the Gospels and Acts, or the essays on religion and ethics contained in the Epistles.[2] There is little danger that the prose of the Bible will be lost or forgotten, neglected or abandoned by scholars, much less by the vast constituency which holds this literature sacred. On the contrary, the Bible will be read and studied, admired and absorbed, primarily as a prose work in the future as in the past.

The case with the great poetic tradition of the Bible is far otherwise. While particular compositions and certain books of the Bible have always been identified and acknowledged as poetic in form and content, much of the poetry of the Bible has been incorporated into the prose tradition. The rediscovery of the poetry of the prophets is a major contribution of modern scholarship, as is the recognition of the poetic tradition behind the earliest prose narratives.[3] Since some large fraction, perhaps a quarter to a third of the Hebrew Bible, must be reckoned as poetry or poetic in character, just its bulk would demand serious attention, but its quality and difficulty make it even more important. In many respects it is older and more basic than the prose materials; at the same time it is more obscure and challenging. The form and style, the selection

*The Presidential Address delivered 29 October 1976, at the annual meeting of the Society of Biblical Literature, held at Stouffer's Riverfront Towers, Saint Louis, MO.

[1] D. N. Freedman, "The Law and the Prophets," *Congress Volume, Bonn 1962* (VT Sup 9; Leiden: Brill, 1963) 250-65; also "Pentateuch," *IDB* 3 (1962) 711-27.

[2] Nevertheless, there is an important poetic component in the NT, which will be discussed later in the paper.

[3] Bishop Lowth, while not the first to make this observation, nevertheless marked a turning point in the study of the prophetic literature and the poetry of the Bible generally. See G. B. Gray, *The Forms of Hebrew Poetry* (New York: Ktav, 1972; reprint of original edition 1915) 6-7; also my comments, "Prolegomenon," to Gray's volume (p. viii).

and order of words, all play a vital role in conveying content, meaning, and feeling. In poetry, the medium and message are inseparably intertwined to produce multiple effects at different levels of discourse and evoke a whole range of responses: intellectual, emotional, and spiritual.

In the present paper, I intend to discuss two aspects of Hebrew poetry in the light of recent research and discussion: (1) its character, including (a) definition; (b) sequence-dating; (c) forms and structures; (2) its function as the vehicle of revelation, including (a) pagan patterns: myth, epic, ritual, oracle; (b) Israelite adaptation: echoes and remnants of epic traditions, surviving poems; (c) continuation: worship (Psalms), wisdom (Proverbs, Job), oracles (Prophets).

I. *The Character of Hebrew Poetry*

(a) *Definition.* Poetry is well delimited by its differences from prose. While there is an area of overlap, generally it is not difficult to distinguish the two without precisely defining the difference. Since the distinction is often quantitative rather than qualitative, and in terms of degree rather than kind, it may be asked why it is important to draw the line at all and try to separate one corpus from the other. The answer is that in spite of some blending of types and blurring of the lines of demarcation, prose and poetry are basically two different ways of using language. Each has its own rules of operation, and it is obligatory to understand each category according to its own pattern, even if the dividing line is not always certain.

We have devised recently a mechanical test to separate poetry from prose in the Bible, and preliminary tests show that it will work efficiently in most cases. The particles *ʾēt* (the sign of the definite direct object), *ʾăšer* (the relative pronoun), and *ha-* (the definite article) all have been identified as prosaic elements, not common in or suitable to poetry.[4] But with one partial exception, no systematic study of the distribution of these elements in biblical literature has been made.[5] In a comprehensive investigation, the results of which are now being prepared for publication, a graduate student of mine, working with statisticians at the University of Michigan, has collected extensive samples of prose and poetry in the Bible, has determined the frequency with which these particles occur, and their distribution and ratios between prose and poetry. Then on the basis of standard formulas and tables, she has been able to fix the value of these particles as a discriminant and calculate the probability that their distribution in the Bible is the result of

[4] W. F. Albright routinely eliminated these particles in his reconstructions of Hebrew poetry, and scholars associated with the Baltimore School have followed the same practice.

[5] The study by Y. T. Radday of the Technion in Haifa was limited to the occurrences of the definite article. In counting, the author made no distinction between the instances of the article indicated by the letter *he*, and those implied by the Masoretic vocalization of the preposition with following nouns. In spite of this qualification, Radday's results are very impressive: poetic books are grouped at the low end of the chart (with minimal use of the article), and prose books at the high end. Books that are mixtures of prose and poetry (as, e.g., Jeremiah and Ezekiel) fall between the extremes.

chance or convention. The conclusion is that the criterion works, *grosso modo*, very effectively and serves to separate prose from poetry without difficulty. Prose passages cluster at the high end of the frequency spectrum while poetry is found at the other extreme. There are exceptions and some overlapping; and we must reckon with a modest amount of contamination: i.e., the addition of one or more of these particles where they did not originally occur, and more rarely their omission where they were present. There is no evidence, however, for the normalization of prose practice through the text or the wholesale revision of "poetry" into "prose," even though no distinction was made in the manner of copying the material, or most of it, in the manuscripts. Otherwise the distinction could not have been preserved, as in fact it has been. In general, these particles occur six to eight times more frequently in prose passages than in poetic ones. Statistically the results are even more important, since they establish beyond cavil that the occurrence of these particles is a valid discriminant, and the difference in distribution reflects an intrinsic distinction between prose and poetry.[6] What it means is that, when a writer composed a prose work, he naturally and inescapably used these particles in the normal fashion described in the grammars; but when he or anyone composed poetry, he naturally did not use them, or if he did, very sparingly. Some of these exceptions can be explained as the result of transmissional errors, since the tendency of scribes would be in the direction of normal prose practice. But the residue would require further investigation and explanation.

Refinements in the use of this criterion may show some fluctuation in the occurrence of these particles in poetry and offer clues to a more discriminating classification of the poems in the Bible. Hypothetically, we might expect this difference between prose and poetry to break down gradually during the long period of biblical composition and compilation. Thus a higher incidence of these particles in poetry might point to a later date of composition, but other potential influences must be reckoned with, screened out, or otherwise accommodated.

We must issue a *caveat* at this point concerning the possible use of this statistically important criterion in textual restoration and in the care and cure of ailing passages in poetry. It would be irresponsible to conclude that these particles were never used in poetry and that all such occurrences in the present text are the result of editorial revision or scribal error. At the same time, some contamination has occurred, and the elimination of intrusive particles will be justified in specific cases, especially where supporting data are available.[7] There must have been a slight tendency to add particles in poetry, chiefly

[6] The key figure for each particle taken separately is less than .001 (and for all three taken together, which is the strongest criterion, even less than for the others), which means that the probability that this is a deliberate difference in the treatment of prose and poetry is so great as to be certain.

[7] Compare Num 24:4b with 24:16c, which are identical except that the particle *ʾšr* occurs before *mḥzh* in v. 4b, whereas it is omitted in v. 16. In view of the metrical balance of the bicolon v. 16cd, we must omit *ʾšr* in v. 4b as a secondary addition. There may be some connection between

because most of the poetry was copied as prose, which would blur this distinction. Furthermore, the Masoretes seem not to have recognized the difference between prose and poetry except where tradition had preserved it in stichometric writing, or in some other fashion.[8] While it is clear that they did not tamper with the existing text (the *kĕtîb*), when it came to vocalization, they followed a uniform pattern marking the presence of the article indiscriminately in prose and poetry wherever it seemed grammatically appropriate.[9]

(b) *Sequence-Dating*. This leads directly to a discussion of sequence-dating in poetry, and the reference to pottery in the title of the paper. Before proceeding on this fragile topic, however, I had best make a more emphatic disclaimer than usual with regard to lack of expertise, especially in the presence of qualified archaeologists. No one — friend or foe — has ever accused me of knowing more than the rudiments of pottery identification or dating. My acquaintance with this intricate science is so passive as to be inert. Nevertheless, the principles of sequence-dating of pottery are simple enough, and the application over the years has proved remarkably successful and perduring. Pottery chronology remains the best and most exact standard of measurement for all periods of the Bronze and Iron Ages (roughly from before 3000 to about 600 B.C.). What makes the lowly potsherd so valuable is that it has extraordinary durability (a quality that also attaches to clay tablets with cuneiform writing on them, as we are being reminded repeatedly in these latter days), occurs in enormous quantities everywhere human beings lived for the last 6000 years and more, and in great varieties of types, sizes, and shapes, and with all kinds of decorations. In addition to these statistically significant characteristics, they also underwent continuous and measurable change and thus constitute an ideal instrument for determining chronological sequence. When combined with accurate stratigraphic analysis, pottery dating is entirely reliable within necessary limits. Except in the most unusual circumstances, dates deriving from the study of pottery cannot be fixed more precisely than within a range of 50 to 100 years. Pottery analysis and sequence dating has been a critical factor in establishing archaeology as a reasonably exact science

the insertion of ʾšr in v. 4b and the fact that the colon v. 16b (*wyrdʿ dʿt ʿlywn*), which is parallel to v. 16a = v. 4a, is missing in v. 4.

[8] Some MSS with stichometric writing have been found at Qumran, e.g., Deuteronomy 32. Cf. P.W. Skehan, "A Fragment of the 'Song of Moses' (Deut. 32) from Qumran," *BASOR* 136 (1954) 12-15.

[9] The statistics show a startling reversal from the pattern established for the use of the three particles, where the proportion is overwhelming, when prose is compared with poetry. When it comes to Masoretic vocalization, however, the difference between prose and poetry is practically erased. If one counts those cases in which, according to the Masoretes, the *he* has been elided and its presence indicated by the appropriate vowels and dagesh forte, the frequency is practically the same (for the entire sample there were 229 occurrences in prose, and 219 in poetry). Even when the greater overall incidence of prepositions in poetry as distinguished from prose is taken into account, the ratio is about 3:2 which is a far cry from the ratio of almost 7:1, which we find when we count only those instances in which the *he* of the article actually appears. It is clear that the Masoretes seriously affected the results where they were able to do so.

and in permitting the material findings to be integrated into the historical framework of the ancient Near East.

In principle, it should be possible to establish criteria for the sequence-dating of Hebrew poetry. As the late W. F. Albright was fond of saying, everything human beings set their minds to and their hands on is susceptible of typological classification and chronological ordering. Everything humans touch evolves in one way or another, and it only requires some experience with the material and the application of good sense to isolate those factors which are diagnostic for the process of change in the phenomena under investigation. By using these criteria adroitly, it should then be possible for us to measure both the direction and the degree of change from one period to the next. What may be relatively simple in principle, however, can turn out to be deucedly difficult in practice.

Albright himself attempted to establish a viable sequence-dating of Hebrew poetry, using as criteria certain widespread stylistic phenomena: repetitive parallelism and paronomasia.[10] As a pioneering effort, it was a brilliant *tour de force* and another example of his extraordinary ability to create new areas of research. The net results, however, can only be regarded as mixed, and he continued to refine the method and reorder the poems during the remaining years of his life. Using the same corpus of early Hebrew poetry, essentially, but applying an entirely different set of criteria, I also have worked out a sequence-dating of these poems, partly as a check on Albright's findings, and to develop a mechanism for dealing with other poems. My study, embodied in a major article, "Divine Names and Titles in Early Hebrew Poetry," has just appeared in the G. E. Wright Memorial Volume (edited by Frank M. Cross and others). I will refrain from repeating myself *in extenso*, except to say that the value for biblical studies of recovering a securely dated corpus of pre-monarchic poetry would be very great and should have an important impact on previous and current reconstructions of early Israelite history.

I can also report a subsidiary gain from the application of the techniques developed in that study to poems outside the corpus mentioned. In a recent examination of the Song of Hannah (1 Sam 2:1-10), another graduate student of mine and I had occasion to compare it with Psalm 113 in view of the close literary connections between them.[11] Converging tests show that the relationship is sequential, though not necessarily direct, and all the relevant indicia point to the Psalm as the older of the two poems. Since the Song, independently of this comparison, has been dated to the period of the United Monarchy (10th century),[12] we are required to date the Psalm earlier, in the

[10] W. F. Albright, *Yahweh and the Gods of Canaan* (Garden City: Doubleday, 1968), chap. 1.

[11] I wish to acknowledge the extensive assistance of Mr. Clayton Libolt, a graduate student at the University of Michigan, in the preparation of this article, "Psalm 113 and the Song of Hannah," which is to appear in the H. L. Ginsberg *Festschrift*, to be published as one of the volumes in the Eretz Israel series.

[12] Cf. "Divine Names and Titles in Early Hebrew Poetry," *Magnalia Dei: The Mighty Acts of*

11th or even the 12th century, a conclusion which was quite unexpected. In the Song of Hannah, there is an explicit reference to the "king . . . anointed one," along with the use of divine names characteristic of the monarchic period; in the Psalm, on the other hand, along with other archaic features, the divine name Yahweh is used repeatedly and exclusively, which is characteristic of the earliest phase of Israelite poetry.

Other scholars have developed different criteria for determining the relative and absolute dates for the ten poems embedded in the narratives of the Pentateuch and Former Prophets (through 2 Samuel). Gradually a consensus is emerging that these poems are to be dated in the Iron I period (from about 1200 to about 900 B.C.), though there are differences about the placement of individual poems.[13] Sequence-dating of poems in the Bible is still in its infancy, but all the ingredients for a successful resolution of one of the most persistent and troubling problems in literary criticism are in hand: an adequate sample of materials, a sufficiently long period of time for the measurement of change, some dated and more datable poems to provide fixed points of reference, and a tested group of criteria which can be used independently or together to fix dates and check results.

(c) *Forms and Structures*. The quest for the key to Hebrew metrics may have reached a turning point. Hitherto the search and the struggle among scholars have been to uncover that governing principle or universal truth that not only would encompass all cases, but would also recover the fundamental patterns adopted by the biblical poets. Needless to say, the quest has proved futile, like some other scholarly quests of the past century; no such magic key has ever been found, or is likely to be. The actual situation is somewhat different. No regular, fairly rigid system will work with any large sample without extensive reshaping of individual poems and verses. The pages of scholarly journals and commentaries are strewn with the wreckage left by the advocates of this approach, and there is a general feeling that while the investment of time, effort, and ingenuity was great, the returns have proved to be small. Not many poetic reconstructions have survived critical scrutiny very long. While newer approaches and methods have been more respectful and conservative regarding the established text and successes have been registered in the case of individual poems, overall the gains have not been impressive. Some poems exhibit formal metrical features, and even regular stanza structure, but it is rare indeed when two or more poems share the same structure. Many poems do not seem to have clear-cut metrical or strophic patterns and may never yield to this sort of analysis. Since an essentially

God (eds. F. M. Cross, W. E. Lemke, P. D. Miller; Garden City: Doubleday, 1976), 55-107; esp. 71-72, 96.

[13] See discussion and bibliography in the following articles: "Divine Names and Titles in Early Hebrew Poetry"; "Early Israelite History in the Light of Early Israelite Poetry," *Unity and Diversity: Essays in the History, Literature, and Religion of the Ancient Near East* (eds. H. Goedicke and J. J. M. Roberts; Baltimore: The Johns Hopkins University, 1975) 3-35; "Early Israelite Poetry and Historical Reconstructions," which is to appear in the Jerusalem Symposium volume to be published by the American Schools of Oriental Research.

descriptive and inductive method requires painstaking treatment of a large number of units, it will be a long time before syntheses and worthwhile generalizations are possible. In the meantime, we should restrict ourselves to modest statements and small claims.

Since we cannot resolve the problem at least on the terms which have been used in the past, we may try to redefine it in ways more appropriate to the tools at our disposal. Our objective is not to find or devise a key to Hebrew metrics, but rather to achieve an adequate description of the phenomena. This is much less ambitious, but by scaling down our expectations we may be surprised by the achievable results. There are three points to be made, and in the process we hope to focus attention on the attainable and dispel some illusions along the way:

(1) There is no single solution to the problem of Hebrew meter and poetic structure, but there are many possible descriptions, some more adequate than others, some more pertinent for different sets of questions than others. In comparing systems, we should give up the notion that the poets of Israel used any of them deliberately, or that our task is to find out which one it was. Lacking any useful literature from antiquity on the subject or clear-cut internal data, the best we can hope for is an evaluation of different systems in terms of economy (or parsimony), efficiency, utility, precision, and comprehensiveness. In general, the system which satisfies these criteria best should be adopted, but different systems may be used for different purposes, and it is always wise to check the results derived from one system by another. It is interesting and may be instructive that practically all the systems which have been devised in the past century have produced positive results in measuring and describing aspects of Hebrew poetry. At the same time none has been generally satisfactory, and all have demonstrable weaknesses. The conclusion is that there is no single best system, but that acceptable results will depend to a great extent on the purpose of the measurement and the kind of description desired. Since all systems reflect a certain rhythmic regularity in much of Hebrew poetry, the principal object is to devise a measuring system that is symmetry-sensitive and will describe the metrical pattern as clearly and as simply as the data permit. That is why I have opted for a syllable-counting system in preference to the more traditional stress-system used by most scholars.[14] Basically, the two methods describe the same phenomena in much the same way, but there are more arguments about the number of stresses than about the number of syllables, or I should say that syllable-counters tend to be more accommodating and less dedicated because one syllable more or less does not make as much difference as one stress more or less. In addition, the

[14] I have described the system in a number of articles: e.g., "Strophe and Meter in Exodus 15," *A Light unto My Path: Old Testament Studies in Honor of Jacob M. Myers* (eds. H. N. Bream, R. D. Heim, C. A. Moore; Philadelphia: Temple University, 1974) 163-203, esp. pp. 168-75; "Acrostics and Metrics in Hebrew Poetry," *HTR* 65 (1972) 367-92, esp. pp. 368-69; with C. F. Hyland, "Psalm 29: A Structural Analysis," *HTR* 66 (1973) 237-56, esp. pp. 238-39; "The Structure of Psalm 137," *Near Eastern Studies in Honor of William Foxwell Albright* (ed. H. Goedicke; Baltimore: The Johns Hopkins University, 1971) 187-205, esp. pp. 188-90.

picture provided by syllable-counting is more precise. An equally simple system that also works with large samples is word-counting. We can define a word as any sequence of Hebrew letters between white spaces on a printed page, leaving open the question of the effect of a *maqqēp* (which is roughly equivalent to a hyphen). I have tried more complex methods of counting, distinguishing between long and short vowels, and even adding in consonants in order to secure an exact calculation of the time-span of a poetic unit. For the most part, I think it has been wasted effort, as poets notoriously bend the rules, written and unwritten, and the point of diminishing returns is reached very rapidly in view of the extraordinary arithmetical effort required.[15]

(2) It is difficult if not impossible to draw the line between the conscious intention of the poet and what the attentive reader finds in a poem. On the whole, I think we have given insufficient credit to the poet for subtleties and intricacies in his artistic creation, and it is better to err on that side for a while. If we find some clever device or elaborate internal structure, why not assume that the poet's ingenuity, rather than our own, is responsible? It is a different matter if it is our ingenuity in restoring or reconstructing the text. In many cases, however, I believe that the process by which the poet achieves an effect is different from the process by which the scholar recognizes and describes it. What is the result of conscious effort on our part, may be spontaneous in the poet, or second nature. For one who is steeped in the tradition and draws on long experience in creating poems, it is not necessary to start from scratch, and the associations and intricate arrangements, which we discover only after painstaking investigation, may be byproducts of which he is not fully aware, while he centers attention on other aspects of composition. Since there is no way finally to resolve such questions about the intention of the poet, it is a safer and better procedure to restrict or extend ourselves to the visible data and describe what we see there, rather than try to probe the recesses of the poet's mind.

(3) Questions concerning oral or written composition and transmission cannot easily be resolved one way or another, and the common discussion does not shed much light on the nature of the process or the end result. These are very important matters, but with respect to Hebrew poetry at least it is difficult if not impossible to disentangle oral and written elements. Both processes are at work in the history of composition and presentation of any biblical poem; all of them finally were written down, no matter how they were composed or how they were transmitted. So there is a written factor at the end of the line, if not earlier, for biblical poems, and undoubtedly an oral factor at some point in the process as well. Needless to say these factors affect each other: oral composition and transmission are very different in a community in which there is a strong writing-tradition from what they are in a community without any writing at all. In the case of the oracles which Jeremiah dictated to the scribe Baruch, there is a mutually interdependent process at work. The original oracles presumably were composed orally. Then they were dictated

[15] See the discussion of these matters throughout the article, "Strophe and Meter in Exodus 15," and especially the tables at the end, pp. 193-201.

by the prophet and written down by the scribe; in principle this was only a change in procedure not in substance. Once written, they begin a new career in manuscript form, with a history to come of editorial revision and scribal alteration. When the autograph is destroyed by the king, another copy has to be compiled, again at Jeremiah's dictation. Is the second version another instance of oral composition, or something else, viz., an effort to reconstitute a previously existing written work, itself a compilation of earlier composed oral pieces. Even without the special complications of the Jeremiah-Baruch composition, the process of composing, reciting, recording, and transmitting is endlessly involved. Rarely if ever can oral and written categories be kept separate, especially in the Near East where writing was a compulsive habit long before the time of the patriarchs.

Thus far I have been able to identify two basic structural types in Hebrew poetry: (1) In the first group are poems of a more traditional type, at least in comparison with the poetry of other cultures. These poems have fairly regular metrical patterns and symmetrical stanza structures, ranging from simple to complex and ornate. To illustrate this type we may consider Psalm 113 in relation to the Song of Hannah.[16] Psalm 113 has a very simple metrical and strophic structure: it consists of three stanzas of three bicola each. The standard line-length is 14 syllables, divided in the middle, 7:7; there is a slight variation in some bicola, which divide 8:6. No alterations or emendations in the text are needed, and except for the question whether the poem is complete or only a fragment, we can consider it a prime example of classic metrical Hebrew poetry. It apparently belongs to the earliest phase of Israelite verse, when presumably poems of this type were prevalent. There are slight deviations from the norm, but these can be regarded as reluctant concessions to the ultimate intractability of language when pressed into metrical patterns or the resistance of the poet to metrical requirements. We can also include transmissional errors as an element in the occurrence of such irregularities, but unless there is other compelling testimony, we need not appeal to such a contingency in order to achieve metrical conformity. Artistic freedom is a more persuasive alternative, or in fact artistic necessity as a guard against mechanical composition and the constant threat of monotony in the creation of metrically repetitive poetry.

Turning to the Song of Hannah, we find a much more complex strophic structure; even after the most painstaking efforts to recover the original, or a more original, form of the poem, it may have eluded us. Still it is possible to identify the basic three-line stanza of 42 syllables in vv. 4-5, and 8a-f. There are elaborations and embellishments, including a formal introduction (vv. 1-2) and complementary closing (vv. 9-10). Similar, though in no case identical, strophic patterns have been identified in other short Psalms (23, 29, 137), all of which have a striking chiasm at the midpoint of the poem. The net effect of these features is to produce an X-like structure within a frame.[17]

[16] See the forthcoming study, "Psalm 113 and the Song of Hannah."

[17] See the following articles: "The Twenty-Third Psalm," *Michigan Oriental Studies in Honor*

(2) Another type of poem exhibits much greater variation in line length and stanza construction, while at the same time there is an overall consistency and regularity which ensure that the poem generally is intact and that the pattern is deliberate. The problem is how to account for the great internal freedom and variety, on the one hand, and the predictable and repeated patterning of the poems as a whole, on the other. The best examples of such poems are the alphabetic acrostics of Lamentations 1–3.[18] Without repeating the extensive analysis of G. B. Gray or my own observations already published, it can be said that within an established framework of 22 stanzas per poem there is considerable freedom in the matter of line length (measured in syllables) and in stanza structure and length. In view of the mechanical structure of the poem, however, such free variations may have been regarded as welcome or obligatory relief from monotony. The great surprise, at least initially, was to discover that in spite of the wide variations from line to line and from stanza to stanza the three poems as a whole were virtually identical in length, again measured by the number of syllables (I: 865; II: 863; III: 868).[19] However we try to explain the matter, the facts are beyond dispute; nor is the situation unique with respect to these three poems. The same results are obtained when eight other acrostic poems are compared: the internal range of variation in line and stanza length is great but the total length of the poems or the averages are again practically identical.[20]

When the distribution of line and stanza lengths (but not the position of the lines) is plotted on a graph, the results overall and for specific poems are the same: an almost perfect bell-shaped curve, which, as we all know, is the pattern for random distribution of practically everything. In this pattern, the bulk of instances will be concentrated around the mean or average figure; the remainder will be spread out above and below the center point, with short lines balancing long ones, thus producing the familiar curve. How do we account for this peculiar phenomenon and correlate a carefully wrought poem with a random-distribution curve for its metrical model? What factors produce uniformity in the overall configuration but a wide range of variation in the component parts?

Parts of the answer lie in the nature and structure of the Hebrew language, and other parts in the complex process of poetry composition. It is difficult to imagine that there was a set of rules governing such a poetic structure. After all, the bell-curve is a description after the fact, not a prescription for would-be

of George G. Cameron (eds. L. L. Orlin et al.; Ann Arbor: University of Michigan, 1976) 129-66; "Psalm 29: A Structural Analysis"; "The Structure of Psalm 137."

18 See Gray's discussion in chap. 3 of *The Forms of Hebrew Poetry*, and elsewhere in his book; cf. my comments in the "Prolegomenon," pp. xi-xxiv.

19 The variation among the poems is less than 1%. Essentially the same results are achieved if we count words, i.e., the combinations of letters between spaces: I: 376; II: 381; III:381. We have ignored the presence of the *maqqēp*, but if we take this Masoretic flourish seriously and regard it as binding words together into single units, then the totals are somewhat different: I: 329; II: 332; III:350. The effect of the Masoretic intrusion is to obscure the equivalence of the poems, but the basic pattern is still visible.

20 D. N. Freedman, "Acrostics and Metrics in Hebrew Poetry," 367-92.

poets to follow. In the case of the poet responsible for Lamentations 1–3, it might be argued that the special metrical pattern reflects the way in which he conceived and executed his work. The whole is a product of his genius, and many of the details are distinctive of this poet. But the distributional pattern we have described seems to be independent of the particular poet. It is observable in practically all the acrostic poems, which cover a wide range of subjects and which were composed by a number of poets, and is clearly the established pattern for poems of this type. For the present, the evidence links the pattern with acrostics, but I am sure that many other poems of different types conform to the same model. Since it is inconceivable that poets counted words or syllables into the hundreds (or thousands) to determine the shape of their poems, especially when they allowed themselves such wide variation in the matter of line and stanza length, we must reckon with a fundamental control deeply ingrained in the consciousness of poets generally. The result was a format at once regular and flexible, within whose fixed but not consciously recognized limts the poet was free to practice his art and express his individuality.

We may summarize the findings in these terms: There is a predictable and repeated total configuration (measured by syllable or word counts), fixed by tradition, experience, and practice. Poets in different places and times conform to this pattern, consciously or not, but inevitably. Within the large structure, however, there is a wide area of free choice, and variation is not only permitted but encouraged. The poet exercises his personal prerogatives in the internal arrangements and expresses his originality not only in the choice and arrangement of words and phrases and clauses, but also in the organization of lines and stanzas. This combination of rigid external control and of internal variety and freedom is distinctive; its roots lie deep in the nature of language, music, and poetry, and it belongs in its history to the sphere of oral composition. Whatever its origin and rationale, the "random-distribution" phenomenon must be reckoned with in the discussion of the nature of Hebrew poetry.

II. *The Function of Hebrew Poetry as a Vehicle of Revelation*

(a) *Pagan Patterns.* From time immemorial the language of heaven and of heroes has been poetic in form. In the ancient Near East and the Mediterranean basin, poetry has served as the vehicle of myth and epic alike; reflecting the same awareness, ritual and liturgy share this quality: oracles, incantations, prayers and hymns customarily appear in poetic guise. The basic and persistent medium of classic religion and revelation is poetry. But this intrinsic association has been obscured somewhat in the Bible, for several reasons: (1) The basic narrative, which is the story of Yahweh and his people Israel, is the first and great prose classic of antiquity. The genre itself is the creation of the biblical writers. There was never anything like it earlier, and there have only been imitators since. The fact that the Primary History — the first Bible — is a prose work has dominated the approach to and evaluation of all the biblical literature. (2) Much of the remainder of the Bible, though actually poetic in character, was copied as prose. (3) The treatment of the Bible as sacred, canonical literature has tended to erase all distinctions among the various types of literature, including the basic one between prose and poetry. Whether the concern was legislative or theological, the objective was to fix the exact wording of the text and establish an authoritative interpretation to settle questions and cases. In the process of making the Bible a constitutional authority, poetry was levelled out as prose. Reverence for the text nearly killed off its spirit and effectively suppressed the special features of its poetry.

(b) *Israelite Adaptation.* Without debating the question of prose versus poetry or denying the predominance of the prose tradition in the Bible, it is legitimate to call attention to the poetic element, which not only lies behind the prose end-product but always persisted alongside of it. With regard to the primary prose narrative, critical scholars have always recognized an important poetic component in it or aspect of it. Various attempts have been made to identify and classify that element: (1) E. Sievers (followed in general respects by E. Brønno) just read the narrative as poetry, in accordance with a very complicated set of rules, to which there was an equally complicated set of exceptions or modifications. The results were very mixed and few contemporary scholars, if any, accept either the premises or the conclusions, much less the rules. But we are all impressed by the incredible energy and ingenuity demonstrated by Sievers. In spite of the shortcomings of the system and of our misgivings about the procedure, we must acknowledge that the exercise has not been in vain; and if he erred, he erred on the right side by emphasizing the presence of poetry in the prose tradition.[21] (2) A second and more successful effort is represented by names like R. Kittel, U. Cassuto, and W. F. Albright, who believed that behind the present prose agglomerate there was a poetic substratum.[22] Moreover, bits and pieces of the original epic have survived, especially in the set speeches or sayings preserved in the present prose framework. Examples may be found by leafing through the pages of the Kittel Bible in which poetic passages have been set off from the prose. Succeeding editions of the Bible have identified more poetic passages but the net effect is about the same: poetry embedded in prose, most often in passages containing dialogue. While the work of the scholars mentioned, and of many others since, has had a massive impact on current scholarship — and a *prima facie* case must be acknowledged — there are difficulties with the position in

[21] E. Sievers, *Metrische Studien* (Leipzig:Teubner, I [1901], II [1904-5], III [1907]). E. Brønno, *Die Bücher Genesis-Exodus: Eine rhythmische Untersuchung* (Stockholm: 1954). There are many other volumes, which include Joshua, Judges, Ruth, Samuel, Kings, Isaiah, Jeremiah, and Psalms.

[22] Albright's views are scattered among his many writings on the subject; Kittel's observations are embodied in his edition of the text of the book of Genesis in the Bible which bears his name. For Cassuto the basic works are: *A Commentary on the Book of Genesis:* Part I: *From Adam to Noah* (English translation; Jerusalem: Magnes, 1961); Part II: *From Noah to Abraham* (English translation; Jerusalem: Magnes, 1964); *Biblical and Oriental Studies. Vol. 1: Bible* (Jerusalem: Magnes, 1973). The translator in all cases was Israel Abrahams.

whatever form it has been advocated. The theory of a poetic substratum or an underlying epic poem remains attractive, but so far it is not only unproved but unprovable. I doubt that this epic ever existed, although I am sure that there were many poems, perhaps some of considerable length, which arose out of and described the early experiences of Israel and its forebears, which did not survive, but which influenced the formation of the prose accounts. In addition there are numerous short passages, mainly in dialogue form, which are clearly poetic, and which form part of the prose narrative. This is simply a fact, but how is the prose-poetry combination to be explained? It is possible that these passages are remnants of an earlier stage of transmission and that the prose writers incorporated these dramatic and lyrical elements from the oral tradition into the larger works. The premise and the argument, however, are open to question: Do the theory and the data really match up? Is not the notion of such carpentering of a narrative rather artificial and out-of-date? (3) These inquiries lead to a third possibility, which combines features of the views just mentioned but presents the case for a poetic component in the prose narrative in a more appealing and less artificial manner. It also reflects the reality of the end-product, which is a genuine work of literature. The essential argument is that the same author is responsible for both prose and poetry in composing his work and has combined them deliberately to enhance the literary quality and dramatic impact. E. F. Campbell, Jr. has proposed just such a solution to the literary problem of the Book of Ruth, which in small compass has many of the same features as the Primary History: a prose framework and narrative with poetic elements (some of extraordinary beauty) embedded in it.[23] It is not necessary or desirable to think in terms of an original poem or poetic narrative, subsequently cast in prose form, while some elements of the older poem have been retained. It is better to regard the work as an independent prose composition in which the convention of putting some of the speeches, especially those of the central characters, in poetic form has been observed. It may be mentioned that in Elizabethan drama, for example, the nobles and other leading characters typically speak in poetry, whereas commoners and comedians are relegated to prose. The same person who composed the prose of Ruth is also responsible for the poetry; no doubt the whole story is based on older oral poetic traditions from the region of Bethlehem and the family of Boaz and his successors. The story itself was not invented, but it was handed down from the time when "the judges judged" in Israel.

Happily, we can leave the question of the poetic elements embedded in the larger prose narratives of the Bible and pursue the great poetic tradition of early Israel in a more fruitful way, by examining several major poems which have been preserved in the Pentateuch and Former Prophets. These poems are independent of their prose contexts, although in each case a title or framework has been provided, indicating that the poem was incorporated into the larger work when the prose narrative had already been composed. In these poems, we have authentic reminiscences of a time earlier than the prose narrative and

[23] E. F. Campbell, Jr., *Ruth* (AB 7; Garden City: Doubleday, 1975) 5-23.

examples of hymnic and lyric composition from the formative period of Israel's existence. The poems, which form a coherent group highlighting the great events and experiences of the early period, are as follows: the Testament of Jacob (Genesis 49); the Song of the Sea (Moses and Miriam, Exodus 15); the Oracles of Balaam (Numbers 23–24); the Song of Moses (Deuteronomy 32); the Blessing of Moses (Deuteronomy 33); the Song of Deborah (Judges 5). The survival and preservation of these poems are quite understandable, even though the prose accounts cover much the same ground (explicitly in the case of Exodus 15 and Judges 5, and in the story of Balaam in which the poems are interspersed among the prose paragraphs, Numbers 22-24). The poems were central and basic to Israel's life and could not be lost or forgotten. They mirrored Israel's self-consciousness as the people of Yahweh, who had led them out of bondage in Egypt, to freedom at Sinai and to nationhood in Canaan. For later generations they remained the fundamental expression of Israel's faith and commitment and served as a constant reminder of its origins and reason for existence. They share in and convey the enthusiasm and exuberance of the early days of Israel and also portray the conflicts and crises of that era. Taken together, the poems form a corpus of tradition about the beginnings of Israel, which is free of later interpretation and adaptation to other situations and circumstances, a unique source from and for the pre-monarchic period in Israel.

Two aspects of the poetry may be distinguished: (1) The date of composition: on the basis of different analyses and by the use of a variety of criteria, it is possible to arrange these poems in a relative order of composition and then fit the whole group into a framework of fixed dates between the 12th and 10th centuries B.C. Since the subject has been treated in some detail elsewhere, I shall only summarize the conclusions. I distinguish three phases of composition, which may be assigned to the 12th, 11th, and 10th centuries respectively: (i) the period of militant Mosaic Yahwism: the Song of the Sea (Exodus 15), during the first half of the 12th century, and the Song of Deborah (Judges 5), during the second half of the same century; (ii) the archaic period, with the revival of patriarchal names and titles for God: the Testament of Jacob (Genesis 49), during the first half of the 11th century, and the Testament of Moses (Deuteronomy 33), during the latter part of the same century; the Oracles of Balaam (Numbers 23–24), perhaps in the middle of the century; (iii) the period of the monarchy: the Song of Moses (Deuteronomy 32), difficult to date, but there are tell-tale signs of later composition in the selection of divine names, which indicate that it belongs to phase iii, not earlier than the 10th-9th centuries, perhaps around 900 B.C.[24] (2) The contents: the poems describe the critical events in the early history of the sacred community, from its origins until its settlement in the land of Canaan.[25] These do not constitute a connected narrative, even in the sense of the prose accounts, but are rather the raw materials of history, selected, collected, reflected, and refracted in poetic form. The poems are only slightly later than the period which they describe

[24] "Divine Names and Titles in Early Hebrew Poetry," pp. 77-80, 96.

[25] "Early Israelite Poetry and Historical Reconstructions."

and are themselves active elements in the material they transmit. The era they cover runs from perhaps the first half of the 13th century B.C. with the formation of the 12 tribe league in Canaan (reflected in the reference to Israel's presence there in the Marniptaḥ stele) to the latter part of the 12th century, when Canaanite resistance to Israelite settlement was crushed at the battle of Taanach by the waters of Megiddo. The Testament of Jacob reflects the establishment of a pre-Mosaic, pre-Yahwistic tribal federation in Canaan, apparently the creation of the patriarchal hero, Jacob. The Song of the Sea recounts the climactic episode in the flight from Egypt, the miraculous deliverance at the crossing of the Red Sea and its aftermath, the journey to the holy mountain of Yahweh, and the initial settlement there. The Oracles of Balaam recall a later phase of this settlement, presumably in trans-Jordan, though details are lacking. The Song of Moses is a long historical and theological survey of Israel's experience in the wilderness, with special concern for the generation that failed, the group that was delivered from bondage, but that was guilty of apostasy and rebellion against its redeemer and suffered the consequences. The Testament of Moses describes a tribal assembly at the time when the two groups and their traditions (patriarchal and Israelite from Canaan, on the one hand; Mosaic and Yahwistic from Egypt by way of the wilderness, on the other) were merged to form Israel, the people of Yahweh.[26] The Song of Deborah records the decisive victory of Yahweh and his people over the kings of Canaan, whereby possession of the land was finally secured, and title was transferred from one people to the other.

These poems were part of a larger corpus, the scope and contents of which are indicated by quotations and references found in the prose narrative, and which were gathered in collections like the Book of Jashar and the Book of the Wars of Yahweh.[27] The emergence of Israel as a small nation-state in the 13th-12th centuries may be one of the minor effects of the great upheaval all along the littoral of the eastern Mediterranean and the surrounding areas, but it must be linked with the saga of the exodus from Egypt and the religious pilgrimage to Sinai, the holy mountain of Yahweh. It is this combination of a new faith embodied in a reconstituted community which gives the story its unique importance and establishes the tradition of exodus, wanderings, and settlement, however difficult it may be to reconstruct it as history, as the major

[26] The setting of the poem is the plains of Moab shortly before the death of Moses, but it already reflects the transition to his successors and is doubtless of later composition, presumably the 11th century.

[27] If Albright was correct in identifying Psalm 68 as a catalogue of *incipits* or opening lines of many different poems, then we have an indication of the extent and variety of ancient Israelite poetry; the Psalm itself may be dated in the 10th century, but that would mean that many of the poems mentioned in it were of pre-monarchic date. The Book of the Wars of Yahweh is mentioned in Num 21:14, in connection with some poetic pieces including the Song of the Well (21:17-18) and the victory song of Sihon (21:27-30); the unnamed book mentioned in connection with the diatribe against Amalek (Exod 17:14) may have been the same, and poems like the Song of the Sea (Exodus 15) and the Song of Deborah (Judges 5) may have been included in such a collection. The Book of Jashar is mentioned in Josh 10:13, in connection with the spectacular miracle of the sun and the moon, and again in 2 Sam. 1:18, in connection with the Lament of David over Saul and Jonathan.

formative factor in the development of Western Civilization. The point which we have been approaching with all deliberate speed is that this handful of biblical poems (along with a few bits and pieces of others now lost) constitute the Israelite version of the mythic-epic tradition of the ancient Near East; this episodic account in poetry was itself superseded by the great prose narrative. Nevertheless, some wise editor preserved the poems alongside the prose, as artifacts and mementos of that creative age when Israel came to be.[28]

The great battle hymns, the Song of the Sea and the Song of Deborah, describe events in Israel's history, victories that were crucial to Israel's survival and success and attributable to the direct intervention of Yahweh. This miracle or wonder, which is at the center of the story in both cases, consists in a sudden rain-storm with a following flood which disables and destroys the chariot force of the enemy, which otherwise would overwhelm the militia of Israel. But it is much more than a natural cataclysm: the violence, the split-minute timing, the complete reversal of fortunes, all point to the hand of God. When a miracle occurs, the causal connection between heaven and earth becomes visible and immediate, as explosive contact is made. As in any mythic or epic situation, involving the divine and the human and communication or action between heaven and earth, the appropriate language is that of poetry. Prose may be adequate to describe setting and circumstances and to sketch historical effects and residues; only poetry can convey the mystery of the miraculous and its meaning for those present. Just as the miraculous participates in history with the mundane and also transcends it, so poetry participates in language with prose but also transcends it. The miraculous action and the poetic utterance have a common source in the powerful spirit of God.

We may summarize this excursus into the realm of esthetics and apologetics by affirming that poetry is the traditional means of expressing and transmitting religious experience: in myth and epic, in ritual and liturgy. In the biblical tradition, the vehicle of communication of the action and word of God is predominantly the prose narrative of the Primary History, but the original medium was poetry (and this pattern persisted through the period of the First Temple), which, like the extraordinary events it embodied and depicted, is also a product of the divine spirit. The chosen leader can only produce signs and wonders through the power of the Spirit, and the poet can only produce his works through the power of the same Spirit. The poetry of religious saga is as much the work of God as the miraculous events it describes. Potentate and poet tend to merge into the same person, so far as tradition is concerned, because the same inspiration is present in the mighty deed as in the mighty word.

28 Comparison with the great Greek epic poems, the *Iliad* and the *Odyssey*, which constitute a literary cornerstone for western culture, is inevitable and necessary. These works are the finest literary achievements of the ancient world (we draw the line in the 6th century B.C. between ancient and modern), with the exception of the Bible, but in terms of poetic art and esthetic quality they are unsurpassed. But they were products of their age and were suited to it; when that world perished, they became relics of a by-gone era.

(c) *Continuations.* This brings us to the next and last proposition: that poetry and prophecy in the biblical tradition share so many of the same features and overlap to such an extent that one cannot be understood except in terms of the other; in short, they are different aspects or categories of the same basic phenomenon, viz., the personal contact between God and man, and the verbal expression of it through the action of the Holy Spirit. The argument is essentially that the prophets were the inheritors of the great poetic tradition of Israel's adventure in faith and maintained, enhanced, renewed, and recreated it in the face of increasingly bitter opposition of those who preferred their religion in more manageable prose forms and who conceded (grudgingly) only the realms of liturgy (hymnody) and wisdom (gnomic and speculative verse) to the poets. There are two points, though not of equal value or importance; nevertheless they complement each other: The first is that the old poems were captured for the prophetic tradition. With few exceptions, the authors were identified as prophets or presented as having prophetic powers, the poem itself being evidence of divine inspiration. Among the poems we have been considering, three are attributed to Moses (Exodus 15, Deuteronomy 32 and 33), who is the prophet par excellence and nonpareil of the Hebrew Bible. Miriam, who is assigned a collaborative role in the presentation and presumably the composition of the Song of the Sea, is explicitly called "prophetess" in that connection (Exod 15:20). Deborah, the composer of the song which bears her name, is also called "prophetess" (Judg 4:4). As for her collaborator, Barak, we are not informed about any prophetic tendencies on his part, only about his military status and prowess. Balaam was a well-known diviner from Aram, whose role in the biblical tradition, however reluctant, was that of an authentic messenger of God. While the term "prophet" or "prophecy" is not used, we may claim his oracles (Numbers 23-24) for that category. A similar argument can be made in the case of Jacob and the Testament attributed to him (Genesis 49). While the term is not used of him directly, the poem is introduced as a prophetic oracle concerning the last times (Gen 49:1).

The correlation between poetry and prophecy is maintained elsewhere in the tradition. David is credited with the composition of several poems which are preserved in 2 Samuel (the Lament over Saul and Jonathan, the Lament over Abner, the Psalm of Salvation, 2 Samuel 22 = Psalm 18, and the Testament of David, 2 Samuel 23:1-7), as well as almost half of the Psalms. The question is whether he also was considered to be a prophet. Generally speaking, the latter role is a late assignment, finding explicit notice in the NT (e.g., Acts 2:30 in connection with the citation of Psalm 110 which was regarded as a messianic, i.e., prophetic utterance). But there is much earlier evidence supporting David's prophetic status. The Testament of David begins with the same words as two of the oracles of Balaam (Num 24:3, 15): *nĕʾum dāwīd,* "oracle of David." The term *nĕʾum* is used almost exclusively of divine oracles in the prophetic literature; and the more archaic usage here, as in the case of Balaam, reflects the conscious recognition that the person named was the bearer of an authentic word from God, precisely the role of the prophet.

The conclusion is confirmed by the passage, 2 Sam 23:2, which reads:

rûaḥ yahweh dibber-bî	Yahweh's spirit has spoken by me,
ûmillātô ᶜal-lĕšônî	and his word is upon my tongue.

The first colon is both difficult and ambiguous: *rûaḥ* is regularly feminine and therefore can hardly be the subject of the verb *dibber;* but even if we took Yahweh as the subject, the meaning would not be affected seriously. Just how to interpret the prepositional phrase *bî* is difficult to decide, but in this case the parallel passage makes it clear that the poet considers himself the messenger by whom God delivers his word. In other words he has a prophetic role. The same expression is used in Hos 1:2, where we read:

tĕḥillat dibber-yahweh bĕhôšēaᶜ	At the beginning (i.e., the first time) when Yahweh spoke by Hosea

The roles of the poet (David) and the prophet (Hosea) are hardly distinguishable.

Among others credited as authors of Psalms, we find the names of Asaph (Psalms 50, 73-83), Heman (Psalm 88), and Ethan (Psalm 89). The first two were called seers, while the third is grouped with them at other places, and no doubt was thought of as having the same status and powers.[29] To sum up, many of the poets of the Bible were considered to be prophets or to have prophetic powers, and in some cases at least, the only tangible evidence for this identification is the poetry itself. On the other hand, most of the prophets for whom we have evidence in the form of speeches or oracles, were in fact poets. While the prose narratives about the prophets in the later historical books (Samuel and Kings) contain very little information about the formal utterances or oracles, there are hints here and there that the prophets composed poems, and were expected to do so in certain circumstances: e.g., Samuel (1 Sam 15:23, which may be authentic); Nathan (the parable of the lamb may be described as poetic prose or prose-poetry, 2 Sam 12:1-4); Micaiah (1 Kgs 22:17); Elisha (2 Kgs 13:17).

The main evidence for prophets as poets comes from the great corpus of the major and minor prophets. While a good deal of prose has been mixed in with the poetry, especially in the Books of Jeremiah and Ezekiel and of postexilic prophets like Zechariah and Haggai, most of these prophets were poets, and their oracles were delivered and have been preserved in poetic form. Most of the prose materials are narratives about the prophets (e.g., the Book of Jonah, which however contains a poem, probably not by the prophet) or paraphrases of their messages written down by others. The fact that a person was a prophet and a poet does not in itself rule out the possibility or even the likelihood that he spoke occasionally in prose, both formally and informally, and might have dictated or written in the same mode. The question is whether the primary equation of prophecy and poetry holds, and I think it is safe to say that from the beginnings of prophecy in Israel at least until the exile, poetry

[29] On Asaph as prophet and seer, see 1 Chr 25:2 and 2 Chr 29:30; on Heman as seer, see 1 Chr 25:5.

was the central medium of prophecy. The pattern persisted after the exile, but the data are less clear; in any case by the 5th century prophecy itself had declined so much that the question becomes academic and irrelevant. The great spiritual leaders of the postexilic period, Ezra and Nehemiah, regarded themselves as conservers and restorers of the old traditions, but by no stretch of the imagination could either have been considered a prophet or a poet. An age had ended.

It may be noted that in subsequent centuries the revival of prophecy brought with it a revival of poetry. The presence of the Holy Spirit of God was considered the necessary sign of the inauguration of a new age of revelation, and in turn prophecy and poetry were products of the Spirit's power. The new form of prophecy in the Greco-Roman age was apocalyptic, and it is in these mostly pseudonymous writings that the genre of prophetic poetry is renewed: the Enoch literature, *The Testaments of the Twelve Patriarchs, The Psalms of Solomon,* etc. The Qumran community also provides an instructive example. The Teacher of Righteousness is not called a prophet (that role is reserved for an eschatological figure of the future) but he is described as an inspired interpreter of the words of the canonical prophets, especially in forecasting future events; in other words he was regarded as having prophetic powers. At the same time, he is apparently the author of the *Hodayot,* or Thanksgiving Psalms, a poet like David.[30]

We may add a cautious note about the NT. With the appearance of John the Baptist and Jesus of Nazareth, it was believed that the age of prophecy had returned in the context of eschatological fulfillment. Luke especially emphasizes this theme in the nativity stories, and true to tradition the speeches of angels and other inspired persons are in the form of poetry, even though the Gospel itself is a prose narrative. Thus the angel makes the first announcement to Zechariah about John in Luke 1:14-17, and to Mary about Jesus in 1:28-34 (several small pieces). Mary herself makes a prophetic announcement in 1:46-55, while Zechariah prophesies under the power of the Holy Spirit in 1:68-79. Simeon, empowered by the same spirit, utters an oracle in 2:29-32, and another in 2:34-35. Anna is not quoted directly, but since she is called a prophetess we may suppose that in her case too there was poetry in the picture.

More difficult and more important is the question concerning the utterances of John the Baptist and Jesus. Here we must be very cautious indeed, but there is some evidence to consider. Probably there is too little left of John's prophetic utterances to make a judgment, but in the case of Jesus a substantial corpus of authentic sayings has survived. How much of what he said belongs to the category of prophecy or apocalyptic, and how much to other categories like wisdom teaching, are serious questions which, however, need not detain us at this point. The classical prophets were not too careful about their categories and wandered from genre to genre in the delivery of

[30] The relevant passage in the Habakkuk *pesher* is 7:1-5: "...its meaning concerns the Teacher of Righteousness to whom God has made known all the mysteries of the words of his servants the prophets. . ." The translation is from W. H. Brownlee, "The Jerusalem Habakkuk Scroll," BASOR 112 (1958) 10.

their oracles. If Jesus was regarded as a prophet, and he seems to have been, then the question with which we are concerned is, Was he also a poet? While the efforts of competent scholars like C. F. Burney and J. Jeremias to recover an original Aramaic substratum in poetic form from the present Greek of the gospels have not achieved universal acceptance, and many details have been rejected or questioned, on the whole the results seem to me plausible and often persuasive.[31] Without pressing the point, it can be argued that there is a poetic quality and perhaps something more rhythmic and regular in many of his utterances. The parables strike me as a kind of prose poetry; while the sayings belong to the category of free verse. While neither his poetry nor his prophecy are in the classic mold, there are haunting reminiscences of both in his recorded utterances. Nor is poetry lacking in other parts of the NT: hymns of one sort or another are embedded in different epistles (e.g., Phil 2:6-10); more specifically the Book of Revelation is a mosaic of poetic compositions within a prose framework. At the same time it is a prophetic work, attributed to John the servant of Jesus.[32]

Our last example may be the most appropriate because while it belongs to the biblical tradition, it lies outside the Bible entirely. In Islam there is one final authentic prophet, Mohammed. The sacred scripture, the Quran, is a transcript of his utterances, and while they vary greatly in length and shape, they are all considered poetic. In this case, prophet and poet are one, and the two categories are coterminous. In the Quran, poetry and prophecy are the same.

What after all was the purpose of this exercise in demonstrating the obvious, that there is a close correlation between classical prophecy and poetry? The answer lies in the effort to come to grips with the larger underlying problem of inspiration, which in turn is related to questions of authority and canonicity. During the period of classical prophecy in Israel, there was a pressing existential question: Did God indeed communicate his will to men as tradition maintained? And how could one choose among the many self-styled messengers of the deity? The test of the prophet was the presence of the Spirit: by the power of the Spirit authentic miracles were performed and authentic oracles were uttered. The miracle or wonder validated the message, and the message interpreted the miracle. It is no accident that miracles and oracles are the province of the prophets. So the prophet could authenticate his mission by wonder as well as by word; but in these latter days miracles were part of the problem rather than the solution. Those in the past were safely embedded in tradition, but in the present, mastery of miracles seemed to have passed into unscrupulous hands, and the subject itself was suspect in the eyes of many. So

[31] C. F. Burney, *The Poetry of Our Lord* (Oxford: Clarendon, 1925); *The Aramaic Origin of the Fourth Gospel* (Oxford: Clarendon, 1922); J. Jeremias, *The Parables of Jesus* (rev. ed.; London: SCM, 1963). For a discussion and evaluation see M. Black, *An Aramaic Approach to the Gospels and Acts* (Oxford: Clarendon, 1954), esp. part III, "Semitic Poetic Form."

[32] Cf. R.H. Charles, *A Critical and Exegetical Commentary on the Revelation of St. John* (*ICC;* 2 vols.; New York: Scribner, 1920); J. M. Ford, *Revelation* (AB 38; Garden City: Doubleday, 1975).

we find frequent warnings in the Old and New Testaments against false prophets and false messiahs who in spite of being false have access to sources of supernatural power and can produce signs and wonders; but they are not to be believed or followed. The Book of Deuteronomy offers two pragmatic tests for dealing with prophets and their claims: (1) They must speak in the name of Yahweh, and not of other gods; (2) Their predictions must come true. Although these tests are simple and clear, they are not workable in all situations. While the first test will screen out interlopers who represent foreign deities, the real problem is with the prophets who speak in the name of Yahweh, but say different and conflicting things. The case of Hananiah and Jeremiah, both of whom claimed to be prophets of Yahweh and who nevertheless offered contradictory diagnoses of the current situation and predictions about the future, exposes the weakness of this test (cf. Jeremiah 28). The second test will work when circumstances allow the community the leisure of delaying a decision about the challenge or the warning of the prophet until his predictions can be checked by events. Most prophecies mix a summons to decide with warnings or predictions about the future, so that people must respond immediately and settle the question as to whether the prophet is true or false long before the test can be applied. There are other ways in which the test might fail: It is entirely possible for a false prophet to make a true prediction; in fact, if two false prophets make opposite predictions, one is certain to be false, but the other may be true. It can also happen that a true prophet makes a false prediction. This may be a little more difficult to explain, but mistakes happen, and a prophet's career and standing could hardly be nullified by one stray prediction. While the situation is complicated, Ezekiel seems to have missed on a prediction about Nebuchadnezzar and the siege of Tyre (cf. Ezek 26:7-14 with 29:17-20); the prophet does not seem to have been unduly disturbed by the outcome and modified his prediction accordingly. There is no clear evidence that the latter forecast, that Nebuchadnezzar would conquer Egypt, was fulfilled either.

This quest too seems to have ended in failure. There are no certain tests, and no infallible guarantees by which to distinguish between true and false prophets. If we revise the question, however, we may find an answer. Instead of trying to decide the ultimate issues of truth and falsehood, which are best left to the *eschaton* and to the Almighty, we may examine the more immediate question facing Israel: the test of a prophet was the presence and power of the Spirit in his message, what he said, and how he said it. Since the Spirit was the direct source of both prophecy and poetry, they were the basic indicators and primary evidence of its presence and activity. In the case of the great prophets, there is a remarkable congruence between content and form, a welding of prophecy and poetry which authenticated both messenger and message. For Israel, the high points of its historical experience were represented, on the one hand, by the great poems of its formative period; and on the other hand, by the prophetic oracles of its later years, in both cases by a happy union of message and medium which directly confirmed the presence and action of the Spirit of God. These compositions, doubly validated as poetry and prophecy, constitute a basic Scripture within the Scriptures, the direct word of God, like one of his thunderbolts hurled from on high.

Pottery, poetry, prophecy. There is an old word-building game called "Anagrams," which can be played in a variety of ways. Here is one: If you add a "t" to "poetry," you can make "pottery." Then if you add a "c" (and make a few other emendations), you can produce "prophecy." As we have suggested, there is more to the connection than mere alliteration and assonance.

PROLEGOMENON TO G. B. GRAY, *THE FORMS OF HEBREW POETRY*

George Buchanan Gray was born in 1865. His education was not typical of nineteenth-century England in that he was not initially a product of the "Oxbridge" establishment. He studied at private schools in Dorset and Exeter, matriculated at London University where he read Greek and Latin, and received his A.B. in 1886. Since his father was a Congregational minister, Gray chose to pursue his interest in Semitic languages and literature at Mansfield College, a non-Conformist hall at Oxford. On completion of his studies, in which he won many distinctions, he was appointed, first, tutor and then Professor of Hebrew and Exegesis of the Old Testament at Mansfield, where he remained for the rest of his life. During the thirty years of his professional career, he wrote numerous articles and eight books, including commentaries on Numbers, I Isaiah, and Job in the prestigious ICC series and a Critical Introduction to the Old Testament (the latter two in collaboration with his senior colleague, S. R. Driver). His final book, *Sacrifice in the Old Testament*, was published posthumously, after his sudden death in November, 1922. G. R. Driver has characterized him as follows, "On critical questions his judgment was shrewd and sane; he distrusted extreme views and advanced cautiously to his conclusions, but, so soon as he was sure of his ground, he could not be shaken."

A bibliography of Gray's works is found in *Sacrifice in the Old Testament* (Oxford, 1925), pp. ix-xi—happily now reissued by KTAV in the *Library of Biblical Studies* (1971; the bibliography on pp. xlvii-xlix), with a Prolegomenon by Baruch A. Levine.

In preparing his classic volume on *The Forms of Hebrew Poetry*, Gray stated his aim as follows: "It is . . . to survey the forms of Hebrew poetry, to consider them in relation to one another, and to illustrate their bearing on the criticism and interpretation of the Old Testament" (pp. v-vi). He goes on to say that he has no new theory of Hebrew meter to present; and at the same time he does not fully accept any past or current theory. His views throughout are characterized by a cautious pragmatism: he affirms the existence of metrical principles in Hebrew poetry, but questions whether enough is yet known to substantiate the "regular symmetrical forms" which other scholars claim to have identified in the poetry of the Old Testament.

The introductory chapter is devoted to a discussion of the formal aspects of Hebrew poetry. In Gray's view, the principal components are parallelism and meter, with strophe as a third but less important factor. The point of departure is the first systematic treatment of formal elements in Hebrew poetry by Robert Lowth whose lectures *De Sacra Poesi Hebraeorum Praelectiones Academicae* appeared in 1753; they were followed by more extended studies in 1778 in connection with his translation of Isaiah. According to Gray, Lowth's contribution was twofold: "He for the first time clearly analysed and expounded the parallelistic structure of Hebrew poetry, and he drew attention to the fact that the extent of poetry in the Old Testament was much larger than had generally been recognized, that in particular it included the greater part of the prophetic writings" (pp. 6-7). Since that time no one dealing seriously with the subject has questioned either the existence or general characteristics of parallelism as described by Lowth, or that it is a central and basic component of Hebrew poetry.

In the remainder of the chapter, Gray reviews the evidence available in Jewish and Christian tradition concerning the nature of Old Testament poetry. Philo and Josephus, Origen, Eusebius, and Jerome all refer to Hebrew poetry, and describe its structure in terms derived from classical Greek metrics. Among a variety of inexact statements, Eusebius alone claims that Psalm 119 consists of hexameters of sixteen syllables. Gray's main point is that formal knowledge of the structure of Hebrew poetry does not seem to have been preserved beyond the second century C.E. if indeed that long. At the same time parallelism, that central feature of such poetry, continues to be characteristic of Jewish poetry well into if not beyond the first century C.E., whether composed in Hebrew or Aramaic and translated into Greek or Latin, or directly in Greek.

Chapter II, "Parallelism: A Restatement," deals in depth with the main subject of Lowth's analysis. After discussing the theoretical and practical distinctions between prose and poetry and the applicability of parallelism and meter to these differences, Gray concludes that parallelism is the only reliable criterion for making an effective determination. As he says, "Parallelism is unmistakable, metre in Hebrew literature is obscure: the laws of Hebrew metre have been and are matters of dispute, and at times the very existence of metre in the Old Testament has been questioned" (p. 47).

He then proceeds to a detailed discussion of the different kinds of parallelism. Lowth distinguished three: synonymous, antithetic, and synthetic. Concerning the first two, Gray has little to say, but points out that the third category, serving as a catchall, has proved to be a vulnerable point in Lowth's exposition. Some of his examples under this third heading exhibit partial parallelism, since the second unit repeats part of the sense of the first, but also adds something new. For this type of couplet (or bicolon), Gray prefers the term "incomplete parallelism" (p. 49). Actually they are variations or by-forms of the first two headings: synonymous and antithetic.

For the other examples under the third heading, Gray readily agrees that the component lines are synthetically related, but without any discernible parallelism. In other words, the term as used by Lowth is extended to material in which there is no sense of parallelism at all; it has become in fact a metrical designation indicating that the two units are parallel in structure. The question is whether the use of the term is justified in such situations, or whether it is not misleading to use it in a radically different sense to describe the changed situation.

In line with his proposed classification of the phenomena under the headings: complete and incomplete parallelism, Gray offers numerous examples of both, with appropriate translations and annotations. With regard to Gen. 49:12 (p. 61) we may suggest the rendering (cf. The New Jewish Version, 1962):

Darker than wine are his eyes,
and whiter than milk are his teeth

in place of

Red-are his-eyes with-wine
and-white-are his-teeth with-milk.

(Cf. *Studies in Ancient Yahwistic Poetry* [AYP], pp. 137, 161.)

To indicate the character and degree of parallelism Gray employed letters of the alphabet to designate the separate terms in the different cola: a . b . c, etc., in the first line, and a′ . b′ . c′ in the corresponding line (pp. 59-60). This system, with some modifications is now universally employed by scholars.

In discussing possible variations of the basic schemes:

a . b and a . b . c
a′ . b′ a′ . b′ . c′

Gray points to

a . b
b′ . a′

and various rearrangements of

a . b . c
a′ . b′ . c′

some of which result in chiastic patterns (e.g.,

a . b . c
c′ . b′ . a′

etc.). Gray does not use the technical term, apparently failing to recognize this significant literary device.

Gray goes on to describe parallelism of paired terms, indicated, e.g., as

a 2 . b
a′2 . b′

As Gray points out, incomplete parallelism offers much greater variety of patterns: e.g.,

a . b or a . b
c . b′ a′ . c

With three or more terms, the number of possible variations increases geometrically. Gray distinguishes two broad classes of incomplete parallelism: with or without compensation (p. 74). Such schemes as

a . b . c or a . b . c
a′ . b′ a′2

are incomplete without compensation, whereas

a . b . c or a . b . c
a′ . d . c′ a′2 . b′

are incomplete parallelism with compensation. The latter subdivision would now be designated a ballast variant (see n. 8 below).

Gray then illustrates the value of such an analytical procedure in dealing with bicola where failure to recognize examples of partial parallelism has resulted in wrong division of the lines, and misunderstanding of the text. These errors are further compounded by mutilation of the passage, disguised as emendation: striking examples from the work of W. R. Harper and C. A. Briggs are offered in evidence.

In Chapter III, Gray discusses Parallelism and Rhythm in the Book of Lamentations. Again his point of departure is Lowth, who treated the Book both in his *Lectures* and *Isaiah*. He pointed to the special features which distinguish the first four chapters from the fifth, especially the falling rhythm and the paucity of parallelism in the former. Budde advanced beyond Lowth in analyzing the exact nature of the "unequal division of the rhythmical periods" and the extent to which this pattern occurs outside of Lamentations (p. 91). With regard to the rhythm, commonly designated *ḳinah*, Budde stipulated that normally the first unit consists of three words or stresses, and the second of two. Variations are possible, but the division is never equal: if the first element has only two words, these are heavier than the corresponding pair.

Lamentations 5 on the other hand consists of balanced lines, with a 3:3 pattern. Seventeen of the twenty verses show strict parallelism between at least one term in each colon. Of the remaining verses, two lack parallelism (vss. 8, 16), while two others seem to be parallel to each other (vss. 9-10). The last (vs. 5) is too obscure to classify.

Gray then returns to a description of chaps. 1-4 which are separate poems in the form of alphabetic acrostics: the first three chapters have three line acrostics: in the first two each three-line stanza begins with a different letter of the alphabet in ascending order from *aleph* to *taw*. In the third, each line of the stanza begins with the same letter. Chapter 4 is a two-line acrostic of the same type as chaps. 1 and 2.

Gray points out that the normal line consists of five words or stresses as against six in chap. 5. He argues from this that the common form of complete parallelism a . b . c / a′ . b′ . c′ does not occur at all in chaps. 1-4; complete parallelism in any form is rare, especially by comparison with chap. 5 in which it is quite frequent.

There follows a discussion of the distinction between "rhythmical parallelism" and "parallelism of thought" on the basis of observations by DeWette and Budde. This distinction, essentially a contrast between form and content, has colored the debate over Hebrew poetry almost throughout its history. Scholars have argued on both sides, in favor of the primacy of one factor over the other, but it must finally be recognized that both are present in Hebrew poetry, often functioning in concord, occasionally in conflict with each other.

Citing Lam. 3, Gray makes the point that parallelism, whether sectional or subsectional (i.e., between bicola or cola) is quite rare, and hence the metrical scheme is sustained by "mere rhythmical parallelism" (p. 102). In chap. 2 on the other hand, parallelism of thought is well-nigh universal, especially between sections (bicola); subsectional parallelism is rare.

His analysis and interpretation of 2:2 deserve discussion. He divides the verse and renders as follows (p. 106):

billaᶜ ᵓădōnāy lōᵓ ḥāmal	The Lord hath destroyed unsparingly
ᵓēt kol-nĕᵓōt yaᶜăqōb	all the homesteads of Jacob;
hāras bĕᶜebrātō	He hath pulled down in his wrath
mibṣĕrē bat-yĕhūdāh	the strongholds of Judah;
higgīaᶜ lāᵓāreṣ ḥillēl	He hath brought to the ground, hath profaned |
mamlākāh wĕśārēhā	the realm and its princes.

While the text is satisfactory and the translation makes sense, there are certain difficulties with Gray's arrangement and analysis of the sections. The division in the third line is awkward, and contrary to the Massoretic punctuation. The second line hardly conforms to the normal *ḳinah* pattern. In addition we should expect a closer linkage between the expressions *mbṣry bt-yhwdh* "the strongholds of Judah" and *hgyᶜ lᵓrṣ* "he hath brought to the ground" (again following the arrangement in MT) than Gray would allow. I suggest the following:

a) *blᶜ ᵓdny lᵓ ḥml*	The Lord devoured, he showed no mercy—
b) *ᵓt kl-nᵓwt yᶜqb*	All the dwellings of Jacob
hrs bᶜbrtw	he tore down in his wrath
c) *mbṣry bt-yhwdh*	the fortresses of Daughter-Judah
hgyᶜ lᵓrṣ	he brought down to the earth—
d) *ḥll-m mlkh wśryh*	He slew her king and her princes.

The key to this analysis is the recognition of the extended parallelism between the two central sections of the verse (*b* and *c*). In similar fashion units *a* and *d* balance. Thus the verbs *hrs* and *hgyʿ* are parallel terms, both referring to the destruction of buildings. A striking illustration is to be found in the roughly contemporary utterance of Ezek. 13:14, "And I will destroy (*whrsty*) the wall . . . and I will bring it down to the earth (*whgʿtyhw . . . ʾl-hʾrṣ*) . . ." Another example from the same period is Isa. 25:12 ". . . and the fortress . . . he brought down to earth . . ." (*wmbṣr . . . hgyʿ lʾrṣ*). Cf. also Isa. 26:5. Similarly the verbs *blʿ* and *ḥll* are to be taken as parallel. I derive *ḥll* from the root "to pierce, slay" rather than "to profane." In view of the reading of the LXX and the parallel expression in 2:9 *mlkh wśryh*, I think we must read the same here: the initial *mem* of *mmlkh* should then be taken as an enclitic with the preceding verb *ḥll.*

On the basis of the proposed analysis, we note that the three-line unit divides into two equal parts, after *bʿbrtw*. A similar structure may be observed in 2:10 which Gray also discusses (p. 107).

yāšěbū lāʾāreṣ yidděmū*	They sat on the ground dumb — |
ziqnē bat-ṣiyyōn	the elders of Sion;
heʿělū ʿāpār ʿal-rōʾšām	Lifted up dust on their head,|
ḥāgěrū śaqqīm	were girded with sackcloth;
hōrīdū lāʾāreṣ rōʾšān	They lowered to the ground their head— |
bětūlōt yěrūšālāyim	the virgins of Jerusalem.

*We read *yāšěbū* instead of MT *yēšěbū*, in view of the other perfect forms at the beginning of cola in this verse. Many other stanzas in this chapter also begin with verbs in the perfect form: vss. 2, 3, 4, 5, 7, 8, 9, 11, 15, 16, 17, 18, 21.

Gray observes correctly the intricate pattern of parallels in the verse. Thus the poet compares the elders with the virgins while contrasting their actions. The former raise dust upon their heads, the latter lower their heads to the ground. Going beyond Gray, we note the chiastic structure which serves to emphasize the point:

zqny bt-ṣywn —— *hʿlw ʿpr ʿl-rʾšm*
hwrydw lʾrṣ rʾšn —— *btwlt yršlm*

We also suggest that the major division in the verse comes in the middle, after *rʾšm*: everything before that refers to the "elders of Daughter-Zion," everything after it refers to the "virgins of Jerusalem." In particular, it is the "virgins" who gird themselves with sackcloth. This analysis produces a more exact balance between the parts, and emphasizes the parallel structure in the description of the two groups: the old men sit (*yšbw*) and lift up dust (*hʿlw*); the virgins gird sackcloth (*ḥgrw*) and lower their heads (*hwrydw*). The juxtaposition of Qal and Hiphil verb forms seems deliberate. It may be added that the distinctions are poetic rather than realistic, and that the two groups chosen are intended to be representative of the surviving population, of whom all the actions described would be typical. Grammatically the clause *ḥgrw śqym* could take the "elders" as subject, or the "virgins" or both.

Gray concludes that parallelism is not a dominant feature in these chapters (2 and 4). But as compared with chaps. 2 and 4, chap. 1 exhibits parallelism, whether sectional or subsectional, even less frequently. Given the relative paucity of parallelism throughout the first four chapters, a question arises concerning the rhythmic character of these chapters. A regular rhythm may well be the product of consistent use of parallelism; thus the pattern a.b.c / a′.b′.c′ would normally produce a 3:3 rhythm. But how does one account for rhythmic regularity when parallelism is a minor element (i.e., incomplete) or absent altogether? The persistence of a distinctive pattern in the first four chapters of Lamentations requires a theory of Hebrew meter to account for the phenomenon. The pattern may be described as a sequence of lines in which there are five words or stress-groups, with a characteristic pause or break after the third. This is what is meant by *ḳinah* meter or rhythm. Unfortunately, as Gray points out, the pattern is not consistent throughout, and in chap. 1 must compete for dominance with another pattern, a more balanced meter which may be characterized as 2:2 instead of the 3:2 of *ḳinah* rhythm. In fact there are a number of other variations from the presumed normal *ḳinah* pattern, but such passages generally are emended to make them conform to one or the other rhythm described. In our judgment Gray has oversimplified the problem, and we have suggested a different and we believe a more objective approach to the phenomenon, the fact of which is widely acknowledged. How to describe, analyze, and control the exact data remain to be considered. In our opinion there was a standard line length (which we can measure in total number of syllables, rather than stresses), which can be determined statistically, as well as a normal range above and below the mean. Measured in this fashion, the separate poems in chaps. 1-3 are practically identical in structure and share a common metrical or rhythmic pattern. In other words, the problem of mixed meter in chap. 1 as over against chaps. 2 and 3, and the related question concerning 2:2 lines as a legitimate variant of the standard 3:2 lines do not seem to have the urgency they once did. The variations are stylistic rather than metrical or quantitative, and well within the overall range which obtains in chaps. 2 and 3, as well as 1.

In Chapter IV, Gray turns to the other main topic: Hebrew rhythm. As he says, ". . . parallelism is but one law or form of Hebrew poetry, and . . . it leaves much to be explained by some other law or form" (p. 123). He goes on to say that, "Some such rhythmical principle, whether or not its nature can ever be exactly and fully explained, seems to govern much of the present text of the Old Testament . . ." (p. 124). To this affirmation there would be widespread agreement, though sharp divergences emerge as soon as the attempt is made to explain or describe that principle more exactly. Gray makes a series of very judicious comments about the difficulties facing the scholar in any attempt at metrical analysis. Given the uncertain state of the present text we could hardly expect to find a precise metrical pattern preserved in it. But if we emend freely, at least in part on the basis of a metrical theory, then we have in effect proved our prejudice; and someone else, emending along other lines, could establish an entirely different metrical pattern.

In developing his views about Hebrew rhythm, Gray begins predictably with parallelism, and affirms that parallelism naturally produces a coincidence between rhythmical periods and sense divisions. He goes further and argues that "parallelism is, broadly speaking, incompatible with anything but 'stopped-line' poetry" (p. 127). This is a plausible conclusion, and applies to sections rather than subsections; it also leaves out of consideration non-parallelistic poetry, where the same criteria do not apply.

Gray then draws a fateful analogy between Hebrew and old Anglo-Saxon poetry (pp. 128ff.). He quotes extensively from G. Saintsbury's *A History of English Prosody* to sketch the principal characteristics of Anglo-Saxon verse: the division of the line into halves, with two accented syllables in each half-line (three of the four being alliterated). The number of unaccented syllables varies widely between half-lines and from line to line. According to Gray, Hebrew poetry shares in several features: "(1) The isolated verse in Anglo-Saxon corresponds to the parallel distich in Hebrew; (2) the strong internal pause in Anglo-Saxon to the end of the first parallel period of the Hebrew distich; (3) there is a correspondingly great irregularity in the number of syllables in successive distichs of Hebrew" (p. 130). As a qualification of the last point, it should be mentioned that there is a greater approximation to regularity in the length of lines in *Piers Ploughman*, which Gray is using as the basis of his comparison (pp. 129-30). (Our own studies and statistical tables on Lamentations and other acrostic poems indicate that the same is true of a number of the Hebrew poems considered by Gray.)

The critical question according to Gray is whether Anglo-Saxon and Hebrew poetry agree as to the constant quantity of stressed syllables in a verse, and the constant ratio of stressed syllables in the two parts of a verse. Part of the difficulty in answering the question is that, as Gray says, "In many Hebrew lines we cannot immediately see for certain either which, or how many, are the stressed syllables . . ." (p. 131). We may add the theoretical consideration that Hebrew may not have had stresses in the commonly assumed sense at all in the early period.

Before proceeding with the question of stress-counting Gray takes up the broader problem of basic rhythmic variety in Hebrew poetry. He distinguishes two broad classes or types of rhythm: *balancing rhythm* and *echoing rhythm*. Thus in Lam. 5 we have lines in which the two parts match (*balancing rhythm*), while in Lam. 4, the lines are unbalanced, the first part being longer than the second (*echoing rhythm*) (p. 133). Nevertheless, exceptions to the norm occur in both poems, so that balancing lines are to be found in chap. 4 and echoing lines in chap. 5.

Gray then seeks to determine the criteria of measurement by which balance and echo are to be distinguished. The first proposal is that all syllables be counted.

A second possibility is to count metrical values, weighing long and short syllables as in Greek and Latin poetry. Thus the number of syllables in a Latin hexameter varies, but the sum is always equivalent to six spondees.

The third is based on the number of stressed words or syllables in each subsection. If they are equal then the line is balanced, if there is a larger number in the first part, then it is echoed.

Gray dismisses the first two without further discussion, and concentrates further attention on the third. As I have suggested elsewhere, this decision was unfortunate, and both of the other hypotheses should have been re-examined. In the study of several poems I have tried to weigh the relative merits of all three systems. While there are difficulties in all of them, there are also positive values. Further investigation is surely warranted.

Gray, however, deals only with the stressed-syllable system, and suggests a number of problems which arise in connection with it. For example, is there any limit to the number of unaccented syllables between accented syllables, or does a secondary stress or counter-tone occur if the number exceeds a certain standard, say three or four? Put another way, may a word bear more than one accent or stress, or does the general correlation of one word, one stress hold throughout? On the other hand, do one-syllable particles like *lʾ* or *ky* take a stress or are they absorbed by neighboring words? As Gray points out, none of these questions can be answered with certainty, but any rigid rule is likely to be wrong. Some flexibility is necessary in dealing with the different phenomena, but the greater the flexibility and the more applicable, the less real utility any system has, since finally it may come down to mere sanction of whatever happens to be the case.

After discussing briefly possible contributions to the elucidation of these problems from the study of Massoretic punctuation and Assyrian poetry, Gray turns to the proposals of E. Sievers, which constitute a detailed and systematic approach to the whole range of metrical issues. His rules are: 1) the number of unstressed syllables attached to a stressed syllable may never exceed four and in most cases three. So every word with more than five syllables must have two stresses; 2) the stressed syllable regularly follows the unstressed syllables associated with it, and no more than one unstressed syllable may follow a stressed syllable (pp. 143-44). Hence Hebrew meter is essentially anapestic, i.e., two unstressed syllables followed by a stressed syllable, though with substantial variations in practice. Gray's conclusion about Sievers' views is that they remain unproved in spite of the erudition and mass of data which Sievers brings to bear on the subject. Gray's comment is pertinent: "The degree of uncertainty which the theory would remove is largely counter-balanced by the insecurity of the basis on which it rests" (p. 147). After examining specific cases in which Sievers alters the pronunciation of Biblical Hebrew: mainly to reduce the number of unstressed syllables, but occasionally to introduce some to avoid the harsh-sounding sequence of two stressed syllables, Gray summarizes Sievers' contribution to the subject as follows: Hebrew poetry is basically anapestic (or iambic) rather than dactylic (or trochaic) in character; there should be some overall balance in total length between parallel units.

At the end of the chapter, Gray proposes a rule of his own: with respect to rhythmically ambiguous terms, he suggests that parallel expressions tended to receive the same treatment; if one was stressed, the other was, and vice versa. He then applies the rule to a number of controversial examples with plausible results. But the arguments are hardly conclusive, and alternate proposals deserve consideration as well. His most detailed discussion is reserved for Lam. 1:1 which on the face of it seems to have an aberrant metrical structure: 3:3, 2:2, 2:2.

<table>
<tr><td>ʾēkāh yāšĕbāh bādād
  hāʿīr rabbātī ʿām</td><td>How doth she sit solitary, |
  —the city (once) great in population!</td></tr>
<tr><td>hāyĕtāh kĕʾalmānāh
  rabbātī baggōyīm</td><td>She is become like a widow, |
  she that was great among the nations:</td></tr>
<tr><td>śārātī bammĕdīnōt</td><td>She that was mistress over provinces, |</td></tr>
<tr><td> hāyĕtāh lāmas</td><td> she hath been (set) to forced labor.</td></tr>
</table>

Budde thought that *hʿyr* in vs. 1a^2 was suspect since a 3:2 meter was desiderated. But Sievers argued that *rbty ʿm* should receive only one stress, and therefore preserved the text. Gray defends Sievers' view, arguing at length that *rbty ʿm* is a closed unit differing in force from *rbty//śrty* in 1bc. The argumentation on both sides, however, seems to me to be special pleading in favor of a metrical scheme which is assumed to be normative. To remove *hʿyr* on metrical grounds (there are no other) would be arbitrary in the extreme, and Sievers and Gray are right in rejecting that proposal. Their defense of the text, however, is forced, and the metrical distinctions too fine to be sustained by the data. Thus 1a would normally be construed as 3:3 except for the notion that such a meter is impermissible in this poem. It is hard to believe that Israelite poets drew such a sharp line. Other criteria, not easily defined, must have played a role in determining metrical structure; but in view of the plethora of doubtful and ambiguous cases, it does not appear that the stressed-syllable count was decisive.

In Chapter V, Gray discusses varieties of rhythm, and then goes on to the subject of strophes. He asserts at the start that there are only two major types of rhythm: balancing, in which the lines or subsections are of equal length, and echoing, in which the second is shorter than the first. He claims that a third type, in which the first part is shorter than the second, is extremely rare and does not warrant the detailed treatment given to the others. Nevertheless, with commendable caution he defends its occurrence against those who would exclude it entirely, and gives several examples.

Under the main headings, Gray lists the following rhythmic types: *balanced*—2:2, 3:3, and 4:4; *echoing*—3:2, but 4:3 occurs as well, though it often breaks down into 2:2:3 which does not convey the same impression as 3:2. There is a certain amount of mixed meter, which may well be deliberate though the situation is complicated by the presence of apparent corruptions in the text. He summarizes as follows: "1) The typical echoing rhythm is 3:2; with this 2:2 alternates, sometimes occasionally, sometimes as in Lam. 1, frequently; other distichs of unequal lines, 4:3 or 4:2, are at best much rarer alternatives. 2) Of the fundamental balancing rhythms 2:2 and 4:4 are closely allied and interchange, and by expansion a further natural and occasional variant is 2:2:2. 3) But this last-mentioned alternative to 2:2 or 4:4 constitutes a link with the third fundamental balancing rhythm, viz. 3:3; for 3:3 and 2:2:2 are but different ways of dividing the same higher unity, viz. the six-stress period, which may yet again divide into 4:2 or 2:4 . . . " (pp. 184-85).

Gray concludes the chapter with a discussion of strophes or stanzas and their occurrence in Hebrew poetry. On the whole there is not much evidence for this practice and what there is is not necessarily convincing. An obvious starting point is the alphabetic acrostics and in Lam. 1, 2, and 4 there is compelling evidence for verse-paragraphs delimited by the successive letters of the alphabet and of equal length throughout the poems. In other acrostics, e.g., Lam. 3 and Ps. 119, no such pattern emerges, however. In some poems, a repeated refrain occurs, which marks off sections or stanzas of the poem. In some poems these units are of approximately equal length, in others they are not. Then there are poems which naturally divide into verse paragraphs of approximately equal length, though there are no formal indications of this division in the text. At the same time, there are many poems in which such paragraphs are very unequal in length, and still others where the lines of demarcation are difficult to determine, if they exist at all. Attempts to discover greater symmetry in the structuring of verse-paragraphs of unequal or irregular length, have proved unsuccessful though the effort has been made with great industry and ingenuity by men like Fr. Köster ("Die Strophen, oder der Parallelismus der Verse der hebräischen Poesie untersucht," *Theologische Studien und Kritiken* [= *TSK*], IV [1831]), and D. H. Müller (*Die Propheten in ihrer ursprünglichen Form* [1896]; *Strophenbau und Responsion* [1898]).

Chapter VI, entitled "The Bearing of Certain Metrical Theories on Criticism and Interpretation," is devoted largely to a critique of the published views of Sievers and Duhm. With respect to Sievers' elaborate demonstration that the books of Genesis and Samuel are poetic in structure sharing rhythmic patterns already attested in the poetic books (*Metrische Studien:* II. *Die hebräische Genesis* [1904-5]; III. *Samuel* [1907]), Gray effectively criticizes Sievers' ambitious attempt as both unproven and improbable, pointing especially to the excessive amount of emendation to which Sievers resorts in order to sustain his theory. Even more destructive of Sievers' theories is the observation that if we begin with a variety of metrical patterns allowing for lines of different lengths, accept run-on lines as a matter of course, allow a wide range of variations and exceptions—not counting emendations—then anything becomes metrical, and it is impossible to distinguish prose from poetry. Once parallelism in both form and sense, and paired cola and larger units are abandoned, then there is little left in the way of criteria to determine the presence of poetry apart from the assertion that it is there. What remains from the wreckage of these monumental schemes is nevertheless considerable. That authentic poems are embedded in the prose of Genesis and Samuel (and the other narrative books of the Pentateuch and Former Prophets) cannot be doubted; now in addition to obvious examples such as Gen. 49; I Sam. 2:1-10; II Sam. 1:19-27; 22; 23:1-7, many other passages can be so identified, especially in speeches and dialogue which lend themselves more easily to poetic presentation. There are, as well, narrative passages which have the rhythm of poetry; and we may recognize the survival in the present prose accounts of an older metrical version or source from which the material has been derived. On the whole, Gray's sober conclusions have stood the test of time, and his views, rather than those of Sievers, have prevailed.

The same can be said also of his judgment against Duhm. Here his quarrel is with the attempt to impose a rigid regularity on the meter of a poem both with respect to distichs (or bicola) and strophes (or stanzas). Duhm is not alone in this camp (Briggs is another with whom Gray crosses swords), but he is an outstanding representative of the surgical school of Hebrew poetry. Gray concedes immediately that the texts of the Prophets, Psalms, and Job, with which Duhm deals, are corrupt, and that not much help is to be had from the versions, the LXX in particular. Hence some room must be allowed for conjectural emendation; but when this procedure is followed in the interests of a metrical theory, then the results are more likely to be harmful than helpful. Gray's words on the subject deserve the most careful and respectful consideration: "But there is need for the greatest possible caution in using a metrical theory as the sole reason for emendation; for one Hebrew metre can be changed into another with fatal ease; drop the verb, or some other parallel term that the sense will spare from the second line of a 3:3 distich, and the result is a very dissimilar 3:2; and, conversely, in a 3:2 distich prefix an infinitive absolute to the verb of the second line and a distich 3:3 is the result" (p. 225).

Gray then discusses examples of Duhm's arbitrary procedures in various parts of Isaiah, but reserves his sharpest criticism for Duhm's treatment of the oracles of Jeremiah. Here in addition to the insistence on regularity in meter and strophe, Duhm maintains that Jeremiah composed in only one meter. The result is catastrophic: very little of the extant book is left to the prophet, and that little is roughly handled. Such practice is a parody of serious scholarship, and has tended to bring the study of Hebrew prosody into disrepute. Over the years Gray's steadying influence has been felt and there is a growing body of opinion that conjectural emendation must be more closely regulated than in the past, if any consensus is finally to be achieved, and that such changes are to be resisted even more rigorously when inspired by metrical considerations. Nevertheless the spirit of Duhm is still abroad in the lands. While deploring the mutilating effects on the text of their labors, we may agree that scholars so inspired stimulate response and reaction, and in their way they contribute to progress in the field.

Gray sums up his inquiry into the nature of Hebrew poetry in the closing pages of the chapter: "The main forms of Hebrew poetry are two—parallelism and rhythm, to which, as a third and occasional form, we may add strophe" (p. 236). Of the two main forms parallelism is most closely connected with sense. The two basic forms of rhythm are balancing and echoing. Anything more than this is fraught with uncertainty. Nevertheless more precision in measurement is desirable, even necessary, so a system of counting stressed syllables serves this purpose. Lines or distichs are defined "by the number of stressed syllables in them. The exact number of unstressed syllables that may accompany a stressed syllable may be uncertain but is certainly not unlimited" (p. 238). We have been able to show that there is a certain regularity and predictability in counting all syllables and that such a method overcomes or avoids some of the subjectivity as well as the seemingly endless and futile debate over how to determine and count stressed syllables.

We subscribe enthusiastically to Gray's final word on the subject: "The best service to the future of Old Testament studies, so far as these can be affected by the examination of those formal elements with which alone these discussions have attempted to deal, will be rendered, I believe, by those who combine with that further study of Hebrew metre which is certainly needed, for it is a subject which still presents many obscurities and uncertainties, an unswerving loyalty to the demands of that other and more obvious form or characteristic of Hebrew poetry which is known as parallelism" (pp. 239-40).

Gray has appended two lengthy studies of specific poems of the Bible (Chapter VII, "The Alphabetic Poem in Nahum," and Chapter VIII, "The Alphabetic Structure of Psalms IX and X") which were originally published elsewhere (*Expositor*, Sept. 1898 and Sept. 1906). In these, Gray has endeavored to practice what he preaches so well, and by and large he has done so. Nevertheless, much time has passed since he did his work, and much has been learned about classical Hebrew and its Northwest Semitic relatives. It would take us too far afield to examine these studies in detail or offer a comprehensive critique. The problems remain very much as Gray described—how to achieve effective results without on the one hand canonizing an admittedly corrupt text (but just where, and in what way), or on the other emending a perfectly sound text (but not immediately intelligible for a variety of other reasons) into something equally appealing and wrong. Many of the other features and devices of Hebrew poets, along with their counterparts in neighboring societies, must be recognized and given their due place in the further studies of which Gray speaks before the reasonable goals which scholars set for themselves in the way of understanding, translation, and interpretation can be reached. If they ever are, then a major part of the credit for such an achievement must be accorded to George Buchanan Gray.

This reprinting of G. B. Gray's classic study, *The Forms of Hebrew Poetry*, provides an excellent opportunity not only to acknowledge his noteworthy contribution to the subject and to appraise his views in the light of the present state of our knowledge, but also to make a few suggestions about research in the future.[1] As stated above, Gray's book first appeared when the scholarly world was being shaken by the brilliant, often conflicting, and sometimes erratic metrical theories of the German specialists Bickell, Ley, Budde, and above all Sievers, to say nothing of the radical and disturbing results achieved by men like Duhm in the analysis of prophetic oracles and Briggs in his treatment of the Psalms. In the face of such an onslaught, Gray supplied a much-needed note of caution in his sober evaluation of the new developments. Partly by appealing to the older tradition in the study of Hebrew poetry initiated by Bishop Lowth of Oxford,[2] and partly by subjecting the newly proposed methods and conclusions to a rigorous, systematic analysis, Gray defined for his day the substantial foundations upon which the study of Hebrew poetry could be built, as well as the limits within which such study could successfully be prosecuted. His work was not notably revolutionary or even novel, but by selecting and adapting wisely among the various principles and techniques then available, he constructed an eclectic and flexible system which served as a framework for the classification and interpretation of the phenomena. In general his findings have proved durable, and scholars have proceeded substantially along the lines he marked out.

Toward the end of the volume (pp. 236-40), Gray listed, in order of importance, three basic factors in Hebrew poetic structure: 1) *parallelism*, which he regards as the central and crucial feature; 2) *rhythm*, which is defined in terms of the number of stressed syllables in the characteristic Hebrew verse-line (i.e., distich or bicolon); and 3) *strophe*, or stanza, which although clearly discernible in certain compositions, is not a regularly repeated or consistently identifiable phenomenon.

Basing his study of parallelism on the famous work of Lowth, and taking into account the contributions of his successors, Gray analyzed and classified once again the various types of parallelism, adding a significant measure of

[1]An excellent summary and accompanying bibliography are to be found in Otto Eissfeldt's *The Old Testament: An Introduction* (trans. P. R. Ackroyd; New York: Harper and Row, 1965), pp. 57-64, with additional comments on pp. 731-32.

[2]Lowth's *De Sacra Poesi*, etc., (1753), was translated by G. Gregory as *Lectures in the Sacred Poetry of the Hebrews* (1835).

clarity and precision to the description of this universally recognized aspect of Hebrew poetry. Certainly his categories of complete and incomplete parallelism are an improvement over previous efforts at classification. Furthermore, he exposed the weakness of Lowth's catchall third category, synthetic parallelism, which all too often disguised or concealed the plain fact that a substantial number of lines of biblical poetry have no parallelism at all. If we now combine these important observations by Gray, we can construct a table or grid on which to plot the whole of biblical poetry with respect to the presence or absence of parallelism. The graph would run from zero (no parallelism) through all the gradations of incomplete parallelism to 100 (complete parallelism); it would then be possible to classify lines and poems according to the degree and distribution of parallelism. Such a table would show at the same time that parallelism could not be regarded as the sole or even sufficient criterion of Hebrew verse, if only because of the large number of lines which have no parallelism. Since, as Gray and others have pointed out correctly, these lines often share a common rhythm or meter with others in the same poem which, however, have parallel elements, it then becomes clear that the overriding consideration in such cases is rhythm rather than parallelism.

If in fact rhythm, with all its deliberate variety and irregularity, is the fundamental criterion of Hebrew verse, then parallelism may be regarded as a stylistic device, the use of which has been influenced, in part at least, by metrical considerations. Thus the poet could use parallel expressions to fill out a line according to the metrical requirements. Such a factor could explain both the presence and the absence of parallelism, as well as the degree or extent of its use in given lines. Viewed in this fashion, the poem expresses the author's thoughts in lines of predetermined length. In those cases in which the poet's thought as expressed coincides in length with the metrical requirement, there will be no parallelism, whereas in those cases in which the basic expression comes short of the requirement, parallel terms would be added to make up the deficiency. In this way we can explain the occurrence of lines without parallelism, with complete parallelism, and with varying degrees of parallelism in the same poem, and having the same rhythm or meter. We are not offering this hypothesis as an analysis of the psychology of the poet, or a probable method of composition, but only as a logical description of the phenomena.

Once it is recognized that parallelism is not a necessary characteristic of Hebrew poetry, and that many lines do not have this feature, it is interesting to observe how the poet deals with this potentially prosaic element. In some cases, the line stands as is, indistinguishable from prose constructions, reflecting either the poverty of poetic imagination or the fact that the dividing line between poetry and prose is not a sharp one; it is also possible that we have an intrusive component not an original part of the poem. In other cases, the poet simply rearranges the parts, often in a provocative way, producing grammatical and syntactical anomalies very different from normal prose practice. Since Gray deals with only one aspect of this important phenomenon, and that tangentially, it may be worthwhile to explore it here, if only briefly, and to cite a few pertinent examples.

One device, often ignored or minimized as an inexact form of parallelism, involves the use, in parallel constructions, of complementary rather than synonymous terms; occasionally because the line of demarcation is not a sharp one, we should speak of overlapping terms. The difference remains, and has important implications for the analysis and interpretation of given texts. That Gray reckons with this factor, is shown by his interpretation (pp. 20-21) of the complementary terms "day" and "night" in Ps. 42:4,9. Taken together they describe continuous time in its totality. In Ps. 72:1-2 there is a series of paired terms which are complementary or overlapping rather than equivalent or synonymous. We may render the verses as follows:

ᵓĕlōhīm mišpāṭĕkā lĕmelek tēn	O God, give your justice to the king
wĕṣidqātĕkā lĕben-melek	And your righteousness to the king's son.
yādīn ᶜammĕkā bĕṣedeq	He will judge your people with righteousness
waᶜăniyyēkā bĕmišpāṭ	And your humbled ones with justice.

The terms *mšpṭ* and *ṣdq* are not equivalent or synonymous, but complementary. Together they describe the nature and process of the divine administration of justice (vs. 1), which serves as a model for the king (vs. 2). Similarly *mlk* and *bn-mlk* are not identical or interchangeable terms (i.e., they are not meant to say the same thing). It hardly needs to be pointed out that not all kings were kings' sons, and contrariwise, kings' sons do not always become kings. The case described here is of a king who was a king's son, and succeeded to the throne of his father; the poet thus emphasizes the stability and legitimacy of the royal line. The proposed interpretation would help to explain the rubric which identifies the king of the Psalm as Solomon rather than David (who, of course, was not a king's son). In vs. 2, the paired terms we wish to consider are *ᶜmk* and *ᶜnyyk*. While the terms are obviously not synonymous, they are nevertheless related. The second defines a special group ("the poor/afflicted") within the first ("the people"). The king is expected to dispense equitable justice to all the people, but the test of his administration will be his treatment of the oppressed, who cannot defend themselves and have no other champion (cf. vs. 12). The sense of the passage would be: "He will judge your people, your afflicted ones in particular, with righteousness and justice." That the principal concern of the poet is with the treatment of the poor and afflicted is amply attested in vss. 4 and 12-14. While we must allow for a certain ambiguity or multiplicity of meaning in the intention of the poet, we contend that the combination *ᶜmk*/*ᶜnyyk* in vs. 2 is equivalent to the construct chain *ᶜnyy-ᶜm* in vs. 4 (which is the normal way of expressing the thought involved).

A similar pattern is to be observed in vs. 9, which may be rendered as follows:

lĕpānāw yikrĕᶜū ṣiyyīm	Before him the desert-dwellers bow down,
wĕᵓōyĕbāw ᶜāpār yĕlaḥēkū	And his enemies lick the dust.

It is clear that the verbal units (*lpnyw ykrᶜw* and *ᶜpr ylḥkw*) are complementary and describe sequential actions. The noun-subjects (*ṣyym* and *ᵓybyw*) are not parallel terms, and their relationship, if any, is not immediately apparent. A number of scholars, including those responsible for the RSV, have found the situation sufficiently disturbing to resort to emendation: *ṣārīm* "foes" for *ṣiyyīm* (it is not necessary to read *ṣārāw*, since the suffix attached to *ᵓōyĕbāw* can serve both nouns). Slight as the emendation is, and appealing as is the resultant reading, it is at the same time unnecessary and unwarranted. The context (vss. 8-11) shows that the poet wishes to emphasize the submission of distant lands and peoples to the king, including not only the coastal areas (vs. 10a) but also the desert regions (Sheba and Seba, vs. 10b). Hence a reference to desert-dwellers in vs. 9 is entirely in order. It only remains to recognize that *ᵓybyw* defines a specific group within the larger category of *ṣyym*, "the desert-dwellers who are his enemies" or "his enemies among the desert-dwellers." The verse may be interpreted as follows: The desert-dwellers, his enemies, bow down and lick the dust before him.

Amos 2:6b reads:

ᶜal-mikrām bakkesep ṣaddīq	Because they sell the righteous for money
wĕᵓebyōn baᶜăbūr naᶜălāyim	And the poor for a pair of sandals.

Both sets of paired terms are to be considered. In spite of arguments to the contrary, and later developments in language and social theory, the terms *ṣdyq* and *ᵓbywn* are not parallel or equivalent. Rather they define and limit each other so as to isolate a single group in society to be distinguished from three others, namely, the righteous poor in contrast to the wicked rich, and the other pair, the righteous rich and the wicked poor. Inevitably the chief concern of the prophet was with the two anomalous groupings: the righteous poor and the wicked rich.[3] The existence of these seemed inconsistent with the prevailing theology, whereas the persistence of the other groups illustrated the

[3]This group is to be identified in Isa. 53:9, where we read:

wayyittēn ᵓet-rĕšāᶜīm qibrō	And his grave was made with the wicked
wĕᵓet-ᶜāšīr bōmātō (IQIs^{a})	And his sepulcher with the rich.

Although *ᶜšyr* is often emended to *ᶜōśē rāᶜ* or the like, there is no textual or other basis for it. The terms "wicked" and "rich" qualify each other in defining the group who are at the opposite pole from Amos' "righteous poor."

divine righteousness in the management of human affairs. Here the prophet calls attention to the anomaly, pointing out that the Israelites make no distinction between righteous (or innocent) and wicked (or guilty), but sell the poor into slavery without discrimination. It seems clear that the prophet accepts the legal stipulation concerning the sale of persons into slavery to satisfy outstanding debts, but protests about the way the law is applied to catch innocent victims. In addition, the prophet raises a serious question about the size of the debt for which these people are sold. The amount of "money" (*ksp*) in the first colon is defined by the "pair of sandals" (*nʿlym*) in the second; the reference is not to the value of the persons sold, but to the amount of the debt for which they are sold. According to the prophet, there is something gravely wrong with a system in which the innocent poor (i.e., through no legally definable fault of their own) are sold into slavery to satisfy debts no greater than the price of a pair of sandals.

Another example is to be found in Ps. 135:5, which reads,

kī ʾănī yādaʿtī kī-gādōl Yhwh	For I know that Yahweh is great,
waʾădōnēnū mikkol-ʾĕlōhīm	And our Lord than all gods.

The RSV resolves the difficulty in the second line by supplying the necessary element of comparison: ". . . and that our Lord is above all gods." But it is surely preferable to recognize the double-duty function of *gādōl* in the first colon, and read: "and that our Lord is greater than all the gods." Next to be noted is that in *Yhwh wʾdnynw* we have the breakup of a stereotyped expression: *Yhwh ʾdnynw* "Yahweh our Lord" which occurs in the opening and closing lines of Ps. 8 (vss. 2 and 10).[4] Finally we observe that the poet has successfully rearranged the words of a simple declarative statement to produce a poetic couplet. Written as prose the sentence would be:

kī ʾănī yādaʿtī kī-gādōl mikkol-	For I know that our Lord Yahweh
ʾĕlōhīm Yhwh ʾădōnēnū	is greater than all the gods.

Still another example of rearrangement is to be found in Ps. 140:10, which reads:

rōʾš mĕsibbāy	The poison of those who surround me,
ʿămal śĕpātēmō yĕkassēmō[5]	The mischief of their lips—let it cover them.

A literal rendering, while correctly representing the individual words of the sentence, does not bring into sharp focus the poet's thought. Since he has

[4]For discussion of this phenomenon, references, and other examples, see M. Dahood, *Psalms I* in *The Anchor Bible* (New York: Doubleday and Co., 1966), pp. xxxiv-xxxv, and Index of Subjects, p. 325, under "Breakup of stereotyped phrases." Cf. also *Psalms II* (1968), Index of Subjects, p. 390, under "Breakup of composite divine names."

[5]In accordance with the Qere. The Kethib (*ykswmw*) has the plural form of the verb which probably reflects the double subject: *rʾš* and *ʿml*. The general sense is not affected, however.

already described his enemies as poisonous snakes with venom on their lips (vs. 4), his intention here is to propose a suitable punishment for these human serpents, namely that they should drown in their own poisonous spittle. Reassembling the component parts, we render: "As for those mischief-makers who surround me (i.e., those who surround me with mischief), may the poison of their lips overwhelm them."

Another difficult passage may suitably be discussed here. Lam. 3:41 reads as follows:

niśśāʾ lĕbābēnū ʾel-kappāyim	Let us lift our hearts and hands
ʾel-ʾēl baššāmāyim	to God in heaven! (RSV)

The translation ignores the problem posed by the preposition *ʾl* in the first colon. Other prepositions are used in the LXX ("upon") and the Vulgate ("with") to smooth out the relationship between the nouns "heart" and "hands." In analyzing the structure of the bicolon, it is clear that *lbbnw* and *kpym* are parallel expressions; and this impression is strengthened by the fact that each term is directly followed by the preposition *ʾl*. In order to make this structural feature apparent, we redivide the line as follows:

niśśāʾ lĕbābēnū ʾel	We lift our heart to—
kappayim ʾel-ʾēl baššāmayim	Our hands to El in the sky.

Needless to say, the first person plural suffix with "heart" applies as well to "hands." In this passage, the repetition of the preposition enhances the parallelism of the terms involved, as well as pointing up their syntactic relationship to the object, El. At the same time, it produces a grammatical anomaly so far as normal prose procedures are concerned.

Another possibility, though less appealing, is to read the *ʾl* after *lbbnw* as the divine name *ʾēl* 'El', as in the next colon. In that case, the preposition *ʾl* after *kpym* must be understood as functioning before El in the first colon as well. The rendering would be:

We lift our heart to El,
our hands to El in the sky.

Although there has always been a wide spectrum of opinions, and the subject continues to be much debated, Gray reflected—if he did not establish—the prevailing view of his day (and probably of ours) that rhythm is important, that it is regular and repeated within broad limits, that it is discernible and that its governing principles are definable. He shied away from those at one extreme who denied that there is meter in Hebrew poetry, and from the rigorists at the other, who insisted that Hebrew meter is quantitative and metronomically regular. Gray held, along with many colleagues before and after him, that Hebrew meter is best defined by the number of stressed syllables in a line or distich, these occurring in a variety of regular and repeated patterns: e.g., 3:3, 2:2, 3:2, etc. He distrusted more elaborate quantitative theories, though he conceded the possibility that the number of unstressed syllables, at least in the aggregate, also figured in the determination of line length. While rejecting Sievers' detailed hypotheses about the sequence and ratio of stressed and unstressed syllables in lines of Hebrew poetry, Gray believed that there were probable practical limitations (both minimal and maximal) as to the total number of unstressed syllables in a line, or between stressed syllables. But his primary concern was with patterns of stressed syllables; in this respect he considered Hebrew poetry to be comparable to Anglo-Saxon poetry.

In spite of the fact that Gray's basic views on meter have prevailed, and that they are held in one form or other by a majority of scholars, I believe that they are one-sided and inadequate. It is important to emphasize, as Gray does (pp. 10 ff.), that we have no information on this subject from the poets themselves or their audiences; and the earliest sources in which the matter is discussed (e.g., Josephus) reflect interpretations of the phenomena rather than authentic traditions. We do not know what principles of meter or rhythm the Hebrew poets acknowledged as authoritative or how they went about meeting the formal requirements. What we are necessarily concerned about, therefore, is an analysis that describes the phenomena adequately, that most faithfully reflects what is actually before us. Without denying either the importance of stressed syllables for determining rhythm, or the possible application of a more precise quantitative system to Hebrew verse, we are persuaded that unstressed syllables played a role in Hebrew poetry along with stressed syllables, and that counting the total number of syllables in lines and larger units produces a more reliable picture of the metrical structure than any other procedure now in use.

On pp. 135-36 Gray discusses all three approaches to the problem of Hebrew meter. Using Lam. 5:3 as an example, he points out that although the syllable count is 8:8, the meter according to a stress-syllable system is unbalanced at 3:2.

yĕtōmīm hāyīnū ʾēn[6] *ʾāb*	Orphans were we, without father,
ʾimmōtēnū kĕʾalmānōt	(And) our mothers (were) as widows[.][7]

[6]The Qere has *wĕʾēn* for Kethib *ʾyn*. The readings may in fact be the same, the only difference being orthographic. When the first of two words in sequence ended with the same letter with which the next word began, the letter was sometimes written only once. Cf. I. O. Lehman, "A Forgotten Principle of Biblical Textual Criticism Rediscovered," *JNES*, XXVI (1967), pp. 93-101; W. Watson, "Shared Consonants in Northwest Semitic," *Biblica*, 50 (1969), pp. 525-33. See also Dahood, *Psalms II*, p. 81 for discussion and additional bibliography. A contrary position is presented by A. R. Millard in "'*Scriptio Continua*' in Early Hebrew: Ancient Practice or Modern Surmise?" *JSS*, XV (1970), pp. 2-15. In the present case we follow the Kethib since it is not clear whether or how such elliptical spelling affected the syllable count. The same possibility occurs in v. 7 where the Kethib has *ḥṭʾw ʾynm* but the Qere reads *ḥāṭĕʾū wĕʾēnām*.

[7]We have given Gray's rendering. However, notice should be taken of certain stylistic

He also notes that the prevailing rhythm of Lam. 5 is balanced, with lines following a 3:3 pattern. While he insists on describing vs. 3 as unbalanced, 3:2, it would appear to be more accurate to say that the line is balanced syllabically, and in this respect conforms to the dominant pattern.[8] There may be only two stresses in vs. 3b, but such a variation may not affect the basic rhythm at all. The same situation occurs in vs. 14, where we read:

zĕkēnīm miššaʿar šābātū	The elders have disappeared from the gate,
baḥūrīm minnĕgīnātām	The young men (have ceased) from their music.

Once again the stress pattern is apparently 3:2, but the syllable count is 8:8 (if we take the segolate *šaʿar* in vs. 14a as monosyllabic).[9] While recognizing the stylistic variation in matching two words against three, we would nevertheless insist that this is not a change in rhythm, which remains balanced (8:8). As already indicated this is the prevailing pattern in Lam. 5. At least half of the lines (distich or bicolon) have 16 syllables, usually divided 8:8 (vss. 3, 4, 5, 14, 16, 20), though occasionally 9:7 (vss. 9, 19), or 7:9 (vss. 11, 12); 10:6 occurs once (vs. 2). Other lines range in length from 12 to 22 syllables, but the mean and average remain at 16. Verse 2 is instructive because the line, unlike vss. 3 and 14, is actually unbalanced. Not only is the stress-syllable pattern clearly 3:2, but the total-syllable count is 10:6 confirming the unbalanced character of the bicolon. At the same time, the total line length is the same as the others, an effect achieved by lengthening the first half of the line, while shortening the second:

---

features which affect the interpretation of the passage. Recognition of the chiastic pattern

ytwmym — *hyynw*
ʾmwtynw — *kʾlmnwt*

helps to focus attention upon the double-duty particle *k-* which qualifies *ytwmym* as well as *ʾlmnwt*. We would translate the verse as follows:

We became as orphans without a father
our mothers as widows.

It is also possible to interpret *k-* as the emphatic particle rather than the preposition of comparison, and read the verse as affirming the equation as a fact:

We became orphans
our mothers indeed, widows.

In either case *ytwmym* and *ʾlmnwt* should be regarded as having the same status in the declaration. If we are orphans, our mothers are widows; if they are like widows, then we are like orphans.

[8] It is a good example of what C. H. Gordon calls a ballast variant. Cf. his *Ugaritic Textbook* (Rome, Pontifical Biblical Institute, 1965), §13.116 (pp. 135-37).

[9] I hope to discuss elsewhere the conventions for syllable counting; cf. the discussion by W. Holladay, "Form and Word Play in David's Lament over Saul and Jonathan," *VT*, XX (1970), pp. 157-59.

naḥ(ă)lātēnū[10] *nehepkāh* *lĕzārīm*	Our inheritance has been turned over to strangers
bāttēnū lĕnokrīm	Our homes to aliens.

We do not wish to dispute Gray's contention that the three lines under discussion have a stress-syllable pattern of 3:2, but we question whether it is appropriate to group them together as having the same rhythmic structure. According to our view, based on a total syllable count, vss. 3 and 14 have a balanced rhythm and are therefore to be grouped with vss. 4, 5, 16, 20 (all 8:8), although these are properly counted 3:3 according to the stress-syllable system. Verse 2, however, is unbalanced with a 10:6 count, indicating a deliberate shift from the frequent 8:8 pattern. The persistence of the total of 16 syllables indicates that the basic unit was the full line (distich or bicolon), and that it was considered a legitimate variation to move the caesura or line division from the center of the line toward one side or the other in an unbalanced construction. Needless to say, these stylistic subtleties or refinements cannot be isolated or even recognized if we are limited to a stress-syllable system. Since the surviving text can hardly be described as errorless, and has certainly undergone both accidental and deliberate changes in the course of transmission, the fact that in its present state it exhibits a high degree of metrical regularity is very impressive. That can hardly be the result of changes introduced into the text, and hence it is likely that the original composition was somewhat more symmetrical and precise in its rhythm. Occasionally, variant readings still attested in the manuscripts or the versions will supply a clue to the more original and metrical reading; more rarely a persuasive conjecture will do the same. It is sufficient for our purposes to uncover the basic patterns without attempting to restore or reconstruct the supposed original.

Other examples of metrical subtleties revealed by a total-syllable count, as contrasted with a stress-syllable count, may be drawn from early poems, e.g., the Song of the Sea (Exod. 15),[11] and David's Lament over Saul and Jonathan (II Sam. 1).[12] In Exod. 15:4 we read:

[10]The *ḥatef pataḥ* after laryngeals is a secondary development, and is not included in the syllable count.

[11]Cf. Cross and Freedman, "The Song of Miriam," *JNES*, XIV (1955), pp. 237-50. A detailed study of the meter and strophic structure of Exod. 15 will appear in the forthcoming J. M. Meyers *Festschrift*. A provisional treatment is to be found in "The Song of the Sea," *A Feeling of Celebration* (*Festschrift* in honor of Professor James Muilenburg; San Anselmo, Calif., 1967), pp. 1-10. For a somewhat different arrangement, see Cross, "The Song of the Sea and Canaanite Myth," *God and Christ: Existence and Province* (*Journal for Theology and the Church* [=*JTC*], 5 [1968]), pp. 1-26.

[12]Pending the publication of a study of the Lament of David in the Geo Widengren *Festschrift*, see an earlier provisional study of the poem Cross and Freedman, *AYP*, pp. 43-50. Cf. also, Gevirtz, *Patterns in the Early Poetry of Israel*, pp. 72-96, and Holladay, *VT*, XX (1970) pp. 153-89.

markĕbōt par^cōh wĕḥēlō	The chariots of Pharaoh and his army
yārāh bayyām	He hurled into the sea;
ūmibḥar šālīšāw	And the choicest of his officers
tubbĕ^cū bĕyam-sūp	Were drowned in the Reed Sea.

The stress-syllable count is clearly 3:2 / 2:2. Since the prevailing pattern in this poem is 2:2 / 2:2 (/ 2:2), (cf. vss. 6, 7, 9, 10, 11, 12, 13, 15, 16a, 17, 18), with occasional lines of 3:3 (cf. vss. 8bc, 14 16b), the text of vs. 4 is often emended (usually by dropping *wĕḥelo*),[13] to produce the expected 2:2 / 2:2. If, however, we use a total-syllable count, the picture is somewhat different. The verse as a whole has 24 syllables, with the major division at *bym* exactly in the middle: the two clauses match at 12 syllables each, and are parallel to each other in structure and content. The only difference between them (aside from the stress-syllable count) is in the placement of the minor pause or caesura. In the first bicolon it comes after *wḥylw* which results in an unbalanced division of the cola: 8:4 according to syllable count. In the second bicolon, the division comes in the middle, resulting in a syllable count of 6:6. In view of the data, the present text is to be defended, rather than emended, on metrical grounds. We may add that the 8:4 pattern in 4a is to be regarded as a permissible variant of the more common 6:6 pattern. In verse 7 we find a similar situation. The total number of syllables is 24, with the major division exactly in the middle of the verse (*qmyk*), producing a pattern 12:12; the two bicola are parallel in structure and content. The minor divisions within the bicola are also in the middle, resulting in patterns of 6:6.

In our opinion, the relative importance of stressed syllables in contrast with unstressed syllables has been exaggerated; a count of all the syllables provides a better clue to the metrical patterns of the poems of the Hebrew Bible. There is no reason why the two procedures cannot be used jointly, to check results, and sharpen insights into the nature of the material.

Gray shows commendable caution in dealing with larger poetic units. That such stanzas or strophes existed may be inferred from the use of certain devices to mark off sections of a poem. The most obvious of these are refrains, that is lines repeated exactly or with slight modifications at regular intervals in the poem. They occur in the Psalter (e.g., Pss. 46, 67), and were used also by the prophets (e.g., Amos 1-2, 4; Isa. 9-10). Difficulties arise when the attempt is made to deduce the principles governing stanza formation, or to define the structure of the strophes set off by the refrains. All too often the stanzas do not have a regular structure, nor do they conform to a standard pattern. There is always the possibility that the extant text is not intact, and that it has suffered losses through scribal error, or has gained accretions by accident or editorial design. Displacement and rearrangement are also to be reckoned with, but to restore a supposed original and symmetrical structure is a hazardous procedure.

[13]We treated the passage as conflate in Cross and Freedman, *JNES*, XIV (1955), pp. 241-44; cf. also Cross, *JTC*, 5 (1968), p. 13, n. 44.

Inclusion in its basic form is characterized by the exact repetition of key words or phrases. When these are extended to clauses or entire verse-lines, they are equivalent to refrains, which serve to define the limits of the poem or the stanzas within it. A more complex and less easily recognized form of inclusion (or envelope construction) does not involve the repetition of terms, but rather the resumption or completion of a thought. It is as though the poet deliberately split a bicolon or couplet, and inserted a variety of materials between the opening and closing halves of that unit to form a stanza. The notion that a grammatical unit may begin at one point in a composition and be continued somewhere else is novel to say the least. Proposed examples must be tested thoroughly, and in any case are not likely to convince all scholars. It may be added that such a view of poetic structure implies, if it does not require, a degree of literary sophistication not usually associated with oral composition or the poets of ancient Israel. Nevertheless the subject deserves attention, and the isolated example offered here may be a harbinger of others not yet detected.

It has been observed that the prophet Hosea often links Egypt and Assyria in parallel construction when speaking of Israel's imminent doom and threatened exile: e.g., 7:11; 9:3; 11:5, 11; 12:2.[14] In 8:9 we have a typical reference to Assyria:

kī-hēmmāh ᶜālū[15] *ᵓaššūr*	For behold they will go up to Assyria.

There is no parallel to this colon in vs. 9, but in vs. 13 we read:

hēmmāh miṣray(i)m yāšūbū	Behold they will return to Egypt.

The latter has no parallel in vs. 13 or its vicinity, but it is clear that the two cola complement each other impressively. Thus we note the repetition of the particle *hmh*,[16] the balancing alternation of the perfect (*ᶜlw*) and imperfect (*yšwbw*) forms of the verb, and the chiasm in *ᶜlw ᵓšwr* and *mṣrym yšwbw*; the syllable count is 7:7. It would occasion no surprise to find these well-matched cola side by side in a poem, but they are four verses apart. Assuming that the positioning of these cola was deliberate, it is inescapable that they form an envelope or framework around a major poetic unit.[17]

[14]An echo of this pattern is to be seen in Lam. 5:6.

[15]In spite of the perfect form, the verb seems to have future force.

[16]While *hmh* is normally taken as the 3rd m. pl. pronoun, it is more likely to be the interjection, "Lo! Behold!" equivalent to Ugaritic *hm/hmt*, cf. Dahood, *Psalms I*, Index, p. 320, and *Psalms II*, Index, p. 383. A good example of similar usage is to be found in Deut. 33:17.

wĕhēm ribĕbōt ᵓeprayim	Now behold the myriads of Ephraim,
wĕhēm ᵓalpē mĕnaššeh	Now behold the thousands of Manasseh.

See Cross and Freedman, *JBL*, LXVII (1948), pp. 195, and 207, n. 62.

[17]This phenomenon has been dealt with in an article on the structure of Ps. 29 which has been prepared by a student, Mrs. Christine Hyland, with my assistance, and which is scheduled to appear in *HTR* (1972).

In his search for the key to Hebrew metrics, Gray devoted considerable attention (Chaps. III, VII, VIII) to the acrostic poems of the Old Testament. Since they are by no means typical of Hebrew poetry generally, it may be doubted whether they provide a suitable base on which to formulate principles governing the nature of the metrical systems employed by the biblical poets. Furthermore the fact that acrostic poems have a rather rigid structure may have encouraged greater independence on the part of the poet in working out internal configurations so that a wider range of variation results, partly from the desire to avoid monotony, than would otherwise be the case.[18] The great virtue of acrostic poems is that lines or stanzas are regularly marked off by words beginning with successive letters of the alphabet. Thus in the Book of Lamentations, the first four chapters are regular acrostics, while the fifth chapter follows the same pattern but without making use of the alphabetic device itself. In the first three chapters, three-line stanzas are the rule; in chaps. 1 and 2 each stanza begins with a successive letter of the alphabet, whereas in chap. 3, each of the three lines of the stanza begins with the same letter of the alphabet. Thus the first word of the first stanza of each of the poems begins with the letter *ʾālef*; in the case of chap. 3, the second and third lines of the stanza also begin with *ʾālef*. The first word of the second stanza begins with *bēt*; again in chapter 3, the second and third lines also begin with *bēt*. Chapter 4 follows the same pattern as chaps. 1 and 2, except that the stanzas have two lines instead of three.

Thanks to this feature, students can determine line and stanza length with a considerable degree of objectivity and accuracy. Since the Book of Lamentations is a relatively homogeneous corpus so far as subject matter and perspective are concerned, it is possible to assemble sufficient data for statistical purposes to describe the typical or standard metrical unit, as well as the range of deviation from the norm. It should also be possible to devise criteria to establish the limits of acceptability, beyond which deviations could be identified as the result of error or editorial modification.

Unless we are to assume gross wholesale corruption of the text, we must recognize that there is considerable variation in the length of lines and stanzas, whatever counting system is used. The evidence for such widespread corruption is negligible, and the assumption is based largely on certain metrical theories about the material. The combination of theories and assumptions is self-defeating, as the reasoning is circular, and results in the creation of a variety of new texts with matching metrical systems. On the contrary there is every reason to believe in the essential soundness of the preserved text, especially in Lamentations, because the editors and scribes had the same acrostic pattern in front of them to help keep the poetic structure intact.

For the reasons given, a statistical approach is likely to yield better results for metrical analysis than the virtuoso handling of individual lines

[18]Of the five poems in Lamentations, chap. 5 is the most regular from a metrical standpoint; at the same time it is the only one without the alphabetic pattern.

which has characterized much of the work to date. In fact, the range of variation is rather limited, and sufficient data seem readily available from Lamentations to fix line and stanza patterns within relatively narrow limits. The writer hopes to publish elsewhere a detailed statistical analysis of the acrostic poems in Lamentations and elsewhere in the Hebrew Bible. It will suffice to summarize the results here:

Poem	*Syllables*	*Lines*	*Average*
Lamentations 5	362	22	16.5
Proverbs 31	360	22	16.4
Psalm 25	362	22	16.5
Psalm 34	351	21	16.7
Psalm 37	719	44	16.3
Psalm 111	169	11	15.4
Psalm 112	169	11	15.4
Psalm 119	2,870	176	16.3
Psalm 145	400	22	18.2

The other group, including Lam. 1-4 exhibits the following pattern:

Lamentations 1	865	67	12.9
Lamentations 2	863	67	12.9
Lamentations 3	868	66	13.2
Lamentations 4	609	44	13.8

There seem to be at least two different structures for acrostic poems in the Bible, with the major group having lines, or bicola, averaging around 16 and 1/2 syllables. A special group represented by Lam. 1-4 has a shorter line of 13-14 syllables. In the poems there is a wide range of variation in the length of lines and stanzas.[19] The deviations form their own patterns, as we have observed, and the end product was strictly controlled by factors of overall length, and a strong sense of balance.

In his discussion of the widespread practice of emending the biblical text through alteration, excision, addition, and rearrangement on the basis of metrical considerations, Gray focussed attention on the arbitrary and subjective character of many of the proposals made by scholars of his day. The destructive results of such scholarship have become only too apparent in the years since, and scholars on the whole are now more careful in dealing with the Hebrew text. The chief danger in invoking the formula *metri causa* lies in the necessarily circular reasoning which is used to support proposed emendations. Since there are no external criteria for determining the meter, it must be derived or calculated from the existing text. Then the same text is corrected or improved on the basis of the meter which was derived from it. The more tightly drawn the reasoning the more vicious the circle.

[19]Except for the short poems, Pss. 111 and 112, which have a narrow range of variation.

Conjectural emendations, whatever their basis or source, are inevitably suspect, and few have survived critical scrutiny. Those which are based upon metrical factors are peculiarly vulnerable, and should be avoided assiduously. Apart from the fact that there has been too much activity of this sort with unconvincing results, there are two important reasons for pursuing a different strategy in dealing with the biblical text:

1. Metrical analysis is now entering a new statistical phase, and can provide an adequate, often detailed, description of the phenomena. We can henceforth be reasonably confident about overall patterns and structures, as well as the numerical limits within which the poets operated; but in the nature of the case these cannot help us decide specific questions about particular lines or words. As we have seen, there are standard deviations from presumed norms, i.e., they are part of the poet's bag of tools, to be used at his option. It would be practically impossible to determine on metrical grounds when such variations were the result of error or later editorial change, and when they were part of the original poet's plan. Earlier approaches to the question of meter were often monotonously mechanical, and the structures on the basis of which emendations were made too rigidly repetitive.

2. Emendations inevitably reflect the state of scholarship at the time the emendations are proposed, and hence have an inhibiting effect on the advancement of knowledge, and the discovery of new features of the language. Emendation often eliminates or obscures devices deliberately used by the poet but not readily recognized by scholars trained in the formal grammar and syntax of Hebrew prose. Much of the progress in analyzing and interpreting the more difficult poetic passages in the Hebrew Bible has been achieved through decipherment of literary materials in cognate languages, especially Ugaritic, and the application of these new data to biblical poetry. The identification of the same and related phenomena in the biblical text has helped to clarify obscure passages, without recourse to drastic or wholesale emendation. Increasingly, new and more refined techniques for dealing with the text are being developed which give promise of achieving more economic, convincing, and satisfying results.

In all this, we do not question the importance or validity of the emendatory process as a scholarly enterprise or obligation. Certainly we do not imply that the preserved Hebrew text is intact. Admittedly numerous errors have occurred in the transmission of the text, as well as deliberate editorial and scribal changes. The difficulty lies in locating, defining, and then correcting them. All too often, the prescribed cure is only another form of the disease, sometimes more virulent. In the case of divergent readings in Hebrew manuscripts or the versions, it is clear that choices must be made. But in the absence of direct manuscript evidence, extreme caution should be exercised, and emendation should be avoided if at all possible. While the Massoretes were fallible, they were also faithful to the tradition. So even changes in vocalization, or the redivision of words and phrases should be justified with care. Recourse to more drastic procedures should be recognized as a last and desperate resort. Conjectural emendations are more likely to be remembered as exercises in scholarly ingenuity than as serious contributions to the recovery of the original reading.

There is every reason to believe that many of the remaining problems in the poetry of the Bible will yield to the vigorous but controlled application of the new methods, disciplined by a rational respect for the extant text, and extreme caution in conjecture. There is always the expectation of new discoveries of literary materials which will enhance our knowledge of the language of the Bible, and the cultural tradition from which it came.

ACROSTICS AND METRICS IN HEBREW POETRY

In his search for the key to Hebrew metrics, George Buchanan Gray devoted considerable attention to the acrostic poems of the Old Testament.[1] Since they are by no means typical of Hebrew poetry generally, it may be doubted whether they provide a suitable base on which to formulate principles governing the nature of the metrical systems employed by the biblical poets. Furthermore, the fact that acrostic poems have a rather rigid structure may have encouraged greater independence on the part of the poet in working out internal configurations so that a wider range of variation results, partly from the desire to avoid monotony, than would otherwise be the case.[2] The great virtue of acrostic poems is that lines or stanzas are regularly marked off by words beginning with successive letters of the alphabet. Thus in the Book of Lamentations, the first four chapters are regular acrostics, while the fifth chapter follows the same pattern but without making use of the alphabetic device itself. In the first three chapters, three-line stanzas are the rule; in chapters one and two each stanza begins with a successive letter of the alphabet, whereas in chapter three, each of the three lines of the stanza begins with the same letter of the alphabet. Thus the first word of the first stanza of each of the poems begins with the letter *'ālef*; in the case of chapter three, the second and third lines of the stanza also begin with *'ālef*. The first word of the second stanza begins with *bēt*; again in chapter three, the second and third lines also begin with *bēt*. Chapter four follows the same pattern as chapters one and two, except that the stanzas have two lines instead of three.

[1] *The Forms of Hebrew Poetry* (London, 1915), Chaps. III, VII, VIII.

[2] Of the five poems in Lamentations, chap. 5 is the most regular from a metrical standpoint; at the same time it is the only one without the alphabetic pattern.

Thanks to this feature, students can determine line and stanza length with a considerable degree of objectivity and accuracy. Since the Book of Lamentations is a relatively homogeneous corpus so far as subject matter and perspective are concerned, it is possible to assemble sufficient data for statistical purposes to describe the typical or standard metrical unit, as well as the range of deviation from the norm. It should also be possible to devise criteria to establish the limits of acceptability, beyond which deviations could be identified as the result of error or editorial modification.

Unless we are to assume gross wholesale corruption of the text, we must recognize that there is considerable variation in the length of lines and stanzas, whatever counting system is used. The evidence for such widespread corruption is negligible, and the assumption is based largely on certain metrical theories about the material. The combination of theories and assumptions is self-defeating, as the reasoning is circular, and results in the creation of a variety of new texts with matching metrical systems. On the contrary there is every reason to believe in the essential soundness of the preserved text, especially in Lamentations because the editors and scribes had the same acrostic pattern in front of them to help keep the poetic structure intact.

For the reasons given, a statistical approach is likely to yield better results for metrical analysis than the virtuoso handling of individual lines which has characterized much of the work to date. In fact, the range of variation is rather limited, and sufficient data are available from Lamentations to fix line and stanza patterns within relatively narrow limits. The following tables give the syllable counts for the poems in Lamentations 1–3. We have avoided emendations entirely, though we acknowledge without dispute that there are corrupt passages and that remedies are available for some of them. But few if any of them have commanded universal assent, and our purpose is to avoid debate over this or that emendation. Since our objective is to establish statistical norms, minor variations will not affect the results, and major ones, being immediately apparent, can be excluded from the calculations. What we are after is the profile of the typical or average line and stanza in the acrostic poems, and the data as preserved in MT are more than sufficient for this purpose. With respect to the vocalization of the words, and the counting of syllables, we have followed MT generally, except where we have convincing evidence for a different vocalization going back behind the Massoretic tradition. Thus we treat segolate formations as originally monosyllabic; we omit secondary vowels (usually *ḥatefs* associated with laryngeals, and including *pataḥ* furtive).

Since we are undecided about the vocalization of certain pronominal suffixes of the 2nd and 3rd person singular attached to verbs, we have supplied two sets of figures, one following the Kethib, the other the Qere.[3] In general the first column reflects the presumed vocalization of the written text: e.g.,* *hsygwh* (1:3) = *hissīgūh*, 3 syllables although vocalized *hissīgūhā*, 4 syllables. The second column, however, reflects the addition of such pronominal endings which are indicated in the vocalization of MT. We have attempted to be consistent throughout, although it is reasonable to believe that the poet himself might have employed somewhat more flexible standards to achieve a more uniform rhythm. Exceptional cases were handled on an ad hoc basis. It should be emphasized that for statistical purposes it does not matter a great deal what counting method is used; for example, had we followed MT exactly, the relative overall results would not have been affected, so long as the principles were applied consistently throughout the material. It is of no particular consequence either if the procedures adopted conform to the actual practice of the 6th century B.C.E., as we hope, or not. The statistical analysis is not impaired, though caution must be exercised in applying the data to the period of composition. So long as we restrict ourselves to descriptions, comparisons, and summaries, we are on safe ground. The degree to which relative conclusions can be objectified will depend upon the soundness of the text, and the validity of the vocalization.

[3] See discussion of this problem in F. M. Cross and D. N. Freedman, *Early Hebrew Orthography* (New Haven, 1952), 65–68. We use the terms in a specialized sense to distinguish the short and long forms of these elements: e.g., the 2nd m. sing. form in the Kethib is written *-t* and occasionally *-th*; the vocalization (i.e., the "Qere") is uniformly *-tā*. The same line of reasoning holds for *-k* and *-kh* (Kethib), but vocalized *-kā* (Qere). We must also allow a reasonable margin for uncertainty or error.

Lamentations

	1		2			3	
	A	B	A	B		A	B
(1)	13	13	14	14	(1)	13	13
	13	13	11	11	(2)	11	11
	12	12	12	12	(3)	11	11
Total	38	38	37	37		35	35
(2)	14	15	14	14	(4)	13	13
	10	11	13	13	(5)	12	12
	14	15	12	13	(6)	13	13
Total	38	41	39	40		38	38
(3)	15	15	11	11	(7)	13	13
	13	13	12	12	(8)	14	14
	12	14	16	16	(9)	14	14
Total	40	42	39	39		41	41
(4)	14	14	14	14	(10)	11	11
	13	15	13	13	(11)	15	16
	10	11	7	7	(12)	15	15
Total	37	40	34	34		41	42
(5)	11	13	13	13	(13)	11	11
	10	11	12	13	(14)	16	16
	11	12	14	14	(15)	13	13
Total	32	36	39	40		40	40
(6)	11	11	12	12	(16)	14	14
	14	15	12	12	(17)	13	13
	11	11	11	11	(18)	14	14
Total	36	37	35	35		41	41
(7)	15	16	13	13	(19)	12	12
	11	12	12	13	(20)	11	11
	12	12	12	12	(21)	10	10
	11	13	37	38		33	33
Total	49	53					
(8)	16	16	12	12	(22)	16	16
	14	16	11	11	(23)	13	14
	10	10	12	12	(24)	14	14
Total	40	42	35	35		43	44
(9)	13	14	16	18	(25)	12	12
	11	11	11	12	(26)	12	12
	12	12	13	14	(27)	10	10
Total	36	37	40	44		34	34

	1 A	1 B	2 A	2 B		3 A	3 B
(10)	10	11	13	13	(28)	12	12
	11	11	12	12	(29)	12	12
	13	13	14	14	(30)	13	13
	34	35	39	39		37	37
(11)	11	11	14	14	(31)	10	10
	13	13	12	12	(32)	12	12
	15	15	13	13	(33)	13	13
	39	39	39	39		35	35
(12)	15	15	13	13	(34)	11	11
	13	13	12	12	(35)	11	11
	12	12	11	11	(36)	14	14
	40	40	36	36		36	36
(13)	14	14	15	15	(37)	13	13
	12	12	15	15	(38)	13	13
	12	12	11	11	(39)	12	12
	38	38	41	41		38	38
(14)	13	13	10	10	(40)	18	18
	10	10	14	14	(41)	14	14
	13	13	11	11	(42)	14	15
	36	36	35	35		46	47
(15)	12	12	12	12	(43)	15	17
	11	11	15	15	(44)	13	13
	13	13	19	19	(45)	14	14
	36	36	46	46		42	44
(16)	16	16	10	10	(46)	12	12
	13	13	14	14	(47)	12	12
	12	12	15	15	(48)	12	12
	41	41	39	39		36	36
(17)	13	14	13	13	(49)	14	14
	12	12	13	13	(50)	11	11
	13	13	12	13	(51)	14	14
	38	39	38	39		39	39
(18)	11	11	13	13	(52)	12	12
	12	12	12	12	(53)	12	12
	14	14	13	13	(54)	12	12
	37	37	38	38		36	36

Lamentations (Continued)

	1		*2*			*3*	
	A	*B*	*A*	*B*		*A*	*B*
(19)	13	13	12	12	(55)	12	12
	12	12	12	12	(56)	17	19
	14	14	11	11	(57)	12	15
	39	39	12	12		41	46
			47	47			
(20)	13	13	13	14	(58)	12	14
	13	13	14	14	(59)	14	14
	10	10	15	15	(60)	13	13
	36	36	42	43		39	41
(21)	14	14	11	11	(61)	14	15
	12	12	13	13	(62)	13	13
	16	19	11	15	(63)	15	15
	42	45	35	39		42	43
(22)	14	15	12	12	(64)	14	14
	11	12	14	14	(65)	13	14
	11	11	14	14	(66)	14	14
	36	38	40	40		41	42
Total:	838	865	850	863		854	868

Distribution Table

No. of Stanzas (A)				*Syllables*	*No. of Stanzas (B)*			
1	*2*	*3*	*Total*		*1*	*2*	*3*	*Total*
1	0	0	1	32	0	0	0	0
0	0	1	1	33	0	0	1	1
1	1	1	3	34	0	1	1	2
0	4	2	6	35	1	3	2	6
6	1	3	10	36	4	1	3	8
2	2	1	5	37	3	1	1	5
4	2	2	8	38	3	2	2	7
2	6	2	10	39	3	6	1	10
3	2	1	6	40	2	3	1	6
1	1	5	7	41	2	1	3	6
1	1	2	4	42	2	0	2	4
0	0	1	1	43	0	1	1	2
0	0	0	0	44	0	1	2	3
0	0	0	0	45	1	0	0	1
0	1	1	2	46	0	1	1	2
0	1	0	1	47	0	1	1	2
1	0	0	1	49	0	0	0	0
0	0	0	0	53	1	0	0	1
22	22	22	66		22	22	22	66

Column A

				Total
Total syllables:	838	850	854	2,542
Average per stanza:	38.1	38.6	38.8	38.5

Column B

Total syllables:	865	863	868	2,596
Average per stanza:	39.3	39.2	39.5	39.3

In spite of considerable variation in the length of individual stanzas (from 32 to 49 syllables in Col. A, from 33 to 53 in Col. B), the totals, and averages, are remarkably close to each other and consistent. For Col. A, the maximum deviation is less than one syllable per stanza (.7 between chaps. 1 and 3, and not more than .4 from the average of 38.5). For Col. B, the maximum deviation is .3 per stanza (between chaps. 2 and 3), while it is less than .2 from the average of 39.3. Even the variant figures resulting from the use of different counting systems do not diverge significantly, the average deviation being .8 of a syllable per stanza, which is well within the margin of uncertainty which must be allowed in calculations of this sort.

The pattern of distribution may be summarized as follows:

Column A

Range	Median 38.5 Stanzas	Percent
37–40	29	44%
36–41	46	70%
35–42	56	85%
34–43	60	91%

Column B

Range	Median 39.0 Stanzas	Percent
37–41	34	52%
36–42	46	70%
35–43	54	82%
34–44	59	90%

If we were to consolidate the data from both columns, we would have the following figures:

Range	Stanzas	Percent
38–40	47	36%
37–40	57	43%
37–41	70	53%
36–41	88	67%
36–42	96	73%
35–43	111	84%
34–44	119	90%

Since our knowledge is less than complete, and our methods rather imprecise, a minimum allowance of one syllable per line (or bicolon) or three syllables per stanza would seem to be in order to account for possible differences in vocalization and syllable counting. Thus while the typical three-line stanza has 39 syllables, stanzas ranging in length from 36 to 42 syllables (over 70% of the total) should be regarded as essentially equivalent. In addition, the poet exercised an option to deviate even further from this norm; but the differences tended to balance out. It is noteworthy that the inclusion of irregular or atypical stanzas does not affect the overall correlation of the poems. Chaps. 1 and 2, in spite of their exceptional four-line stanzas, have almost exactly the same total length as chap. 3. The differences among the poems as a whole are practically nil.[4] We conclude that the poet was free to choose from a variety of stanza lengths, clustering around 39 syllables. At the same time, he was guided or limited by factors governing overall length, and the need to achieve an effective balance between longer and shorter stanzas.

The statistical picture presented by chap. 4 is comparable, though the details differ. In the following tables we continue to provide two sets of figures, reflecting the different methods of counting already described in connection with chaps. 1–3.

LAMENTATIONS 4

	A	*B*		*A*	*B*		*A*	*B*
(1)	12	12	(2)	13	15	(3)	13	13
	12	12		15	15		12	12
	24	24		28	30		25	25
(4)	12	12	(5)	14	14	(6)	13	13
	12	12		14	14		14	14
	24	24		28	28		27	27

[4] To remove these lines (1:7 and 2:19) as editorial additions would create an imbalance in the total syllable count between chaps. 1 and 2 on the one hand, and chap. 3 on the other, where none exists now. These extended stanzas are apparently part of the overall scheme, which includes several abbreviated stanzas as well. Similar variations occur in chap. 3. The present correlation in total syllable count, surely not the product of editorial activity, deliberate or accidental, remains a factor of crucial importance in determining principles and procedures.

LAMENTATIONS 4 (Continued)

Stanza	A	B
(7)	12	13
	13	13
	25	26
(8)	14	15
	13	13
	27	28
(9)	14	14
	15	15
	29	29
(10)	14	15
	12	12
	26	27
(11)	14	14
	14	15
	28	29
(12)	14	14
	14	14
	28	28
(13)	12	14
	11	11
	23	25
(14)	13	13
	12	12
	25	25
(15)	17	17
	18	18
	35	35
(16)	14	14
	16	16
	30	30
(17)	15	15
	14	14
	29	29
(18)	13	13
	16	16
	29	29
(19)	13	13
	16	16
	29	29
(20)	14	14
	13	13
	27	27
(21)	14	14
	13	13
	27	27
(22)	14	14
	14	14
	28	28
Total:	601	609

DISTRIBUTION TABLE

Number of Stanzas (A)	*Syllables*	*Number of Stanzas (B)*
1	23	0
2	24	2
3	25	3
1	26	1
4	27	4
5	28	4
4	29	5
1	30	2
1	35	1
22		22

	COLUMN A	COLUMN B
Total syllables:	601	609
Average per stanza:	27.3	27.7

The size of the sample is insufficient to permit definite conclusions, but the general picture is similar to what we have seen in chaps. 1–3. The average and median fall between 27 and 28 for both columns (the difference between A and B is mathematically insignificant). Most of the stanzas cluster in the range between 27 and 28 (13 stanzas or about 60% of the total), with the rest distributed from 23 (or 24) to 35.[5] Once again we observe the phenomenon of longer and shorter stanzas balancing off. Unfortunately we do not have another acrostic poem of the same kind with which to compare chap. 4.[6]

Turning now to the calculation of line length, we have the following data for chaps. 1–3:

DISTRIBUTION TABLE

No. of Lines (A)				*Syllables*	*No. of Lines (B)*			
1	*2*	*3*	*Total*		*1*	*2*	*3*	*Total*
0	1	0	1	7	0	1	0	1
7	2	3	12	10	3	2	3	8
13	11	8	32	11	12	9	8	29
13	20	17	50	12	15	17	15	47
17	14	15	46	13	16	16	13	45
10	11	15	36	14	8	13	16	37
4	5	4	13	15	8	6	5	19
3	2	2	7	16	4	1	3	8
0	0	1	1	17	0	0	1	1
0	0	1	1	18	0	1	1	2
0	1	0	1	19	1	1	1	3
67	67	66	200		67	67	66	200

	COLUMN A *Syllables*	*Average*	COLUMN B *Syllables*	*Average*
Chap. 1	838	12.5	865	12.9
Chap. 2	850	12.7	863	12.9
Chap. 3	854	12.9	868	13.2
Total:	2,542	12.7	2,596	13.0

As was true of the stanzas, there is considerable variation in the length of individual lines. Nevertheless, the average line length hardly varies at all from poem to poem. It is 12.7 in Col.

[5] Lam. 4:15 is an exceptional stanza with 35 syllables. The rest are two-line units ranging from 23 (or 24) to 30 syllables in length.

[6] Ps. 37, which is also a two-line alphabetic acrostic, has a substantially different structure. See discussion below.

A, with a maximum deviation of .2 in either direction; it is 13.0 in Col. B, with an even smaller range (from 12.9 to 13.2). The median is in approximately the same position, just under 13. The distribution pattern can be summarized as follows:

Range	Column A Lines	Percent	Range	Column B Lines	Percent
12–14	132	66%	12–14	129	64.5%
11–15	177	87.5%	11–15	177	87.5%
10–16	196	98%	10–16	193	96.5%

Taking 13 as our midpoint, we find almost 2/3 of all the lines within a single syllable of this number in either direction (i.e., 12–14). If we extend the range by another syllable (to 11–15), then we can account for 7/8 of all the lines. Within this normal range, the poet was expected to compose his lines; rarely and for special reasons, he could go beyond these limits. Once again and in even more impressive fashion, we observe a pattern of overall regularity, along with considerable flexibility in individual lines.

The figures for chap. 4 are as follows:

Distribution Table

Number of Lines (A)	*Syllables*	*Number of Lines (B)*
1	11	1
9	12	7
10	13	10
16	14	14
3	15	7
3	16	3
1	17	1
1	18	1
44		44

	Column A	Column B
Total syllables:	601	609
Average per line:	13.7	13.8

The average line length is 13 and 3/4, with the median about the same. The distribution may be summarized as follows:

Range	Column A Lines	Percent	Range	Column B Lines	Percent
13–15	29	66%	13–15	31	70%
12–16	41	93%	12–16	41	93%

The statistics for chap. 4 are somewhat different from those for the first three chapters. The average (and median) line length is almost a syllable longer, though this is still within the margin we have allowed for uncertainty. Within chap. 4, the concentration of lines within the normal range is notable: the bracket 13–15 accounts for about 2/3 of the total; if the range is extended by an additional syllable in either direction, then almost all of the lines (93%) are included.

While these statistics cannot be used to control or emend specific lines or stanzas, since deviations and other eccentricities are an integral and inescapable part of poetic strategy, nevertheless they give a thoroughly adequate metrical description of prevailing usage in the 6th century B.C.E. The evidence provided by Ps. 137 supports the general conclusions drawn from chaps. 1–4 of Lamentations. This is of particular interest because the Psalm shares a common theme and period of composition with Lamentations.[7] In Ps. 137, the Opening (vss. 1–2) and Closing (vss. 8–9) have 37 and 38 syllables respectively, thus conforming in overall length to the normative pattern of Lam. 1–3. The body of the poem, vss. 3–7, consists of an introductory stanza (vs. 3), a double stanza in the center (vss. 4–6), and a following stanza (vs. 7). Structurally, vss. 3 and 7 complement each other, and together balance off vss. 4–6. Vss. 3 and 7 have 27 syllables each, while the double stanza (vss. 4–6) has 54 syllables. These are all well within the normative range determined for Lam. 4. The fact that Ps. 137 has stanzas of different length is of interest in itself, and offers some hint of the rich variety available to the Hebrew poets. The greater regularity in basic stanza structure in the poems we have been considering may be attributed to the acrostic pattern.

Returning to Lamentations, we wish to emphasize certain data which have been noted, namely, the frequency and distribution of anomalous features. The most striking phenomenon of this sort is the occurrence of a single four-line stanza in each of the first two poems (1:7 and 2:19), a marked deviation from the

[7] A detailed study of the metrical structure of this psalm is to be found in The Structure of Psalm 137, *Near Eastern Studies in Honor of William Foxwell Albright,* ed. Hans Goedicke (Baltimore, 1971), 187–205.

prevailing three-line pattern. Closer inspection of these stanzas is in order.

Lam. 1:7 reads as follows:

zākerāh Yerūšālēm [8]	Jerusalem ponders
yemē 'onyāh ūmerūdēh(ā) [9]	the days of her affliction and homelessness —
kōl maḥmudēh(ā)	all the precious possessions
'ašer hāyū mīmē qadm	which were hers from ancient times —
binpōl 'ammāh beyad-ṣār	when her people fell by the hand of the foe
we'ēn 'ōzēr lāh	and there was no one to aid her.
rā'ūh(ā) ṣārīm śāḥaqū	The foes gloated over her, they laughed
'al-mišbatteh(ā) [10]	at her destruction.

The second line is usually omitted in order to achieve the standard three-line pattern. It is true that the line disturbs the syntactic connections, especially between *ymy 'nyh* etc. and *bnpl 'mh.*[11] It also introduces a diversionary element, the glory of the early days, into an otherwise cohesive unit dealing with the current tragedy. Nevertheless, the vocabulary is characteristic of Lamentations, as well as the association of ideas.[12] The con-

[8] The four-syllable pronunciation *Yerūšālēm* undoubtedly prevailed during the classical period. The Qere *Yerūšālayim* is already reflected in the orthography of some of the Dead Sea scrolls, but cannot be traced to an earlier period.

[9] The sense of the word is indicated by its association with *'ny*; cf. Lam. 3:19 and Isa. 58:7.

[10] The term is a *hapax*; it may be that the initial *mem* should be construed as enclitic with the preceding *'l*. In any case the meaning, "cessation, destruction," and derivation from *šbt* seem clear. Cf. T. McDaniel, Philological Studies in Lamentations: I, *Biblica* 49 (1968), 53.

[11] RSV renders:

> Jerusalem remembers in the days of her affliction
> and bitterness
> all the precious things that were hers from
> the days of old.

This is unsatisfactory, since "the days of her affliction" must be taken as the direct object of "remembers." We note that at 3:19, where the same terms occur in combination, RSV renders correctly: "Remember my affliction."

[12] For *mḥmd,* cf. 1:10, 11; and for *ymy qdm,* cf. 2:17.

trast between the former splendor and the present misery of Jerusalem and its people is a major theme of the first poem.

Lam. 2:19 reads:

qūmī rōnnī ballayl(ā)	Rise, cry out in the night
l^{e}rō’š ’ašmurōt	during the first of the watches.
šipkī kammaym libbēk	Pour out your heart like water
nōkḥ p^{e}nē ’^{a}dōnāy	in the presence of the Lord.
ś^{e}’ī ’ēlāw kappayk	Lift your hands to him
‘al- napš ‘ōlālayk	for the lives of your children
hā‘^{a}tūpīm b^{e}rā‘āb	who faint from hunger
b^{e}rō’š kol-ḥūṣōt	in all the main streets.

It is customary to excise the fourth line for strophic reasons. A case can be made that the line is excessive, and disturbs the homogeneity of the three-line unit to which it is attached. Note the sequence of verbs in the imperative 2nd f. s., and the close parallelism between the second and third lines. On the other hand, the fourth line balances the first line metrically (both are $7 + 5 = 12$); it also fits the immediate context, and shares both terminology and mood with the rest of the poem.[13]

The fact that the same deviation, one four-line stanza in a poem of three-line stanzas, occurs in both poems, suggests the possibility that it is a deliberate device. Hesitation to emend away the fourth line is strengthened when we examine chap. 4, and find a single expanded stanza (vs. 15) conspicuously longer than and divergent from the two-line stanzas, which otherwise follow in regular unbroken sequence.[14] The structure of the stanza may be analyzed as follows:

sūrū ṭāmē’	"Depart, you unclean,"
qār^{e}’ū lāmō	they cried to them,

[13] Cf. 2:11–12, where the same terminology occurs, including *‘tp* and *‘ll*. For *ḥwṣwt* in 2:19, however, we have *rḥwbwt* in vss. 11 and 12. There are other minor differences as well, showing that there is no question of direct copying.

[14] In Prov. 31:10–31, which is an alphabetic acrostic, there is a single tricolon (vs. 15) in an otherwise unbroken sequence of bicola. This phenomenon seems too widespread and patterned to be the coincidental result of changes, accidental or editorial, independently introduced into the several poems.

sūrū sūrū	"Depart! depart!
'al- tiggā'ū	do not trespass!"
kī nāṣū gam nā'ū	"For they are homeless, even wanderers,"
'ām^{e}rū baggōyīm	they said, among the nations,
lō' yōsīpū lāgūr	"they shall not stay any longer."

The stanza apparently consists of a long bicolon (2:2/3 or 4/3), followed by a tricolon (2:2:2). The syllable count is:

$$9 + 8 = 17$$
$$6 + 6 + 6 = 18$$

Other arrangements are possible,[15] but the shift from the 2nd to the 3rd person after *tg'w* seems to mark the major division in the stanza. However we classify the component parts, it is clear that the stanza is substantially longer than any of the others in the poem,[16] and is constructed differently.

Irregular stanzas with 3 and 1/2 lines (i.e., a colon added to the third line) turn up in chaps. 1 and 2, again one in each.

At 1:21 we read:

šām^{e}'ū kī ne'^{e}nāḥāh 'ānī	They heard how I groaned
'ēn m^{e}naḥēm lī	there was no one to console me.
kol-'ōy^{e}bay šām^{e}'ū	All my enemies heard
rā'ātī śāśū	they rejoiced at my trouble;
kī 'attāh 'āśīt(ā)[17]	But you, may you achieve it,
hēbē't(ā) yōm qārā't(ā)	may you bring the day which you proclaimed

[15] MT has the major pause at *n'w*. If we accept this division, we would have a three-line stanza, as follows:

$$4 + 5 + 4 = 13$$
$$4 + 6 = 10$$
$$6 + 6 = 12$$

[16] With 35 syllables it is about one-third longer than the average. There is approximately the same ratio between the four-line and three-line stanzas in chaps. 1 and 2.

[17] We interpret *'śyt* and *hb't* as precative perfects, in accordance with the context. On the phenomenon in Hebrew poetry, cf. DAHOOD, *Psalms I* (*Anchor Bible*; New York, 1966), Index, 328; *Psalms II* (*Anchor Bible*; New York, 1968), Index, 396.

w^{e}yihyū kāmōnī	and let them become as I am.

At Lam. 2:15 we read:

sāp^{e}qū ʿālayk kappaym	They clap their hands at you,
kol-ʿōb^{e}rē dark	all who pass along the way.
šār^{e}qū wayyānīʿū rō'šām ʿal-bat Y^{e}rūšālēm	They hiss and shake their heads at Daughter Jerusalem.
h^{a}zōʾt hāʿīr šeyyō'm^{e}rū	Is this the city of which they said,
k^{e}līlat yōpī	"Perfection of beauty,
māśōś l^{e}kol-hā'ārṣ	joy of the whole earth."

The two stanzas are quite similar in structure:

1:21	2:15
$9 + 5 = 14$	$7 + 5 = 12$
$7 + 5 = 12$	$9 + 6 = 15$
$6 + 7 + 6 = 19$	$8 + 5 + 6 = 19$

A similar phenomenon occurs in Lam. 4:18, where the second line has been expanded by the addition of a single colon. We read as follows:

ṣādū ṣ^{e}ʿādēnū	They tracked our steps
millikt birḥōbōtēnū	so that we could not walk in the squares.
qārab qiṣṣēnū	Our end has drawn near
māl^{e}'ū yāmēnū	our days are completed
kī-bā' qiṣṣēnū	indeed our end has come.

As we have already observed, there are a number of short stanzas to offset the lengthened ones. One of these deserves special attention because it lacks a colon or half-line. We read 2:4 as follows:

dārak qaštō k^{e}'ōyēb	He drew his bow as at an enemy
niṣṣōb [18] y^{e}mīnō k^{e}ṣār	His right hand was poised as at a foe.

[18] Since *ymynw* is feminine, we interpret *nṣb* as the inf. abs. in parallel construction with the perfect *dārak*.

wayyahrōg kol maḥmaddē-ʿāyn	Then he slew all those most precious in our sight
beʾōhl bat-Ṣiyyōn	in the tent of Daughter Zion.
šāpak kāʾēš ḥamātō	He poured out his wrath like fire.

The structure may be analyzed as follows:

$$7 + 7 = 14$$
$$8 + 5 = 13$$
$$7 = 7$$

Precisely the same phenomena do not occur in chap. 3, which has a somewhat different internal structure. The stringency of the requirement that each line of the three-line stanza begin with the same letter of the alphabet apparently ruled out the occurrence of the four-line variant noted in the other chapters. Nevertheless, we have something comparable to the extended lines of the other chapters. We offer the following examples:

At 3:40 we read

naḥpeśāh derākēnū wenaḥqōrāh	Let us search out our ways and let us examine (them)
wenāšūbāh ʿad-Yhwh	and let us return to Yahweh!

The words *nḥpśh* and *nḥqrh* are synonymous and interchangeable. They could be regarded as doublets, or alternate expressions preserved in a conflate text. If we omitted one of them, the resulting meter, $7 + 7 = 14$, would be closer to the norm instead of the present somewhat anomalous $11 + 7 = 18$. Nevertheless, the variation corresponds to others already noted, and may therefore go back to the author himself.

At 3:56 we read

qōlī šāmāʿt(ā)	Hear my call
ʾal-taʿlēm ʾoznek(ā)	Do not cover your ear
lerawḥātī	for my relief
lešawʿātī	to my outcry.

The verse is longer than most in chap. 3 (17 or 19 syllables depending upon the counting method used), and poses certain problems in meaning and syntax. It has been suggested that *lšwʿty* is a gloss on *lrwḥty*, itself an error for an original *lᵉṣiwḥātī* "to my outcry." However, such a speculative reconstruction is less than convincing. The best clue to the solution of the problem of the text is to be found in the curious arrangement of the words, whereby the verbs and their direct objects are both in the first half of the verse, while the indirect objects are grouped together in the second. The first two elements, *qwly šmʿt* and *ʾl-tʿlm ʾznk*, are synonymous expressions in chiastic order. The alternation of perfect and imperfect forms of the verb is a well-known device in Hebrew and Ugaritic poetry. In this case the verb *šmʿt* is to be taken as the precative perfect, in agreement with the jussive form *ʾl-tʿlm*.[19] The indirect objects, *lrwḥty* and *lšwʿty*, are not synonymous, but balance each other structurally. Each one completes one of the clauses in the first part of the verse. Thus *lrwḥty* goes naturally with *qwly šmʿt* ; and *lšwʿty* fits with *l-tʿlm znk*. To bring out the syntactic relationships more clearly, we have arranged the text in the conventional way:

qōlī šāmaʿt(ā) lᵉrawḥātī	Hear my call for relief for me,
ʾal-taʿlēm ʾoznᵉk(ā)	Do not close your ear
lᵉšawʿātī	to my outcry

The poet has varied the usual practice by juggling the order of the words, thus intertwining the two clauses of the verse.

To test further the hypothesis of patterned deviation from a statistical norm, we append an analysis of several other acrostic poems: Lamentations 5, Proverbs 31:10–31, and Psalms 25, 34, and 145. While Lam. 5 is technically not an acrostic because the alphabetic sequence is not used, it is generally agreed that all the other characteristics are present in this poem, and that it should be treated as belonging to that class. In the following tables, the figures given reflect the inclusion of pronominal endings which are indicated in the vocalization but not in the orthography (corresponding to Col. B of the earlier charts): [20]

[19] See fn. 17.

[20] As already indicated, the major consideration is general consistency. Overall the differences are not significant.

	Lam. 5		*Prov. 31*		*Ps. 25*		*Ps. 34*		*Ps. 145*	
	1)	20	10)	14	1)	9	2)	18	1)	21
	2)	16	11)	12	2)	20	3)	18	2)	20
	3)	16	12)	14	3)	18	4)	17	3)	17
	4)	16	13)	14	4)	18	5)	21	4)	18
	5)	16	14)	16	5)[21]	22	6)	17	5)	18
	6)	12	15)	22		10	[22]		6)	22
	7)	22	16)	20	6)	19	7)	19	7)	17
	8)	14	17)	17	7)	28	8)	16	8)	14
	9)	16	18)	15	8)	15	9)	16	9)	13
	10)	17	19)	17	9)	16	10)	15	10)	19
	11)	16	20)	18	10)	20	11)	21	11)	19
	12)	16	21)	16	11)	17	12)	15	12)	20
	13)	17	22)	15	12)	15	13)	15	13)	20
	14)	16	23)	15	13)	12	14)	17	13a)	16[23]
	15)	15	24)	18	14)	14	15)	15	14)	19
	16)	16	25)	15	15)	15	16)	15	15)	23
	17)	18	26)	16	16)	16	17)	15	16)	14
	18)	14	27)	15	17)	17	18)	17	17)	16
	19)	16	28)	17	18)	15	19)	17	18)	20
	20)	16	29)	15	19)	17	20)	16	19)	18
	21)	20	30)	18	20)	17	21)	15	20)	18
	22)	17	31)	21	21)[24]	12	22)[25]	16	21)[26]	18
Total		362		360		362		351		400
Average		16.5		16.4		16.5		16.7[27]		18.2

The correspondence among the first four columns is so close that we are justified in speaking of at least one normative line

[21] There is some confusion in the text, with the *he* and *waw* stanzas apparently mixed together. The most widely adopted procedure involves reading *w* before *'wtk* with some Hebrew MSS and the LXX; then that is regarded as the beginning of the *waw* stanza. The total of 31 (actually 32 with the added *w*) syllables is appropriate for two stanzas.

[22] The *waw* stanza has been lost. We make our calculations on the basis of 21 stanzas.

[23] The *nun* stanza has fallen out of MT, but can be supplied on the basis of one Hebrew MS, LXX, and other versions. The reading has now been confirmed by 11QPs^a (with the exception that the first *kl* is omitted). Cf. J. A. Sanders, *The Psalms Scroll of Qumran Cave 11 (11QPs^a)* (Oxford: Clarendon Press, 1965), 38; and *The Dead Sea Psalms Scroll* (Ithaca, N.Y.: Cornell University Press, 1967), 66–67.

[24] There is an additional verse (22) which does not form part of the alphabetic pattern, though it belongs to the poem.

[25] Cf. fn. 24.

[26] The added words *l'wlm w'd* belong to the refrain which is preserved in full in 11QPs^a. Cf. Sanders, *The Psalms Scroll of Qumran Cave 11*, 38, and *The Dead Sea Psalms Scroll*, 66–67.

[27] The average is calculated on the basis of 21 lines (cf. fn. 22).

length for alphabetic acrostics. This holds true in spite of the fact that the poems vary in subject matter, are by different authors, and come from different periods in all likelihood. It is also of importance that the average line-length of these four one-line acrostics differs markedly from that of chaps. 1–4 of Lamentations (i.e., 16.5 compared with 13–14). The difference is sufficient to indicate that the poet had a limited choice among fixed basic structures in the composition of acrostics of different kinds. This seems also to be true of Ps. 145, which varies substantially from the others, and deserves further investigation.[28]

Among the four acrostics with the same basic line-length, the distribution is as follows:

Syllables	*Lam. 5*	*Prov. 31*	*Ps. 25*	*Ps. 34*	*Total*
9	0	0	1	0	1
10	0	0	1	0	1
12	1	1	2	0	4
14	2	3	1	0	6
15	1	6	4	7	18
16	11	3	2	4	20
17	3	3	4	5	15
18	1	3	2	2	8
19	0	0	1	1	2
20	2	1	2	0	5
21	0	1	0	2	3
22	1	1	1	0	3
28	0	0	1	0	1
	22	22	22	21	87

	Lam. 5	*Prov. 31*	*Ps. 25*	*Ps. 34*	*Total*
Total syllables:	362	360	362	351	1,435
Averages:	16.5	16.4	16.5	16.7	16.5

The median and average both fall between 16 and 17. The great bulk of the lines cluster around those numbers. In the normal range from 15 to 18 we find a majority of the lines in every one of the poems for a total of 61 out of 87 overall, or 70%. If we extend the range to include lines from 12 to 20, we have 78 lines or almost 90% of the total. Lam. 5 shows remarkable consistency with half of the lines having exactly 16

[28] The non-alphabetic acrostic, Ps. 38 (cf. DAHOOD, *Psalms I*, 234) has a total number of 406 syllables, and may have the same basic structure as Ps. 145.

syllables. Prov. 31 is more diffuse, but the shorter lines are balanced by the longer ones to produce practically the same total and average. Ps. 25 is an extreme example of dispersion, with both the shortest and longest lines of the group: the nine-syllable half-line in vs. 1, and the double-line stanza in vs. 7 (12 + 16 = 28 syllables). In the same Psalm, vs. 5, a complex which includes both the *he* and *waw* lines, has 31 or 32 syllables. It is a good illustration of the technique of balancing. We have suggested a division of 22 (for *he*) and 10 (for *waw*), which is rather irregular for the individual lines; but nevertheless, the total is well within the normal range for two lines. There is a similar situation in Lam. 5, where the shortest (vs. 6 = 12 syllables) and longest (vs. 7 = 22) lines are juxtaposed. Taken together they average out well within the normal range. Ps. 34, in contrast with Ps. 25, shows much greater consistency, with 18 of its 21 lines coming within the 15–18 range.

Other acrostic poems bear a close family resemblance to the ones just considered. In Psalms 111 and 112 the basic alphabetic unit is the half-line or single colon. In the following table we have paired successive half-lines in order to provide a basis of comparison with the one-line acrostics:

	Psalm 111	*Psalm 112*
1)	8 + 8 = 16	8 + 8 = 16
2)	7 + 8 = 15	8 + 7 = 15
3)	7 + 8 = 15	6 + 8 = 14
4)	8 + 7 = 15	9 + 8 = 17
5)	6 + 8 = 14	7 + 9 = 16
6)	8 + 8 = 16	7 + 8 = 15
7)	9 + 7 = 16	9 + 9 = 18
8)	8 + 9 = 17	7 + 8 = 15
9)	7 + 8 = 15	8 + 7 = 15
9–10)	7 + 8 = 15	7 + 7 = 14
10)	7 + 8 = 15	7 + 7 = 14
Totals	169	169

Average per colon:	7.7
per line:	15.4

The distribution according to the basic half-line unit is as follows:

Syllables	*Psalm 111*	*Psalm 112*	*Total*
6	1	1	2
7	7	9	16
8	12	8	20
9	2	4	6
	22	22	44

The regularity of the poems is immediately apparent. The average and median fall between 7 and 8, and the overwhelming majority of the cola are in the 7–8 bracket (36 out of 44 lines, or 82%). If we count bicola, we have the following distribution:

Syllables	*Psalm 111*	*Psalm 112*	*Total*
14	1	3	4
15	6	4	10
16	3	2	5
17	1	1	2
18	0	1	1
	11	11	22

Almost half of the lines or bicola have 15 syllables. If we extend the range one syllable in either direction, we include practically all of them (19 out of 21 or 90%). While the average of 15.4 is somewhat lower than the prevailing figure for the one-line acrostics, the range and concentration of lines in these poems are generally comparable. The half-line acrostic is built according to the same basic scheme, and the ratio to the full-line acrostic is approximately 1:2, as we should expect.

Psalm 37 consists of a two-line acrostic, like Lam. 4, but its line length is rather different.

Psalm 37

1)	16	3)	18	5)	16	7)	17	8)	15
2)	17	4)	18	6)	16		7	9)	19
	33		36		32		24		34
10)	21	12)	14	14)	25	16)	14	18)	18
11)	17	13)	14	15)	15	17)	19	19)	17
	38		28		40		33		35
20)	17	21)	17	23)	15	25)	24	27)	13
	7	22)	18	24)	13	26)	14	28)	15
	24		35		28		38		28
28)	16	30)	16	32)	15	34)	10	35)	16
29)	16	31)	14	33)	21		16	36)	18
	32		30		36		26		34

37)	15	39)	16
38)	17	40)	27
	32		43

Total syllables: 719
Average per stanza: 32.7

The average for the two-line stanza is just about double that of the one-line acrostics previously considered, showing that Ps. 37 has the same basic pattern as the others, but adapted to the two-line format. The difference between this poem and the other two-line acrostic, Lam. 4, is noticeable, not only with regard to line length but also in the wide variation in stanza length and structure. The distribution in Ps. 37 is as follows:

Syllables	*Stanzas*	*Syll.*	*Stan.*	*Syll.*	*Stan.*
24	2	26	1	28	3
30	1	32	3	33	2
34	2	35	2	36	2
38	2	40	1	43	1

The median is 33, close to the average. While the length of stanzas varies from a low of 24 to a high of 43, there is a careful balancing of long and short stanzas. Almost half of the stanzas are found in the normal range from 30 to 35. There are four in the low range from 26 to 28, and these are matched by four in the high range from 36 to 38. Two very short stanzas of 24 syllables each (actually tricola) are balanced against two extended stanzas of 40 and 43 syllables each.

Finally we turn to the longest acrostic poem in the Bible, Ps. 119. It has 22 eight-line stanzas; each of the eight lines begins with the same letter of the alphabet, as is the case with the three-line stanzas of Lam. 3. The statistics are as follows:

Psalm 119

Alef		*Bet*		*Gimel*		*Dalet*	
1)	15	9)	15	17)	16	25)	15
2)	15	10)	17	18)	15	26)	17
3)	13	11)	16	19)	16	27)	19
4)	13	12)	13	20)	16	28)	16
5)	13	13)	12	21)	16	29)	15
6)	14	14)	12	22)	16	30)	14
7)	16	15)	16	23)	19	31)	15
8)	14	16)	15	24)	13	32)	12
	113		116		127		123

He		*Waw*		*Zayin*		*Ḥet*	
33)	15	41)	20	49)	15	57)	13
34)	20	42)	16	50)	17	58)	16
35)	15	43)	22	51)	18	59)	17
36)	13	44)	15	52)	16	60)	14
37)	15	45)	17	53)	18	61)	17
38)	17	46)	18	54)	14	62)	17
39)	17	47)	14	55)	19	63)	21
40)	18	48)	23	56)	13	64)	17
	130		145		130		132

Ṭeṭ		*Yod*		*Kaf*		*Lamed*	
65)	14	73)	24	81)	17	89)	14
66)	17	74)	19	82)	18	90)	16
67)	17	75)	19	83)	16	91)	17
68)	13	76)	20	84)	17	92)	16
69)	19	77)	19	85)	15	93)	16
70)	16	78)	20	86)	16	94)	16
71)	13	79)	16	87)	18	95)	18
72)	13	80)	15	88)	15	96)	17
	122		152		132		130

Mem		*Nun*		*Samek*		*Ayin*	
97)	15	105)	14	113)	14	121)	16
98)	19	106)	16	114)	15	122)	14
99)	17	107)	15	115)	17	123)	16
100)	15	108)	17	116)	20	124)	18
101)	17	109)	16	117)	18	125)	17
102)	15	110)	18	118)	15	126)	14
103)	16	111)	17	119)	18	127)	15
104)	16	112)	14	120)	18	128)	16
	130		127		135		126

Pe		*Ṣadde*		*Qof*		*Reš*	
129)	15	137)	13	145)	17	153)	18
130)	13	138)	14	146)	16	154)	17
131)	17	139)	17	147)	17	155)	17
132)	17	140)	16	148)	15	156)	16
133)	17	141)	16	149)	18	157)	17
134)	15	142)	15	150)	16	158)	21
135)	18	143)	15	151)	14	159)	19
136)	17	144)	15	152)	16	160)	17
	129		121		129		142

Šin		*Taw*	
161)	18	169)	19
162)	15	170)	19
163)	16	171)	18
164)	14	172)	15
165)	17	173)	17
166)	18	174)	18
167)	15	175)	19
168)	20	176)	21
	133		146

Total syllables:	2,870
Average per stanza:	130.5
Average per line:	16.3

The distribution according to stanzas is as follows:

No. of Syllables	*No. of Stanzas*	*Syllables*	*Stanzas*
113	1	130	4
116	1	132	2
121	1	133	1
122	1	135	1
123	1	142	1
126	1	145	1
127	2	146	1
129	2	152	1

Stanza length varies from a low of 113 to a high of 152, with the majority of the lines clustering around the average and median of 130. Ten stanzas are in the range from 127–132; six are in the bracket from 113–126, matched by six which run from 133–152.

The distribution according to line length is as follows:

Syllables	*Lines*	*Syllables*	*Lines*
12	3	18	19
13	13	19	12
14	16	20	6
15	32	21	3
16	34	22	1
17	35	23	1
		24	1

Line length ranges from 12 to 24, but the main concentration is in the 15–17 bracket with 101 lines out of 176, or 57% of the total. If we extend the range two syllables in either direction (13–19), then 161 lines or over 91% are included.

As the figures show, Ps. 119 is constructed on the same basic plan as the others. A summary table indicates the correlations among the different acrostic poems considered:

Poem	*Syllables*	*Lines*	*Average*
Lamentations 5	362	22	16.5
Proverbs 31	360	22	16.4
Psalm 25	362	22	16.5
Psalm 34	351	21	16.7
Psalm 37	719	44	16.3
Psalm 111	169	11	15.4
Psalm 112	169	11	15.4
Psalm 119	2,870	176	16.3
Psalm 145	400	22	18.2

The other group, including Lam. 1–4, exhibits the following pattern:

Lamentations 1	865	67	12.9
Lamentations 2	863	67	12.9
Lamentations 3	868	66	13.2
Lamentations 4	609	44	13.8

There seem to be at least two different structures for acrostic poems in the Bible, with the major group having lines, or bicola, averaging around 16 and 1/2 syllables. A special group represented by Lam. 1–4 has a shorter line of 13–14 syllables. In the poems there is a wide range of variation in the length of lines and stanzas.[29] These deviations form their own patterns, as we have observed, and the end product was strictly controlled by factors of overall length, and a strong sense of balance.

[29] Except for the short poems, Pss. 111 and 112, which have a narrow range of variation.

3. *Divine Names and Titles in Early Hebrew Poetry*

IN A RECENT SURVEY of early Hebrew poetry, the late Professor W. F. Albright proposed a basic sequence dating, using certain stylistic phenomena as determinative criteria.[1] Chief among these were repetitive parallelism and paronomasia or wordplay. Relative chronology is fixed by reference to Ugaritic poetry which is substantially older than practically all surviving biblical verse. Since repetitive parallelism is frequent in Ugaritic poems, its occurrence in Hebrew poetry would be an indicator of early date. On the other hand, paronomasia is rare in Ugaritic, so its occurrence in Hebrew poetry would point to a somewhat later date of composition. Albright was able to discern a pattern in early Hebrew poems exhibiting a gradual decline in the use of repetitive parallelism with a corresponding increase in the use of paronomasia.[2] This discovery permitted an arrangement of the poems in sequence, between the thirteenth and tenth centuries B.C., with more specific dates being assigned on the basis of historical allusions and other information in the poems. Albright fixed the order and dates of the poems as follows:

1. Song of Miriam (Exodus 15)—early thirteenth century
2. Song of Deborah (Judges 5)—ca. 1150
3. Oracles of Balaam (Numbers 23–24)—ca. 1200
4. Testament of Moses (Deuteronomy 33)—middle of eleventh century
5. Song of Moses (Deuteronomy 32)—ca. 1025
6. Testament of Jacob (Genesis 49)—late eleventh century
7. Song of Hannah (I Sam. 2)—late eleventh
8. David's Lament (II Sam. 1)—early tenth
9. Oracle of David (II Sam. 23)—first half of tenth
10. Royal Psalm (II Sam. 22=Ps. 18)—tenth
11. Psalm 78—tenth
12. Psalm 68—tenth

13. Psalm 72—tenth
14. Psalm 29[3]

The following comments about the list may be in order:

1) While the Song of Deborah precedes the Oracles of Balaam in Albright's list, he dated the Oracles earlier than the Song. On the basis of stylistic criteria, he recognized that the Song was more archaic: e.g. it exhibits extensive repetitive parallelism, while the Oracles have very little. The overriding consideration for Albright, however, was the presence of specific historical information in the Oracles, especially among the isolated utterances in Num. 24:20–24, which pointed to a date around 1200, necessarily earlier than the Song of Deborah.[4] But these utterances are not integral parts of the Oracles, and even if Albright's analysis were correct, the data would be insufficient to fix the date of the Oracles as a whole. Our investigation tends to confirm Albright's stylistic order, and points to a later date (in the tenth century) for the Oracles.

2) In further notes on the early poems, Albright expresses some reservations about his placement of the Testament of Jacob (Genesis 49), and concludes that the content is "surprisingly heterogeneous."[5] He then assigns a number of oracles to "Late Patriarchal" times, including the Joseph sayings (vss. 22–26), with which we are primarily concerned.[6]

The general purpose of the present paper is essentially the same as Albright's, to fix the chronological sequence of the early poems of Israel, as these have been preserved in the Bible. However, I expect to use an entirely different set of criteria in determining the sequence, thus providing an independent basis for comparing and evaluating results. In what follows, I wish to focus attention on the use of divine names and epithets in the poetry under consideration. The underlying assumption is that such usage, while at the option of the poet, reflects prevailing religious patterns, and the changes which took place during the creative and adaptive years of Israel's history. From an examination of the incidence and distribution of divine names and epithets, I can distinguish three phases in the development of Hebrew poetry during this early period:

1. *Militant Mosaic Yahwism* (*twelfth century*): the name Yahweh is used exclusively or predominantly.

Exodus 15
Psalm 29
Judges 5

2. *Patriarchal Revival* (*eleventh century*): in addition to Yahweh, the name El is used in parallel with it. The equation Yahweh=El (i.e. the God of the Fathers) opens the way to the introduction or reintroduction of divine epithets associated with the patriarchal deity in the Genesis traditions: in particular *šadday, ʿelyōn,* and *ʿōlām.*

Genesis 49
Numbers 23–24
Deuteronomy 33

3. *Monarchic Syncretism* (*tenth century or later*): in this period a new set of titles and epithets appears, reflecting the syncretistic tendencies of the religion of the monarchy. The date of most of these poems is secured by explicit reference to the monarchy and David in particular.

I Samuel 2
II Samuel 1
II Samuel 23
II Samuel 22=Psalm 18
Deuteronomy 32
Psalm 78
Psalm 68
Psalm 72

The variations between my list and Albright's are relatively few, especially considering the differences in method. My approach and conclusions will be defended in the analysis of the individual poems, and comments on selected divine names and epithets. The data on the incidence and distribution of the latter will be summarized in accompanying charts.

Phase I

1. The Song of the Sea: Exod. 15:1–18, 21[7]

Many scholars regard the poem as composite, with only the opening couplet (vs. 1, repeated with slight change in vs. 21) original, going back to Mosaic times. The rest is considered a later composition, and is dated anywhere from early monarchic to late post-exilic times. In my opinion, vss. 1 and 21 constitute a refrain, sung antiphonally by different groups at the beginning and end of the poem, and forming an envelope around the main section of the poem. A comparable arrangement is to be found in David's lament over Saul and Jonathan (II Sam. 1:19–27) in which a refrain is repeated in the opening and closing lines: *'ēk nāpᵉlū gibbōrīm.*[8] For the rest, I consider the poem a unified composition, with the possible exception of vs. 2 which seems to be a separate liturgical exordium delivered by the temple precentor, dating from the tenth century.

Returning to vss. 1 and 21, the only divine name which occurs is Yahweh, which is in accord with the hypothesis presented above. To be compared with this is the other brief war song associated with the wanderings in the wilderness, the attack on Amalek (Exod. 17:16). In the latter, the name

Yahweh appears; the abbreviated form Yah also seems to occur, but the text is difficult and may be corrupt.[9]

In addition, there are the songs of the ark, Num. 10:34–35, which probably belong to the period after the settlement in the land. The only divine appellative is Yahweh (cf. the adaptation in Ps. 68:2 which is substantially the same as Num. 10:34). The same pattern holds for the Aaronic benediction (Num. 6:24–26; Yahweh occurs three times), but this factor alone does not demonstrate an early date of composition.

In vs. 2 there is a series of divine names and epithets. The combination *'ozzī wᵉzimrāt,* "my mighty fortress," occurs only here and in the parallel passages, Isa. 12:2 and Ps. 118:14.[10] Taking the terms separately, and limiting the references to poems on Albright's list, *'z* as a divine epithet is found in Ps. 29:1="Mighty One."[11] With respect to *zmrt,* the plural form *zᵉmīrōt* is found in II Sam. 23:1="Defense (of Israel)."[12]

The shortened form Yah also appears in vs. 2. Among the listed poems it occurs here and in Psalm 68 (twice, vss. 5, 19). Apart from these instances (and the possible occurrence in Exod. 17:16) its usage is specialized and in general late: as part of a liturgical formula in the Psalter, *hallᵉlūyāh;* sporadically in the Psalms and late poetry. None of these can be attested before the tenth century at the earliest (e.g. Ps. 89:9). If we suppose that the name Yahweh was introduced by Moses in the thirteenth century, we would hardly expect such an abbreviated form to be in general use before the tenth century, and the evidence generally supports this view. If the reading here is correct, then it seems to me that the verse is a later addition; or put another way, the poem in its present completed form is not earlier than the tenth century.[13]

The form *'ēlī,* "my God" (divine name with suffix), occurs in Pss. 18:3, 68:25, both of which date to the tenth century (or later) but not in any of the earlier poems on the list. Parallel to it is the expression *'ᵉlōhē 'ābī,* "my father's God." The construct form *'ᵉlōhē* turns up regularly on the list, but the absolute form, *'ᵉlōhīm*=God, does not appear until the monarchic period. The combination *'ᵉlōhē 'ābī* does not occur elsewhere in our poetry, but it does appear in prose dealing with the period of the patriarchs and Moses: e.g. Gen. 31:5, 32:10; Exod. 18:4 (cf. Gen. 26:24, 28:13, 46:3, etc.).

In the main part of the poem, vss. 3–18, the name Yahweh predominates, occurring eight times (vss. 3, 3, 6, 6, 11, 16, 17, 18). In two cases, there are parallel expressions: *n'dr, nwr', 'śh pl'* (vs. 11) and *'dny* (vs. 17). With respect to the former, *n'dr* is unique as an epithet of God, while *nwr'* occurs again in Ps. 68:36; the third expression has a parallel in Ps. 72:18, while the participle with a different object is also found in Num. 24:18 and II Sam. 22:51 (=Ps. 18:51).

The occurrence of *'dny* in vs. 17 poses a problem. While normal canons of poetic parallelism support MT (Yahweh in 17a is balanced by *'dny* in 17b), there is substantial textual evidence in favor of an original reading

Yahweh which was subsequently changed to *'dny*, i.e. a number of manuscripts of MT and the Samaritan have Yahweh.[14] There is no doubt that *'dny* is a legitimate surrogate for Yahweh and is often used in combination with it, sometimes in a parallel construction with Yahweh or *'ᵉlōhīm*. Just when it was introduced, however, remains a question. The only attested instances in our list of poems are in Psalms 78 (vs. 65) and 68 (vss. 12, 18, 20, 23, 27, 33), neither of which can be earlier than the tenth century. Furthermore, in view of the fact that *'dny* became a permanent substitute for Yahweh in the reading of the text (confirmed as early as the third century B.C. by the standard rendering of the Tetragrammaton in the LXX as *kyrios*), it is very difficult to distinguish between cases in which *'dny* is original, and in which it has been substituted accidentally for an original Yahweh. In the present instance it seems more likely that Yahweh was the original reading, and that *'dny* was introduced into the text secondarily. It is more difficult to imagine the reverse.

In addition there are terms for divine beings other than Yahweh. Thus the words *'ēlīm* and *qōdeš* occur in vs. 11, which reads:

> Who is like you, Yahweh,
> among the gods?
> Who is like you, Awesome One,
> among the holy ones?

The term *qōdeš* is an abstract or collective term, equivalent to the expected *qᵉdōšīm*, which may be reflected in the LXX of this passage.[15] The connection is well attested in Ps. 89:6–8 where both *qᵉdōšīm* and *'ēlīm* occur in parallel phrases. Behind the parallel pattern in poetry lies a stereotyped expression attested in a Phoenician inscription of the tenth century B.C. from Byblos: *'l gbl qdšm*, "the holy gods of Byblos."[16] The meaning of the passage in Exodus 15 could be expressed as follows: "Who is like you, among the holy gods, Yahweh the Awesome One?"

In the light of the data, my conclusion is that the original poem consisted of vss. 1, 3–18, and 21 and was composed in the twelfth century.[17] The dominant divine name is Yahweh; in addition there are a few qualifying adjectives or epithets but these tell us very little. Subsequently, vs. 2 was added, and with it were introduced several names and epithets, which derive from the period of the early monarchy. In its present expanded and revised form, the poem may be dated as late as the tenth century.[18]

Distribution

1. Yahweh: vss. 1, 3, 3, 6, 6, 11, 16, 17, 18, 21
   a. Without parallel: vss. 1, 16, 18, 21
   b. In parallel with other divine names
      1) *Adonay:* vs. 17
   c. In parallel with various terms and phrases

1) *'īš milḥāmāh:* vs. 3
2) *ne'dār:* vs. 11
3) *nōrā':* vs. 11
4) *'ōśēh pele':* vs. 11

2. *Yah:* vs. 2
   a. In parallel with other terms:
      1) *'ozzī:* vs. 2
      2) *zimrāt:* vs. 2
3. *Eli:* vs. 2
   a. In parallel with other terms:
      1) *'elōhē 'ābī:* vs. 2
4. *Adonay:* vs. 17 (cf. Yahweh, 1.b.1)

2. PSALM 29[19]

Albright did not attempt to place Psalm 29 in his sequential scheme, but he speaks of it as being "very archaic" (*YGC,* p. 21) and "clearly archaic" (p. 27).[20] Nevertheless an effort can and should be made to fix a date partly on the basis of his stylistic criteria, and partly on the basis of the use of divine names. With respect to the former, Psalm 29 employs repetitive parallelism to an extraordinary extent, comparable to both the Song of the Sea and the Song of Deborah, perhaps with greater affinity for the more elaborate patterns of the latter.[21] With respect to divine epithets, the picture is very similar, though here there is a closer correlation with the Song of the Sea.[22] The name Yahweh is emphasized overwhelmingly, occurring no fewer than eighteen times in the short span of eleven verses. The only other divine designation is *'ēl,* which occurs twice (vss. 1 and 3).

In vs. 1, we have the phrase *benē 'ēlīm,* which may be rendered "sons of the gods," i.e. divine beings, like *ben-re'ēmīm,* "a calf of wild bulls," i.e. a young wild bull, or the familiar expression *benē hannebī'īm,* "the sons of the prophets," i.e. members of the prophetic guild. The phrase, however, is a designation of the divine assembly, derived directly from Canaanite mythopoetic language, and should be translated "sons of El." The word *'ēlīm* should be interpreted, therefore, as the divine name, El, with the genitive case ending and the enclitic *mem.*[23] The phrase is equivalent to *'ēlīm,* "gods," in Exod. 15:11.

In vs. 3, it is combined with the term *hakkābōd.* The phrase may be rendered "the God of glory" or "the glorious God," or "El, the Glorious."[24] That a divine title is intended is shown by the usage in vs. 2: *hbw lyhwh kbwd šmw,* which may be translated, "Give praise to Yahweh, whose name is Glorious." The same term (*kbwd*) occurs in conjunction with *'z* in vs. 1: "Give praise to Yahweh, the Glorious and Victorious"; it also stands alone in vs. 9: "O Glorious One!"[25]

This generic use of *'ēl,* "God," in a construct chain, which is attested again in certain poems of Phase III, e.g. I Samuel 2 and Deuteronomy 32, is to be distinguished from its specific employment as the personal name of the deity, El, the patriarchal appellation which appears in Phase II poems, Genesis 49, Numbers 23–24, Deuteronomy 33.

In Psalm 29 reference is made to the people of Yahweh (vs. 11), but without further explicit identification. This usage corresponds to the pattern in Exodus 15 rather than that of Judges 5 where the equation with Israel is made directly. In view of its affinities with the poems in Phase I, and possible thematic dependence on the Song of the Sea, Psalm 29 should be assigned to the latter part of the twelfth century, and in any case not later than around 1100.[26]

Distribution

1. Yahweh: vss. 1, 1, 2, 2, 3, 3, 4, 4, 5, 5, 7, 8, 8, 9, 10, 10, 11, 11
    a. Without parallel (or parallel with Yahweh): vss. 1a, 2b, 3ab, 4ab, 5ab, 7, 8ab, 9, 10ab, 11ab
    b. In parallel with other divine names and epithets
        1) *El:* vs. 3
        2) *Kabod:* vss. 1, 2, 3, 9
        3) *Oz:* vs. 1
2. El: vs. 3 (cf. Yahweh, 1.b.1)

3. THE SONG OF DEBORAH: JUDG. 5:2–31[27]

In this poem there is an overwhelming preference for Yahweh, which occurs fourteen times. There are only two other epithets used: *'ᵉlōhē yiśrā'ēl,* "the God of Israel" (vss. 3, 5) and *zeh sīnay,* "the One of Sinai" (vs. 5). In all three occurrences, the terms are directly parallel with Yahweh, emphasizing the identification of Yahweh with the revelation of Mount Sinai, and as the God of Israel.

The designation, "the One of Sinai," is archaic in form, possibly pre-Mosaic in origin, and reflects the wilderness experience. If any epithet is basic and indigenous to Yahwistic religion, it is this one. The only other occurrence of that expression is in Ps. 68:9, a passage which is dependent upon Judg. 5:5.

The case is not so clear with respect to the other title, "God of Israel." It is the classical historical characterization of Yahweh, just as Israel is designated "the people of Yahweh" (vss. 11, 13; cf. Exod. 15:13, 16). While the term may also go back to Moses or the Mosaic experience, it seems to be more applicable to the community after its entry into the promised land. While the term *'am,* "people," is used repeatedly in both poems, Exodus 15 and Judges 5, and they are identified as Yahweh's people, the term Israel does not occur in Exodus 15.

It is only when they have arrived in the land that the *'am* is called Israel. According to the biblical tradition, however, both the name Israel and the designation "God of Israel" are pre-Mosaic and find their origin in the patriarchal stories. Thus Israel is the name acquired at a certain point in his career by Jacob, and continues as the name of his clan (Gen. 32:29, 35:10). Furthermore, Jacob's God, "El," is given the explicit title *'ᵉlōhē yiśrā'ēl,* "God of Israel," in connection with the erection of an altar at Shechem (33:18–20). In view of the biblical traditions, supported by archaeological evidence, there is no reason to doubt that Israelites (i.e. *bny yśr'l*) were settled in the Shechem area during pre-Mosaic times. Their God was El, the patriarchal deity whose sway extended throughout the region, and who was worshipped at Bethel (cf. Gen. 35:7) in addition to Shechem and other places.

What is reflected in the Song of Deborah is not the equation of Yahweh with El and the blending or merging of domains, characteristics, and the like, but the attribution of El's title as God of Israel to Yahweh. This is an indication of the continuing militance of the Mosaic movement, laying claim to the loyalty of Israelites in the central highlands. They had joined the people of Yahweh in the struggle against the Canaanites on the basis of the exclusive demands of Yahweh. Only one step in the direction of accommodation to the descendants of the patriarchs was made: the appropriation of the title, God of Israel. Whatever the etymology and original meaning of the name may be, *yiśrā'ēl* is a verb compounded with the divine element *'ēl,* and must therefore derive from an El-worshiping community. That suits very well the region around Shechem in the period down to the twelfth century B.C.

The word *'ᵉlōhīm* occurs in vs. 8. The passage is difficult and so far has eluded successful analysis and interpretation. If the apparent connection between the phrase *'lhym ḥdšym* here and the same words in Deut. 32:17 is valid, then *'lhym* in both places refers to "gods," not "God."[28] There is a consistent pattern in the early poetry that the term *'ᵉlōhīm* is not used for God, although the construct form *'ᵉlōhē* and the equivalent form with pronominal suffixes are so used. It is not until we come to the Psalms in the so-called Elohistic Psalter that *'lhym* is used regularly for God, generally as a substitute for Yahweh (though Yahweh also appears in these poems).[29] The only other example of *ᵉlōhīm,* "God," from our list is found in II Sam. 23:3, *yir'at 'ᵉlōhīm,* "the fear of God," which is a stereotyped expression for "piety." The natural pair *yhwh//'lhym* does not appear in our poetry.

In general the Song of Deborah shares with the Song of the Sea an intense concentration on the name Yahweh, to which it adds the unique but indigenous epithet *zh syny,* "the One of Sinai." In Judges 5 the people of Yahweh is explicitly identified as Israel, and Yahweh is explicitly called the God of Israel, whereas in Exodus 15, the people is called simply *'am,* though the special relationship to Yahweh is spelled out just as emphatically. In Judges 5 as well, Israel is defined as a congeries if not a confederation of tribes (i.e. territorial and political units) and a list of them is given. Except for the appropriation of the title *'ᵉlōhē yiśrā'ēl,* no link with the patriarchs or their religion is asserted, or even implied. This is the period of militant Mosaism:

Yahweh is emphasized to the exclusion of the normal parallel El; and Israel is stressed to the exclusion of the logical complement, Jacob. Those combinations were yet to be made; they belong to Phase II.

Distribution

1. Yahweh: vss. 2, 3, 3, 4, 5, 5, 9, 11, 11, 13, 23, 23, 23, 31
   a. Without parallel: vss. 2, 3a, 4, 9, 11a, 11b, 13, 23a, b, e, 31
   b. In parallel with (other) divine names and epithets:
      1) *'ᵉlōhē yiśrā'ēl:* vss. 3, 5
      2) *zeh sīnay:* vs. 5

Phase II

4. THE TESTAMENT OF JACOB: GEN. 49:1–27

Apart from the blessing of Joseph (vss. 22–26), the poem is almost entirely devoid of divine names or epithets. The only exception is the name Yahweh in vs. 18, but this verse is universally regarded as a secondary addition.

The blessing of Joseph requires special attention, not only because it is replete with archaic titles and epithets, but because this is the only clear example of non-Yahwistic El poetry in our corpus. Albright regarded this passage as stemming from late patriarchal times, and that judgment may be correct.[30] It reflects the religion of the El worshipers in the central highlands (Joseph territory) who traced their descent from the patriarchs and formed the core of the pre-Mosaic tribal league Israel. In its present form, however, the blessing has been accommodated to the historical-political realities of the eleventh century.

The key names are El and Shadday (vs. 25). According to the priestly writer the compound name El Shadday was the designation of the God of the Fathers par excellence (cf. Exod. 6:3, which is the pivotal statement about the relationship between the patriarchal name El Shadday and the new Mosaic name Yahweh) and is used by him in the patriarchal narratives: Gen. 17:1, 28:3, 35:11, 43:14, 48:3. It occurs in some of the poems of Phase II, including the present instance, Num. 24:16, and Ps. 68:15.

While Psalm 68, following Albright, is best understood as a catalogue of song titles or a compendium of opening lines, covering the whole period of our poetry from the twelfth century or earlier down to the tenth century, most of the contents must be pre-monarchic.[31] After Phase II, however, the term drops out of use, and is characteristically omitted in poetry from the monarchic period. Psalm 91, the date of which is uncertain, may be an exceptional instance from the monarchic period. In vs. 1, Shadday occurs in parallel with Elyon as is the case in Num. 24:16.

Otherwise usage is limited and follows a curious but significant pattern. It occurs in prophetic prose and poetry of the sixth century, a period of nostalgic revival in Judah and throughout the Near East, i.e. Ezek. 1:24, 10:5; Isa. 13:6=Joel 1:15 (*yhwh//šdy*).[32] It also occurs frequently in Job (thirty-one times), more than all the rest of the occurrences put together (seventeen times). Since Job probably dates from the same general period (seventh–sixth century),[33] the usage may reflect similar interests. It is likely that some other, stronger influence stemming from patriarchal or pre-monarchic traditions is at work here, however.

Finally we may point to the occurrence of the term twice in the Book of Ruth (1:20, 21). Naomi is quoted as referring to the deity by this title (parallel with Yahweh, vs. 21). While the date of Ruth is uncertain, the book may well be a product of the seventh–sixth centuries in its present form.[34] The pattern is therefore essentially the same as Isa. 13:6=Joel 1:15 of approximately the same date. The story, however, is about events in the period of the judges (twelfth–eleventh centuries), and may reflect actual usage of *šadday* quite accurately, since the term occurs in two poems which are dated to that period on other grounds.

To summarize: (1) The epithet *šadday* is attributed to the patriarchal period by the priestly writer. (2) It was used along with other patriarchal names during the period of the judges (eleventh century) as attested by contemporary poems, and indirectly by evidence in the Book of Ruth. (3) Then it disappeared almost entirely from use during the monarchic period (with the possible exception of Psalms 68 and 91, as noted), only to be revived in the period of national nostalgia beginning in the late seventh century B.C.

The reading El Shadday (*'ēl šadday*) in Gen. 49:25, supported by the Samaritan and the Septuagint as well as a few manuscripts of MT, is to be preferred to the standard reading of MT *w^{e}'ēt šadday* which is anomalous at best. The parallel expression is *mē'ēl 'ābīkā* which may be rendered either "From the God of your father" (so RSV), or "From El, your Father." While the former is entirely possible, the latter may be preferable, since the term "father" is a characteristic designation of El in the Ugaritic texts, and was transferred to Yahweh in Israelite tradition; cf. Deut. 32:6; Ps. 68:6.

Just as the evidence from the poems of Phase I tends to support the view that the name Yahweh was introduced by Moses and used exclusively in the early period by his followers, so the evidence from Genesis 49 points to the conclusion that the patriarchal names of God, and the compound El Shadday in particular, were used by Israelites, who claimed descent from the fathers and continued to worship the fathers' God under the name and titles of that earlier experience.

In the preceding verse (Gen. 49:24) there are two other epithets which require our attention: *'^{a}bīr ya'^{a}qōb and rō'eh 'eben yiśrā'ēl*. The former, which is commonly rendered "Mighty One of Jacob" (RSV, etc.), or "Champion," is more literally "Bull," an appropriate designation of the god El in Canaanite tradition and presumably true of the patriarchal El as well. The terms in Ugaritic and Hebrew are not identical, however; apparently certain distinctions were recognized and maintained. The phrase occurs in the royal, possibly Davidic Psalm 132 (vss. 2 and 5). It is interesting to note that the term *'ᵃbīr* otherwise turns up only in Isaiah, but in all parts of it: 1:24 (*'ᵃbīr yiśrā'ēl*), 49:26 and 60:16 (*'ᵃbīr ya'ᵃqōb*). Presumably the epithet was adopted by the early monarchy, and it remained associated with the worship of Jerusalem and its traditions thereafter.

The other phrase, *r'h 'bn yśr'l,* poses textual and exegetical problems which so far have defied adequate analysis and solution. The essential elements are *rō'eh* and *yiśrā'ēl*="Shepherd of Israel," as comparison with Ps. 80:2 makes clear (cf. also Gen. 48:15, *hārō'eh 'ōtī,* which connects the epithet directly with Jacob/Israel). The word *'bn* may be understood as a by-form of *bn,* "son."[35] Further it should be read as plural: **'ibnē* or the like. The omission of the final *yod* may be understood as an instance of early consonantal spelling, or the initial *yod* of the next word *yśr'l* may be regarded as serving double duty.[36] The rendering would then be "Shepherd of the sons of Israel"; cf. *bny y'qb* in vs. 2 of the same poem.

Other possible divine epithets may be looked for in vs. 26. As in vs. 25, *'ābīkā* may refer to El or God rather than to a human father, though such an interpretation hinges to some extent upon the proper understanding of the pair *šādayim wārāḥam* in vs. 25. If that is ultimately a reference to the Mother goddess, though somewhat generalized and demythologized, then we would be justified in seeing in *'byk* a reference to the divine Father, a more appropriate source of exceptional blessing. The following words, *gābᵉrū 'al,* are more difficult and do not make sense in the MT. Accepting the consonantal text but redividing the words (cf. the wrongly divided *'qb m'šr* in vss. 19–20), I vocalize and render as follows: *gibbōr wᵉ'al,* "Warrior and Exalted One," i.e. "the Exalted Warrior." For *gibbōr* as a divine title, see Ps. 24:8, especially the pair *'izzūz wᵉgibbōr,* "Mighty One and Warrior," i.e. "the Mighty Warrior"; and Isa. 10:21 *'ēl gibbōr,* "El the Warrior," in which *gibbōr* is an epithet of El. The second term *'al* has been identified as a divine epithet in Ugaritic, and is preserved, though not recognized as such by earlier grammarians and scholars, in several ancient poems, e.g. Deut. 33:12; I Sam. 2:10; II Sam. 23:1 (cf. the name *'ēlī* in I Sam. 1 ff. and the Northwest Semitic name *yᵉḥaw-ēlī*).[37]

Finally in Gen. 49:25 we note the pair *'ad//'ōlām.*[38] It is possible that these are divine epithets here and that the mountains mentioned are not merely aged or ancient, but specifically associated with the Ancient//Eternal God.[39] The same pair *hrry 'd//gb'wt 'wlm* occurs in the archaizing poem in Habakkuk 3 (vs. 6). The equivalent usage is found in the parallel blessing of Joseph in Deut. 33:15, *hrry qdm//gb'wt 'wlm;* cf. *'lhy qdm// zr't 'wlm* (vs. 27), already noted, which is to be rendered "the ancient

God . . . the arms of the Eternal One." The conclusion is that the term *'ōlām,* with its parallels *'ad* and *qedem,* was an ancient designation of the patriarchal God, El, and that its usage was revived or continued in the community which worshiped El, and brought its divine terminology with it when it merged with the Yahweh-worshiping group from the wilderness. Cross has established the pre-Mosaic date of the epithet *'lm* as a designation of El in the proto-Canaanite inscriptions from Sinai dating to the fifteenth century B.C.[40] Dahood has identified the divine name Olam in a number of psalms and other poetic passages:[41] cf. Isa. 40:20 and Pss. 66:7, 89:2 (*yhwh 'wlm,* "Yahweh the Eternal").

In the blessing of Joseph, there are three of the characteristic divine epithets associated with the patriarchal age in biblical tradition: El, Shadday, and possibly Olam. In addition we have *'al* (or *'ēlī*) which is derived from the same root as a fourth patriarchal title, Elyon, and semantically equivalent. The absence of the principal name Yahweh may be inadvertent, but it is more likely that this passage comes from the El-worshiping community in the Shechem area in pre-Mosaic times. In its present form, however, the Testament of Jacob reflects the formal organization of the twelve-tribe amphictyony; the repeated occurrence of the pair Jacob//Israel (vss. 2, 7, 24) confirms this view. The poem as a whole is to be assigned to Phase II, and may be dated in the first half of the eleventh century.[42]

Distribution

1. Yahweh: vs. 18 (no parallel)
2. El: vs. 25, (25)
   a. In parallel with other divine names and epithets
      1) Shadday: vs. 25
      2) *'ābīkā:* vs. 25
      3) *'ᵃbīr yaʿᵃqōb:* vs. 24
      4) *rō 'eh ('eben) yiśrā'ēl:* vs. 24
3. Shadday: vs. 25 (cf. 2.a.1)
4. Ad: vs. 26
   a. In parallel with other divine names
      1) *'ōlām:* vs. 26
5. Olam: vs. 26 (cf. Ad, 4.a.1)

5. THE ORACLES OF BALAAM: NUMBERS 23–24[43]

In these poems, the principal divine name is El, which occurs eight times, 23:8, 19, 22, 23, 24:4, 8, 16, 23. The first seven are in the major oracles, while the last occurs in one of the brief sayings appended to the oracles, and is apparently the only divine name in them (24:20–24).

The name Yahweh also occurs, but less frequently: 23:8, 21, 24:6. It is used once in each of the first three oracles, but not at all in the fourth utterance or the appended sayings.

The equation Yahweh=El appears twice: (1) Num. 23:8 where the order of MT (El//Yahweh) is reversed in the LXX which is probably original; (2) 23:21–22, where the order is Yahweh//El. This all-important identification was not present in the earlier poems of Phase I (see discussion above). It is matched by the combination Jacob-Israel, which occurs seven or eight times in these oracles (23:7, 10, 21, 23, 23, 24:5, 17, 18–19 with order reversed if the text is correct), and represents the classic designation of the tribal league.

It should be pointed out that the occurrence of Yahweh and El in parallel cola or lines does not represent the break-up of the divine name Yahweh-el (perhaps "El will create, bring to pass"), which may well have been the original full name of Yahweh, but rather the equation of separate divine names here drawn together from different traditions.[44] In our opinion, Yahweh was deliberately and explicitly separated from the El tradition with which he may have been associated earlier in pre-Mosaic times. While the story of the golden calf (Exodus 32) has been colored by reminiscences of and attitudes arising out of the division of the kingdom and the use of similar figures in the temples at Bethel and Dan, the original nucleus reflects the emphatic rejection of El worship by the militant followers of Moses during a crisis in the wilderness. Only later, after the settlement in the land, and the time of Deborah, was the breach repaired, and an agreement between the respective worshipers of Yahweh and El achieved.

The term *'ᵉlōhāw,* "his God," is joined to Yahweh in 23:21. The pronominal suffix refers to Jacob-Israel mentioned in the preceding verse, confirming the consolidation of the two segments of the confederation, and identifying Yahweh as the God of the entire community.

In the second group of oracles, other divine epithets appear: El and Shadday are associated in 24:4. In the parallel passage, 24:16, there is an additional colon which includes the title Elyon. It is clear that vs. 16 has the original form of the couplet while vs. 4 is a defective, and erroneously revised, version of the former. In any case, it is important to note the occurrence of three names or titles of the patriarchal deity in the poems, and in proximity to each other.

The names El and Shadday have already been discussed, though it may be emphasized that together they are the basic designation of the God of the fathers. Along with it we have Elyon which is associated specifically with Abraham and the dialogue with Melchizedek at Salem (Gen. 14:18, 19, 20, 22; note the combination El Elyon). Besides its occurrence in the Oracles of Balaam, Elyon also is found in Deut. 32:8 (probably an extract from an older cosmogony), II Sam. 22:14=Ps. 18:14 (to which should be compared I Sam. 2:10 where we have the epithet *'lw* for original Al or Eli in place of Elyon in the same clause), and Ps. 78:17, 35, 56.

The Oracles of Balaam are representative of Phase II. We may isolate the following features:

1) identification of Yahweh with El, the God of the fathers;
2) the divine epithets used are those associated with the patriarchs: specifically Shadday and Elyon, while others are avoided or employed sparingly. The occurrence of Shadday is especially noteworthy, since this term was in use mainly during the period of the judges and apparently fell into disfavor during the monarchy. It does not reappear until the seventh–sixth centuries in biblical usage.

In view of the evidence a date in the eleventh century for the Oracles is entirely reasonable.

Distribution

1. El: 23:8, 19, 22, 23; 24:4, 8, 16, 23
   a. Without parallel: 23:19, 22, 23; 24:8, 23
   b. In parallel with other divine names and epithets
      1) Yahweh: 23:8
      2) Elyon: 24:(4), 16
      3) Shadday: 24:4, 16
   c. In parallel with other terms
      1) *mōṣīʾ:* 23:22; 24:8
2. Yahweh: 23:8, 21; 24:6
   a. Without parallel: 24:6
   b. In parallel with other divine names
      1) El: 23:8 (cf. El, 1.b.1)
      2) *ʾᵉlōhāw:* 23:21
3. Elyon: 24:(4), 16 (cf. El, 1.b.2)
4. Shadday: 24:4, 16 (cf. El, 1.b.3)

6. THE TESTAMENT OF MOSES: DEUTERONOMY 33[45]

The distribution of divine names and epithets in Deuteronomy 33 is very similar to that in Genesis 49 and Numbers 23–24. The patriarchal terms El and Olam occur as well as Eli (which is equivalent to Elyon). Only Shadday is missing, and this may indicate that Deuteronomy 33 is slightly later in date than the other two, a view which may be sustained on other grounds as well.

The principal divine name in this poem, unlike both the preceding ones, is Yahweh which occurs eight times: vss. 2, 7, 11, 12, 13, 21, 23, 29. Unlike the Testament of Jacob, the name Yahweh occurs repeatedly in the individual sayings concerning the tribes: Judah, Levi, Benjamin, Joseph, Naphtali. It also appears in the opening and closing units showing that the entire composition is thoroughly Yahwistic.

The opening verses are admittedly difficult and obscure if not corrupt. It is possible that there is a divine epithet in the phrase *ḥōbēb ʿammīm*, "lover of peoples" (vs. 3), but if so, it is unique in our collection.

In vs. 12 it is possible to read *ʿlyw* in either position as the divine title Al or Eli, "the Exalted One." The sequence is similar to I Sam. 2:10 where *ʿlw*, "the Exalted," is parallel to Yahweh.[46]

The sequence *hrry qdm//gbʿwt ʿwlm* occurs in vs. 15. This pair has been discussed earlier in connection with the Joseph saying in Genesis 49 where a similar combination appears (vs. 26). It remains a question whether the phrases are best rendered "ancient mountains//eternal hills" or "mountains of the Ancient One//hills of the Eternal," but the latter is at least plausible if not probable.

In vs. 16 we have the unique designation *šōkᵉnī sᵉneh*, "the dweller in the bush," apparently a reference to the episode of the burning bush (cf. Exod. 3:1–5). The archaic and poetic character of the epithet is indicated by the survival of the genitive case ending on the participle (*šōkᵉnī*) which is grammatically correct.[47]

The expression *marḥīb gād*, "the enlarger of Gad," occurs in vs. 20. Although the sentiment is echoed repeatedly in connection with the occupation of the land, the word *marḥīb* does not occur again in the Bible.

In vs. 26, we meet the traditional patriarchal name El, and along with it the phrase *rōkēb šāmayim*, "Rider of the skies." With this is to be compared the expression *lārōkēb bišmē šᵉmē qedem*, "O Rider of the ancient and most remote skies," lit. "in the skies of the skies of antiquity" (Ps. 68:34). Cf. also Ps. 68:5, *lārōkēb bāʿᵃrābōt*, "O Rider of the clouds."

In the following verse we find *ʾlhy qdm*, "the ancient God," and *zrʿt ʿwlm*, "the arms of the Eternal One." The parallelism confirms the interpretation of *ʿwlm* as the divine epithet, while *ʾlhy qdm* is simply the extended form of *qdm*, "the Ancient One."

In both the framework and the blessings, Deuteronomy 33 exhibits a range of divine names and epithets comparable to the Testament of Jacob and the Oracles of Balaam. Yahweh is emphasized as in the Song of the Sea and the Song of Deborah. The combination Jacob-Israel occurs several times, vss. 4–5 (not parallel, but associated), 10, 28, as in Genesis 49 and Numbers 23–24. The name Israel occurs independently (vss. 21, 29), however, which reminds us of the Song of Deborah.

There is an interesting reference to Moses (vs. 4) which is unique in the early poetry. Although several poems are attributed to Moses including this one, the connection is late and editorial. The next verse (5) speaks of a king, which suggests, if the verse itself is not secondary, that the framework was added in the monarchic period, or that the poem as a whole reflects the transition period from tribal confederacy to monarchy, i.e. the time of Saul. This historical situation presupposed in the individual sayings, and the description of Benjamin especially, point to the latter part of the eleventh century as the time of composition.[48]

It may be added that the unusual designation *yᵉšūrūn* for Israel which occurs twice in the poem (specifically in the framework—vss. 5 and 26) occurs again only in Deuteronomy 32 among our poems, which on other grounds should be dated to the monarchic period. The term must have had special and rather exclusive connotations because it is dropped entirely until Second Isaiah picks it up at the height of the nostalgic period (Isa. 44:2).

Characteristic of the Phase II poems is the continued use of the name Yahweh, but not the overwhelming preponderance evident in Phase I. It is frequent in Deuteronomy 33, but in Numbers 23–24 it is less common, preference being shown for the designation El. In Genesis 49 it does not appear at all in the sayings, though it occurs once in a secondary insertion (vs. 18). In this respect Genesis 49 is unique among all the poems in the list; the general omission of Yahweh must be the result of some special circumstance about which we can only speculate at this point.

All of the poems have the name El, and one or more of the epithets explicitly associated with the patriarchs: Shadday (Genesis 49 and Numbers 23–24), Elyon (Numbers 23–24), and Olam (Genesis 49 and Deuteronomy 33). It would be appropriate to speak of a revival of patriarchal religion or religious terminology during this period. Several indicators point to the eleventh century as the date of composition for these poems, with their strong emphasis on the tribal confederation (Genesis 49 and Deuteronomy 33), but there are some hints as well of the earliest phases of the monarchy (Numbers 23–24 and Deuteronomy 33).

Distribution

1. Yahweh: vss. 2, 7, 11, 12, 13, 21, 23, 29
    a. Without parallel: vss. 2, 7, 11, 13, 21, 23, 29
    b. In parallel with other divine names
        1) *ʿal* or *ʿēlī:* vs. 12
2. Al or Eli: vs. 12 (cf. 1.b.1)
    a. In parallel construction or combination
        1) *ḥōpēp:* vs. 12
3. El: vs. 26
    a. In parallel with other terms
        1) *rōkēb šāmayim:* vs. 26
4. *ʾᵉlōhē qedem:* vs. 27
    a. In parallel with other divine names
        1) *ʿōlām:* vs. 27
5. Olam: vss. 15, 27
    a. In parallel with other divine names and epithets
        1) *qedem:* vss. 15, 27 (cf. *ʾᵉlōhē qedem,* 4.a.1)

PHASE III: TENTH CENTURY OR LATER

7. THE SONG OF HANNAH: I SAM. 2:1–10

The predominant divine name in this poem is Yahweh, which occurs nine times in MT (eight, if we substitute *bē'lōhay* for the second *byhwh* in vs. 1 with LXX, which is reasonable). No other epithet or qualifying term occurs more than once, except for *'lhy* which appears twice with suffixes: *'lhy* in vs. 1 and *'lhynw* in vs. 2.

The term *qādōš*, "holy," appears in vs. 2. While the expression is an old one, deriving from Canaanite mythology, and is used as a collective singular or plural of the divine beings who participate in the heavenly council (cf. Exod. 15:11 *qdš//'lym;* Deut. 33:2[?], 3; Ps. 89:6, 8), it is not used of God in any of the poems so far considered. It appears in our corpus only in Ps. 78:41, where we have *qᵉdōš yiśrā'ēl//'ēl,* i.e. El, the Holy One of Israel. The expression becomes dominant in Jerusalem usage of the eighth century and is very frequent in First Isaiah. It is also common in the later prophets, especially Second Isaiah.

The term *ṣūr,* "mountain," also makes its appearance as an epithet of God for the first time (vs. 2). This is one of the more common titles in Phase III poems, and is distinctive of songs associated with the monarchy: cf. II Sam. 23:3; II Sam. 22:2, 32, 47, (47)=Ps. 18:2, 32, 47; Ps. 78:35; it also occurs frequently in Deuteronomy 32. Apart from these occurrences, the term as a divine epithet (either *ṣūr, ṣūrī,* or the like) occurs only in a number of psalms and prophetic materials: Isa. 17:10, 30:29; Hab. 1:12. There are no occurrences in the Pentateuch or Historical Books (apart from the poems in our group), showing there was no tradition associating the epithet with patriarchal religion. This is supported by the fact that although the equivalent term occurs in the Ugaritic texts it is not used as a divine title. There remains the curious, apparently archaic name *ṣūrīšadday,* "Zurishaddai" ("Shadday is my Mountain"; Num. 1:6, etc.) which was borne by the father of the tribal leader of Simeon at the time of the census. In our poetry, however, the two terms *šadday* and *ṣūr* do not occur in the same composition. Just as *šadday* is typical of Phase II poems, so *ṣūr* is characteristic of Phase III.[49] Since the terms are nearly equivalent in meaning, it would appear that Canaanite (=Hebrew) *ṣūr* displaced older Amorite *šadday* during the period of the monarchy.

In vs. 3 Yahweh is identified as *'ēl dē'ōt,* "the God of knowledge." The formation reminds us of similar constructions, e.g. *'ēl hakkābōd,* "the God of glory" (Ps. 29:3);[50] *'ēl 'ᵉmūnāh,* "the God of faithfulness" (Deut. 32:4); the patriarchal formula *'ēl rᵒ'ī,* "the God of my vision"(?) or "El who sees me" (Gen. 16:13); *'ēl qannā',* "the God of zeal (or passion)"

(Exod. 34:14); *'ēl raḥūm wᵉḥannūn,* "the God of love and grace" (Exod. 34:6).

In vss. 6–8 a long series of participles is associated with the name Yahweh: *mmyt, mḥyh, mwryd, mwryš, m'šyr, mšpyl, mqym.* A similar arrangement occurs in the Royal Psalm, II Sam. 22:2–3=Ps. 18:3 though the specific terms are different. The multiplication of qualifying adjectives has a liturgical character and may well reflect temple practice.

The term *'lw* (vs. 10), Al or Eli, "the Exalted One," has been noted.

A monarchic date for the poem is established by vs. 10 (i.e. *malkō*// *mᵉšīḥō*=his anointed king), assuming that it is an original part of the poem. That a distinct series of divine epithets and adjectives is associated with poems of the monarchy seems evident.

Distribution

1. Yahweh: vss. 1, [1], 2, 3, 6, 7, 8, 10, 10
   a. Without parallel (or with Yahweh as parallel): vss. 1ab, 8, 10a
   b. With other divine names
      1) *'ᵉlōhay:* vs. 1
      2) *'ᵉlōhēnū:* vs. 2
      3) *'ēl (dē'ōt)*: vs. 3
      4) *'al:* cf. *'lw*
      5) *qādōš:* vs. 2
      6) *ṣūr:* vs. 2
   c. With other terms
      1) *mēmīt:* vs. 6
      2) *mᵉḥayyeh:* vs. 6
      3) *mōrīd:* vs. 6
      4) *mōrīš:* vs. 7
      5) *ma'ᵃšīr:* vs. 7
      6) *mašpīl:* vs. 7
      7) *mᵉrōmēm:* vs. 7
      8) *mēqīm:* vs. 8
2. El: vs. 2 (cf. Yahweh, 1.b.3)
3. Al: vs. 10
   a. With parallel divine names
      1) Yahweh: vs. 10
4. Qadosh: vs. 2 (cf. 1.b.5)
5. Ṣur: vs. 2 (cf. 1.b.6)

8. DAVID'S LAMENT OVER SAUL AND JONATHAN: II SAM. 1:19–27[51]

Unfortunately for our purposes, no divine names or epithets appear in this poem. This is especially regrettable, since the date of the poem can be fixed with reasonable certainty at about 1000 B.C.

9. THE LAST WORDS OF DAVID: II SAM. 23:1–7[52]

Unlike the preceding item, this short poem is practically a compendium of current divine names and epithets: the direct association with David ensures a tenth-century date.

In the opening line of vs. 1 we find the divine title *ʿl*, "the Exalted One": i.e. "oracle of the man, raised up by the Exalted One."[53] This term has been discussed in connection with Gen. 49:26; Deut. 33:12; and I Sam. 2:10.

In the second line of the same verse, we find the terms *ʾlhy yʿqb*//*zmrwt yśrʾl*, "the God of Jacob//the Defense of Israel." The formal pattern is very much like that of Deut. 33:27 *ʾlhy qdm*//*zrʿt ʿwlm*, "the ancient God//the arms of the Eternal." For the expression *zmrwt*, "defense," see the comments on *zmrt* in Exod. 15:2.

In vs. 2 Yahweh appears for the only time in the poem.

In vs. 3 MT has *ʾlhy yśrʾl*, "the God of Israel," but it is likely that the original reading was *ʾlhy yʿqb*, "the God of Jacob," since we have "Israel" in the parallel expression, *ṣwr yśrʾl*, "the Mountain of Israel," and one would expect the same pairing of Jacob and Israel here as in vs. 1. It has already been observed that the use of *ṣwr* as a divine epithet is characteristic of Phase III poems.

The word *ʾᵉlōhīm*, "God," in the absolute form appears for the first time in our poetry in vs. 3. It occurs in the expression *yirʾat ʾᵉlōhīm*, "the fear of God," which is quite rare; cf. Gen. 20:11 and Neh. 5:15. The phrase, which conveys the basic idea of "piety" or "reverence," describes the attitude and behavior of a *ṣaddīq*, "righteous one" (which is the parallel or complementary term in our passage). The common expression is *yirʾat Yahweh* which occurs frequently in the wisdom literature and later poetry (note Isa. 11:2–3, where it is used of the ideal king of the house of David). The word *ʾᵉlōhīm* occurs in Judg. 5:8, but there it must be a numerical plural and refer to "new gods."[54] A similar usage occurs in Deut. 32:17 (where *ʾlhym* is parallel to *ḥdšym*); in Deut. 32:39 *ʾlhym* is also probably a numerical plural, and in any case refers to a god or gods other than Yahweh.[55] It is interesting to note that the construct form *ʾlhy* and the form with suffixes invariably refers to Yahweh in the early poems, cf. Exod. 15:2; Judg. 5:3, 5; Num. 23:21; Deut. 33:27; I Sam. 2:(1), 2; etc. while the absolute form *ʾlhym* is not used at all of God, but only as a numerical plural referring to other gods.

The divine name *ʾēl*, "El, God," occurs in vs. 5, and parallel to it is the term *ʿōlām*. I take this to be the divine epithet, "the Eternal One" forming part of the traditional combination *ʾēl ʿōlām* (cf. Gen. 21:33), "El the Eternal."[56] The word *ʿōlām* is usually construed with *bᵉrīt* and rendered "an eternal covenant." Since the expression occurs frequently in the Bible, it cannot be ruled out. Nevertheless it should be noted that the other occurrences of the expression in the Bible are all late. It appears only in the prose of the Pentateuch and is used only by P: Gen. 9:16; 17:7, 13, 19; Exod. 31:16; Lev. 24:8; Num. 18:19. For the rest it is found only in exilic and post-exilic prophecy: Isa. 24:5, 55:3, 61:8; Jer. 32:40, 50:5; Ezek. 16:60, 37:26; and a late Psalm (105:10=I Chron. 16:17). Under the circumstances it would be unusual, though not impossible to find it in an early Davidic poem, especially since the covenant with David is not elsewhere called a *bᵉrīt ʿōlām,* "everlasting covenant": cf. Pss. 89:4, 29, 35, 40; 132:12; Jer. 33:21. What is to be everlasting is the promised kingship. The idea but not the wording occurs in Ps. 89:29—"For ever will I maintain my kindness toward him / and my covenant will stand firm for him." Isa. 55:3 echoes a similar sentiment though it speaks of a future rather than a historic covenant: "I will make with you an everlasting covenant (*bᵉrīt ʿōlām*), my steadfast sure love for David." Hence, I would render II Sam. 23:5 as follows:

> Utterly secure is my dynasty with El
> For the Eternal has executed a covenant in my behalf.

In estimating the date of this poem consideration should be given to the opening formula: *nᵉʾum dāwīd ben-yišay / ūnᵉʾum haggeber* . . . , "The oracle of David ben-Jesse / yea the oracle of that man . . ." The formula is the same as that of the Oracles of Balaam (Num. 24:3–4, 15–16):

nᵉʾum bilʿam bᵉnō-bᵉʿōr	The oracle of Balaam the son of Beor
ūnᵉʾum haggeber . . .	yea the oracle of that man . . .

Except for Prov. 30:1 which has an abbreviated form of this introduction (*nᵉʾum haggeber*) in an obscure context and Ps. 36:2, these are the only instances in which *nᵉʾum* is used of a human speaker. Otherwise it is always used of God.

The opening formula in the Oracles of Balaam and David's Testament belongs to a formal style which seems to have flourished in the eleventh–tenth centuries. Then it dropped out of use in relation to human beings, surviving only in combination with God in liturgical formulae. It is restricted almost entirely to prophetic utterances (cf. the exceptional *nᵉʾum Yahweh,* Ps. 110:1; the psalm may be of early date).

Distribution

1. Al: vs. 1
2. *ʾᵉlōhē* ——: vss. 1, 3
   a. In parallel with other divine names and epithets
      1) *zᵉmīrōt:* vs. 1.
      2) *ṣūr:* vs. 3
3. Yahweh: vs. 2
4. Elohim: vs. 3

5. El: vs. 5
    a. In parallel with other divine names
        1) *'ōlām:* vs. 5
6. Ṣur: vs. 3 (cf. 2.a.2)
7. Olam: vs. 5 (cf. 5.a.1)

10. A ROYAL SONG OF THANKSGIVING: II SAMUEL 22=PSALM 18[57]

This poem, which is preserved both in the books of Samuel and of Psalms was considered by more than one editor to be characteristically Davidic. Among other features, it shares with II Samuel 23 and I Samuel 2 a similar selection of divine names and epithets.

The name Yahweh dominates the poem, occurring sixteen times in the Samuel version (S) and in the Psalms edition (P).

In the opening verses (2–3), after the initial occurrence of Yahweh, there is a series of qualifying nouns, including participles, all referring to the deity and having the first person pronominal suffix:

	S		P
1.	*sal'ī*	My Rock	*sal'ī*
2.	*m^eṣūdātī*	My Stronghold	*m^eṣūdātī*
3.	*m^epalṭī*	My Deliverer	*m^epalṭī*
4.	*'^elōhay* [MT *'^elōhē*]	My God	*'ēlī*
5.	*ṣūrī*	My Mountain	*ṣūrī*
6.	*maginnī*	My Suzerain	*maginnī*
7.	*qeren yiš'ī*	The Horn of My Salvation	*qeren yiš'ī*
8.	*miśgabbī*	My Redoubt	*miśgabbī*
9.	*m^enūsī*	My Refuge	————
10.	*mōšī'ī*	My Savior	————

The series may be compared with the list of participles detailing Yahweh's powers and activities already noted in I Samuel 2. This group, however, has a devotional and personal quality lacking in the other.

From this list, the terms that are of particular interest to us are *'^elōhay* (S)=*'ēlī* (P), and *ṣūrī,* which occur elsewhere in this poem, and others of our collection:

The construct form *'^elōhē* occurs in combination with *yiš'ī* in vs. 47 (P), "the God of my salvation."[58] The parallel terms are Yahweh and *ṣūrī*. The form with first person singular suffix, *'^elōhay,* occurs in vss. 7, 22, and 30. In vss. 7 and 22 it is balanced by Yahweh, while there is no correlative in vs. 30. In vs. 32, we have the form with the first person plural suffix *'^elōhēnū*. Parallel terms are *'ēl* (S)=*'^elōah* (P), Yahweh, and *ṣūr*. We note the first appearance of *'^elōah* in our group of poems. It occurs twice in Deut. 32 (vss. 15, 17) but otherwise is not present. It is very common in Job (forty-two times) and occurs in other archaizing poetry of the later period: e.g. Hab. 3:3; cf. Pss. 50:22, 114:7, 139:19; Prov. 30:5; Isa. 44:8. The distribution is similar to that of *šadday,* already noted, though *'ᵉlōah* is not genuinely archaic in the same sense as *šadday* which has roots in patriarchal times. The term *'ᵉlōah* does not seem to have been used earlier than the monarchy and then only for a brief period, presumably in the tenth–ninth centuries. After a gap, it was revived in the nostalgic era, previously mentioned.

The name El (in addition to the suffixed form in Ps. 18:3) occurs in vss. 31, 32 (S), 33, and 48. In vs. 31 *hā'ēl,* "the God, El himself," is parallel to Yahweh and *māgēn,* "Shield," or "Suzerain, Benefactor."[59]

The pronoun *hū',* "He," is used as a designation for God in conjunction with *māgēn.* A random distribution of this term among the poems in our list might have been expected, but in fact it is restricted entirely to Phase III, and particularly to the last four poems in this group. Besides the occurrence here, it appears in Deut. 32:4, 6, 6, 39; Ps. 78:38; Ps. 68:36. In view of the unusual and consistent pattern displayed, we may regard its use as a feature of Phase III poetry. In vs. 33, *hā'ēl* has *mā'uzzī,* "my Refuge," as a complement in S, but in P there is a participial expression *ham'azzᵉrēnī,* "the One who girds me."

The epithet *ṣwr,* "Mountain," occurs in vss. 2, 32, 47 (S has it twice). These instances have all been noted previously.

The epithet *'elyōn* occurs in vs. 14 in parallel with Yahweh. The verse itself echoes I Sam. 2:10 in part, where we have the divine name Al which is related to Elyon. Its occurrence in the Oracles of Balaam has been noted.

The term *nērī,* "my Lamp," occurs in vs. 29, in parallel with Yahweh and *'ᵉlohay* (P).

More participles turn up in vss. 34–35: *mᵉšawweh,* "the One who sets," and *mᵉlammēd,* "the One who teaches." In vs. 49, we have *mōṣī'ī,* "the One who brings me out" (S), and *mᵉpalṭī,* "the One who delivers me" (P).

The closing verse, if part of the original poem, fixes the date of composition in the monarchy and attaches it to David and his posterity. The parallel terms *malkō//mᵉšīḥō* are the same as in I Sam. 2:10.

Distribution

1. Yahweh: vss. 2, (3P), 4, 7, 14, 16, 19, 21, 22, 25, 29, (29S), 31, 32, 42, 47, 50
   a. Without parallels: vss. 4, 16, 19, 21, 25, 29ab(S), 42, 50
   b. With divine names and epithets:
      1) *sal'ī:* vs. 2
      2) *mᵉṣūdātī:* vs. 2
      3) *mᵉpalṭī:* vs. 2
      4) *'ᵉlōhay:* vss. 3(S), 7, 22, 29(P), 30
      5) *'ēlī:* vs. 3 (P)
      6) *ṣūrī:* vss. 3, 47

7) *maginnī:* vs. 3
8) *qeren yiš'i:* vs. 3
9) *miśgabbī:* vs. 3
10) *m^{e}nūsī:* vs. 3
11) *mōšī'ī:* vs. 3
12) *'elyōn:* vs. 14
13) *nērī:* vs. 29
14) *hā'ēl:* vs. 31 (cf. El 2.a.1)
15) *'^{e}lōhēnū:* vs. 32 (cf. El 2.a.2)
16) *'^{e}lōhē yiš'ī:* vs. 47

c. With other terms
1) *m^{e}hullāl:* vs. 4
2) *māgēn:* vs. 31
3) *magdīl:* vs. 51
4) *'ōśeh-ḥesed:* vs. 51

2. El: vss. 31, 32(S), 33, 48
a. With divine names and epithets
1) Yahweh: vss. 31, 32
2) *ṣūr:* vs. 32
3) *'^{e}lōhēnū:* vs. 32
4) *mā'uzzī:* vs. 33

b. With other terms
1) *māgēn:* vs. 31
2) *hū':* vs. 31
3) *hannōtēn n^{e}qāmōt:* vs. 48
4) *mōrīd:* vs. 48
5) *mōṣī'ī:* vs. 49

3. Ṣur: vss. 3, 32, 37, 47(S)
a. With other divine names
1) Yahweh//*'^{e}lōhay:* vss. 2–3 (cf. 1.b.6)
2) El//Yahweh//*'^{e}lōhēnū:* vs. 32
3) Yahweh//*'^{e}lōhē yiš'ī:* vs. 47 (cf. 1.b.16)

4. Elyon: vs. 14 (cf. 1.b.12)
5. Eloah: vs. 32(P)
a. In parallel with divine names and epithets: (cf. 2.a.2)
1) Yahweh: vs. 32
2) Ṣur: vs. 32
3) *'^{e}lōhēnū:* vs. 32

6. *Hū':* vs. 31 (cf. 2.b.2)

11. THE SONG OF MOSES: DEUTERONOMY 32

The pattern of selection and distribution of divine names and epithets in Deuteronomy 32 is very similar to that of the poems just considered and of Psalm 78. We may have in these data an additional and possibly helpful clue to the dating of this poem, which has proved a difficult problem to scholars, who have tested an assortment of dates from Moses to the exile and beyond.[60]

The principal divine name is Yahweh which occurs eight times, as was also the case with Deuteronomy 33 and I Samuel 2 (on a corrected basis).

In vs. 3, we have *'ᵉlōhēnū,* "our God," which is parallel to Yahweh. In vs. 37 the archaic form *'ᵉlōhēmō,* "their God," occurs, in parallel with *ṣūr,* "Mountain."

The term *ṣūr* occurs seven times; in six instances the reference is to the God of Israel: vss. 4, 15, 18, 30, 31, 37. In vs. 4, the word *haṣṣūr,* "the Mountain," has a parallel in *'ēl 'ᵉmūnāh,* "the God of truth." In addition the terms *ṣaddīq,* "Righteous One," and *yāšār,* "Upright One," are used of God. In vs. 15, *ṣūr* is paralleled by *'ᵉlōah,* "God," which has already been discussed in connection with its appearance in Ps. 18:32. In vs. 18, *ṣūr* is balanced by *'ēl,* "El, God," while in vs. 30, the matching term is Yahweh. In vs. 31, *ṣūr* occurs twice in the sequence *kī lō' kᵉṣūrēnū ṣūrām,* "For their mountain is not like our Mountain." A comparison of deities is involved, though it is interesting that the same epithet is used of both the true and a false god. Verse 37 combines *ṣūr* with *'ᵉlōhēmō,* "their God," as already mentioned.

The divine name or qualifying designation *'ēl* is also common in this poem, occurring a total of five times (vss. 4, 8, 12, 18, 21), including a highly probable reading in vs. 8 on the basis of the LXX and a Qumran document of Deuteronomy 32, i.e. *bny 'l* (or *'lhym*) for *bny yśr'l.*[61]

In vs. 12, *'ēl* is modified by *nēkār,* "strange, foreign," in reference to another god as a possible companion of Yahweh: "Yahweh alone guided him / and there was no strange god with him." In vs. 21, there is a different sort of negative formulation: *lō'-'ēl,* "a no-god," i.e. a false deity. The line reads: "They aroused my resentment with a no-god / they provided me with their vanities (i.e. idols)." It will be seen that the term *'ēl* in this poem is not restricted to the divine appellation "El" (vs. 18, already noted) but is used in a more generic sense as well: e.g. *'ēl 'ᵉmūnāh* (vs. 4), "God of truth" or "the faithful God"; *'ēl nēkār,* "a strange god"; *lō'-'ēl,* "a no-god."

In vs. 8, the patriarchal epithet *'elyōn* makes its appearance; its occurrence in Numbers 23–24 and II Samuel 22=Psalm 18 has already been noted. The passage here has an archaic ring, reflecting mythologic traditions about the origins of the nations: a poetic version to be compared and contrasted with the story of the tower of Babel (Gen. 11:1–9). There is an apparent equation of Elyon with El, if we accept the reading of LXX and 4Q Deuteronomy: cf. Gen. 14:18, 20, 21, where the combination occurs. The identification of this God with Yahweh is certainly intended by the poet (cf. vss. 12 and esp. 39), though vs. 9 has been interpreted as reflecting a subordinate status for Yahweh in the pantheon headed by Elyon.

The term *'ᵉlōah,* "God," occurs twice, once in parallel with *ṣūr* (see above), once in vs. 17 where it stands for the true God in contrast with *šēdīm,* "demons, evil spirits," and *'elōhīm,* "gods."

In vs. 39, *'elōhīm,* "gods," (though possibly "god") is comparable to *'ēl nēkār* in vs. 12:

> And there was no strange god with him (12)
> And beside me there are no gods (39).

Additional terms for "God" (*'l* or *'lhym*) and "gods" (*'lhym*) probably occurred in an earlier form of vs. 43 which is truncated in MT (cf. LXX and 4Q Deuteronomy).[62] If *'lhym,* "God," is the correct reading here (and possibly vs. 8), then these instances would parallel the usage noted in II Sam. 23:3.

On the basis of the selection and distribution of divine names and epithets in this poem, I would assign it to the latter part of Phase III, and date it in the latter part of the tenth century at the earliest, or in the ninth century. At the same time, it should be noted that there is no explicit reference to the monarchy or historical events later than the settlement. There are other affinities with earlier poems, especially the Blessing of Moses and the Oracles of Balaam. Apparently the poet had in mind a setting in the pre-monarchic period and composed his piece accordingly. A later editor correctly perceived this intention and quite naturally attributed the utterance to the principal figure of early Israel, Moses himself.

Distribution

1. Yahweh: vss. 3, 6, 9, 12, 19, 27, 30, 36
   a. Without parallels: vss. 9, 19, 27, 36
   b. In parallel with divine names and epithets
      1) *'elōhēnū:* vs. 3
      2) *hū'* vss. 6ab
      3) *'ābīkā:* vs. 6
      4) *'ēl nēkār:* vs. 12
      5) *ṣūrām:* vs. 31 (cf. *ṣūr,* 2.a.7)
2. Ṣur: vss. 4, 15, 18, 30, 31, 37
   a. In parallel with other divine names
      1) *'ēl 'emūnāh:* vs. 4
      2) *ṣaddīq:* vs. 4
      3) *yāšār:* vs. 4
      4) *hū':* vs. 4
      5) *'elōah:* vs. 15 (cf. 6.a.1)
      6) *'ēl:* vs. 18
      7) Yahweh: vs. 30
      8) *'elōhēmō:* vs. 37
   b. In parallel with other terms

1) *ṣûrām:* vs. 31 (*keṣûrēnû*): I assume that Israel is speaking in this verse. In any case one term refers to the God of Israel and the other *ṣûr* refers to another god.

3. El: vss. 4, (8), 18
   a. Without parallel: vs. 8 (but linked with Elyon)
   b. In parallel with divine names
      1) *haṣṣûr:* vs. 4 (cf. 2.a.1)
      2) *ṣaddîq//yāšār:* vs. 4
      3) *hû':* vs. 4
      4) *ṣûr:* vs. 18 (cf. 2.a.6)
4. *Hû':* vss. 4, 6, 6, 39
   a. In parallel construction
      1) *haṣṣûr:* vs. 4 (cf. 2.a.1)
      2) *'ēl 'emûnāh:* vs. 4 (3.b.3)
      3) *ṣaddîq//yāšār:* vs. 4
      4) Yahweh: vs. 6 (cf. 1.b.2)
      5) *'ābîkā:* vs. 6
5. *Elyon*: vs. 8
6. *Eloah:* vss. 15, 17
   a. Without parallel: vs. 17
   b. In parallel construction
      1) *ṣûr:* vs. 15

12. PSALM 78

Since this Psalm is located in the Elohistic Psalter, the dominant divine name is Elohim (eight times) instead of Yahweh (twice). Almost as frequent as Elohim is El which occurs seven times. The name Yahweh appears in vss. 4 and 21; in both verses it stands by itself, without a parallel term.

In the Elohistic Psalter, the name Elohim is used where in the same or similar lines in a Yahwistic compendium the name Yahweh would appear.[63] As we have seen, the emergence of Elohim as a distinctive name for God is rather late in our poetry (II Samuel 23 and perhaps Deuteronomy 32); its use in the Elohistic Psalter is rather unusual and reflects the special circumstances under which that part of the Psalter was composed or compiled. It occurs in vss. 7, 10, 19, 22, 31, 35, 56, 59. Thus in vs. 7, Elohim is set in parallel with El as elsewhere in our poetry it is Yahweh and El that are conjoined. The same pairing of Elohim and El occurs in vss. 19 and 35. In the latter verse, two additional terms occur, forming double pairs:

'elōhîm ṣûrām	God (was) their Mountain
'ēl-'elyôn gō'ᵃlām	El-Elyon (was) their Redeemer

In vs. 56, Elohim is paired with Elyon: "And they tested and rebelled against God Most High." In vs. 59, Elohim is paralleled by *m'd,* "the

Mighty One." The passage may be rendered: God heard and was angered / and the Mighty One rejected Israel."[64] In the other instances, Elohim has no explicit parallel (vss. 10, 22, 31).

El occurs in vss. 7, 8, 18, 19, 34, 35, 41. Several of these have already been noted (vss. 7, 19, 35). El in vs. 18 balances Elyon in vs. 17. In vs. 41, El is identified as *qᵉdōš yiśrāʼēl,* "the Holy One of Israel." The occurrence of *qādōš* in I Sam. 2:2 has already been noted, as well as its distribution in the Bible. The combination *qᵉdōš yiśrāʼēl* is the distinctive title used by I and II Isaiah; but it also occurs in Ps. 89:19 which is a royal psalm of approximately the same date as this poem.[65] In vss. 8 and 34, El stands alone.

The epithet Elyon occurs three times (vss. 17, 35, and 56), all of which have been noted previously: (1) parallel to El in vs. 18; (2) combined with El and parallel to Elohim (vs. 35); *ṣûrām,* "their Mountain," also occurs in this verse, parallel to *gōʼᵃlām,* "their Redeemer"; (3) linked with Elohim (vs. 56).

The term Adonay occurs once, in vs. 65. The only other instance in the poetry studied so far is the disputed occurrence in Exod. 15:17 (MT). There are several more examples in Psalm 68. It is clear in any case that Adonay was not in general use before the tenth century which is the earliest possible date for this Psalm and Psalm 68 in their present form.

The general selection and distribution of divine names and epithets in Psalm 78 correlate well with the other poems in this group, and tend to support a date in the early monarchy. The specific references to Judah, Zion, and David confirm the supposition. The shift in usage away from Yahweh to Elohim seems to reflect the special circumstances of the editorial format of the Elohistic Psalter and is not necessarily a reflection of the original pattern of the poem. The same is true of the other poems from this section of the Psalter which are yet to be examined.

Distribution

1. Elohim: vss. 7, 10, 19, 22, 31, 35, 56, 59
   a. Without parallel: vss. 10, 22, 31
   b. In parallel construction
      1) *ʼēl*: vss. 7, 19, 35
      2) *ṣûrām:* vs. 35
      3) *ʻelyōn:* vss. 35, 56
      4) *gōʼᵃlām:* vs. 35
      5) *mʼd:* vs. 59
2. El: vss. 7, 8, 18, 19, 34, 35, 41
   a. Without parallel: vss. 8, 34
   b. In parallel construction
      1) *ʼᵉlōhîm:* vss. 7, 19, 35 (cf. 1.b.1)
      2) *ʻelyōn:* vss. 17 (cf. 3.a.1), 35

3) *ṣūrām//gō'ᵃlām:* vs. 35
4) *qᵉdōš yiśrā'ēl:* vs. 41
3. Elyon: vss. 17, 35, 56
a. In parallel construction
1) El: vss. 17, 35 (cf. 2.b.2)
2) Elohim: vss. 35, 56 (cf. 1.b.3)
3) *ṣūrām//gō'ᵃlām:* vs. 35
4. Yahweh: vss. 4, 21
5. Adonay: vs. 65
6. *Hū':* vs. 38
a. In parallel construction
1) *raḥūm:* vs. 38

13. PSALM 72

This poem begins with the word *'ᵉlōhīm,* "God," a usage which is to be expected in this section of the Psalter. There are no other divine names and epithets, however, until the concluding lines of the poem, vss. 18–19. These do not appear to have been part of the original poem, but constitute a liturgical conclusion to this second book of the Psalter. In any case the divine names and titles are as follows: (1) Yahweh; (2) *'ᵉlōhīm;* (3) *'ᵉlōhē yiśrā'ēl.* The phrase "Yahweh, the God of Israel" goes back ultimately to the Song of Deborah. Apparently *'ᵉlōhīm* was inserted in keeping with the character of the Elohistic Psalter; the combination Yahweh Elohim is reminiscent of the curious pattern in the J source at the beginning of Genesis (2:4 ff.).

The evidence is insufficient to make a judgment, but there is nothing in the poem, and certainly in the divine nomenclature to preclude a tenth-century date.

14. PSALM 68[66]

Albright described this poem as a catalogue of *Incipits* or first lines of early Israelite songs dating from the period between the thirteenth and tenth centuries. On the basis of our analysis and grouping of divine titles, Psalm 68 exhibits similar heterogeneous characteristics, with a varied collection of such terms belonging to all three phases of early Israelite poetry. In other words, the diversity of divine names conforms to the hypothetical model posited by Albright. Furthermore the distribution, with few exceptions would point to a collection of songs that was predominantly pre-monarchic in date (i.e. before Phase III).

For reasons already adduced, the principal name of God used in this Psalm is Elohim (twenty-four times); in many if not most cases, it can be shown that the more original form of the line or couplet had the name Yahweh. Nevertheless, Yahweh does appear three times; and El is present in five places. The construct form *'ᵉlōhē* occurs twice and *zh syny,* "the One of Sinai," once; *šadday* also appears once. The relatively late term *'dny*, "my Lord," appears six times (in some cases apparently as a substitute for a more original Yahweh). The short form Yah occurs twice. In such a catholic collection, certain omissions are surprising: *'elyōn*, "Most High," *ṣūr*, "Mountain," and *'elōah*, "God," do not occur. The absence of the latter two suggests that few of the opening lines derive from the period of the monarchy, though the compilation can hardly antedate the tenth century in view of vss. 30 ff. which mention Jerusalem and presuppose the existence of the temple. A more detailed study of the divine names and epithets follows:

In vs. 2 there is a clear echo of the Song of the Ark (Num. 10:35), but Elohim has been substituted for the original Yahweh. There is no parallel term, as is also true in vss. 3 and 4.

In vs. 5, there is a parallel expression for Elohim: *lārōkēb bā'arābōt*, "O Rider of the Clouds," which is derived from a Canaanite expression used of Baal.[67] The term Yah also occurs in this verse, but the exact meaning of the passage is unclear. In vs. 6 Elohim is designated *'abī yetōmīm*, "Father of the fatherless," and *dayyan 'almānōt*, "the Legal Guardian of the widows." In vs. 7, Elohim serves as subject of two participles: *mōšīb*, "Who settles singles in households," and *mōṣī'*, "Who brings forth prisoners."

In vss. 8–9, there is an adaptation of a well-known passage in the Song of Deborah (Judg. 5:4–5), in which Elohim has been substituted for the more original Yahweh (three times). In addition we have the familiar *zh syny*, "the One of Sinai," and *'lhy yśr'l*, "the God of Israel."

In vs. 10, Elohim stands by itself, without a parallel term. The same is true of vs. 11. In vs. 12 Adonay, "my Lord," occurs, in place of the expected Elohim. In vs. 15, we have the only occurrence of Shadday in the poem.

In vss. 16–17, Elohim occurs twice; the second is balanced by Yahweh. In vs. 18, Elohim occurs in the first colon, and Adonay in the second. Since the second colon is evidently a slightly corrupted version of the first colon of Deut. 33:2, *yhwh msyny b'*, "Yahweh came from Sinai," it is probable that Adonay has been substituted for a more original Yahweh here. I render the colon as follows:

'dny b' msyny bqdš	My Lord came from Sinai among the holy ones

The term *bqdš* is to be interpreted as a collective: holy ones. The same usage occurs in vs. 25 of this psalm, and in Exod. 15:11; cf. also *rbbt qdš*, "myriads of holy ones" (Deut. 33:2).[68]

In vs. 19 we have the unusual combination *yh 'lhym*. The initial term (*yh*) is probably the exclamation, "O!" rather than the divine name Yah.[69]

In vss. 20–21, there is a chiastic arrangement featuring Adonay and El, as follows:

'ᵃdōnay//*hā'ēl* (20)
hā'ēl//*'ᵃdōnay* (21)

In vs. 21, enclosed within the outer pair is another combination: El and Yahweh.

In vs. 22, we have Elohim alone; in vs. 23, the divine name is Adonay. In vs. 25, Elohim is matched by *'ēlī,* "my God," which in turn is in apposition with *malkī,* "my King." The passage as a whole may be rendered:

Behold the marches of God
The marches of my God,
My King among the holy ones.[70]

In vs. 27, Elohim is balanced by Yahweh. In vs. 29, *'ᵉlōhēkā,* "your God," is in parallel construction with Elohim. In vs. 30, the divine appellative *'l,* "Exalted One," occurs. I follow Dahood generally in analyzing and rendering: "Your temple, Exalted One, is in Jerusalem."[71] In vs. 32, Elohim has no parallel. In vs. 33, Elohim is balanced by Adonay. In vs. 34, the epithet, *rōkēb,* occurs in the expression: *lārōkēb bišmē šᵉmē-qedem,* "O Rider of the most ancient skies." Cf. vs. 5.

In vs. 35, Elohim occurs in parallel with *'l yśr'l,* "the Exalted One of Israel." In vs. 36, Elohim occurs with the participle *nwr',* "the Terrible One"; it is balanced by the expression *'ēl yiśrā'ēl,* "the God of Israel," which reminds us of the patriarchal *'ēl 'ᵉlōhē yiśrā'ēl,* "El, the God of Israel" (Gen. 33:20) as well as the common expression *'lhy yśr'l,* "the God of Israel." The Psalm ends with Elohim (*bārūk 'ᵉlōhīm,* "blessed be God").

Distribution

1. Elohim: vss. 2, 3, 4, 5, 6, 7, 8, 9, 9, 10, 11, 16, 17, 18, 19, 22, 25, 27, 29, 32, 33, 35, 36, 36
   a. Without parallel: vss. 2, 3, 4, 8, 10, 11, 22, 32, 35, 36
   b. In parallel with other divine names
      1) Yah: vs. 5, cf. vs. 19 (?)
      2) Yahweh: vss. 17, 27
      3) Adonay: vss. 18, 33
      4) El: vss. 25 (*'ēlī*), 36 (*'ēl yiśrā'ēl*)
      5) Elohim: vs. 9 (*'ᵉlōhē yiśrā' ēl*); cf. vs. 29 (*'ᵉlōhēkā*)
      6) Al: vs. 35 (*'l yśr'l*)
   c. In parallel with various epithets and phrases
      1) *rōkēb:* vs. 5 (*lārōkēb bā'ᵃrābōt,* "O Rider of the clouds"; cf. vs. 34)
      2) *'ᵃbī yᵉtōmīm wᵉdayyan 'almānōt:* vs. 6
      3) *mōšīb yᵉḥīdīm* and *mōṣī' 'ᵃṣīrīm:* vs. 7
      4) *zeh sīnay:* vs. 9
      5) *malkī:* vs. 25
      6) *nōrā':* vs. 36
      7) *bārūk:* vs. 36

2. Adonay: vss. 12, 18, 20, 21, 23, 33
   a. Without parallel: vss. 12, 23
   b. In parallel with other divine names
      1) El: vs. 20 (*hā'ēl*); cf. vs. 21
      2) Elohim: cf. vss. 18, 33
3. El: vss. 20, 21, 21, 25, 36
   a. Without parallel
   b. In parallel with other divine names
      1) Adonay: vs. 21, cf. vs. 20
      2) Yahweh: vs. 21
      3) Elohim: cf. vss. 25, 36
4. Yahweh: vss. 17, 21, 27
   a. Without parallel
   b. In parallel with other divine names
      1) Elohim: cf. vss. 17, 27
      2) El: cf. vs. 21
5. Al: vss. 30, 35
   a. Without parallel: vs. 30
   b. In parallel with Elohim: vs. 35
6. Shadday: vs. 15 (no parallel)
7. Yah: vss. 5, 19 (both instances are uncertain)

Summary: The Chronology of the Poems

From the data on divine names and epithets and certain other key terms assembled and analyzed in the foregoing presentation it is possible to present certain conclusions about the relative and absolute chronology of the poems under consideration.

First of all, the selection and distribution of divine names do not appear to be haphazard but follow a traceable evolutionary pattern. We believe that we can distinguish three major phases during the period from the twelfth through the tenth–ninth centuries B.C., and arrange the poems in a general chronological sequence according to specific criteria. We restrict ourselves to divine nomenclature and a few other terms, but recognize that there are a number of other factors to be considered in making a determination of date, whether relative or absolute or both. Such factors include content and style in the broad sense as well as numerous details of different kinds. But our purpose here is to present the case for the particular criterion described and to show its relevance for arranging the poems chronologically.

Secondly, we have assumed generally the integrity and accuracy of the received Hebrew text (MT), i.e. that the poems are unified compositions and that the text has been transmitted faithfully, in particular with respect to the divine names and epithets. With certain exceptions, the data support the presupposition: there has been very little tampering or alteration. With respect to integrity, the danger zones are at the beginning and ending of the poems, where introductory or concluding matter could have been and occasionally may have been added (Exod. 15:2 is the single most striking example though there are others). With respect to accuracy, there are two principal difficulties both having to do with the substitution of one appellation for another though each occurred or developed under different circumstances and presumably at a different time:

1. The substitution of Adonay for Yahweh, which ultimately became universal in reading the Scriptures and examples of which crept into the text as a result. The title Adonay must also have had an independent history so it is difficult to determine when it is an original reading and when it is a secondary substitution for Yahweh. Again with a rare exception or two, the evidence from our poems is that Adonay was not in use in Israelite poetry until Phase III.

2. The substitution of Elohim for an original Yahweh. This practice, which is evident in the so-called Elohistic Psalter, presumably reflects the same ambience and literary usage that we find in the E-source of the Pentateuch, and may date back to the tenth–ninth centuries. While the term *'ᵉlōhīm* was certainly known and in use from earliest times, its specific employment as a name for God (as against the numerical plural "gods") is not attested until Phase III in our collection of poetry. Even then we must distinguish between its natural appearance (e.g. II Sam. 23:3) and its extensive use as a surrogate for a more original Yahweh in Psalms 68 (especially) and 78. In spite of these difficulties, what is surprising is the degree to which the nomenclature remains characteristic and distinctive; the inevitable conclusion is that there has been no wholesale substitution or alteration of names. A good illustration of the very limited extent of such changes may be seen in the comparison of II Samuel 22 with Psalm 18: in vs. 3, S has *'ᵉlōhē* while P has *'ēlī* (probably the better reading); in vs. 29, S has Yahweh, while P reads *'ᵉlōhay* (again the preferred reading); in vs. 32, S has *'ēl* while P reads *'ᵉlōah* (presumably a secondary reading and a sign of later compilation); in vs. 47, S has *ṣūr*, while P omits the word (also correct, since *ṣūr* is intrusive in the passage). Otherwise the distribution of divine names is the same.

Thirdly, the pertinent data have been assembled on a chart, to indicate at a glance the distribution and arrangement of the terms which have been isolated in this study. In setting up the chart the list of terms has been coordinated with the list of poems. The sequence of poems has been derived essentially from Albright with occasional rearrangement as indicated by the occurrence or absence of key epithets. These adjustments reflect the theory on which the investigation is based and in turn affect the conclusions. In other words, a certain degree of circular reasoning is inevitable as well as desirable in formulating the hypothesis. By this process of double approximation, a greater precision is achieved in organizing the material and ordering the poems. The test of the theory is likewise twofold: (1) inner consistency, which may be a matter of scholarly ingenuity, but not less important for that reason; and (2) conformity to external data, that is, data external to the hypothesis or the materials used in arranging the poems: e.g. historical references and allusions, independent scholarly reconstructions and conclusions, etc.

Taking the group of poems as a whole, it is immediately obvious that there are a plethora of names, epithets, and other terms descriptive of the deity, so many, in fact, that it would be very difficult if not impossible to handle them effectively in trying to determine chronological relationships among the poems. A striking illustration would be the long lists of participles and similar expressions used of God in the Song of Hannah (I Samuel 2) and the Royal Song of Thanksgiving (II Samuel 22=Psalm 18). The available information is outlined in Chart A (pp. 125-26).

Once the over-all pattern has been established, then important but incidental details of this kind shed significant light on the nature of Israelite hymnody in the period to which these poems belong. In general, however, terms which occur in only one of the poems in the group are not immediately pertinent to our investigation and these have been excluded from a more concentrated summary of the evidence provided in Chart B (pp. 127-28).

Even this compilation is too cluttered and confusing, though the basic data are present. Further reduction in the number to a select group of diagnostic and determinative expressions is necessary, along with appropriate adjustments in the sequence of the poems, in order to produce a consistent evolutionary and intelligible sequence dating. We have restricted the study to the dozen key terms in categories A and B under divine epithets, and half-a-dozen other terms which bear on the questions of order and chronology. Similarly, we have reduced Albright's list of poems from fourteen to twelve because two of the compositions have insufficient data to allow for adequate analysis and comparison (David's Lament, II Sam. 1:19–27, and Psalm 72). The resultant correlations and adjustments are presented in Chart C (p. 129). The following comments are in order:

The Terms:

A. Terms for God

1. Names

a. Yahweh and Yah

In these poems the name Yahweh is practically ubiquitous, and generally dominant. Since there is every reason to believe that the name was introduced into general use in the course of the thirteenth century B.C., and not before, a clear *terminus a quo* is provided for the poems in which Yahweh appears. No serious scholar has ever suggested otherwise, and the tradition uniformly assigns the poems to Moses, his contemporaries, or successors. The single exception is all the more striking because not only is the poem in Genesis

49 attributed to a pre-Mosaic figure (the patriarch Jacob) but the name Yahweh is conspicuously absent.[72] Since this is not the case even with the Elohistic Psalms 78 and 68 in which Elohim predominates, or the Oracles of Balaam in which El has the leading role (Yahweh occurs two or three times in each of the three poems mentioned), the omission as well as the tradition behind it may be significant, and may point to a non-Yahwistic origin for the Testament of Jacob.

The short form Yah, in contrast with Yahweh, is rare, occurring three times in all (as against ninety plus for Yahweh): once in Exodus 15, twice in Psalm 68. All three examples are suspicious, and its absence from the rest of the poems indicates that the form was not known or not in use for most of the period. One would normally expect an abbreviated form to be introduced after the full form had been in use for some time. Its appearance in Psalm 68, which is placed at the end of the sequence, would be in conformity with this expectation.[73] The problem of its appearance in Exodus 15 has already been mentioned. Essentially the conclusion is that the poem in its present final form including vs. 2 (with Yah and *'ēlī*) and the title Adonay in vs. 17 reflects a monarchic setting and should be dated in the tenth century. However, there is excellent reason to believe that the poem in a more original form consisted of an opening and closing (vss. 1 and 21) and a corpus beginning with vs. 3 and extending through vs. 18. In addition there is convincing textual evidence to support the reading Yahweh instead of Adonay in vs. 17. Under the circumstances, an earlier date, and a position at the head of the line would be appropriate for this song.

b. Elohim

1) The independent form, *'ᵉlōhīm,* occurs only once in these poems, with the exception of the Elohistic Psalms, 78, 68, where it is the dominant name (eight times in Psalm 78, and twenty-four times in Psalm 68). It appears in II Sam. 23:3, which cannot be earlier than the second quarter of the tenth century. It should be added that the word *'ᵉlōhīm* with the meaning "gods, divine beings" occurs in some of our poems: Judg. 5:8 and Deut. 32:17, 39, but there is no overlap. In poems where *'ᵉlōhīm* means "God," the word is not used for "gods," and vice versa.[74] The conclusion is that until the tenth century the term *'ᵉlōhīm* was used only as a numerical plural, and applied to other gods. From the middle of the tenth century on, its predominant use was as a designation of God, and a surrogate for Yahweh. It would be fair to link this usage in the Elohistic Psalms, especially 78 and 68, with the practice of the Elohist in the Pentateuch: the dates would be reasonably close as well.

2) If the independent or absolute form *'ᵉlōhīm* is used as a numerical plural in early poetry and only later as a name of God, the same cannot be said of the construct form *'ᵉlōhē,* which is used of God in several early poems, i.e. from the beginning of our sequence: the form *'ᵉlōhē yiśrā'ēl* occurs twice in the Song of Deborah, as well as in Psalms 68 and 72, while

its counterpart *'ᵉlōhē yaʿᵃqōb* appeared twice (in all probability) in II Samuel 23.[75] Other forms are attested in Deuteronomy 33 (*'ᵉlōhē qedem,* vs. 27) and Exodus 15 (*'ᵉlōhē 'ābī,* but this is in vs. 2). In any event the construct form is present in poetry from all three phases, stretching from the twelfth through the tenth centuries. It should be added that the suffixed form *'ᵉlōhāw* in Num. 23:21 is equivalent, since the antecedent for the pronominal suffix is Jacob/Israel of the same verse. The same argument can be used in connection with other plural pronominal suffixes: *'ᵉlōhēnū* and *'ᵉlōhēmō* which occur in third phase poems I Samuel 2, II Samuel 22 =Psalm 18, and Deuteronomy 32.

3) Two other suffixed forms remain: *'ᵉlōhay* which has a personal, devotional tone, and is more appropriate for the king than the nation. Typically this form occurs in Royal Psalms: I Samuel 2, and II Samuel 22=Psalm 18. The remaining form *'ᵉlōhēkā* occurs in Ps. 68:20 in an obscure passage. It is difficult to say just who is meant by the pronoun, or if, finally, it is the pronominal suffix.[76]

c. El (and *hā'ēl*)

1) The independent form *'ēl* (or *hā'ēl*) occurs in most of the poems in the group, showing that the divine name or designation El is second in importance only to Yahweh in these poems. Thus it is present in all three of the poems in Phase II, and five of the six in Phase III.[77] A point of major interest is that the independent form does not appear in any of the poems of Phase I: Exodus 15, Psalm 29, and Judges 5. It is to be noted that the suffixed form *'ēlī* occurs in Exod. 15:2, a verse which has already been discussed. The suffixed form also appears in Pss. 18:3 (but not in II Samuel 22) and 68:25, pointing to a somewhat later date for the introduction of this form than the independent form. Furthermore, the independent form *'ēl* also appears in both Psalms 18 and 68, along with the suffixed form, which is not the case with Exodus 15. We reserve judgment about *'ēlī* in Exodus 15 on two grounds: (1) that it is not the same as *'ēl*=El, and (2) that it may be a secondary intrusion (i.e. as part of vs. 2). The conclusion is that the divine name El was not in use during the earliest phase of Israelite poetry: neither Exodus 15 nor Judges 5, which are overwhelmingly Yahwistic in character and tone, have it. With respect to Psalm 29, the title occurs only in the phrase *'ēl hakkābōd* (vs. 3), which should be analyzed as a construct chain and rendered "the God of glory" or "the glorious God." In defense of this analysis we may point to the parallel expression *melek hakkābōd* in Ps. 24:7–10 which is also to be interpreted as a construct chain. In addition, there is no traditional association of El with the term *kābōd,* as there is with *ʿelyōn, ʿōlām,* and *šadday;* (3) the imagery and allusions of the poem are associated with the figure of Baal, rather than El; the former is more likely to have been the model for "the God of glory."

2) There are a handful of other instances of the term *'ēl* in a construct

relationship. Considered alphabetically, the first of these, *'ēl 'ābīkā* (Gen. 49:25) is a doubtful case. The normal rendering: "the God of your father" (RSV) is possible but not likely. The translation should reflect the apposition of the two nouns: "El, your Father." The term *'ābīkā* in vs. 26 also has a divine reference in our opinion: "the blessings of your father . . ." The identification is unmistakable in Deut. 32:6, "Is not He your Father . . . ?" The forms *'ēl 'emūnāh* (Deut. 32:4) and *'ēl dē'ōt* (I Sam. 2:3) are more clearly construct chains, and here the meaning is "God of truth or faithfulness," and "God of knowledge." The same is true of *'ēl hakkābōd,* "the God of glory," in Ps. 29:3, as already observed. The use is generic, and *'ēl* in these passages is equivalent to Elohim, or rather the construct *'elōhē*. That seems to be the only reasonable way to interpret the peculiar form *'ēl yiśrā'ēl,* "the God of Israel." The original form of this patriarchal designation was *'ēl 'elōhē yiśrā'ēl,* "El the God of Israel" (Gen. 33:20). Apparently it has been telescoped in Ps. 68:36. Three of the four occurrences of *'ēl* in a construct chain are in Phase III poems, indicating that the widespread use of this formation was relatively late, and raising a question, perhaps, about the date of the final version of Psalm 29.

3) The suffixed form *'ēlī* has already been discussed. Two of the three occurrences of this form are found in Phase III poems: Psalms 18 and 68. The form in Ps. 18:3 is matched by *'elōhē* (to be corrected to *'elōhay*) in II Sam. 22:3, showing that the terms were equivalent in meaning. Our conclusion about the suffixed form is that in general its use is a later development than the use of the independent form. It is a feature of Phase III poems, while the appearance of El as an independent form belongs to Phase II.

d. Eloah

1) The term, which is the formal singular of *'elōhīm,* is not at all common in Biblical Hebrew, and very rare in the group of poems under consideration. It occurs twice in Deuteronomy 32 (vss. 15, 17), and once in Psalm 18 (vs. 32; II Sam. 22:32 has *'ēl,* presumably the more original reading). The inference to be drawn on the basis of admittedly limited data is that the name Eloah was not in use during Phases I and II of the early poetry, and makes its first appearance around the middle of Phase III (late tenth century). Beyond this it appears sporadically in a few Psalms, Habakkuk, and Second Isaiah; but very frequently in Job (forty-two times out of a total of fifty-seven in the Hebrew Bible). The pattern resembles the distribution of Shadday at least superficially: some early use (though Shadday has much better attestation) and a revival in the nostalgic period (seventh–sixth centuries), with a heavy concentration in Job, a strongly archaizing poetic work.

2. Principal titles and epithets

a. Elyon

The title Elyon, which biblical tradition traces back to patriarchal times (cf. Gen. 14:18, 19, 20, 22) is well attested in our list, occurring in four poems: Numbers 23–24, II Samuel 22=Psalm 18, Deuteronomy 32, and Psalm 78. The combination El Elyon, which is found in Genesis, recurs in Ps. 78:35, while the pair is split in Num. 24:16 (cf. 24:4), a common device in Hebrew poetry. To summarize: Elyon as an epithet for God does not appear in poetry of Phase I, but does occur in Phase II along with other archaic (i.e. patriarchal, according to the tradition) names and titles: El, Shadday, and Olam. It continues in use in Phase III, and occasionally thereafter in a number of Psalms (including Psalms 47 and 91, which employ other archaic and archaizing terms).

b. Al (or Eli)

The related term Al (or Eli), "the Most High," has a similar distribution through Phases II and III, appearing in Genesis 49, Deuteronomy 33, I Samuel 2, II Samuel 23, and Psalm 68. Curiously enough the form Al does not occur in the poems in which Elyon appears, and Elyon does not appear in the poems which have Al. They appear to be alternate forms of the same basic attribute of God. That the expressions are equivalent and interchangeable is shown by the parallel passages:

I Sam. 2:10	II Sam. 22:14=Ps. 18:14
'al baššāmayim yar'ēm	*yar'ēm baššāmayin Yahweh*
Yahweh yādīn 'apsē 'āreṣ	*we'elyōn yittēn qōlō*

The different forms *'al, 'lyw, 'lw* may reflect an original **'aliyu>'alu>'al,* though the variety may be due in part at least to the fact that the later editors and scribes did not recognize the existence of the epithet and invariably read the term as a form of the preposition *'al,* by itself or with suffixes. Our vocalization is hypothetical, though the form is derived from the root *'ly,* which also underlies *'elyōn.*[78]

c. Shadday

The designation Shadday, like Elyon, is traced to patriarchal times in the biblical tradition, specifically by the priestly writer or editor, who states that the name of God par excellence for the patriarchs was El Shadday (Exod. 6:3). At the same time he asserts that the name Yahweh was first revealed to Moses and by him to the people. The compound form El Shadday is standard usage in the P material of the Pentateuch (Gen. 17:1, 28:3, 35:11, 43:14, 48:3; Exod. 6:3); it also occurs in Ezek. 10:5 (but cf. Ezek. 1:24 where Shadday alone appears). In Num. 24:4, 16, Shadday occurs by itself, but in parallel sequence with El and Elyon, suggesting a break-up of the traditional combination. In this case, El forms a natural pair with both Elyon and Shadday (as in the patriarchal narratives). In Gen. 49:25, El and Shadday are in parallel cola according to MT, but the reading *we'ēl šadday* for *we'ēt šadday* is attested by some manuscripts of MT, the Samaritan and Septuagint, and is to be preferred: *'ēl 'ābīkā*//*'ēl šadday.* In Ps. 68:15 Shadday stands by itself.

For the rest, the term occurs in Psalm 91 in parallel with Elyon (vs. 1), a poem of uncertain but possibly early date, since the same pair of terms occurs in the Oracles of Balaam. It also occurs in Isa. 13:6=Joel 1:15, both of which can be dated in the sixth century, during the nostalgic period. As in the case of Eloah, the majority of occurrences of Shadday is in Job (thirty-one out of a total of forty-eight). Finally, we note the occurrence, twice, of the title in Ruth (1:20, 21). While in its present form Ruth is relatively late, perhaps seventh–sixth centuries B.C.,[79] it purports to deal with the period of the judges. Apparently the use of Shadday was intended to reflect actual practice in that period, and was probably accurate in that respect. It is precisely in the poetry of Phase II (eleventh century) that we find Shadday, so the evidence of the poems corroborates the data in Ruth, which in turn support the proposed dating of the poems.

d. Olam

This is another term with roots in the patriarchal tradition: cf. Gen. 21:33, where the combination El Olam, "El the Eternal," appears. Since *ʿōlām* is a common noun to begin with, and the divine title is indistinguishable from it in form, the identification of the latter cannot be regarded as certain in all cases, though in some it is highly probable. The best example is Deut. 33:27 in which *ʿōlām* is in parallel construction with *ʾᵉlōhē qedem,* "the ancient God."[80] It may well be that the construct *ʾᵉlōhē* is intended to serve double duty, controlling *ʿōlām* as well as *qedem,* i.e. "the God of eternity." But the difference between that and "the Eternal One" would be slight, and in time the term Olam would gain independent status as in fact it did in later Phoenician tradition. Whether the phrases combining *ʿōlām* with *gbʿwt*//*hrry* are also to be interpreted in this fashion, "the hills of the Eternal One" rather than in the customary way, "the eternal hills," depends partly on the interpretation of the rather vague translation "eternal hills" and partly on the degree to which mythological notions of the sacred mountain (-range), i.e. the mountains//hills of the gods are reflected in this poetry (cf. Gen. 49:26=Deut. 33:15—*gbʿwt ʿwlm*). The remaining instance, in II Sam. 23:5, is also debatable, but there is a strong case for rendering the clause "for the Eternal has ordained a covenant for me" rather than "He has ordained an eternal covenant for me."[81]

The divine term *ʿōlām,* like the other patriarchal epithets of El, is found in the poetry of Phase II (Deuteronomy 33 and Genesis 49), and may also appear in Phase III (cf. II Sam. 23:5). It was never very popular and did not catch on as a title of God, though it was used extensively in liturgical phrases preserved in the Psalms. Its use as a divine epithet seems to be concentrated in the latter part of Phase II, and the first half of Phase III, roughly 1050–950 B.C.

e. Ṣur

The next term to be considered is *ṣūr,* the basic meaning of which is "mountain." As a title or name for God, its use is concentrated in the poetry of Phase III. It is found in practically all the poems of that phase, but not at all in the poems of Phases I and II. Comparison between *ṣūr* and its apparent cognate *šadday* is instructive and may be important.[82] Its presence in poetry which cannot be earlier than the tenth century gives it a reasonable connection with the monarchy, while its absence from all twelfth- and eleventh-century poetry is equally significant. The frequent occurrence of *ṣūr* in Deuteronomy 32 also helps to fix the date of that elusive poem.

1) The independent forms *ṣūr* and *haṣṣūr* occur in I Sam. 2:2; II Sam. 22:32=Ps. 18:32; II Sam. 22:47 (omitted in Ps. 18:47, which is the superior reading); and Deut. 32:4, 15, 18, 37. These poems are concentrated in Phase III, and if we add the construct form in the phrase *ṣūr yiśrā'ēl,* "the Mountain of Israel," which appears in II Sam. 23:3, we would have a solid group of four consecutive poems from the beginning of Phase III to a point well past the middle.

2) The distribution of suffixed forms of *ṣūr* (e.g. *ṣūrī, ṣūrēnū, ṣūrām*) is also restricted to Phase III, but there seems to be a slight shift toward a later date for these forms. While the independent and construct forms occur in the first four poems of Phase III, the suffixed forms occur in the third, fourth, and fifth poems in the group. Thus the two earliest poems in Phase III (I Samuel 2 and II Samuel 23) have the independent form only, while the fifth poem (Psalm 78) has the suffixed form only. The third and fourth poems, II Samuel 22=Psalm 18, and Deuteronomy 32, have both independent and suffixed forms:

	I Sam. 2	*II Sam. 23*	*Ps. 18= II Sam. 22*	*Deut. 32*	*Ps. 78*
(*h*) *ṣūr*	X	X	X	X	—
ṣūr+suff.	—	—	X	X	X

The divine title *ṣūr* is characteristic of Phase III poetry. The independent form seems to have flourished earlier in this period and the suffixed form somewhat later though there is a considerable overlap, which is hardly surprising. The general picture conforms to what we have seen to be the case with *'ēl* and its suffixed form.

f. *hū'*

Since *hū',* "he, that one," is a pronoun which could have been substituted for, or used in parallel with, any divine name or title, a random distribution among the poems in our group might have been expected. On the contrary, it is entirely absent from Phases I and II; and its use is concentrated in Phase III. It appears in the last four poems on the list: II Samuel 22=Psalm 18, Deuteronomy 32, Psalm 78, and Psalm 68, and nowhere else in the group, indicating that its use is characteristic of Phase III, especially the middle and latter part of that period.

g. Adonay

The last title to be considered is Adonay, which occurs three times in the poems on our list. Aside from the example in Exod. 15:17 already considered, it appears only in the last two poems of Phase III: Psalms 78 and 68. It occurs once in Psalm 78 (vs. 65), and six times in Psalm 68 (vss. 12, 18, 20, 21, 23, 33). On the whole, it appears to be a substitute for another divine name, usually Yahweh, rather than a new title, though it may well have served the latter function as well. As a surrogate, its distribution is much like that of Elohim and the pronoun *hū'*. During the latter part of Phase III, there was a significant development in the use of equivalent or substitute terms for the principal name, Yahweh, along with the general proliferation of divine names and epithets already described. It would be entirely reasonable to associate this development with the worship at the temple and the adaptation of the rich Canaanite musical and poetic traditions for liturgical use there.

As previously indicated we will not deal with the long list of qualifying nouns and participles applied to the deity in the poems. They deserve more detailed classification and analysis than is possible in the present paper, though such analysis should yield supporting or corrective data for the conclusions drawn from the primary evidence provided by the principal divine names and titles.

There is a group of other terms in the poems which may provide clues to the proposed sequence dating. An examination of words used for other divine beings is not particularly fruitful, chiefly because there are very few of them, and they do not exhibit any clear pattern of distribution. Thus *'ēlīm,* "gods," turns up in Exod. 15:11. Ps. 29:1 has *bᵉnē 'ēlīm,* probably "sons of El" (with enclitic *mem* attached to *'ēli,* singular with genitive case rather than the plural ending). The singular *'ēl nēkār,* "foreign god," occurs in Deut. 32:12, however. The collective term *qdš,* "holy ones," also appears in Exod. 15:11, and apparently in Deut. 33:2; the plural form occurs in the latter, vs. 3. Finally *'ᵉlōhīm* as a numerical plural, "gods," appears in Judg. 5:8 and Deut. 32:17. All these terms appear early in the list, and reappear later, but the incidence is too sporadic and the distribution too scattered to offer a basis for making useful inferences.

The case is somewhat different with certain other nouns, proper and common. If we concentrate attention on the words referring to the people of Yahweh, we find the following data of interest. The term *'am,* "people," is used throughout Phases I and II, appearing in all six poems of those groups. In Phase III the use is less consistent, though the term turns up in Deuteronomy 32 and Psalm 78. It does not appear in the three poems which mark the initial period of Phase III, but these focus explicitly on the anointed one, the king, who displaces the people as the immediate object of divine attention: I Sam. 2:10 and II Sam. 22:51=Ps. 18:51 have the parallel terms *malkō//mᵉšīḥō*. In II Sam. 23:1, *mᵉšīaḥ* (construct) occurs but not *melek;* however, David the king is referred to by name. The shift from people to king is made evident by the following comparison:

Ps. 29:11	I Sam. 2:10
Yahweh *'ōz lᵉ'ammō yittēn*	*wᵉyitten-'oz lᵉmalkō*

It may be added that the term *mšyḥ* occurs only in the three poems in which the term *'am* does not. None of these terms occurs in Psalm 68, which is distinguished by other special features.

The name Israel appears for the first time in our poetry in the Song of Deborah (eight occurrences: vss. 2, 3, 5, 7, 7, 8, 9, 11). It does not occur in Exodus 15 or Psalm 29, though in both of these poems the term *'am* is used with direct reference to Yahweh as possessor and/or creator of his people. In Judges 5, the expression *'am Yahweh* is used along with Israel, but the name Jacob is conspicuously absent. In practically all the other poems in our list, the two names are linked: e.g. Numbers 23–24, Genesis 49, Deuteronomy 33, II Samuel 23, Deuteronomy 32, Psalm 78. The exceptions are Pss. 68:9 and 72:18. In those passages, the formula used is *'ᵉlōhē yiśrā'ēl,* "the God of Israel," which is the same as in Judg. 5:3, 5. Thus the pair Jacob//Israel is typical of Phases II and III, but does not appear in Phase I. It is tempting to see the reflection of historical developments in the shifts in usage from *'am* alone, as in Exodus 15 and Psalm 29, to the pair *ya'ᵃqōb//yiśrā'ēl* (along with *'am*) in Phases II and III. In addition, there is the exotic term *yᵉšūrūn* which occurs only three times in our poetry, and once thereafter in the Hebrew Bible.[83] These occurrences are in Deuteronomy 33 (vss. 5 and 26), and Deuteronomy 32 (vs. 15), which represent Phases II and III respectively. The selection and distribution of the terms for the people of Yahweh, *'am, yiśrā'ēl, ya'ᵃqōb,* and *yᵉšūrūn* are almost exactly the same in Deuteronomy 33 and Deuteronomy 32, and following Albright, it would seem logical to date their composition in the same period. On the other hand, there is a significant divergence in their use of divine names and epithets, which justifies the somewhat greater gap in time between them that I have estimated, and their assignment to different phases. The explanation of these apparently conflicting or divergent tendencies may lie in the presumed effort of the poet to imitate an older style and set his poem in an earlier historical setting.

The remaining terms *melek//*māšīaḥ* appear in poems of the monarchy (both in I Samuel 2 and II Samuel 22=Psalm 18, *mšyḥ* alone in II Samuel 23). The term "king" appears as well in Num. 24:7 (*malkō*) and Deut. 33:5 (*melek*). In neither case is it entirely clear whether the divine or a human king is meant, but we must allow for the latter possibility. If so, and if the reference is to the Israelite monarchy, then we must reckon with a date of composition during the monarchy in both instances. In my opinion Deuteronomy 33 as a whole reflects the election and consecration of Saul as king by the tribal confederation, and vs. 5 in particular contains an allusion to the inauguration of his reign. The passage in the Oracles of Balaam is more obscure and it is better to suspend judgment about that particular question. A date in the eleventh century for the Oracles of Balaam seems probable to me, as also for Deuteronomy 33.

Conclusion

To summarize: comparison with the conclusions of Albright and Robertson show relatively modest divergences in the ordering of the poems, and their chronology, both relative and absolute, although the approach and criteria employed were very different. In the following table I have listed the poems once more, giving the dates proposed by Albright, Robertson, and me.

Poem	*Albright*	*Robertson*[84]	*Freedman*
Exodus 15	1. 13th century	1. 12th century	1. 12th century
Judges 5	2. 1150	2. end of 12th	3. 12th
Numbers 23–24	3. 1200		4. 11th
Deuteronomy 33	4. mid 11th		6. late 11th
Deuteronomy 32	5. ca. 1025	3. 11th–10th	11. 10th–9th
Genesis 49	6. late 11th		5. 11th
I Samuel 2	7. late 11th		7. 11th–10th
II Samuel 1	8. early 10th		8. early 10th
II Samuel 23	9. first half 10th		9. first half 10th
II Samuel 22-Psalm 18	10. 10th	4. 11th–10th	10. 10th
Psalm 78	11. 10th	5. 10th–9th	12. 10th–9th
Psalm 68	12. 10th		13. 10th–9th
Psalm 72	13. 10th		14. 10th–9th
Psalm 29	14. [5th]		2. 12th

The essential differences in order are as follows:

1) Albright discusses Psalm 29, describes it as very archaic, but finally suggests that it dates in final form from the fifth century B.C.[85] In my opinion it is very archaic and belongs to Phase I, in the twelfth century.

2) After placing Genesis 49 sixth in his list, and dating it late in the eleventh century, Albright modified his views and suggested that parts of it may be considerably older, going back to late patriarchal times. I have placed it fifth, and dated it to the eleventh century.

3) Albright has Deuteronomy 33 before Genesis 49, while I reverse the order since I believe, as Albright suspected, that Genesis 49 is more archaic.

4) There is a major divergence in dealing with Deuteronomy 32. Albright puts it fifth, and dates it about 1025, but I find many marks of later composition, and put it eleventh in order, placing it in Phase III, not earlier than the tenth century, and very likely the ninth century.

5) I have insufficient data to place or date II Samuel 1 and Psalm 72 but have no reason to disagree with Albright's dates.

6) Albright places Judges 5 before Numbers 23–24 on stylistic grounds, but dates Numbers 23–24 before Judges 5. My data support Albright's stylistic analysis, but not his dating, so I date Judges 5 earlier than Numbers 23–24.

With respect to specific dates, there are some variations. Albright dates Exodus 15 to the thirteenth century and Numbers 23–24 to 1200, while I find nothing earlier than the twelfth century, to which period I assign both Exodus 15 and Judges 5. Numbers 23–24, on the other hand, belongs to the eleventh century in my opinion. I date Deuteronomy 33 slightly later than Albright and Genesis 49 slightly earlier. I also put Deuteronomy 32 at least a century later than Albright does. The rest are the same, or practically so.

There is a striking agreement with Robertson on the poems to which he is willing to assign dates. Thus we agree on a twelfth-century date for Exodus 15 and Judges 5, as well as on the order of composition of these poems. We also agree on a tenth-ninth-century date for Psalm 78. We diverge slightly on II Samuel 22=Psalm 18, which he dates a little earlier than I do, and more seriously on Deuteronomy 32. He is closer to Eissfeldt and Albright, dating the poem in the eleventh–tenth centuries, whereas I am closer to Wright and Cross, placing it in the tenth–ninth centuries.

While the order of the poems cannot be fixed with certainty, and all proposed dates are approximate, a consensus on the corpus of early Hebrew poetry and the broad outlines of its chronology seems to have emerged.

A NOTE ON THE NAME YAHWEH

In all the poems, the term *yhwh* functions clearly as a proper noun both grammatically and syntactically. Its original verbal form and force have left no trace in the poetry under consideration, any more than such factors survive in names like *ya'ᵃqōb* and *yiśrā'ēl*. This fact is both interesting and a little disturbing, especially if the name were of recent origin (thirteenth century), and if it still retained its verbal force for some time after its adoption.[86]

There are several expressions in which the verbal force has been preserved, and which can only be understood in the light of the original meaning of the form *yhwh*:[87] e.g. such phrases as *yhwh ṣᵉbā'ōt*, "he creates the hosts," *yhwh šālōm*, "he inaugurates peace" (Judg. 6:24). Neither of these appears in any of our poems, nor anything like them, so we must suppose that these expressions while correctly reflecting the etymology of the term *yhwh* do not underlie its use as a name, but were introduced secondarily, i.e. after the adoption of Yahweh as a name, the name of God. The expression *yhwh ṣᵉbā'ōt*, "he creates the hosts," does not occur in the Pentateuch at all, but first appears in the stories in the books of Samuel (cf. I Sam. 1:3, 11,

4:4, 15:2, etc.). According to repeated testimony, it was part of the legend on the ark (cf. I Sam. 4:4; II Sam. 6:2), and there is little reason to doubt that this was the original locus of the expression in pre-monarchic times. The expression *yhwh šālōm* (Judg. 6:24) seems to come from the same period. Of these expressions, only *yhwh ṣᵉbā'ōt* became a factor in Israelite poetry and its appearance is largely late and secondary since in the majority of instances it has the form *yhwh 'ᵉlōhē ṣᵉbā'ōt,* "Yahweh, the God of hosts," in which the verbal force of *yhwh* has been lost entirely. Nevertheless, the verbal force is preserved in the original form, reflected in the prose tradition, and some account must be taken of this.

Our proposal is briefly as follows:

1) The original form *yahweh* was a verb, and was used in a variety of liturgical utterances relating to the patriarchal God El.[88] Thus El was the God who created the hosts, peace, and the rest. During the period of the judges some of these expressions were introduced at the time that the name El was itself officially accepted by Israel and identified with Yahweh the God of Moses.

2) Yahweh as the personal name of God had been introduced earlier by Moses and it was used and understood as a name. Afterwards, when Yahweh and El were identified, the archaic expressions which originally described activities of El were adopted along with the divine titles and epithets associated with patriarchal El. The expressions containing the verb *yahweh* were introduced but there must have been some confusion about their meaning and significance. Very soon the verbal element was interpreted as the name, and the result was the misinterpretation of the expression. This comes out clearly in the modification of the original *yhwh ṣᵉbā'ōt* to *yhwh 'ᵉlōhē ṣᵉbā'ōt,* a necessary change on the part of those who saw in *yhwh* only the sacred name of God, and not a verb previously associated with a different theological tradition.

3) As already indicated, our poetry is entirely unaffected by this development, indicating that the traditions on which the earliest Israelite poems rested began with Yahweh as the personal name of God and only later incorporated the expressions which retained the verbal force of the underlying root (the hiphil form of **hwy*).

NOTES

1. W. F. Albright, *YGC,* pp. 1–28, 42–52. The individual poems were analyzed in a series of articles spanning his career as a scholar: e.g. "The Earliest Forms of Hebrew Verse," *JPOS* 2 (1922), 69–86; "The Oracles of Balaam," *JBL* 63 (1944), 207–233; "The Psalm of Habakkuk," *Studies in Old Testament Prophecy* (Edinburgh, 1950), pp. 1–18;

"A Catalogue of Early Hebrew Lyric Poems (Psalm 68)," *HUCA* 33, Part 1 (1950–51), 1–39; "Some Remarks on the Song of Moses in Deuteronomy XXXII," *VT* 9 (1959), 339–346. For discussion of the dates of various poems in the group, see F. M. Cross and D. N. Freedman, *Studies in Ancient Yahwistic Poetry* (henceforth *SAYP;* Baltimore, 1950), and D. A. Robertson, *Linguistic Evidence in Dating Early Hebrew Poetry* (henceforth *LEDEHP;* New Haven, 1966).

2. *YGC*, pp. 10 ff.

3. Albright makes several comments about the age of the poem, but does not fix a date; see discussion, p. 60.

4. *YGC*, pp. 15–16. 5. *YGC*, p. 265.

6. *YGC*, p. 266. See the discussion of Genesis 49, p. 63.

7. There is a number of recent and forthcoming studies of this poem: *YGC*, pp. 11–13, 45–47; *SAYP* [N 1], pp. 83–127; F. M. Cross and D. N. Freedman, "The Song of Miriam," *JNES* 14 (1955), 237–250; Cross, "The Song of the Sea and Canaanite Myth," in *God and Christ: Existence and Province, JTC* 5 (1968), 1–25; note the references in fn. 27, pp. 9–10; P. C. Craigie, "An Egyptian Expression in the Song of the Sea (Ex. XV 4)," *VT* 20 (1970), 83–86, with a bibliographical summary on p. 83; the same author has an extensive study of the poem which will be published in the near future. See also "Strophe and Meter in Exodus 15," my lengthy study of the structure of the poem in *A Light Unto My Path*, the J. M. Myers *Festschrift* (Temple University Press, 1974), pp. 163–204. Cf. G. W. Coats, "The Traditio-Historical Character of the Reed Sea Motif," *VT* 17 (1967), 253–265; B. S. Childs, "A Traditio-Historical Study of the Reed Sea Tradition," *VT* 20 (1970), 406–418.

8. Cf. D. N. Freedman, "The Refrain in David's Lament over Saul and Jonathan," in *Ex Orbe Religionum (Studia Geo Widengren)*, Studies in the History of Religions, No. 21 (1972), 115–126.

9. The older printed editions of the Hebrew Bible have *ks yh* as two words, but Kittel, *Biblia Hebraica*³, reads *ksyh* as a single expression. Neither the form nor the meaning is clear, though the verbal root *ksy* may be discerned (as suggested by Cross).

10. Cf. Cross and Freedman, "The Song of Miriam" [N 7], 243.

11. For discussion on the structure and meaning of Psalm 29, see D. N. Freedman and C. F. Hyland, "Psalm 29: A Structural Analysis," *HTR* 66 (1973), 237–256.

12. Cf. H. N. Richardson, "The Last Words of David: Some Notes on II Samuel 23:1–7," *JBL* 90 (1971), 257–266, esp. pp. 261–262.

13. See Cross, "The Song of the Sea and Canaanite Myth" [N 7], p. 13, fn. 42.

14. Ibid., p. 16, fn. 57. 15. Ibid., p. 14, fn. 49.

16. Cf. Albright, "The Phoenician Inscriptions of the Tenth Century B.C. from Byblus," *JAOS* 67 (1947), 153–160; the phrase occurs in the Yeḥimilk inscription, lines 4–5, dated by Albright to the middle of the tenth century, pp. 156–157.

17. This date is supported by Cross, "The Song of the Sea and Canaanite Myth" [N 7], p. 11 (late twelfth or early eleventh century; Robertson, *LEDEHP* [N 1], p. 231 (twelfth); P. C. Craigie, unpublished monograph.

18. It is likely that many if not most of the poems in our list appeared in one or the other of two early anthologies which are mentioned in the Bible: the Book of the Wars of Yahweh (Num. 21:14), and the Book of Jashar (Josh. 10:13; II Sam. 1:18). The earliest editions of these collections may well go back to the time of the judges, but the final published form must be dated in the monarchic period. In fact there is a reference to the Book of Jashar in the LXX of I Kings 8:13, as the source for a poetic utterance attributed to Solomon at the dedication of the temple.

19. For recent discussion of Psalm 29, see P. C. Craigie, "Psalm XXIX in Hebrew Poetic Tradition," *VT* 22 (1972), 143–151, and literature cited. Cf. Hyland and Freedman [N 11].

20. Albright also states that it is impossible to date accurately but suggests a "fifth(?) century B.C." date for its final redaction (*YGC*, p. 255).

21. On the similarities and differences between Exodus 15 and Judges 5, see Albright, *YGC*, pp. 12–14.

22. On the similarities between Psalms 29 and Exodus 15, see Craigie [N 19].

23. Cf. M. Dahood, *Psalms I,* AB, vol. 16 (1966), pp. 175–176; and on Ps. 89:7, *Psalms II,* AB, vol. 17 (1968), p. 313.

24. In Ps. 24:7–10, the equivalent expression *melek hakkābōd,* "the king of glory" or "the glorious king," occurs five times as a title of Yahweh. This evidence strengthens the view that *'ēl hakkābōd* should be analyzed as a construct chain. The passage in Psalm 24 belongs to the same genre as Psalm 29, and may also date to the pre-monarchic period.

25. See discussion in Hyland and Freedman [N 11].

26. H. L. Ginsberg, "A Strand in the Cord of Hebraic Hymnody," *EI* 9 (1969), 45–50, dates it to the pre-monarchic period (p. 45), while Cross, "The Song of the Sea and Canaanite Myth," [N 7], 10, and Craigie [N 19], 144, place it somewhat later.

27. For recent discussion see P. C. Craigie, "The Song of Deborah and the Epic of Tukulti-Ninurta," *JBL* 88 (1969), 253–265; and "Some Further Notes on the Song of Deborah," *VT* 22 (1972), 349–353. Cf. also R. G. Boling in *Judges,* AB, vol. 6A (1975).

28. Following A. Weiser, "Das Deboralied," *ZAW* 71 (1959), 75, and D. R. Hillers, "A Note on Judges 5:8," *CBQ* 27 (1965), 124; against Craigie, "Some Further Notes on the Song of Deborah" [N 27], 350–351.

29. Cf. Albright, *YGC,* pp. 31–34, citing work by Boling, "'Synonymous' Parallelism in the Psalms," *Journal of Semitic Studies* 5 (1960), 221–255.

30. *YGC,* pp. 255–256.

31. *YGC,* pp. 26–27, and references in fn. 60 on p. 26.

32. The passage in Isaiah is generally dated to the sixth century B.C. or later; cf. R. B. Y. Scott, "Isaiah: Chapters 1–39," IB, V (1956), 254–255. On the date of Joel, see J. M. Myers, "Some Considerations Bearing on the Date of Joel," *ZAW* 74 (1962), 177–195; his conclusion (p. 195) is that a date around 520 B.C. is the most likely.

33. On the date of Job, see D. N. Freedman, "Orthographic Peculiarities in the Book of Job," *EI* 9 (1969), 35–44. Albright's conclusions as to the date of Job are given on pp. 43–44.

34. E. F. Campbell, Jr., recommends an earlier date (in the ninth century) for the composition of Ruth; cf. *Ruth,* AB, vol. 7 (1975), pp. 23–28.

35. See M. Dahood, *Psalms III,* AB, vol. 17A (1970), p. 324; cf. Isa. 14:19 and Job 5:23. The same word, with prosthetic *aleph* occurs in Phoenician.

36. For discussion and evaluation see D. N. Freedman, "The Structure of Psalm 137," in *Near Eastern Studies in Honor of William Foxwell Albright,* ed. Hans Goedicke (Baltimore, 1971), p. 195 and fn. 9; and Freedman, "Prolegomenon," *The Forms of Hebrew Poetry,* by G. B. Gray (New York, 1972), p. liv, fn. 6.

37. For discussion of the term, see F. M. Cross and D. N. Freedman, "The Blessing of Moses," *JBL* 67 (1948), 194 and 204–205, fn. 38; also Richardson [N 12], 260–261, and fns. 16–18.

38. The word *hwry* may be an error for *hrry,* "mountains" (to be vocalized *harᵉrē* as a construct before *'ad,* which has mistakenly been interpreted as the preposition and linked with the following word *ta'ᵃwat*), in parallel with *gib'ōt,* "hills." See *SAYP* [N 1], pp. 141 and 182, fns. 82, 83.

39. The use of *'ōlām* as a divine epithet is even more probable in Deut. 33:27; cf. Cross and Freedman [N 37], pp. 196 and 209, fn. 85. Another possible instance occurs

in II Sam. 23:5; cf. Richardson [N 12], 259, 263–264. See the discussion of this verse, p. 73.

40. F. M. Cross, "Yahweh and the God of the Patriarchs," *HTR* 55 (1962), 238–239.

41. Cf. *Psalms I*, Index, p. 322; *Psalms II*, Index, p. 386 [N 23].

42. Cf. *SAYP* [N 1], pp. 129–233.

43. The best study of this poem is still that of Albright, "The Oracles of Balaam," *JBL* 63 (1944). More recent comments are to be found in ch. 1 of *YGC*.

44. On the original form of the name Yahweh, see Dahood, *Psalms I*, Index, p. 320; *Psalms II*, Index, p. 384 [N 23]; *Psalms III* [N 35], Index, p. 472. Cf. also D. N. Freedman, "The Name of the God of Moses," *JBL* 79 (1969), 151–156, esp. p. 156; and Cross [N 40], pp. 250 ff.

45. For detailed discussion, see Cross and Freedman [N 37].

46. See discussion p. 65, and N 37.

47. Cf. Cross and Freedman [N 37], pp. 194 and 206, fn. 53.

48. On the date of composition, "The Blessing of Moses" [N 37], p. 192.

49. As already noted *šadday* appears in Psalm 68 (vs. 15), which we have assigned to Phase III. However, Psalm 68 contains much older material and the passage in question may derive from an earlier period. The absence of *ṣûr* from Psalm 68 is another indication of its archaic character.

50. See discussion of this expression and the general formulation, p. 60.

51. For recent discussion of this poem and bibliography, see Freedman [N 8].

52. For recent discussion, see Richardson [N 12], and D. N. Freedman, "II Samuel 23:4," *JBL* 90 (1971), 329–330.

53. For *'l* in MT, the reading in 4QSam^{a} is *'l*, "El, God," which may be more original (so Cross). See Richardson [N 12], pp. 260–261.

54. See discussion p. 62 and N 28.

55. At Deut. 32:8, the reading in MT, *bny yśr'l*, "sons of Israel," is secondary. The original Hebrew was *bny 'l* (or possibly *'lym* or *'lhym* since the manuscript breaks off after the letters *'l*), "the sons of El." See P. W. Skehan, "A fragment of the 'Song of Moses' (Deut. 32) from Qumran," *BASOR* 136 (1954), 12. At Deut. 32:43, the Qumran scroll has the phrase *kl 'lhym*, "all the gods," clearly the numerical plural. Skehan, ibid., pp. 13–15, restores a line with the phrase *bᵉnē 'ēlīm*, while F. M. Cross, *ALQ*², pp. 182–183, supplies *bny 'lhym*, "sons of God." The reading is based on an unpublished 4Q reading.

56. See Richardson [N 12], pp. 263–264.

57. For detailed discussion, see F. M. Cross and D. N. Freedman, "A Royal Song of Thanksgiving: II Samuel=Psalm 18," *JBL* 72 (1953), 15–34.

58. The parallel passage (S) has *'ᵉlōhē ṣûr yiš'ī*, a contaminated text in which the word *ṣûr* is intrusive.

59. On this meaning of *mgn*, perhaps *māgēn* or *māgōn*, see Freedman [N 8], pp. 122–123. Cf. Dahood, *Psalms I*, Index, p. 321, and *Psalms II*, Index, p. 384 [N 23].

60. For discussion of the problem and various solutions, see the following: Albright, *YGC*, pp. 17 ff., and "Some Remarks on the Song of Moses in Deuteronomy XXXII," pp. 339–346 [N 1]; O. Eissfeldt, *Das Lied Moses Deuteronomium 32, 1–43 und das Lehrgedicht Asaphs Psalm 78 samt einer Analyse der Umgebung des Mose-Liedes*, Berichte über die Verhandlungen der Sächsischen Akademie der Wissenschaften zu Leipzig. Phil.-hist. Klasse, 104–5 (Berlin, 1958); P. W. Skehan, "The Structure of the Song of Moses in Deuteronomy," *CBQ* 13 (1951), 153–163; G. E. Wright, "The Lawsuit of God: A Form-Critical Study of Deuteronomy 32," in *Israel's Prophetic Heritage*, eds. B. W. Anderson and W. Harrelson (New York, 1962), pp. 26–67; Robertson, *LEDEHP* [N 1], p. 231.

61. See Skehan [N 55], p. 12.

62. See ibid., pp. 13–15; Cross, *ALQ²*, pp. 182–183; Albright, *YGC*, p. 18 and fns. 46 and 46a.

63. Cf. Boling, [N 29], pp. 221–255; Albright, *YGC*, pp. 31 ff.

64. See my note "God Almighty in Psalm 78:59," *Biblica* 54 (1973), 268. A parallel instance occurs in Ps. 46:2; cf. Dahood, *Psalms III*, pp. 136 and 318–319, correcting his analysis in *Psalms I*, p. 278.

65. Cf. Ps. 71:22.

66. For discussion see Albright, *YGC*, pp. 26–27; "A Catalogue of Early Hebrew Lyric Poems (Psalm 68)" [N 1].

67. Ibid.

68. Cf. Cross and Freedman [N 37], pp. 193, 198–199, fns. 8–9. The emendation of *qdš* to *qdšm* is not necessary.

69. I owe this observation to F. M. Cross.

70. For the rendering of *bqdš*, "among the holy ones," see N 68. Contrast Dahood, *Psalms III* [N 35], p. 147, who translates "from his sanctuary."

71. *Psalms III*, pp. 132, 149. The same epithet occurs in vs. 35 in association with Israel, "the Exalted One of Israel."

72. The single line, vs. 18, which contained the name Yahweh is not a part of the original poem, but a later insertion.

73. See comments p. 83 on the examples in vss. 5 and 19.

74. On a possible exception in Deuteronomy 32, see discussion p. 73, esp. N 55. It is important to emphasize that the reading *'lhym*, "God," is not directly and explicitly attested in any manuscript or version available to us.

75. See comments p. 73 on the reading in II Sam. 23:3; cf. Richardson [N 12], p. 262.

76. See the discussion of this point by Dahood, *Psalms II* [N 23], p. 149.

77. While it does not occur by itself in I Samuel 2, it appears as a construct with *dē'ōt*, "the God of knowledge," or "the (all-) knowing God."

78. That the third stem consonant was *yod* is confirmed by Ugaritic *'ly;* cf. Gordon, *Ugaritic Textbook* (Rome, 1965), p. 456; Dahood, "The Divine Name *'ēlî* in the Psalms," *Theological Studies* 14 (1953), 452–457; *Psalms I*, Index, p. 322; *Psalms II*, p. 386 [N 23]; *Psalms III* [N 35], p. 475.

79. See discussion p. 64, and N 34.

80. See discussion p. 65, and N 39.

81. See discussion pp. 65, 73 and NN 39, 56.

82. See discussion p. 71, and N 49.

83. It occurs in Isa. 44:2, from the nostalgic period (sixth century).

84. *LEDEHP* [N 1], p. 231. Robertson regards only five of the poems listed as demonstrably or probably early.

85. See discussion p. 60, and N 20.

86. Albright's effort to read the verb *yahweh* in Exod. 15:3 *yahweh 'īš milḥāmāh*, "he creates the army," i.e. the men of war (*YGC*, p. 13, fn. 34), deserves consideration, but is hardly compelling when the normal reading makes reasonable sense in the context. The poem is about Yahweh as the Divine Warrior, who unaided, destroys the Egyptians and strikes terror in the hearts of all other enemies of his people, so it is difficult to see the rationale or purpose in a reference to the creation of fighting hosts whether divine or human.

87. See Albright, *YGC*, p. 33, and review of B. N. Wambacq, "L'épithète divine *Jahvé Seba'ôt:* Étude philologique, historique et exégetique," *JBL* 67 (1948), 377–381; F. M. Cross, "Yahweh and the God of the Patriarchs," *HTR* 55 (1962), 250–259; D. N. Freedman, "The Name of the God of Moses," *JBL* 79 (1960), 151–156.

88. See Cross [N 87].

Chart A: The Terms

I. Terms for God
  A. Names
    1. Yahweh and Yah
    2. Elohim
      a. Independent form
      b. Construct chain:
        1) *'elōhē yiśrā'ēl/ya'aqōb*
        2) *'elōhē 'ābī*
        3) *'elōhē qedem*
      c. Suffixed forms:
        1) *'elōhay*
        2) *'elōhēkā*
        3) *'elōhāw*
        4) *'elōhēnū*
        5) *'elōhēmō*
    3. El (and hā'ēl)
      a. Independent form
      b. Construct chain
        1) *'ēl 'ābīkā* (?)
        2) *'ēl 'emūnāh*
        3) *'ēl dē'ōt*
        4) *'ēl yiśrā'ēl*
        5) *'ēl (hak)kābōd*
      c. Suffixed form: *'ēlī*
    4. Eloah
  B. Principal titles and epithets:
    1. Elyon
    2. Al
      a. Independent forms: *'l, 'lw, 'lyw*
      b. Construct chain: *'l yiśrā'ēl*
    3. Shadday
    4. Olam
    5. Ṣūr (and haṣṣūr)
      a. Independent form
      b. Construct chain: *ṣūr yiśrā'ēl*
      c. Suffixed forms
        1) *ṣūrī*
        2) *ṣūrēnū*
        3) *ṣūrām*
    6. Hū'
    7. Adonay
  C. Qualifying Nouns and Phrases
    1. Nouns
      a. Independent forms
        1) *zmrt*
        2) *yāšār*
        3) *kābōd*
        4) *m'd*
        5) *māgēn*
        6) *melek*
        7) *'ad*
        8) *'ōz*
        9) *ṣaddīq*
        10) *qedem*
        11) *qādōš*
        12) *raḥūm*
      b. Suffixed forms
        1) *'ābīkā*
        2) *ḥizqī*
        3) *māginnī*
        4) *malkī*
        5) *menūsī*
        6) *mā'uzzī*
        7) *meṣūdātī*
        8) *miśgabbī*
        9) *nērī*
        10) *sal'ī*
        11) *'ozzī*
    2. Phrases
      a. *'abīr ya'aqōb*
      b. *'īš milḥāmāh*
      c. *zeh sīnay*
      d. *qeren yiš'ī*
  D. Participles
    1. Qal (G-stem)
      a. *bārūk*
      b. *gō'alām*
      c. *ḥōbēb*
      d. *ḥōpēp*
      e. *(han)nōtēn*
      f. *'ōśeh ḥesed*
      g. *'ōśeh niplā'ōt*
      h. *'ōśeh pele'*
      i. *rōkēb*
      j. *rō'ēh*
      k. *šōkenī seneh*
    2. Niphal (N-stem)
      a. *ne'dār*
      b. *nōrā'*
    3. Piel - Pual (D-stem)
      a. *mehullāl*
      b. *meḥayyeh*
      c. *melammēd*
      d. *mepalṭī*
      e. *merōmēm*
      f. *mešawweh*

4. Hiphil (H-stem)
   a. *magdīl*
   b. **mōṣī'*
      1) *mōṣī'ī*
      2) *mōṣī'ō*
      3) *mōṣī'ām*
   c. *mōrīd*
   d. *mōrīš*
   e. *mōšī'ī*
   f. *mēmīt*
   g. *ma'ᵃšīr*
   h. *mēqīm*
   i. *marḥīb*
   j. *mašpīl*

II. Other terms
   A. For divine beings
      1. *'ēl (īm)*
      2. *qdš (īm)*
      3. *'ᵉlōhīm*
      4. *šēdīm*
   B. Proper nouns
      1. *'ᵉdōm*
      2. *ya'ᵃqōb*
      3. *yiśrā'ēl*
      4. *yᵉšūrūn*
      5. *kᵉna'an*
      6. *mō'āb*
      7. *miṣrayim*
      8. *sīnay*
      9. *pᵉlešet*
      10. *śē'īr*
   C. Common nouns
      1. *melek*
      2. **māšīaḥ*
      3. *nᵉ'um*
      4. *'am*

CHART B.1[a]

	Exod. 15	Judg. 5	Num. 23-24	Deut. 33	Deut. 32	Gen. 49	I Sam. 2	II Sam. 1	II Sam. 23	Ps. 18 II Sam. 22 S	P	Ps. 78	Ps. 68	Ps. 72	Ps. 29
יהוה	10[b]	14	3	8	8	1	8[c]		1	16	16	2	3	1	18
עז	1														1
זמר[ו]ת	1								1						
יה	1												2		
אל	1		8	1	4[d]	2[e]	1		1	4	4	7	5		1
אלהים	1	2	1	1	2		2[f]		3	6	6	8	26	3	
נורא	1												1		
אדני	1[g]											1	6		
זה סיני		1											1		
מלך			1										1		1
מוציא			2							1	0		1		
עליון			2[h]		1					1	1	3			
שדי			2			1						1			
על[יו]				1		1	1		1				2		
רכב				1									2		
עולם				1					1						
צור					6		1		1	4	3	1			
אב					1	2									
הוא					4					1	1	1	1		
אלוה					2					0	1				

[a] This chart includes divine names and epithets which occur in more than one poem in the group. The order of the poems follows Albright's arrangement. The numbers are derived from MT except where otherwise indicated.

[b] For statistical purposes I consider vs. 21 to be part of the poem. If we accept the reading *yhwh* for *'dny* in vs. 17, the total would be 11.

[c] Reading *b'lhy* for *byhwh* in vs. 1; in MT the total is 9.

[d] Including the reading *'l* in vs. 8, on the basis of 4QDeut. and LXX, but excluding *'l* in vs. 12, which is listed in B.2 under other gods.

[e] Reading *'l šdy* in vs. 25 with Samaritan, LXX, etc. against MT, *'t šdy*.

[f] See fn. c.

[g] If *yhwh* is the original reading in vs. 17, then *'dny* would be dropped.

[h] Restoring *'lywn* in Num. 24:4 on the basis of Num. 24:16.

CHART B.2

	Exod. 15	Judg. 5	Num. 23-24	Deut. 33	Deut. 32	Gen. 49	I Sam. 2	II Sam. 1	II Sam. 23	Ps. 18 II Sam. 22 S	P	Ps. 78	Ps. 68	Ps. 72	Ps.
אל [ים]	1				1										1
קדש [ים]	1			2											
עם	3	4	2	3	4	1						5		3	2
אלהים		1			2										
נאם			6						2						
מלך			1	1			1			1	1				
משיח							1	1	1	1	1				
דוד									1	1	1	1			
אדום	1	1	1												
כנען	1	1													
מואב	1		2												
ישראל		8	8	5	1	4		1	2[a]			7	3	1	
שעיר		1	1	1											
סיני		1		1									2		
יעקב			8	3	1	3			2[b]			3			
מצרים			2									3	1		
ישרון				2	1										

[a] Reading *'lhy y'qb* for *'lhy yśr'l* in vs. 3, on the basis of the parallel construction in vs. 1.
[b] Cf. fn. a.

CHART C

	PHASE I			PHASE II			PHASE III						
	12th Century			11th Century			10th Century				9th Century		
	Exod. 15	Ps. 29	Judg. 5	Gen. 49	Num. 23-24	Deut. 33	I Sam. 2	II Sam. 23	Ps. 18 II Sm. 22 S	Ps. 18 II Sm. 22 P	Deut. 32	Ps. 78	Ps. 68
יהוה	X	X	X	(X)[a]	X	X	X	X	X	X	X	X	X
אל[b]	(X)[c]	X					X			X	X		X
אלהי	(X)[c]		X		X	X	X	X	X	X	X		X
אל[d]				X	X	X	X	X	X	X	X	X	X
שדי				X	X								
על[י]				X		X	X	X					X
עליון					X				X	X	X	X	
צור							X	X	X	X	X	X	
אלהים								X				X	X
הוא									X	X	X	X	X
אלוה										X	X		
אדני	(X)[e]											X	X
עם	X	X	X	X	X	X					X	X	
ישראל			X	X	X	X		X			X	X	X
יעקב				X	X	X					X	X	
מלך					X	X	X		X	X			
משיח							X	X	X	X			
דוד								X	X	X		X	

The poems are listed in order of composition and the terms in order of appearance.

[a] The name Yahweh appears only once, in vs. 18, which is a secondary insertion.
[b] The term *'lhym* here is generic, i.e. "God." It occurs either as a construct, *'ᵉlōhē,* or with the suffix *-y,* "my God."
[c] These forms occur in vs. 2, which is not part of the original poem in my opinion.
[d] The term *'l* here is the personal name of the deity, "El."
[e] The word *'dny* occurs once in Exodus 15 (vs. 17) and is textually suspect. The original reading probably was *yhwh.*

EARLY ISRAELITE HISTORY IN THE LIGHT OF EARLY ISRAELITE POETRY

In a previous paper I attempted to establish a sequence dating for the early poems of Israel.[1] A principal conclusion was that the oldest substantial poems of the Israelite confederacy which have survived are the Song of the Sea (Exod. 15) and the Song of Deborah (Judg. 5). In my opinion, both poems belong to the earliest phase of Israel's national existence, and their original composition may be dated with some confidence to the twelfth century B.C. Of the two, the Song of the Sea is older: it describes the episode in which corporate existence effectively began for this people, and may be assigned to the first half of the twelfth century, or about 1175. The Song of Deborah describes the major victory of the Israelites over the Canaanites near Taanach, as a result of which Canaanite political hegemony and military superiority were overthrown, and Israelite possession of the land was confirmed. This poem may be assigned to the third quarter of the twelfth century, or not later than about 1125.

The conclusions reached in the previous article, which form the premise of the present study, do not depend for their acceptance entirely on the validity of the criteria or the reliability of the procedures adopted. Other scholars, using different criteria and methods, have arrived at very similar results with respect to the two poems under consideration.[2] We may affirm a growing consensus about their early date. Regardless of the merit of my particular analysis of the material and the proposed identification and sequence dating of the corpus of early biblical poetry, there is a sound basis for the early dating of these poems, and hence for their use in the reconstruction of the initial phases of Israelite history.

[1]The article, "Divine Names and Epithets in Early Israelite Poetry," will appear in the forthcoming *Festschrift* in honor of G. Ernest Wright, to be published by Doubleday and Co.

[2]On the early dating of the Song of the Sea, see *YGC*, 12-13; *LEDEHP*, 153-56, esp. 155; P.C. Craigie, "An Egyptian Expression in the Song of the Sea (Exodus XV 4)," *VT* 20 (1970) 83-84; and "Psalm XXIX in the Hebrew Poetic Tradition," *VT* 22 (1972) 144-45; and F. M. Cross, "The Song of the Sea and Canaanite Myth," chap. 6 in *CMHE*, 112-44, esp. 121-25.

The antiquity of the Song of Deborah is affirmed by most scholars, with slight variations as to the precise date; see, e.g., G. Fohrer, *Introduction to the Old Testament*, trans. D. Green (Nashville, 1965) 209; O. Eissfeldt, *The Old Testament: An Introduction*, trans. P. R. Ackroyd (New York, 1965), 100-101; P. C. Craigie, "The Song of Deborah and the Epic of Tukulti-Ninurta," *JBL* 88 (1969) 253-65, esp. 253-55; and "The Conquest and Early Hebrew Poetry," *Tyndale Bulletin* 20 (1969); D. Harvey, "Deborah," in *The Interpreter's Dictionary of the Bible*, ed. G. A. Buttrick (New York, 1962), vol. 1, 809.

The purpose, therefore, of the present paper is to examine the two songs and attempt to extract from them valid historical data for a reconstruction of Israel's earliest national experience. The assumption is that these are the oldest sources available for such a reconstruction, are roughly contemporary with the events, and should therefore provide an accurate description of the central and most important occurrences in the saga of early Israel. At the same time, it must be borne in mind that we are dealing with poetry with its characteristic literary features and emphases, not a journalistic report of battle actions. That means that we cannot expect a simple, sober, sequential account, but must deal with an impressionistic reflection and refraction of the events as they impinged on the creative, emotive mind of the poet. By balancing the various factors, it should be possible to recover significant historical information, not only about the events, but the impact they had on the people who participated in them, and how they perceived their importance and meaning.

Clearly the two poems do not provide anything like a complete or continuous account of Israel's early days, or even of the central events themselves. But they are the primary witnesses to those events, and their testimony must be weighed accordingly. They constitute the foundation upon which a more complete reconstruction may be attempted, and the standard by which the prose data of the Bible are to be measured and evaluated. It is of interest that in the case of both poems there is an accompanying prose narrative (Exod. 14 for the Song of the Sea; and Judg. 4 for the Song of Deborah). The priority of the Song of Deborah and its superiority as a historical source in relation to the prose account have been widely acknowledged.[3] The opposite has been the case with the Song of the Sea, though no adequate reasons have ever been adduced for this reversal in method and treatment of essentially equivalent phenomena.[4] It is my intention to rectify this distortion in scholarly tradition and custom, and treat the literary remains consistently, and in the same order of priority.

THE SONG OF THE SEA (EXOD. 15:1-18, 21)[5]

Both of the biblical poems belong to the genre of victory hymn, examples of which happily have survived from neighboring cultures. Thus we have the Egyptian poems which celebrate the victories of Rameses II over the Hittites at

[3]See J. M. Myers, "The Book of Judges," in *The Interpreter's Bible* (New York, 1953), vol. 2, 717-18.

[4]See the discussion of this point in F. M. Cross and D. N. Freedman, "The Song of Miriam," *JNES* 14 (1955) 237-50, esp. 237-39. See S. R. Driver, *The Book of Exodus*, in "The Cambridge Bible" (Cambridge, 1911) 113-40.

[5]For a basic bibliography, see the article "The Song of Miriam" mentioned in n. 4; for more recent literature, see n. 2.

Kadesh on the Orontes, and of Marniptah over the Libyans and others,[6] as well as the Assyrian poem about Tukulti-Ninurta's triumphant campaign against the Kassites of Babylon.[7] All three of these date to the thirteenth century B.C. and are, therefore, somewhat older as well as being much longer than the biblical examples.

It is not my intention to compare these poems or their formal characteristics in detail, but rather to emphasize certain points in common about their structure and the mode of treatment of the central subject matter. While the poems tell a story which is generally consecutive, there are variations in detail from a strict chronological sequence. Attention is focused on the central event or series of actions which culminate in the utter defeat and rout of the enemy. The total time span is relatively short: the story line includes some background material, preliminary actions leading to the central event, the decisive engagement itself, and something of the immediate consequences for both victor and vanquished.

Typically, the poems establish the fact of victory as well as its importance. Then there are flash-backs, filling in details of the preparations and preliminaries leading to the decisive engagement. The victory is again celebrated, and the consequences described.[8]

The Song of the Sea opens with a vivid couplet summarizing the victory at sea (v. 1), which is repeated as a closing refrain (v. 21):

> I will sing to Yahweh for he has triumphed gloriously,
> Horse and its charioteer he hurled into the sea.[9]

[6]For a translation of the victory narrative of Rameses II, see J. H. Breasted, *Ancient Records of Egypt* (Chicago, 1906-7), vol. 3, §§ 298-351; pertinent sections are given by John A. Wilson, in *ANET*, 255-56. Wilson has also translated the Marniptah victory hymn, *ANET*, 376-78. See the discussion by Sir Alan Gardiner, *Egypt of the Pharaohs*, paperback ed. (New York, 1964) 259-64, 272-74.

[7]P.C. Craigie provides bibliographical data on the Epic of Tukulti-Ninurta in "The Song of Deborah and the Epic of Tukulti-Ninurta," 255, n. 13.

[8]The Song of Deborah is much longer than the Song of the Sea, and supplies more details of the engagement and its immediate aftermath: e.g., the death of Sisera at the hands of Jael. Nevertheless, it may not be complete, and seems to break off abruptly in the course of a vivid description of Sisera's mother, expectant yet anxious, not yet aware of the disaster that had befallen her son and his army. From a literary point of view the poem seems to be a torso, lacking at least a concluding section (not to speak of other narrative parts relating to Deborah and Barak), which would balance the lengthy Introduction (vv. 2-9). The Song of the Sea is a more symmetrical composition, and seems to be complete as it has come down to us (see my forthcoming article, "Strophe and Meter in Exodus 15," in the Jacob M. Myers' *Festschrift*).

[9]The first person singular form of the verb is probably original, as the same form is found in the Song of Deborah (Judg. 5:3); but see Cross, *CMHE*, 127 and n. 47. The plural imperative form (v. 21) is appropriate as a summons to the people, or the choir representing them.

The account of the sea victory is filled out in verses 3-5, and reaches a climax in the description of the mighty storm at the Reed Sea generated by Yahweh himself. It was not a battle in the usual sense, since only Yahweh was active against Pharaoh and his host, not the people of Yahweh. Under the circumstances it is difficult to reconstruct the episode with any precision, although the prose compilers made a valiant stab at it, aided presumably by other source materials.[10] There is enough evidence to make it clear that the decisive moment came with the destruction of the Egyptian chariot force by a violent storm at the Reed Sea. It is noteworthy that the song celebrates the defeat of an armored contingent (i.e., chariotry), as does the Song of Deborah. Possession of chariots was the sign of military superiority in the world of the second millennium B.C., and under normal circumstances a show of this force would have been sufficient to intimidate any rebellious band armed only with hand weapons. For a militia without sophisticated weapons or training, to challenge a chariot army would seem to be the height of folly, and victory could only come about through the miraculous intervention of God. Just that is precisely the theme of both poems. In Israel's infancy, when it was little better than a rabble in arms, crucial victories over heavily armed opponents were achieved by Yahweh, the God of Israel.

There is a break in the sequence after verse 8; verse 9 is a flash-back, depicting the boastful enemy equipped and ready to set forth in pursuit of Yahweh's people, to overtake, destroy, and despoil them. While the language is typical, and should not be pressed for historical details, nevertheless it provides background for the central event. With verse 10, the unit resumes the theme of victory at sea, and closes with the drowning of the Egyptians.

It is not until the next section that the aftermath or consequences of Yahweh's triumph is described. The main result is the liberation of the people from Egyptian domination and further military intimidation, and their subsequent march through the wilderness under divine guidance to his holy habitation (v. 13).[11] The same theme is continued in verse 17, with 16cd serving as a link. But at the same time, or rather, prior to the movement of the people from the sea to the mountain, another consequence or by-product of the victory is described. This lengthy digression (vv. 14-16ab) concerns the neighboring peoples who are involved in the aftermath for two reasons: (1) they occupy land still claimed by Egypt as part of its Asiatic empire, and hence must be considered vassals of the pharaoh. While Egyptian power was somewhat

[10]For the most recent and efficient treatment of the problem, see the discussion in Cross, *CMHE*, 121-44.

[11]For the identification of the "holy habitation" with the wilderness sanctuary, see *CMHE*, 125, and n. 41; see also Cross and Freedman, "The Song of Miriam," 248, n. 42. I think that a location in the wilderness is virtually certain, and that Sinai is a much more likely site than Shittim (against Cross, *CMHE*, 141). For additional details and discussion, see below.

attenuated in this period (the first quarter of the twelfth century B.C. in my opinion), nevertheless the pharaoh (presumably Rameses III) was a powerful monarch, and after the repulsion of the sea peoples, exercised some control over the remaining Asiatic territories, including Philistia, Canaan, Edom, and probably Moab[12] and (2) the second consideration is that the line of march of the people of Yahweh took them near or into regions claimed by one or more of the nations mentioned. While no direct encroachment of their territories is affirmed or even hinted at, the movement of a sizable group in proximity to ill-defined border regions would be enough to generate concern. When such a movement is associated in popular report with a spectacular victory over one of the major powers, that concern would naturally escalate into consternation.

According to the poet, the magnitude of the victory is best seen in the reaction of the neighboring vassal domains. Terror and dread overwhelm them; they are paralyzed by sheer fright. This theme, which is common to campaign oratory of the ancient Near East and a cliché in the prose Assyrian annals, is used to heighten the political impact of the engagement at the Reed Sea. The poet links the primary victory over the Egyptians with the secondary effect on their vassals through a play on the word "stone," two properties of which are exploited in his imagery. Thus the chariot army of Pharaoh is said to sink into the depths "like a stone" (v. 5); and the four nations which occupy the Asiatic territory of Egypt are said to be struck dumb "like a stone" (v. 16).[13]

Instead of coming to the aid of the suzerain in his hour of need, or afterward, they remain silent and motionless behind their borders; they permit, and by their cowardly inaction, encourage the second aftermath—the march through the wilderness of the people of Yahweh. Thus the latter not only escape from Egypt and the armored pursuit force, but are able to turn their flight into a triumphal parade across potentially hostile regions to the sacred area surrounding Yahweh's holy mountain.

The passage of the people through this region is recorded in verse 16cd, which connects the terrified acquiescence of the peoples in this trespass with the advance of Yahweh's people through the wilderness and ultimate arrival at its destination. Thus verse 13 summarizes this aspect of the aftermath, with

[12]There is evidence to support these claims, though only for Palestine and the southern regions around the Dead Sea. Syria definitely had been lost, in spite of the survival of traditional and anachronistic phraseology in the wall inscriptions at Medinet Habu, and the remaining Asiatic territory would disappear in the course of the twelfth century; see Gardiner, *Egypt of the Pharaohs*, 283ff. and 288. See also A. Malamat, "The Egyptian Decline in Canaan and the Sea-Peoples," chap. 2 in *Judges*, ed. B. Mazar (Tel-Aviv, 1971), vol. 3 in "The World History of the Jewish People; First Series: Ancient Times," 34-35.

[13]Against the argument of M. J. Dahood, "*Nāda* 'To Hurl' in Ex 15, 16," *Biblica* 43 (1962) 248-49, I hold that v. 16 refers to the condition of the four nations mentioned in vv. 14-15, not to that of the Egyptians. Thus the standard analysis and interpretation of the passage are to be preferred; see *CMHE*, 130 and n. 66.

emphasis on Yahweh's faithful and powerful guidance, and the people's safe arrival at the sacred area. Verses 16 and 17 spell out the details of the movement across the wilderness (v. 16cd) and the entry and settlement in the holy territory of Yahweh (v. 17).

The identification and location of the sacred habitation of Yahweh (v. 13; see related expressions in v. 17) is the principal remaining problem of the poem.[14] With respect to this question, I propose the following: (1) that *nĕwē qodšekā* "your holy habitation" and *har naḥălātĕkā* "your mountain possession" are parallel or complementary expressions for the same place; (2) that the action in the verses under consideration (vv. 13 and 17) is all in the past, in spite of the variation in the form of the verbs employed (two suffixed forms in v. 13, two prefixed forms in v. 17a), as already observed many years ago by S. R. Driver;[15] and (3) that the place in question is none other than the mountain of God at Sinai or Horeb. According to the tradition this area was the immediate goal of the people who left Egypt, and it fits well into the context of the victory at sea,[16] whereas a location elsewhere, e.g., in the land of Canaan, not only disrupts the unity and continuity of the poetic narrative, but represents the entry and settlement in the promised land as peaceful and without the resistance of the inhabitants, contrary to the practically unanimous testimony of all other sources.[17]

[14]The most recent discussion is that in *CMHE*, 141-43. In an unpublished manuscript on the "History of the Religion of Israel," Albright deals with the question of the location of the sanctuary in v. 17; he suggests two possible solutions: Sinai or Canaan, but is unable to decide between them.

[15]*The Book of Exodus*, 139-40. Cross comes to the same conclusion, *CMHE*, 125, as does Robertson, who has made a thorough study of verb forms in Hebrew poetry, *LEDEHP*, 8-55.

[16]See Exod. 3:1-12, esp. v. 12: "And he said, 'Indeed I shall be with you, and this is the sign that I have sent you. When you bring the people out of Egypt, you shall serve God at this mountain.'" The association between Yahweh and Sinai is very ancient and must be pre-Mosaic. One of the oldest and most distinctive epithets of Yahweh is *zeh sīnay* "the One of Sinai" (Judg. 5:5; Ps. 68:9).

[17]The common view, that the land of Canaan is meant by the description in v. 17, is expressed by Driver and others; see, e.g., Cross and Freedman, "The Song of Miriam," 249-50, n. 59. Since there is no mention of an armed invasion or military conquest of the land in the poem, the difficulty with this identification of the sanctuary of Yahweh with the later shrines at Shiloh or Jerusalem becomes apparent. Cross (*CMHE*, 141ff.) plausibly suggests a location for this shrine at Gilgal, which served as the first cult center for the confederation in the land of Canaan; and this was before any military action in Canaan itself. In order to justify the proposal, Cross points out that the mountain terminology, which may have been associated with Sinai originally, might well have been transferred even to an unimpressive site like Gilgal, in much the same way that similar terms were later applied to Mt. Zion, which is a rather modest hill.

Nevertheless, I find it hard to believe that a poet, recounting the decisive moments in the formation of the community, would omit entirely any reference to the original sacred

That the phrases *nwh* (*qdšk*) and *hr* (*nḥltk*) are in fact complementary is confirmed by a passage in Jeremiah where we find the same terms paired: *nĕwē* (*ṣedeq*) and *har* (*haqqōdeš*).[18] In the latter passage, the reference is certainly to the land of Canaan, very likely to the holy city Jerusalem and Mt. Zion. The terms would inevitably be applied to the central sanctuary of Yahweh wherever that happened to be. From the tenth century on, it was at Jerusalem, to be sure, but before that time it was elsewhere. In Jer. 31:23, we have a good example of transference, since the terms are more appropriate to a wilderness region (i.e., *nāweh* is a pastoral habitation) and an authentic mountain range. Such terms would not have been used to describe Jerusalem and Mt. Zion, if they had not been hallowed by tradition, a tradition originally associated with Sinai/Horeb and its great mountain.[19] They are especially appropriate to that place in the period to which the poem has been assigned by me and other scholars on independent grounds. The preservation of the terminology and its adaptation to other sanctuaries in other places is typical of the conservatism of all religious groups, and only serves to emphasize the antiquity and tenacity of these original traditions. Parallel to this phenomenon is the persistent assertion, found in several early poems (and restated in the archaizing Psalm of Habakkuk) that Yahweh came from Sinai, i.e., from the southland (his primordial dwelling among men) to acquire a new permanent abode in Canaan (Judg. 5:4-5, Deut. 33:2-3, Ps. 68:8-9; cf. Hab. 3:2-3).

Furthermore, the description of the divine throne (*mākōn lĕšibtĕkā* "dais of your throne," i.e., the platform on which the throne of Yahweh is set) and sanctuary (*miqdāš*) in Exod. 15:17 reflects the heavenly or mythic palace and throne-room of the deity, made by his own hands, and hence to be distinguished from man-made temples wherever they may have been erected. Yahweh's own palace was in the heavens at the top of the sacred mountain, generally hidden from view by the clouds. Such a picture of Yahweh's residence made by him fits the scene at Sinai and nowhere else.[20] The use of the critical

---

mountain of Yahweh, i.e., Sinai, which figures so prominently in all surviving traditions, in favor of a secondary and temporary center of worship, without further specification. Unless the obvious, primary reference can be shown to be impossible or highly improbable, it is a better choice, especially in an early poem, than a secondary transferred reference.

[18]Jer. 31:23 reads as follows: "Thus has said Yahweh of hosts, the God of Israel, 'Again they will say this word in the land of Judah and in its cities, when I restore their fortunes, "May Yahweh bless you, legitimate habitation, O holy mountain."'"

[19]For discussion of this point, see *SITP,* 105-6, n. 14.

[20]According to later tradition Sinai was the place, not only where the first tabernacle was erected, but indeed where Moses received detailed directions concerning its construction. The point is emphasized that Yahweh showed Moses "the pattern of the Tabernacle and the pattern of its furnishings" (Exod. 25:9). The key term is *tabnīt,* which is rendered "pattern" in the standard translations. It is derived from the root *bnh* "to build," and normally signifies something constructed. In other words, Moses was

phrase at the dedication of the temple in Jerusalem in the days of Solomon brings out the distinction between the heavenly and earthly sanctuaries; the Massoretic Text of 1 Kings 8:13 reads:

bānōh bānītī bēt zĕbūl lāk	I have surely built a royal house for you
mākōn lĕšibtĕkā ᶜōlāmīm	A dais for your eternal throne.

This is an adaptation of the original mythical reference to the current occasion.[21]

My conclusion is that verses 13 and 17 refer to the march through the wilderness from the sea to the mountain. The various nouns *nwh qdšk*, *hr nḥltk*, *mkwn lšbtk*, and *mqdš* all describe the holy abode of Yahweh in the southland. Similarly, the verbs *nḥyt*, *nhlt*, *tbᵓmw*, and *ṭṭᶜmw* describe the march through the wilderness and the entry into and settlement at the holy site. That place was surely Sinai/Horeb (the exact location of which remains uncertain), though Kadesh-Barnea has some claim to be considered as an alternate site. In any case, the poet had in mind a settlement in the vicinity of the holy mountain, which was dedicated to the worship and service of Yahweh.

The phrase *hr nḥltk* "the mountain of your possession" (i.e., the mountain to which you have rightful claim, or your own mountain which belongs to you by right) establishes legal ownership, whether that possession is a matter of inheritance or conquest. As has been noted by scholars, an almost identical expression, *ǵr nḥlty*, has turned up in Ugaritic as a description of the mountain sacred to Baal. The mountain itself, while draped in mythological terms and associations, not only bears a distinctive name, *ṣāpōn* "North" (i.e., the

---

shown something constructed on top of the mountain (see Exod. 24:17), rather than a blueprint. The heavenly tabernacle itself, in my judgment, served as the model for the earthly replica; that is what Moses saw when he ascended the mountain to confer with God.

[21] C. D. Ginsburg, in his *Biblia Hebraica, Massoretico-Critical Text of the Hebrew Bible*... (London, 1906), offers a slightly different reading: *bānītā* "you have built" for *BH* *bānītī* "I have built." The second person singular reading may be a legitimate variant, corresponding to the viewpoint expressed in Exod. 15:17, in which Yahweh's own action in erecting his temple is emphasized. The Solomonic edifice is only the earthly replica of the glorious heavenly original, which was made without hands (i.e., by God's rather than man's hands). The ambiguity reflected in the shift between the first and second person forms of the verb, is also present in the opening line of the couplet (v. 12; see LXX 1 Kings 8:53 which is the corresponding text, but has an additional colon, which may well be original): "Yahweh said that he would dwell in thick darkness." Here we have a reference to the cloud which surrounded the divine presence, and protected the privacy of his heavenly abode; at the same time it has an earthly counterpart in the incense cloud which rises in the temple and obscures the holy of holies and the sacred objects on solemn occasions (e.g., the Day of Atonement as described in Lev. 16:12-13).

northern peak), but has been identified with classical Mt. Casius, modern Jebel Aqraᶜ, just north of Ras Shamrah.[22]

In addition, Cross has shown that a particular mountain was sacred to the god El, chief of the Canaanite pantheon, namely, Mt. Amanus, which is even higher than Mt. Casius.[23] In other words, the expression is to be understood as the designation of a real mountain which has a special role in relation to a particular deity, i.e., it is his own mountain. In the original instance, it will be a towering peak (at least in relation to its environment), on which the palace of the god is located, where he holds sway, and where his retinue of heavenly servants wait upon him. In this respect, Yahweh is like El and Baal, having his own sacred mountain. It is Sinai/Horeb, traditionally identified with Jebel Musa, an imposing peak in the Sinai peninsula. Questions have been raised about the location, and other sites (and other mountains) have been proposed, including the volcanic peaks in the northern Hejaz.[24]

Wherever it was in the southern region, that mountain was known to Israel and identified as Yahweh's own, just as he was identified as the God of this mountain: *zeh sīnay* "the One of Sinai." In Cross's view, which I have adopted, Yahweh was the patron deity of a Midianite league (which included Kenites as a specialized group) in the general area around the Gulf of Akaba (the region variously called Seir, Edom, Paran).[25] The association of Yahweh with Sinai is therefore pre-Mosaic, and may be reflected in the place-name *yhwꜣ* preserved in a thirteenth-century Egyptian list.[26] Presumably the full name would have been *bēt yahweh*; both name and location are appropriate for the Midianite sacral center including both settlement (at Qurayya) and mountain (Sinai).[27]

We may suppose that the Midianite settlement there was of relatively recent origin (Late Bronze Age), and that the phrase *hr nḥltk* reflects the establishment of the cult of Yahweh at Sinai. The language used to describe Yahweh's ascendancy there is typically mythical and belongs to the pre-Mosaic form of this religion. Other echoes of the older tradition may be found scattered through the poetry of the Hebrew Bible, though the mixture of presumed Midianite motifs with those of Canaanite religion cannot easily be untangled (e.g., Rahab, the mythical monster in Ps. 89:11, may be Midianite; Leviathan, on the other hand, has a cognate in Canaanite mythology). It is only after the

[22]See *YGC*, 117-18.

[23]See *CMHE*, 37-38.

[24]On the location of Sinai, see M. Noth, *The History of Israel*, trans. S. Godman, rev. ed. (New York, 1960) 127-33.

[25]See *CMHE*, 71.

[26]See *CMHE*, 61-62 and n. 63; also *SITP*, 105-6, and n. 14.

[27]On the Late Bronze settlement at Qurayyah, see the preliminary reports by P. J. Parr, G. L. Harding, and J. E. Dayton, "Preliminary Survey in N. W. Arabia, 1968," *Bulletin of the Institute of Archaeology* 8/9 (1970) 219-41; and J. E. Dayton, "Midianite and Edomite Pottery," *Proceedings of the Fifth Seminar for Arabian Studies* (London, 1972) 25-33.

transfer of Yahweh's earthly center from Sinai to Canaan that such language would be applied to one or more sites in Canaan. Not until the capture of Jerusalem and the erection of the sanctuary there, is the shift in language and terminology completed.

There is an interesting parallel passage in Ps. 78, a lengthy historical poem which deals primarily with the Exodus and Wanderings, though it carries the story as far as the accession of David and the establishment of his dynasty.[28] After an extended introduction (vv. 1-8), the narrative opens with the deliverance from Egypt and continues through the Wanderings in the wilderness and the miracles and murmurings which punctuated them (vv. 9-39). Then, beginning with verse 40, the poet returns to the Plagues in Egypt and the Exodus. With the slaying of the first-born (v. 51), the stage is set for the departure of the people, which is then described in language reminiscent of Exod. 15:13, 16-17. Thus we read:

52) Then he led forth his people like sheep,
and guided them in the wilderness like a flock;
53) He led them to a safe place so that they would have nothing to fear,
but the sea overwhelmed their enemies;
54) Then he brought them to his sacred region,[29]
to the mountain which his right hand had created;
55) He drove out the nations before them, and assigned their landed property to them by lot,
he settled the tribes of Israel in their tents.

It is important to recognize that this is a summary statement covering the period from the departure from Egypt down to the occupation of the land of Canaan, including as principal and representative events the drowning of the Egyptians, the Wanderings in the wilderness, and the entry into the land. It is clear that verses 52-53 deal with the complex of incidents leading up to the destruction at the sea. On the other hand, verse 55 presumptively refers to the invasion of Canaan and the apportionment of the conquered land.

The question is: to what does verse 54 refer? Since it is placed between the departure from Egypt and the drowning of the Egyptians, on the one hand (vv. 52-53), and the forcible dispossession of the nations and the division of the land among the Israelite tribes, on the other (v. 55), it would be reasonable to see in

[28]See O. Eissfeldt, "Das Lied Moses Deuteronomium 32:1-43 und das Lehrgedicht Asaphs Psalm 78 samt einer Analyse der Umgebung des Mose-Liedes," *Verh. Sächs. Acad. Wiss. Leipzig, Phil.-hist. Kl.* 104, no. 5 (Berlin, 1958) 26-41; also *YGC*, 17, n. 41; 25, n. 58.

[29]Dahood renders Hebrew *gbwl* as "mount" on the basis of Ugaritic *gbl* "mountain" (*Psalms* II [New York, 1968] 237, 245; also Albright, *YGC*, 26, and n. 59). If the translation is correct, then it would serve to strengthen the case for connecting the various expressions in Exod. 15 (*nwh qdšk, hr nḥltk*) and Ps. 78 (*gbwl qdšw, hr zh qnth ymynw*).

verse 54 a description of the Wanderings in the wilderness and the sojourn at the holy mountain there. After all, the poet was fully aware of the wilderness tradition, having devoted the bulk of his composition to a detailed account of Israel's experience there. It would be strange if in the resumé all reference to the wilderness were omitted, or if that part of the tradition were simply submerged in the account of the Conquest.[30] Prevailing scholarly opinion to the contrary notwithstanding, any reference to the hill country of Judah here or Mt. Zion in particular would be out of order, and would disturb the dramatic build-up of the poem, which reaches its climax with the explicit designation of Judah and Mt. Zion as the real focus of God's interest in verses 68-69; David is mentioned in verse 70 as the one who attained this goal. Any such reference would be premature before the historical narrative in verses 56-67 (note, e.g., the mention of Shiloh, vv. 60f., which preceded Jerusalem as the site of the central sanctuary), and especially so before the invasion and occupation of the land, v. 55.[31]

In my opinion, Ps. 78:54, like Exod. 15:13 and 17, describes the wilderness mountain sanctuary as the initial goal of the march from Egypt. This is the natural reading and interpretation of the passages in both poems, and there is nothing in either of the latter to suggest otherwise. It is only the accumulated weight of scholarship that has obscured this point. Furthermore, we note that Ps. 78:55, with its clear statement of the dominant themes of the conquest of Canaan and the division of the territory, has no echo in Exod. 15. There is no hint in the latter of either of these matters, or of any other element in the Conquest tradition.

If the scope of the poem in Exod. 15 is limited to the victory at the Reed Sea and its immediate consequences—the march through the wilderness and the settlement at the holy mountain there—what can we say about the date of these events, on the basis of the internal data of the poem? The principal clue is to be found in the list of four peoples in verses 14-15. These are described as having heard the news of the Egyptian disaster at the sea, and as responding with shock and great fright, so much so that they were paralyzed with fear and unable to impede the triumphal march of Yahweh's people through the wilderness. The identity and collocation of these peoples are both interesting and important. The order of the names is geographical and stylistic: (1) The news of the Egyptian catastrophe reached the Philistines in southwest Palestine first, since they were nearest to the place where it occurred; from there the word was passed on to the Edomites in the southeast quadrant, and then to the

[30]See H.-J. Kraus, *Psalmen*, vol. 15, pt. 7, in the *Biblischer Kommentar* (1960) 547; Dahood, *Psalms II*, 245.

[31]It is possible that the movement in v. 53a is to be understood as subsequent to the victory at sea in v. 53b, but even that would only signify that the people had escaped from Egyptian territory and power: the flight to a place of safety is the counterpoint to the destruction of the Egyptian force. The poet has already alluded to the safe departure of the Israelites (vv. 12ff.) and may well have that aspect of the episode in mind in v. 53.

Moabites in the northeast. Finally it came back across the Jordan to the Canaanites in the northwest.[32] (3) The phrases are organized in an envelope construction, in which the first and last terms form a linked pair, while the second and third terms form a balancing pair:

1) *yšby plšt*	//	4) *yšby knᶜn*
2) *ᵓlwpy ᵓdwm*	//	3) *ᵓyly mwᵓb*

From a historical and chronological point of view, there is only one period during which these four peoples coexisted in the area from the border of Egypt to the northern perimeter of Palestine: the twelfth century B.C. The critical terms are the first (*plšt*) and the fourth (*knᶜn*), though all are important. There is no explicit mention of the Philistines in Egyptian sources before the early twelfth century (during the reign of Rameses III, who repelled an invasion of the sea peoples, among whom they are listed).[33] Doubtless they were present in the area earlier (in the thirteenth century, certainly, perhaps even before that), but they were not settled as a national entity in Palestine before the first quarter of the twelfth century, so far as one can tell from the records.[34] The reference here, in which Philistia is grouped with other settled peoples cannot be earlier, but might be later. It is often claimed, moreover, that it must be much later, since other occurrences of the term *pělešet* are in either late (e.g., Isa. 14:29, 31; Joel 4:4) or undatable poetry (Pss. 60:10, 83:8, 87:4, 108:10).[35] Standard usage in prose (and other early poetry, e.g., 2 Sam. 1:20) is the masculine plural form, *pělištīm*. While this argument may carry some weight, it is clear that the singular form, *plšt*, was in use in a neighboring culture (Egypt) as early as the twelfth century, and must therefore have been known by the Israelites. Its haphazard and sporadic use in Hebrew poetry can hardly be used to prove anything about its introduction into the language.

It may also be argued that the term *yšby*, which I have rendered "enthroned ones,"[36] is inappropriate for the Philistines, who did not have kings

[32] It is possible to see in this arrangment a reflection of the traditional line of march of Yahweh's people, who came near but did not enter the territories of the Philistines, Edomites, and Moabites in that order before finally reaching the land of the Canaanites. See Craigie, "The Conquest and Early Hebrew Poetry," 86. However, the passage in Exod. 15 makes no distinction between Canaan and the other three nations; it does not imply contact with any of them, much less conquest.

[33] See Gardiner, *Egypt of the Pharaohs*, 284-85; Albright, *YGC*, 157-64; Malamat, "The Egyptian Decline in Canaan," 32-35.

[34] See Malamat, "The Egyptian decline in Canaán," 23-25. For a contrary view, see *CMHE*, 124-25, where Cross places the settlement of the Philistines in the thirteenth century. The fact that the name does not occur in the records of either Rameses II or Marniptah is difficult to explain if the Philistines were organized as a political entity in Palestine in the thirteenth century.

[35] See *YGC*, 46-47; Cross and Freedman, "The Song of Miriam," 248, n. 44; also my discussion in "Divine Names and Epithets."

[36] See Albright's comment, quoted in "The Song of Miriam," 249, n. 49.

(*mĕlākīm*) in this period, but were governed by a council of tyrants or lords (*sĕrānīm*, which is etymologically related to Greek *tyrannos*). The word *yōšēb* is less specific than *melek*, and hence may have served as an equivalent for *seren*; at the same time, it could represent "kings" in the complementary phrase *yšby knᶜn* "kings of Canaan." In the eyes of the Israelites, the formal distinction between Philistine and Canaanite political structures may have been obscured by the functional similarities, especially in the leadership. It is also possible that in Exod. 15:14, the phrase *yšby plšt* simply means "the inhabitants of Philistia,"[37] though in view of the expressions in verse 15 referring to the leaders of Edom and Moab (and presumably Canaan), it is not likely.

At the other end of the period, i.e., by the eleventh century, the situation on both sides of the Jordan had changed drastically: on the east bank the Ammonites had intruded upon the domestic tranquility of the Moabites by seizing large chunks of their territory; and on the west bank the Israelites and Philistines had practically demolished the Canaanites. It is instructive that after the decisive defeat of the Canaanite kings recorded in the Song of Deborah there is no further mention of the Canaanites in any early poem of Israel, or in the prose accounts after the period of the Judges (except for an occasional stereotyped phrase: 1 Kings 9:16, 2 Sam. 24:7; cf. Neh. 9:8, 24). If the battle of Kishon, celebrated in the Song of Deborah, occurred around 1150 B.C., or slightly later, then we could fix the events described and the situation reflected in the Song of the Sea in the first half of the twelfth century, preferably in the first quarter. I do not see any sufficient basis for pushing the principal occurrence—the victory at the sea—back into the thirteenth century, though that is possible. The further back it is set, the greater the discrepancy in the picture of the four nations in verses 14-15. The earliest possible date for the Exodus would then be the last quarter of the thirteenth century, while a preferable date would be around 1200, or very early in the twelfth century.

An apparent conflict between this proposal and the evidence in the Marniptah "victory stele," in which "Israel" is mentioned in a series of peoples and cities located in Syria-Palestine may be resolved in the following manner. If the identification with biblical "Israel" is accepted, and there seems to be no significant argument against the equation, we would agree that there was a confederation of political units in the land of Canaan collectively called "Israel" during the thirteenth century B.C. or even earlier.[38] Already in the thirteenth century the league had gained sufficient autonomy to merit mention in Marniptah's list of enemies in the Asiatic provinces. But it had not yet attained

[37]For this translation, see "The Song of Miriam," 242; and *CMHE*, 130.

[38]The fact that the determinative preceding the name is that of a people rather than of a state indicates that in Egyptian eyes "Israel" was either a recent arrival in the country, or as a political confederation a recent development. The name "Israel" is pre-Mosaic, non-Yahwistic; it is patriarchal in origin and was applied to a tribal league which was already in existence in Palestine for some time before the Exodus or the emergence of Mosaic Yahwism. See my discussion in "Divine Names and Epithets."

statehood or adopted Yahwism, which was introduced into the country at a later date. It seems likely that many if not most of the tribal names were attached to districts in Palestine in pre-Mosaic times.[39] In other words, the framework or territorial structure of the twelve-tribe confederation was already present in Palestine at least a half-century before the movement initiated by Moses under the banner of a militant and triumphant Yahweh penetrated the west bank of the Jordan river.

Having attempted to determine the chronological horizon of the poem, and to fix the approximate date of the events and circumstances described in the poem, namely, the first quarter of the twelfth century, we may proceed to consider the date of the poem itself. A substantial mass of evidence and argumentation has been assembled by a number of scholars pointing to a very early date for the composition of the Song of the Sea; in fact it is held by several to be the oldest of all Yahwistic poems of any length in the Bible.[40] More specifically, a date in the twelfth century for its composition seems very reasonable.[41] On the basis of the present analysis and some of the inferences drawn from it, I now propose a date of composition in the second quarter of the twelfth century, and in any case before 1150. In my opinion, the poet was restricted in his vision of the historical experience of his people, the people of Yahweh, to the period ending with the settlement at the southern wilderness sanctuary. He was, therefore, acquainted with Mosaic Yahwism in its pristine form, before its first radical adaptation to a territorial state with a developed political structure. He lived within a generation of the events described in the poem, and may even have been a participant in or observer of them. The conclusions to which I have come, while not quite as traditional as those of the compilers of the Pentateuch, who attributed the poem to Moses himself and the refrain to Miriam and her companions, are nevertheless sufficiently drastic to pose questions for orthodox critical scholarship, as well as to offer suggestions for the reconstruction of biblical history.

The picture presented by the poem and supplemented by extrabiblical data may be described as follows:

[39]See *YGC*, 20, 265-66.

[40]See my discussion in "Divine Names and Epithets"; Albright dates the poem in the thirteenth century (*YGC*, 12, 45-47); Robertson assigns it to the twelfth century (*LEDEHP*, 135, 153-156, esp. 155); Cross and I put it in the twelfth or eleventh century (*CMHE*, 124).

[41]Albright's date in the thirteenth century seems too early to me; in order to maintain it, he must emend *plšt* out of the text (*YGC*, 46-47). The presence of that word in the text would not bother Cross, but his date for the poem is a bit low in my opinion. My present view is about the same as the one expressed in "The Song of Miriam," i.e., not later than the twelfth century in its original form, and not later than the tenth century in its final form (see my discussion in "Divine Names and Epithets").

1. Behind the poem is the flight from Egypt, here barely touched on by the enemy in his speech in which he boasts that he will overtake, put to the sword, and plunder the people.

2. The central content of the poem is the miraculous deliverance of the people at the Sea of Reeds. While numerous details are provided, including information about Pharaoh's chariotry and officers, about the violence of the storm which wrecked the armored force and drowned the fighting men, it is extremely difficult to reconstruct a rational sequence of events or the exact circumstances of the occurrence.[42] That there was a decisive shift in the fortunes of the fleeing group seems certain.

3. From that time on they were free of the threat of Egyptian reprisals or punitive action. According to the poet, the effect of the victory was not limited to Egypt, but extended to overwhelm the other neighboring and interested states: Philistia, Edom, Moab, and Canaan. Paralyzed by fear at the awesome display of Yahweh's power against the most powerful nation in that part of the world, these lesser peoples could offer no opposition as the people marched across the wilderness from the sea to the holy mountain of Yahweh. The poem closes with the vivid description of the people planted in the sacred precinct, the peculiar possession of Yahweh, where his sanctuary stands, the dais of his throne, all made by his own hands. The language is rich with mythic terminology, derived from the older religious traditions preserved in Canaanite literary texts. Such expressions, which were used of other gods and their sacred areas and temples,[43] were applied to Yahweh and his sacred mountain in this passage, and would be adapted to worship at the different central shrines of Israel and Judah in the centuries to come, finally being fixed on Jerusalem and Mt. Zion, Yahweh's permanent earthly abode in the biblical tradition.

The poem is also important for what it does not say: there is no mention or presumption of the Conquest, i.e., the entry into and the settlement in Canaan. Furthermore, there is no reference to the patriarchs or awareness of the theme of the promised land. The objective of the people who fled from Egypt was the holy land of Yahweh, but that territory was in the southern wilderness, Yahweh's traditional home, not Canaan.

In short, there is no obvious link between Yahweh and the God of the Fathers.[44] In this poem we have a clear expression of a new religion, not simply

[42]For a persuasive and probable account of what happened, see Cross, *CMHE*, 126-32; cf. Albright, *YGC*, 45-46; "The Song of Miriam," 238-39.

[43]Cross has shown that Canaanite El is associated specifically with Mt. Amanus (*CMHE*, 24-39); Baal's mountain, on the other hand, is Mt. Casius (*YGC*, 118, 125, 128).

[44]Exod. 15:2, with its reference to "the God of my father," may represent an attempt to link Yahweh to patriarchal religion. Two observations are in order, however: (1) The verse as a whole seems to be secondary, a later interpolation designed to serve a liturgical purpose (see our comments in "The Song of Miriam," 243-44; and mine in

the adaptation of an old one. The accommodation of the new faith introduced by Moses to the traditional El religion of Israel was the work of a later generation.[45] Furthermore, the group that was the object of divine intervention, who were rescued from the pursuing chariots, is known only as the people of Yahweh. Although they have been redeemed by him, even created by him, they are not called Israel and claim no patriarchal descent: they are not necessarily children of Abraham, Isaac, and Jacob. The group is perhaps best described as a heterogeneous collection: an undefined mixture of the stateless people at the bottom of the Egyptian class and power structure, sharing little more than a common language (in biblical terms, *ᶜereb rāb* and *ᵓăsapsūp*).[46] But these slaves secured a unique leader, were delivered by a miracle; they were welded into a community through a common faith, hardened and toughened by a terrible ordeal in the wilderness, to emerge as the people of Yahweh. That is their only designation in the Song of the Sea. There is no confederation called Israel (or Judah) in the poem, no tribal divisions with the familiar names of Jacob's sons, no traditions of the past, no promise of posterity, no conquest of the land—only permanent dwelling with Yahweh and continued life under his protection.[47]

"Strophe and Meter in Exodus 15" and "Divine Names and Epithets"). (2) A distinction is to be drawn between the singular form "father," used here, and the plural "fathers" which is the standard designation of the patriarchs. In other words, the term does not identify the deity as the "God of the Fathers," but only as the family God; see J. P. Hyatt, "Yahweh as the 'God of my Father,'" *VT* 5 (1955) 130-36; also "The Origin of Mosaic Yahwism," *The Teacher's Yoke: Studies in Memory of Henry Trantham* (Waco, Texas, 1964) 75-93. If the wording derives from an old tradition, and is to be considered as anything more than a poetic equivalent to *ᵓēlī* "my God," then we may see here an allusion to Moses' adopted family in Midian, whose God he (and Israel) came to worship (cf. *CMHE*, 71).

[45]See my discussion in "Divine Names and Epithets"; but cf. *CMHE*, 71 for a somewhat different view. I would agree that the name Yahweh originates in a liturgical formula describing El. By the time of Moses there was a sharp disjuncture, so that in all the early poems, Yahweh appears only as a name, and never with its original verbal force. The link with El had been broken, and was not forged again until after the settlement in Canaan.

[46]For the Hebrew words see Exod. 12:38 and Num. 11:4. While the biblical editors are careful to distinguish between the Israelite core and the accompanying rabble, the description probably fit the whole group. See G. E. Mendenhall, "Early Israel as the Kingdom of Yahweh," chap. 1 in *The Tenth Generation* (Baltimore, 1973), esp. 5, 19ff., 21-23.

[47]For a provocative analysis of the nature of early Israelite society under the impact of Mosaic Yahwism, see Mendenhall, "Tribe and State in the Ancient World," chap. 7 in *The Tenth Generation*, 177-87.

THE SONG OF DEBORAH (JUDG. 5)[48]

A drastically altered scene is reflected in the Song of Deborah, to which we now turn. The battle between Israel and Canaan at Taanach by the waters of Megiddo (Judg. 5:19) was the decisive episode in the struggle for control of the central and northern areas of Palestine. With the destruction of Sisera's chariot force, and the defeat of the Canaanite kings allied with him, the main phase of the warfare between Israelites and Canaanites was over.[49]

The central action is described briefly but vividly in verses 19-22, with the preceding sections of the poem being devoted to preliminary and preparatory actions and summary statements, while the particular fate of Sisera is narrated in the succeeding units of the poem (verses 24-27 and 28-30, which relate the concern of his mother). The time-span of the poem is relatively brief, a characteristic of victory odes.[50] The major battle and its immediate aftermath take place on a single day, while the specific preparations for the battle, including the muster of the Israelite militia are a matter of a few weeks or months, hardly more. The only extended flash-back is to be found in verses 4-5, which refer to Yahweh's march from the southland to Canaan. While it is sometimes argued that this passage reflects only the immediate situation in which Yahweh, the One of Sinai, comes from the region of Edom//Seir, i.e., the location of his terrestrial base, to the aid of his beleaguered people in their

[48]For recent discussion of the Song of Deborah, see Craigie, "The Song of Deborah and the Epic of Tukulti-Ninurta," 253-65, esp. 254-55 with bibliographical references. See *YGC*, 13-14, 48-51; R. G. Boling deals with the Song in detail in his forthcoming volume on *Judges* in the Anchor Bible series. [Published in 1975, see chap. 9.]

[49]For the distribution of the term "Canaan," see the discussion above and my article, "Divine Names and Epithets." Except for an occasional allusion to the past or in a stereotyped expression, the word Canaan is no longer functional as a historical-political title. It is not found in any early poem later than the Song of Deborah, though it occurs in the prophetic oracles of the eighth century and following, and in a few Psalms as well. The title "Canaan" and the gentilic "Canaanite" occur repeatedly in the Pentateuch and Joshua, as expected. The usage continues in Judges through chap. 5 (and once more in Judg. 21:12). It appears twice more in the Deuteronomic History: 2 Sam. 24:7 and 1 Kings 9:16; and crops up occasionally in the Chronicler's Work (1 and 2 Chron. and Ezra-Neh.). Among the prophets, it occurs in Isaiah (19:18, 23:11), Hosea, Zephaniah, Obadiah, and Ezekiel. It appears in the historical Pss. 105 (v. 11), 106 (v. 38), and 135 (v. 11): these are all references to the past, when Canaan was an active political entity. The contrast in usage is dramatic, and clearly deliberate. In the eyes of the biblical writers, Canaan ceased to exist as a geopolitical entity after the great battle between Israel and Canaan described in Judg. 4 and 5.

[50]See Craigie, "The Song of Deborah and the Epic of Tukulti-Ninurta," 256-64. The same considerations are applicable to the narrative of Rameses II.

critical encounter with the Canaanites, that is a questionable inference.[51] The passage reflects rather the permanent displacement of Yahweh's earthly abode from the southern wilderness to the land of Canaan, and corresponds to the movement of his people from Sinai or Kadesh to the northern region. That this migration of God and people was not immediately related to the battle at Taanach described in the Song of Deborah, but had an independent status in the traditions of Israel, is to be seen in the fact that several versions of the divine march from the southern plains to Canaan occur in various early or archaizing poems: e.g., Deut. 33:2-3, Ps. 68:8-9, and Hab. 3:3.[52] None of these refers directly to the episode described in Judg. 5, but rather imply that Yahweh's march north was at the head of his people and took place in preparation for the entry into the settlement in the land of Canaan. While the southern mountain range, where Yahweh revealed himself to Moses and was worshipped by his people in their first permanent settlement, would always retain its sacred associations and have a central place in the traditions of the founding of the community, it is instructive that its importance was only in terms of reminiscence, and the ongoing cult could accept the transfer of holiness to the land of Canaan as permanent and complete. The tabernacle and ark symbolized the continuing presence of Yahweh whether in motion or at rest in one or another of the major shrines of early Israel. This practice continues until the final stabilization of worship in the temple at Jerusalem. There were deviations from this norm in later times, e.g., the persistent heresy of the northern kingdom with its sanctuaries at Dan and Bethel, but the official view was held firmly in the biblical writings. There is only one recorded instance of a pilgrimage to the ancient mountain of Yahweh: Elijah's flight to Horeb after the episode at Mt. Carmel.[53] There may have been others, but their absence from the record indicates that there was no regular practice of this sort. In short, the transfer of sanctity was complete and irreversible. The God of Sinai became in turn the God of the promised land (Canaan, including Trans-Jordan), and ultimately the resident deity of Jerusalem on Mt. Zion.[54]

[51]See G. F. Moore, *A Critical and Exegetical Commentary on Judges*, ICC (New York, 1895) 139-40.

[52]See *CMHE*, 86, n. 17; 100-102, 157.

[53]1 Kings 19. In spite of persistent efforts to reconstruct a ritual pilgrimage to Sinai//Horeb and a celebration there, the paucity of supporting data is noteworthy. Cf. *CMHE*, 308-9 and n. 56.

[54]The special association of Yahweh with different local sites in no way conflicts with his character as a cosmic deity. The tension between the local and particular manifestations of the deity, on the one hand, and his transcendent, universal aspects, on the other, is characteristic of biblical religion, and higher religion in the Near East generally. See Cross's perceptive remarks in "The Priestly Tabernacle," in *The Biblical Archaeologist Reader* 1 (Anchor Books; New York, 1961) 225-27.

Even though the march from the south is not directly related to the battle at the Kishon river, it forms a necessary part of the story of the Conquest, and serves also as the link between the Exodus and Wanderings on the one hand, and the Wanderings and the Conquest on the other. The sequence of events is closely knit, and while the poems emphasize only the most important occurrences, there are no significant gaps, from the beginning with the Exodus from Egypt until the final displacement of the Canaanites. According to the chronology proposed above, not more than one or two generations were involved, perhaps only forty to sixty years. If the Exodus and initial settlement in the south are to be dated around 1200 or shortly thereafter, then the march from the sacred mountain north should be placed in the second quarter of the same century, with the climactic battle at Taanach around 1150 or a little later. If the Song of the Sea was composed in the second quarter of the twelfth century or roughly around 1175, then we should date the composition of the Song of Deborah in the third quarter of the century, hardly later than about 1125. In other words, both poems were occasional pieces composed to celebrate recent decisive victories.[55]

The next unit of the Song of Deborah, verses 6-7, which begins in the epic manner, "In the days of Shamgar ben-Anat / in the days of Jael . . . ," is usually taken to be retrospective, describing the desperate condition of the Israelites before the appearance of Deborah and the great victory at Taanach. The disappearance of the yeomanry or militia (*ḥdlw przwn*, v. 7)[56] was difficult to square with their victorious reappearance (v. 11), while the references to the "days of Shamgar," apparently a contemporary, and Jael, an active participant in the victory, were seen to be problems if not outright errors (Jael has often been emended right out of the text).[57] In the light of a new analysis of the content of the verses, however, it has become clear that they describe the consequences of Deborah's leadership and the victory in battle, not its antecedents. Hence the references to Shamgar and Jael are quite appropriate, and the retrospective tone reflects the standpoint of the poet who views the scene as a whole, including the background, the preparations, the battle, and the aftermath.

The unit may be read as follows:[58]

[55]On the dating of these poems, see my discussion in "Divine Names and Epithets."

[56]On the translation of the key term, see *YGC*, 49, n. 101.

[57]Albright changes "Jael" to "Jabin"; see *YGC*, 49, n. 99.

[58]The translation and analysis are based upon the work of Professor Marvin Chaney of San Francisco Theological Seminary, who graciously provided the relevant material from his unpublished doctoral dissertation, and through oral communication. The material can be divided into eight lines with the following syllable count: 7 + 7, 10 + 10, 6 + 8, 6 + 8. The second bicolon seems to overbalance the other lines, and perhaps a slightly different strophic arrangement is in order (see my translation): 7 + 7 + 10 = 24; 10 + 6 + 8 = 24; 6 + 8 = 14.

bīmē šamgar ben-ʿănāt	(6) In the days of Shamgar ben-Anat,
bīmē yāʿēl ḥādĕlū	In the days of Jael, they enriched themselves,
ʾŏrāḥōt wĕhōlĕkē nĕtībōt	From caravans and highway travelers,
yēlĕkū ʾŏrāḥōt ʿăqalqallōt	From caravans which travel the crooked roads,
ḥādĕlū pĕrāzōn	(7) The yeomanry enriched themselves.
bĕyiśrāʾēl ḥādēllū ʿad	In Israel, they enriched themselves on booty,
šaqqamtī dĕbōrāh	Because you rose up, Deborah,
šaqqamtī ʾēm bĕyiśrāʾel	Because you rose up, a mother in Israel.

The new analysis and interpretation of this passage depend upon the identification of the root *ḥdl* II in the three-fold occurrence of the verb *ḥdlw*. In contrast with *ḥdl* I, which means "to cease, leave off," *ḥdl* II means "to become fat, rich, prosperous," and then also "gross, stupid"; but we are concerned with the basic meaning of this root. The decisive evidence for this interpretation is to be found in the Song of Hannah (1 Sam. 2:1-10), where the phrase *ḥādēllū ʿad* is found (1 Sam. 2:5), and where the meaning cannot be questioned: "(The hungry) have grown fat on booty." The identical expression in Judg. 5:7, including the peculiar Massoretic vocalization, requires the same translation, which dramatically alters the sense of the whole unit.

The success of the yeomen of Israel in amassing booty is thus a consequence of Deborah's leadership, and easily understood in the light of the smashing victory over the Canaanites. The two occurrences of *ḥdlw* in verse 7 must be understood in the same way, as describing the recent prosperity of the Israelite militia; the pattern of repetition is found throughout the unit: e.g., *bymy . . . bymy*, *ʾrḥwt . . . ʾrḥwt* (v. 6); *šqmty . . . šqmty*, *byśrʾl . . . byśrʾl* (v. 7). The proper interpretation of *ḥdlw* in verse 6 is less certain. If the subject of the verb is *ʾrḥwt* "caravans," then the meaning should be "cease"; the thought would be that the rich caravan trade conducted by and in behalf of the merchant princes of the Canaanite cities, and protected by their chariot forces, had been forced to stop by the threat and actual depredations of the Israelite militia, who were essentially guerilla fighters. Alternatively, if the verb is to be identified as another instance of *ḥdl* II, then the meaning would be that the same militia was enriching itself by plundering the aforementioned caravans. It seems to me that the latter understanding is more in keeping with the data already adduced, and presents a consistent picture of Israel's position after the victory at Taanach.

If there is material reflecting the period before Deborah's activity, it may be found in verse 8. The first part remains difficult, and may be beyond recovery or restoration, but I believe that it should be analyzed and interpreted in the light of Deut. 32:17.[59] The explicit remark in the latter part of the verse about the lack of heavy-duty weapons for the infantry would seem to reflect the sad state of Israelite military strength before Deborah. The usual rendering of the number of men in the army of Israel as 40,000 is obviously questionable, but it is not just a case of poetic hyperbole. The term *ᵓelep* is to be understood in its etymologic sense as a village or a population center, which was responsible for providing a unit of troops.[60] Apparently there was a potential army of forty such units in Israel. If the average number of men in an *ᵓelep* was 10, that would make up a fighting force of 400 at full strength, a substantial army for the hill country of Palestine.[61] In the prose account of the battle in Judg. 4, reference is made to Barak's army of 10,000 men (vv. 6 and 14); we can interpret this figure as signifying ten units (perhaps 100 men) from two tribes, Naphtali and Zebulun (see Judg. 5:18). How many additional troops were provided by the remaining eight tribes is not clear, especially since several of them may not have sent any at all (e.g., Reuben, Dan, Gilead, and Asher; vv. 15-17), but if the total was around 400 (official strength), then the share of the four other participating tribes (Ephraim, Benjamin, Machir, and Issachar) would have been 300.

The first major unit of the poem closes with verse 9, which forms an envelope construction with verse 2: note the repetition of the expression *brkw yhwh* "Bless Yahweh," and the subtle interchange between *byśrᵓl . . . ᶜm* (v. 2) and *yśrᵓl . . . bᶜm* (v. 9). We may render as follows to show the interconnection:

biprōaᶜ pĕrāᶜōt bĕyiśrāᵓēl	(2) When locks were long in Israel,
bĕhitnaddēb ᶜām	When the people volunteered,
bārăkū yhwh	Bless Yahweh!
libbī lĕḥōqĕqē yiśrāᵓēl	(9) My heart was with the commanders of Israel,
hammitnaddĕbīm bāᶜām	Who volunteered among the people,
bārăkū yhwh	Bless Yahweh!

The next unit, verses 10-13, initiates the celebration of the great victory: verse 10 is the announcement to the audience; verse 11 is the recitation of the mighty deeds of Yahweh; verse 12 recalls the beginning of the action, with the

[59]See D. R. Hillers, "A Note on Jdg. 5:8," *CBQ* 27 (1965) 124-26. For comments on the relationship between the two passages, see *CMHE*, 122-23, n. 34.

[60]See G. E. Mendenhall, "The Census Lists of Numbers 1 and 26," *JBL* 77 (1958) 52-66.

[61]For example, King Mesha of Moab reports that he led a fighting force of 200 men against Jahaz, a town in Israel (line 20 of the Mesha Inscription); see Albright's translation in *ANET*, 320.

summons to the leaders, Deborah and Barak; and verse 13 is a reprise of some kind (see v. 11).

The central unit of the poem in its present form concerns the mustering of the tribal units for the battle (vv. 14-18). The material is in some disarray and not always intelligible. But it seems to be a roll call of the tribes or political units which were expected to supply troops for the engagement. It is clear that some tribes were more enthusiastic about the battle than others, and perhaps more to the point, some participated and others did not.[62] It is important to note that tribes which did not take an active part in the struggle are listed along with those which did. That means that the list does not derive from the circumstances of the battle, but rather reflects an already existing organization, i.e., a confederation of some kind. While the sequence is irregular and there is some unexplained overlapping and repetition, the list appears to be complete (at least in the mind of the poet). It is always possible that lines and names have dropped out of the poem, which may be only a torso,[63] and there is the glaring omission of three well-known tribes (Simeon, Levi, and Judah). But until and unless convincing evidence is forthcoming, it is methodologically more reliable to suppose that the list reflects the reality in the twelfth century B.C.[64]

The list gives the impression of originality and authenticity. It does not conform to the standard lists of the prose materials with respect to number, order, or designation, though there is sufficient correspondence and overlap to show that we are dealing with essentially the same groups.[65] At the same time, the divergences are so striking, that we must regard the list in Judg. 5 as

[62]The latter is emphasized by the curse hurled at Meroz, which must have been notably delinquent (v. 23). This verse, which is often challenged as secondary and intrusive, actually closes the unit dealing with the battle itself, vv. 19-23. The key word is *bāʾū,* which controls both the first line of the unit (v. 19) and, with the negative particle *lōʾ*, the last line (v. 23). The enemy, the kings of Canaan, came to the battle, but the people of Meroz, who belonged to the federation, did not, though under covenant obligation to help in time of need. The verse is also a link to the next major unit, vv. 24-30. Note the contrast between *ʾōrū* "curse" (v. 23), and *tĕborak* "let her be blessed" (v. 24).

[63]It is difficult to imagine that the poem proper ended with v. 30 (v. 31 is commonly understood to be a liturgical signature, which is linked thematically and grammatically with vv. 4-5; note, e.g., the agreement in second person singular pronominal suffixes). At the same time, this impression of incompleteness cannot be demonstrated, and nothing more than educated guesses can be made about the supposedly missing parts.

[64]In view of the persistent tradition of a twelve-tribe league, and the prevalence of twelve- and six-tribe groups in the surrounding regions (as reported in the Bible), it may be agreed that the original configuration included twelve units. That the number and names of the tribes may have varied from time to time, and that there were changes in the participating units is also clear from the biblical records.

[65]Eight of the tribal names given in the Song of Deborah are identical with those in the standard lists: Ephraim (v. 14), Benjamin (14), Zebulun (14, 18), Issachar (15), Reuben (15, 16), Dan (17), Asher (17), Naphtali (18). The other two are related to known tribal

independent of the others, and not influenced by the traditions reflected in Gen. 49, Deut. 33, or the prose accounts. As is well known, Judg. 5 includes the ten northern tribes, but not the southern tribes, Simeon and Judah, or the tribe of Levi. It is often supposed that the southern tribes were cut off from the north by a line of fortified Canaanite cities, and that they are not mentioned in the poem because there was no way for them to join in the affair.[66] But this is conjectural and depends upon the view that the traditional twelve- (or thirteen-) tribe structure was operational in the twelfth century.

I believe that the Song of Deborah reflects the actual state of affairs at that time: namely, that there was a ten-tribe league which bore the name Israel.[67] The existence of such a confederation can be traced back to or postulated for the thirteenth century on the basis of the Marniptah stele, while certain tribal (and territorial) designations in Palestine may be even older.[68] But of the geographic extent of such a confederation, or the number and names of its constituent elements, we must rely on biblical evidence which is not available before the twelfth century, although presumably more ancient data are embedded in some of the sources. For the twelfth century we have only the Song of Deborah, which is the subject of debate. The earliest biblical evidence for the twelve-tribe federation is to be found, in our opinion, in the Testaments of Jacob (Gen. 49) and Moses (Deut. 33), which are to be dated in their present form not earlier than the eleventh century B.C.[69] Other lists come from different literary strata and sources, reflecting a basic consensus about the number and distribution of the tribes, though with variations in detail.[70]

---

names, and can be regarded as valid surrogates: Machir (14) for Manasseh (in the tradition he is identified as Manasseh's first-born son); Gilead (17) for Gad (although Gilead is represented as the son of Machir, Num. 26:29, 30; etc.).

[66] See Y. Aharoni, "The Settlement of Canaan," chap. 6 in *Judges*, ed. Mazar, 109.

[67] See J. Liver, "The Israelite Tribes," chap. 9 in *Judges*, ed. Mazar, 201-4, esp. 203, n. 34. See E. Meyer, *Die Israeliten und ihre Nachbarstämme* (Halle a. S., 1906) 232-35 on the subject of a ten-tribe league; also S. Mowinckel, *Zur Frage nach documentarischen Quellen in Josua 13-19* (Oslo, 1946) 21ff.; and A. Malamat, "The Period of the Judges," chap. 7 in *Judges*, ed. Mazar, 138-39.

[68] See Aharoni, "The Settlement of Canaan," 115-16; and H. H. Rowley, *From Joseph to Joshua* (London, 1950) 3, 33-35.

[69] In my opinion, both poems contain older materials, see Albright, *YGC*, 265-66, on the Blessing of Jacob. The presence of Judah in both lists reflects developments toward the end of the eleventh century.

[70] The classic treatment of the tribal lists is that of M. Noth, *Das System der zwölf Stämme Israels* (Stuttgart, 1930). The order of the tribes in Gen. 49 is as follows: Reuben, Simeon, Levi, Judah, Zebulun, Issachar, Dan, Gad, Asher, Naphtali, Joseph, Benjamin. The Leah group (six tribes) comes first, followed by the children of the concubines (four tribes), with the Rachel group (two tribes) coming at the end. The basic pattern is indicated in Gen. 35:22-26 (after the narratives detailing the births of the successive children of Jacob, Gen. 29:31-30:24, and 35:16ff. for Benjamin). The following table indicates the range of variation among representative lists:

As pointed out in another place, I believe it is significant that the poems containing the twelve-tribe lists also regularly couple Israel with Jacob,

Judg. 5	*Gen. 49*	*Deut. 33*	*Gen. 29, 30, 35*	*Gen. 35:22-26*
Ephraim	Reuben	Reuben	Reuben	Reuben
Benjamin	Simeon	Judah	Simeon	Simeon
Machir	Levi	Levi	Levi	Levi
Zebulun	Judah	Benjamin	Judah	Judah
		Joseph		
Issachar	Zebulun	Ephraim	Dan	Issachar
Reuben	Issachar	Manasseh	Naphtali	Zebulun
Gilead	Dan	Zebulun	Gad	Joseph
Dan	Gad	Issachar	Asher	Benjamin
Asher	Asher	Gad	Issachar	Dan
Naphtali	Naphtali	Dan	Zebulun	Naphtali
	Joseph	Natphali	Joseph	Gad
	Benjamin	Asher	Benjamin	Asher

Gen. 46	*Exod. 1*	*Num. 1:5-15*	*Num. 1:20-43*	*Num. 2*
Reuben	Reuben	Reuben	Reuben	Judah
Simeon	Simeon	Simeon	Simeon	Issachar
Levi	Levi	Judah	Gad	Zebulun
Judah	Judah	Issachar	Judah	Reuben
Issachar	Issachar	Zebulun	Issachar	Simeon
Zebulun	Zebulun	Ephraim	Zebulun	Gad
		Joseph		
Gad	(Joseph)	Manasseh	Ephraim	Ephraim
			Joseph	
Asher	Benjamin	Benjamin	Manasseh	Manasseh
Joseph	Dan	Dan	Benjamin	Benjamin
Benjamin	Naphtali	Asher	Dan	Dan
Dan	Gad	Gad	Asher	Asher
Naphtali	Asher	Naphtali	Naphtali	Naphtali

Num. 7	*Num. 13*	*Num. 26*	*Num. 34*	*Deut. 27:12-13*
Judah	Reuben	Reuben	Judah	Simeon
Issachar	Simeon	Simeon	Simeon	Levi
Zebulun	Judah	Gad	Benjamin	Judah
Reuben	Issachar	Judah	Dan	Issachar
Simeon	Ephraim	Issachar	Manasseh	Joseph
Gad	Benjamin	Zebulun	Ephraim	Benjamin
Ephraim	Zebulun	Manasseh	Zebulun	Reuben
		Joseph		
Manasseh	Manasseh	Ephraim	Issachar	Gad
Benjamin	Dan	Benjamin	Asher	Asher
Dan	Asher	Dan	Naphtali	Zebulun
Asher	Naphtali	Asher		Dan
Naphtali	Gad	Naphtali		Naphtali

whereas in the Song of Deborah, with its ten-tribe list, only Israel is named.[71] Whatever this datum may imply about the particular relationship between Judah (and perhaps Simeon and Levi) and Jacob, it seems clear that there was a distinctive correlation between the name Israel and the ten northern tribes. That correspondence is fully attested at the time of the divided kingdoms, when the northern group of ten tribes separated from the dynasty of David to establish its own realm.[72] That this move was a restoration rather than an innovation is confirmed by the fact that after Saul's death, Ishbaal, his son, was crowned king of Israel (2 Sam. 2:8-9), while David became king of Judah at Hebron (2 Sam. 2:1-4). Thus as early as 1000 B.C. there were two nation-states, Israel and Judah, the former of which consisted of ten tribes, while the latter may have included other units besides Judah, as for example, Simeon, which were fully absorbed.

According to the tradition, David reigned for seven and one-half years at Hebron before becoming king of both Israel and Judah (2 Sam. 5:1-5). Ishbaal is said to have reigned for two years over Israel before his assassination. The discrepancy of five and one-half years is curious; if we assume that the figures

---

Josh. 13-19	*Ezek. 48:1-29*	*Ezek. 48:30-35*	*Apoc. 7*
Reuben	Dan	Reuben	Judah
Gad	Asher	Judah	Reuben
1/2 Manasseh	Naphtali	Levi	Gad
Judah	Manasseh	Joseph	Asher
1/2 Manasseh	Ephraim	Benjamin	Naphtali
Ephraim	Reuben	Dan	Manasseh
Benjamin	Judah	Simeon	Simeon
Simeon	Benjamin	Issachar	Levi
Zebulun	Simeon	Zebulun	Issachar
Issachar	Issachar	Gad	Zebulun
Asher	Zebulun	Asher	Joseph
Naphtali	Gad	Naphtali	Benjamin
Dan			

Except for Num. 34 (in which the Trans-Jordanian tribes have been omitted) and Judg. 5, all the lists count twelve tribes, although the names and the order vary. In general, the lists from Genesis and Exodus give the twelve sons of Jacob, including Levi and Joseph. From Numbers on, Levi is generally omitted and Joseph is divided into two tribes, Ephraim and Manasseh. In Deut. 33, Simeon is dropped rather than Levi, while Ephraim and Manasseh are appended to the Joseph oracle, which otherwise is similar to the Joseph oracle in Gen. 49. Ezekiel has both kinds of lists: in the geographic distribution of the tribes, Levi is omitted (he is located in the sacred precinct) while Ephraim and Manasseh are included (Ezek. 48:1-29); in the list of the gates of Jerusalem, Levi is included, along with Joseph, which displaces Ephraim and Manasseh (Ezek. 48:30-35).

[71]See discussion of this point in "Divine Names and Epithets."

[72]See 1 Kings 11:26-39, esp. vv. 30-32, 35-36.

are correct, then we may explain the circumstances in one of several ways:[73] (1) If David and Ishbaal began to rule over their respective kingdoms at the same time, then we must suppose that there was a five-year interregnum in Israel before David became king there. (2) If, on the other hand, there was little or no gap between the death of Ishbaal and the accession of David over Israel, then we must suppose that David became king of Judah five and one-half years before Ishbaal became king of Israel, i.e., while Saul was still alive. So far as the biblical narrative is concerned there is no support for either supposition: David's accession to the throne of Judah is placed immediately after the death of Saul, and his accession to the throne of Israel is similarly placed after the death of Ishbaal. Of the two alternatives proposed, the former seems less likely; it is difficult to imagine that there was any significant delay in making David king of Israel after the death of Ishbaal. In my opinion it is more likely that David became king of Judah during Saul's reign as king of Israel, and as a consequence of the rupture between them. Since David became a vassal chieftain under the authority of Achish, the Philistine ruler of Gath, after David's break with Saul, it is not difficult to imagine that he was installed as king of Judah with Philistine approval. Judah, after all, had been a protectorate of the Philistines since the time of the Samson stories (see Judg. 15:9-13, esp. v. 11). The question may legitimately be raised as to whether Saul was ever king of both Israel and Judah or, put another way, whether Judah was part of the kingdom of Israel over which Saul reigned as king. It is my judgment that if Saul ever exercised even nominal rule over Judah, it was through an arrangement separate from that which bound Saul to the northern kingdom; and that such an arrangement with Judah was terminated when David broke with Saul, and in effect became his successor as ruler of Judah. The effective establishment of a dual monarchy united in the person of a single king was the achievement of David and Solomon.

Briefly, we suggest that the original twelve-tribe league, located in Canaan and dating back to pre-Mosaic times, included Simeon and Levi, as well as the ten mentioned in the Song of Deborah (possibly with some name changes). The two "missing" tribes (Simeon and Levi) were banished from the league, as the result of some serious breach of confederation regulations, as indicated by the severe condemnation pronounced against both of them in Gen. 49:5-7. There may be a connection between this pronouncement and the scandalous events at Shechem involving the two brothers reported in Gen. 34, but it is difficult to say. If the same episode is in mind, then it would seem that the poet and the prose writer saw things somewhat differently (see Gen. 34:7 and vv. 30-31). The inference that the two tribes were banished from the league is based on a new interpretation of Gen. 49:7, which I render as follows:

[73] H. W. Hertzberg, *I and II Samuel: A Commentary*, trans. J. S. Bowden (Philadelphia, 1964) 249-51, questions the validity of the figure for Ishbaal.

ʾārūr ʾappām kī ʿāz	(7) Cursed be their wrath—how fierce it was!
wĕʿebrātām kī qāšātāh	And their rage—how cruel it was!
ʾăḥallĕqēm bĕyaʿăqōb	I will divide them from Jacob,
waʾăpīṣēm bĕyiśrāʾēl	and I will banish them from Israel.[74]

In accordance with this interpretation, I suggest that both groups moved off in a southerly direction, with Simeon finding refuge and settling in the territory of Judah. The account of this settlement in Josh. 19:1-9 implies that Simeon's move into territory assigned to Judah was secondary and unplanned. Levi seems to have relinquished its territorial claims, and left the country, ultimately finding its way to Egypt. There is no reason to doubt the tradition that Moses and his family belonged to this group, or that Levites were among those at the center of the Exodus movement.

To summarize: It is my contention that an original twelve-tribe league in Canaan bore the name of Israel, and included Simeon, Levi, and the ten tribes mentioned in the Song of Deborah, but not Judah, which had a separate history. The two tribes, Simeon and Levi, were dropped from membership, and the remaining ten-tribe group, pictured in the Song of Deborah, constituted the Israelite federation in the twelfth and early part of the eleventh century B.C. It is possible that efforts were made to reconstitute a twelve-tribe league including Judah and Simeon during the eleventh century under the leadership of Samuel, but clear evidence is lacking.[75] Out of this league, the monarchy emerged, with Saul as the first king (*melek*) or dynastic ruler (*nāgīd*) of Israel. A similar development took place in the south with David becoming king of Judah, apparently before the death of Saul. After the death of Ishbaal, under David's forceful leadership the two kingdoms were united,[76] only to fall apart again after the death of his son Solomon.[77]

[74] In archaic poetry the preposition *bĕ* often has the meaning "from" as in Ugaritic. The force of the verb *pwṣ* in the Hiphil is illustrated by Gen. 11:8, "And Yahweh dispersed them from there...." Similarly the basic meaning of *ḥlq* in the Piel is "to divide, separate"; see Ps. 60:8 = 108:8.

[75] In Deut. 33, Judah apparently has been substituted for an original Simeon in v. 7, where the verb *šĕmaʿ* (the same root as in the name *šimʿōn* "Simeon") and the sentiment expressed would seem to suit Simeon better than Judah. Since the statement is vague, and the particular circumstances are not known to us, it is best not to press the point. Since Simeon was actually part of Judah by this time, the substitution is quite understandable (see Josh. 19:1).

[76] Note that in 2 Sam. 19:43 the status of Israel as a ten-tribe entity during the reign of David is emphasized in the controversy between Israel and Judah.

[77] See 1 Kings 11:31,35, in which Israel is described as consisting of ten tribes, while Judah is offered one tribe as a consolation prize. Traditionally, this extra tribe would have been Simeon, since Simeon apparently was transferred from Israel to Judah in earlier times; but in the immediate historical context, it was understood to be Benjamin (cf. 1 Kings 12:21 in the light of 1 Kings 11:32 and 36). The latter shift

The remaining parts of the Song of Deborah deal with matters relating more directly to the battle and its outcome: i.e., verses 19-22, the destruction of the Canaanite forces by the torrential wady Kishon; verse 23, the cursing of Meroz; verses 24-27, the execution of Sisera by Jael; and verses 28-30, the mounting concern of Sisera's mother over the absence of news and the delay in the return of her son. There may be some reasonable doubt as to whether the poem is complete as we have it in the biblical text, but we must deal with it in its present form. Aside from a possible resolution of the tension created by the juxtaposition of the two dramatic scenes in the latter part of the poem—Jael and Sisera, on the one hand, and Sisera's mother and her chief lady-in-waiting, on the other—the essential story of the battle and the events leading up to and away from it is in the record.

A brief summary, in general chronological sequence, follows:

1. The earliest point of reference in the poem is the march of Yahweh, the God of Sinai, from the region of Seir//Edom (vv. 4-5). This event is subsequent, in my opinion, to anything recorded in the Song of the Sea, including the Exodus, the Wanderings through the wilderness, and the settlement at the Sinai sanctuary by the people of Yahweh. What this mythopoeic statement signifies in historical terms is not entirely clear, but we may infer reasonably that a movement both of ideas and of people is involved. While Yahweh's march northward is linked to the subsequent battle at Taanach in the poem, there is no suggestion that Yahweh returned safely to his mountain abode once the victory was achieved. A permanent change of address was involved, though it seems clear that the southern mountain, Sinai, and the holy encampment there, remained identified with and sacred to Yahweh. It is not, however, a crude shift of residence and jurisdiction on the part of a local deity, but the transfer of a distinctive religious faith to a new community. Ideas, especially of this kind, do not travel by themselves, but are carried by people, so at least some segment of the population that worshipped and served Yahweh at Sinai must have accompanied him on his march to Canaan, or to reverse the image, he must have accompanied them on their march north. The new Mosaic faith attracted adherents along the way, and rapidly became the religion of important elements in the population of Canaan. This group included settlements scattered through the hill country especially, and constituted the Israel of pre-Mosaic times. The migrants from the far south merged into the larger entity with its geographic base in Palestine to form Israel, the people of Yahweh, to use the language of the Song of Deborah.[78]

---

should have been reflected in a reduction in the number of tribes assigned to Israel (i.e., nine), but the tradition of ten was too strong to be altered at this late date.

[78]According to tradition, the route followed by the people of Yahweh took them past the territory of the Edomites and the Moabites, and into direct conflict with the Amorite kingdoms of Og and Sihon in Trans-Jordan. I wish neither to deny nor to

2. There is an apparent reference to an earlier period in Israel's experience, though the precise chronological relationship to Yahweh's march from the south is not clear. The mention of *ʾĕlōhîm ḥădāšîm* "new gods" (v. 8), is suggestive of a time of conflicts, especially if it is related historically to a similar passage in Deut. 32 (v. 17). The confederation seems to have been in a state of military disarray then, in contrast with the later situation described in verses 6-7 and summarized in verse 11.

3. This people, which had lived in an uneasy, generally subordinate relationship to various Canaanite city-states, now under the impetus of the new faith, and doubtless influenced by other socioeconomic and political factors (including the steady decline of Egyptian power and influence), challenged Canaanite hegemony. The next scene is the mustering of the militia: a roll call of the tribal units or politicomilitary districts is given, along with the responses of the tribes in terms of providing manpower and active participation. According to the text, five of the tribes responded favorably (vv. 13-15): Ephraim, Benjamin, Machir (for Manasseh), Zebulun, and Issachar; four others failed to show any enthusiasm for the enterprise (vv. 15-17): Reuben, Gilead, Dan, and Asher. In an appendix (v. 18), Zebulun and Naphtali are cited for conspicuous bravery on the field of battle. The two latter tribes are also mentioned in the prose account (Judg. 4) as the principal participants in the struggle against Sisera.

4. The battle itself is described briefly but dramatically. In ordinary terms, the odds against Israel were overwhelming, but with Yahweh on their side, the outcome could not be in doubt. Divine power was manifested in the sudden flooding of the Kishon; the Canaanite chariot force was wrecked by the river, and the battle ended. The summation in the Song of the Sea applies as well to Sisera and his army as it did to Pharaoh and his host (Exod. 15:1).

> I sing of Yahweh that he is greatly exalted,
> Horse and charioteer he hurled into the sea.

5. The story then focuses on Sisera and his unseemly fate. To fight and die in battle was tragic but honorable; a man could be a hero even in a lost cause. But to die at the hands of a woman was a disgrace, an irreparable blow to the warrior's name and reputation. The poet has taken full advantage of Sisera's mischance to immortalize the enemy and oppressor, who fell by a woman's wile and mighty stroke. For he is not merely recording the circumstances and outcome of the battle, but expressing exultation at victory over a hated foe, and special satisfaction at the scandalous demise of their leader. The dramatic and emotional possibilities of this drastic judgment on any who dared to oppose the will of Yahweh for the well-being of his people are exploited, not only in the

diminish the importance of the tradition, but simply to note that the two poems with which I am dealing say little if anything about the experience of Israel in this region. One must look to poems like the Song of Heshbon (Num. 21:27-30) and the Oracles of Balaam (Num. 23-24) for possible information on this point.

grim account of Sisera's death, but also in the story of Sisera's mother and her attendants vainly waiting for the news of expected victory, and nervously reassuring themselves with unlikely reasons for the delay.

6. The aftermath of victory is described, according to a new interpretation, in verses 6-7.[79] Freed from the intimidation and menace of Canaanite forces, the Israelites were able to regulate commerce in their territories, or in other words, intercept and plunder the caravans as they crossed over the mountain passes. Thanks to the great victory engineered by Deborah and Barak, the Israelites achieved a considerable measure of security, stability, and prosperity, in stark contrast with the deplorable conditions which prevailed before the battle.

7. Finally, there is the summons to everyone in Israel to sing and celebrate, to rehearse and proclaim the great triumph of Yahweh and his militia; there is also a proud if not boastful warning to kings and princes to give heed and pay close attention to this new and dominant force in international affairs (vv. 2-3, 9-11). The liturgical close (v. 31) makes it clear that the ancient victory, which gave Israel its place in the sun, has continuing and repeated relevance in the life of the community of faith.

SUMMATION

The two poems under consideration, the Song of the Sea and the Song of Deborah, are the oldest substantial compositions preserved in the Hebrew Bible, in my opinion, and both may be dated in the twelfth century B.C. As such, they offer both historical data and immediate reactions to the circumstances of Israel in its formative years. Always remembering that lyric poetry is not prose narrative, still less journalistic reporting, we may nevertheless learn much from these ancient sources, both from what they include and omit, and how they treat central and peripheral matters.

Essentially, the poems taken together confirm the historicity of key events, and establish their chronological relationships. Thus the Song of the Sea links the flight from Egypt with the deliverance of the people from the Egyptian chariotry at the Reed Sea. The victory at the sea is also tied to the march through the wilderness, and the settlement at the holy mountain, Sinai. The basic sequence—Exodus, Deliverance, Wanderings, Settlement at the sacred mountain—is attested by the poem. The Song of Deborah, for its part, confirms the settlement in the southern plateau (in the region of Seir//Edom), and the subsequent march north by Yahweh. The occupation of Canaan is presumed, but what is proclaimed now is decisive victory and effective control of that land.

The story of the twelfth century for Israel the people of Yahweh, according to the poems, is as follows:

[79]See discussion above.

1. Exodus from Egypt and deliverance at the sea.
2. Wandering through the wilderness and settlement at Sinai/Horeb.
3. Yahweh's march north at the head of his people.
4. The conversion of Israel, or parts of it, already in being as a confederation of tribes, to faith in Yahweh.
5. The struggle against Canaanite oppression, which comes to a climax in the battle at Taanach and results not only in the defeat of Sisera and his chariot army, but in the effective elimination of the Canaanites as a political force in the country. Israel, as the successor of Canaan, enters a new phase of its national existence.

The summary just given is in general conformity with the dominant tradition in the various prose strands of the Pentateuch or Primary History, and it may be wondered whether such an apparently harmonious result is really justified.[80] Actually, the placid surface is deceptive, and there are a number of radical divergences from the traditional reconstruction. A critical point is the continuity posited in the prose narrative from the patriarchs through the sojourn in Egypt, and the subsequent events culminating in the return to Canaan and settlement there. The poems offer a significantly different picture, revealing the tell-tale seams by which originally independent and disparate traditions have been sewn together.

In the Song of the Sea there is no mention of the patriarchs or any traditions derived from them. According to our analysis there is no direct link to the land of Canaan, either of a patriarchal past there, or of a promised future. So far as the poem is concerned, Yahweh is not just a new name for the God of the Fathers, but a new God.[81] He has no primary connections with the Fathers or the land of Canaan. Similarly, the people of Yahweh are just that, and not Israel at all, or as yet. They were redeemed and acquired (or created) by him, and owe their freedom and status to him. Their origins, which are not traced beyond their presence in Egypt, may well be complex, and included in the Exodus group may be elements which traced their descent to the patriarchs, and claimed kinship with Israelites; but they are defined in the poem only as Yahweh's people.[82]

[80]See the discussion by Craigie, "The Conquest and Early Hebrew Poetry," 76-93.

[81]See the discussion of Exod. 15:2, above. The issue is a subtle one, since in matters of religion and culture nothing is brand new: there are always antecedent models and influences. The origins of the term *yahweh* in a sacral context are to be found in the cultic traditions associated with the God El; on this point I agree fully with Albright and Cross; see Cross, *CMHE*, 1-77, especially the section on Yahweh and El. Albright's formulation of the matter is found in a variety of his writings; a useful summation appears in an unpublished manuscript on the "History of the Religion of Israel." In the earliest poems of Israel, however, Yahweh is a fully autonomous deity, independent of El, and with his own history.

[82]A link through the family of Moses with the tribe of Levi, and hence with Israel, is at least plausible and may be probable. Given a cultural-linguistic continuum, other connections between the Exodus and patriarchal groups are also likely.

Whatever may be Yahweh's own background, geographically, linguistically, or mythologically,[83] by the time he is introduced in the poems of the twelfth century, he is a distinct deity, independent of the chief gods of the Canaanite or Amorite pantheons.[84] In the poems, the term Yahweh is used only as a name, and not as a verb, which it is formally.[85] Even if the original form of the name was *yahweh-ʾēl*, as I believe, any ultimate connection with El, the principal deity of one or another of the northwest Semitic pantheons, has long since been severed.[86] In short, the Song of the Sea tells us of a new religion, and a new people, and a new experience.

We have argued for a date in the twelfth century, preferably in the first half of that century for the Song of the Sea. It is also our contention that the events which it reports occurred at the beginning of the same century. Taking the names and places, as well as the rest of the data at face value, there can hardly be any other conclusion. The mention of *pělešet* "Philistia" in precisely the same form in which it appears in the inscriptions of Rameses III (the earliest recorded references) strongly supports a twelfth-century date.[87] While Philistines were undoubtedly present in the area at an earlier date, there is no significant evidence for the systematic occupation of the southwestern coastland of Palestine until after the attacks on Egypt by the Sea Peoples had been repulsed. These date from the early years of Rameses III at the beginning of the twelfth century.[88]

[83]Cross's analysis of the origins and setting of the worship of Yahweh is persuasive, see *CMHE*, 71ff. It may be observed that Yahweh emerged from a description of El as the creator; the classic expression *yahweh ṣěbāʾōt* "he creates the armies" must be predicated of El, not Yahweh. Later editors misunderstood the construction, and saw in the word *yhwh* not a verb but the name of the deity; so they inserted the word *ʾělōhē* before *ṣěbāʾōt*, to ease what they considered to be a grammatical anomaly. See Albright's review of B. N. Wambacq, *Lʾépithète divine Jahvé Ṣěbāʾôt: Étude philologique, historique et exégétique*, in *JBL* 67 (1948) 377-81. Yahweh, for his part, is an *ʾēl* "god," and from early times he is so designated: e.g., *ʾēl ḥannūn wěraḥūm, ʾēl qannāʾ*.

[84]So far as I am aware, the term *yhwh*, as the name of a deity, has not turned up in any religious literature outside of Israel. All known nonbiblical occurrences are either explicit references to the God of Israel (e.g., *yhwh* in the Mesha Inscription), or are otherwise associated with the same God (e.g., the place-name in the region of Edom mentioned earlier).

[85]See my discussion in "Divine Names and Epithets."

[86]See my discussion of the original form of the name in "The Name of the God of Moses," *JBL* 79 (1960) 151-56. The revival of old formulas like *yahweh ṣěbāʾōt* and *yahweh šālōm* "he creates peace" (Judg. 6:24) in the period of the Judges reflects a rapprochement between the groups worshipping Yahweh and those worshipping El; see "Divine Names and Epithets," Appendix.

[87]See A. Malamat, "The Philistines and their Wars with Israel," chap. 8 in *Judges*, ed. Mazar, 164-79.

[88]See W. F. Albright's discussion, "The Sea Peoples in Palestine," chap. 33, pt. 1, in *Cambridge Ancient History* (Cambridge, 1973) vol. 2, 26-28, 33; Malamat, "The Philistines and their Wars with Israel," 170ff.

The flight from Egypt was followed immediately by the deliverance at the Reed Sea, which liberated the people of Yahweh from further Egyptian oppression or intimidation. The march across the plain and settlement at the holy mountain followed soon after. Here the community of God was established and cultic and civil life was organized.

At this point we postulate that a series of critical episodes affected the life of the community and drastically altered the course of its history.[89] Successful wars of defense may have encouraged the group to expand in a northerly direction.[90] At the same time, divisions and controversies may have produced severe strains in the community, which are amply reflected in a variety of prose accounts.[91] Dissidents were thus forced out and obliged to make their way to other places. One way or another, reports of the new movement along with advocates and adherents reached civilized centers on both sides of the Jordan. Undoubtedly visitors came south to observe and left to proclaim the wonder of what they had seen.[92]

The response to the new faith would have been mixed, and this situation is reflected in the literary sources. Yahwism apparently took hold among the *bĕnē yiśrāʾēl* "the sons of Israel," a federation of ten tribes then occupying the hill country of central and northern Palestine. It was subject to various forms of political and economic pressure by the rulers of the Canaanite city-states which claimed possession of that territory. After a series of engagements which began in an earlier period (fourteenth-thirteenth centuries),[93] the Israelites under new leadership represented by Deborah and Barak, and as a result of Yahweh's

[89]Other poems in the Pentateuch and the prose narratives undoubtedly preserve historical details of Israel's experience in the wilderness and subsequent march northward, but a precise chronology or exact determination of the events eludes us.

[90]The reliability of the traditions concerning Og and Sihon has been questioned repeatedly, and most recently and vigorously by J. Van Seters, "The Conquest of Sihon's Kingdom: A Literary Examination," *JBL* 91 (1972) 182-97. In spite of Van Seters's direct challenge, I believe that the poem preserved in Num. 21:27-30 is very old and supports the tradition; see P. D. Hanson, "The Song of Heshbon and David's *NÎR*," *HTR* 61 (1968) 297-320.

[91]For example, the stories of the murmurings in the wilderness, of the golden calf, of the controversial report of the spies, of the rebellion of Dathan and Abiram, and of Korah, and of the episode of Baal-Peor.

[92]The story of Balaam, who was brought in to curse and remained to bless and praise the unique people of God, is a prime example. While the Oracles of Balaam can hardly be dated in their present form before the eleventh century, they doubtless contain accurate historical information about the early period of Israel's existence; see my discussion in "Divine Names and Epithets." The isolated sayings at the end of Num. 24 may be somewhat older than the longer poems; in Albright's judgment, they reflect the movements of the Sea Peoples toward the end of the thirteenth century B.C. (see "The Oracles of Balaam," *JBL* 63 [1944] 207-33, esp. 227-31).

[93]The stories in Joshua, and especially Judg. 1, may reflect the struggles of pre-Yahwistic Israel to gain and maintain a foothold in Canaan, as well as later activity in those areas.

personal intervention, were able finally to overthrow Canaanite authority and eliminate the oppressive system under which they had suffered.[94]

The stories in Joshua and especially Judg. 1 may well reflect efforts by the tribes individually and in various groupings to establish a footing on the west bank of the Jordan in the fourteenth-thirteenth centuries, before their conversion to Yahwism. Their God, El Shadday, probably of Amorite origin and associated with the patriarchs who migrated from Harran in the Middle Bronze Age, was identified with El, the chief god of the Canaanite pantheon, as seen in the adoption of certain epithets: El Elyon, El Olam.[95] He was typically the God of revelation, law, and justice, bound by covenant ties of promise and obligation to his people. The claim to possession of the land was based upon the patriarchal presence in various localities, certain shrines dedicated to El, and the tradition of a divine commitment to the Fathers. The tribal league was organized around a common religious commitment to the patriarchal God, who was worshipped in these places, e.g., Shechem and, above all, Bethel. We may suppose that patriarchal religion was reactivated by the new faith in Yahweh, and the community was infused with a new spirit of militancy which won the day and established the federation as master of the former Canaanite enclave.

A similar process may be posited for the southern group of tribes, including Judah and Simeon, where Yahwism must also have penetrated, as reflected in archaic traditions preserved in Judg. 1 and 3, and Josh. 15.[96] Many of the connecting pieces are missing, however, so a detailed reconstruction is not yet possible.

Cross has recently proposed a new view of the history of the priesthood in Israel on the basis of an ancient rivalry between a Mosaic or Mushite priestly group and one derived from Aaron.[97] The Mushite priesthood apparently had its point of origin and headquarters in the far south, in Yahweh's homeland; but it also established centers in Israel, in the northern part of Canaan, at Shiloh and Dan among other sites. The Aaronids, on the other hand, were in control in the sanctuaries in the area between, stretching from Hebron in the south to Bethel in the central part of the country, and including Jerusalem. Lines of demarcation could hardly be maintained rigidly, but in general the Mushite priests would have been responsible for the form of Yahwism adopted in the north, while the Aaronids would have determined the character of the faith in

[94]See G. E. Mendenhall, "The Hebrew Conquest of Palestine," *BA* 25 (1962) 66-87; reprinted in *The Biblical Archaeologist Reader* 3 (New York, 1970) 100-120. For a recent discussion of the Conquest traditions, see Weippert, *SITP*.

[95]See Cross's discussion of these epithets, *CMHE*, 3-12; M. Haran, "The Religion of the Patriarchs, an Attempt at a Synthesis," *ASTI* 4 (1965) 30-55; also "Divine Names and Epithets."

[96]The Caleb traditions, including the story of Othniel (Judg. 1:11-21, and 3:7-11), must be very old; as Albright has shown, there is an archaic poem embedded in the text: Judg. 1:14-15 = Josh. 15:18-19 (*YGC*, 48).

[97]*CMHE*, 195-215.

the south. The Song of Deborah in particular would have been a product of Mosaic Yahwism, reflecting a special interest in Jael, whose family was related to the Mushite priesthood.[98]

We can set up a series of correlations as a general guide to the division between Mushites and Aaronids:

	Mushite	*Aaronid*
Geographic distribution	North (and far south)	South (and central)
Collective designation	*bĕnē yiśrāʾēl* Israel	*bĕnē yaʿăqōb* (?) Judah
Chief deity	Yahweh	El (with Yahwistic component)
Iconography	Cherubim	Bull images
Origins	Exodus, Wanderings, Sinai	Patriarchs Promise of the land

By the time the formal twelve-tribe pattern emerged in the eleventh-century Testaments of Jacob (Gen. 49) and Moses (Deut. 33),[99] several significant changes from the Song of Deborah may be noted:

1. For "Israel, the people of Yahweh" in the Song of Deborah, there is now a fixed pair, "Jacob//Israel," which is used repeatedly in the two Testaments (and in the Oracles of Balaam, which we have also dated to the eleventh century).[100] In other words, the ten-tribe league called Israel has become a twelve- (or thirteen-) tribe federation called properly Jacob-Israel, though the term Israel could be used for the expanded group. In time the two major units would be identified as Israel and Judah, though the former would continue in use as the more generic term.

2. With respect to divine nomenclature, we find that the nearly exclusive use of the name Yahweh, characteristic of the twelfth-century poems, has yielded to an expanded list of names including in particular the patriarchal designation, El, along with the epithets for this deity recorded in the Book of Genesis: Shaddai, Elyon, Olam.[101] These poems reflect an accommodation or blending of Mosaic and patriarchal traditions: Yahweh and El have come together as a single God. Such a development must also reflect political adjustments of some kind. The most obvious is the union of northern and

[98]On this relationship, see B. Mazar, "The Sanctuary of Arad and the Family of Hobab the Kenite," *JNES* 24 (1965) 297-303; and *CMHE*, 201.

[99]On the dating of the Testaments of Jacob and Moses, see "Divine Names and Epithets." As Albright maintains, individual blessings may be considerably older (see *YGC*, 265-66). I would now hold that the incorporation of Judah in the lists reflects the attempts to amalgamate the northern and southern groups. These efforts were initiated in the eleventh century, perhaps by Samuel and Saul, but did not reach fruition until the time of David.

[100]See discussion in n. 92, above.

[101]See discussion in "Divine Names and Epithets."

southern tribes to form a larger and more powerful confederation. The occasion for such unifying activities can only have been the emergence of a greater threat than the one posed by the now defeated Canaanites. By the end of the twelfth century, the Philistines had established themselves as the major power in Palestine, and with the collapse of other resistance, the Israelites had to face this enemy alone.

The process of consolidation must have been encouraged by the severe pressures exerted by the Philistines, and it may have come to a head after the fall of Shiloh around 1050 B.C. Under the leadership of Samuel, the Israelites were still unable to offer effective resistance, but he initiated the process which led to success. First, he established a permanent executive authority in the person of Saul, the *nāgīd* "chieftain." Second, David, a Judahite military genius, was recruited as Saul's lieutenant, thus combining the forces of north and south. If the anointing of David by Samuel has a basis in fact, we may regard it as the proleptic or actual coronation of David as king of Judah, just as Samuel anointed Saul to be king of Israel. We may also see in David's marriage to Michal, Saul's daughter, a diplomatic attempt to cement the ties between Israel and Judah, looking forward to a merger not only of families but of states. The latter was in fact achieved by David after the collapse of the house of Saul.[102]

[102]See discussion above.

EARLY ISRAELITE POETRY AND HISTORICAL RECONSTRUCTIONS

In a series of papers of which this is the third, I have presented the thesis that the early poetry of Israel constitutes a prime source for the reconstruction of Israel's history and that these materials have, to a considerable extent, been neglected or misinterpreted and misapplied to the questions at hand.[1] In my view, this corpus of poetry should be restudied in an attempt to recover authentic historical information, to supplement, correct, and revise existing models of the early Israelite experience. In order to accomplish this objective, several problems need to be resolved, including the following: (1) To determine the scope and date of the corpus; I note in passing that the date of a poem is not necessarily correlative with the accuracy of its contents. An early date does not guarantee historical validity or precision, a late date does not exclude them. In general, however, the earlier the date, the greater the reliability of the contents. (2) To assess the contents of the poems for their historical usefulness. It is important to bear in mind that poetry is not prose, that we cannot expect in the poems to have a journalistic account of events and circumstances, or a chronicle produced by a historian as a result of research and reflection. There are, however, corresponding advantages in poetry roughly contemporary with the events and circumstances: songs often capture the spirit of the occasion and focus on what is centrally important. Inevitably they also contain direct factual information, which can be appropriated by the careful historian. (3) To cope with methodological issues, such as the comparative value of arguments from evidence and arguments from silence. The former as a class are superior to the latter, but occasionally inferences based on the absence of data can be quite compelling.

Then the relationship between the poems and the prose narratives needs to be considered. Traditionally, the approach has been harmonistic, and in practice this has meant the subordination, if not suppression, of the poetic tradition, in favor of the more comprehensive and coherent prose account. As a result there has been a marked tendency to minimize or ignore the contribution of the poems to historical reconstructions. Without elevating a contrary procedure to the level of principle, namely, that there is a necessary conflict between the poems and the prose accounts, nevertheless, each should

[1]The two earlier papers are now in print: (1) "Divine Names and Titles in Early Hebrew Poetry," in F. M. Cross et al., eds., *Magnalia Dei* (Essays in Honor of G. Ernest Wright; New York: Doubleday and Co. 1976) 55-107; (2) "Early Israelite History in the Light of Early Israelite Poetry," in H. Goedicke and J. J. M. Roberts, eds., *Unity and Diversity: Essays in the History, Literature and Religion of the Ancient Near East* (Baltimore: Johns Hopkins University, 1975) 3-35. Other studies in the series are in preparation.

be dealt with independently of the other and analyzed, interpreted, and evaluated in terms of its own content and structure. In the general comparison of poetic and prosaic sources, two points may be made: (1) that the early poems are closer to the events than any surviving prose accounts (e.g., the Song of Deborah in Judges 5, and the prose account in Judges 4; the Song of the Sea in Exodus 15 and the prose account in Exodus 14; (2) the transmission of poetry tends to be more faithful than that of prose, even though the former may be predominantly an oral phenomenon and the latter a written tradition. This is so because word selection and placement as well as rhythmic and stylistic factors are central in poetic composition and contribute to the preservation of the material in its original form. Contrariwise, except for mechanical blunders, it is easier to protect the sense of a prose composition, while indulging in editorial revisions.

There have been numerous studies of individual poems in the premonarchic corpus, and important historical inferences have been drawn from them: I need only mention the classic studies of W. F. Albright and those of his pupils.[2] Few scholars, if any, have doubted the importance of the Song of Deborah as a historical source, difficult as the poem is to interpret, or that it mirrors the circumstances and occurrences at a particular time and place in the period of the Judges (probably the latter half of the 12th century B.C.). In a very vivid way it brings us into direct contact with the actions and thoughts, the manners and morals of particular people in that context. The same would be true of the Lament of David over Saul and Jonathan of a later time. It is our contention, however, that there is a substantial corpus of such poetry, which can be profitably considered, and that valuable historical information can be gleaned from this material. Furthermore, any general reconstruction of early Israelite history would have to incorporate the data of the poems, and in other ways deal with the picture they present.[3]

The corpus of which we have been speaking consists essentially of the pre-monarchic poems which have been preserved in the biblical text, having survived the wholesale reordering of priorities and restructuring of Israelite traditions which took place under the impact of the monarchy.[4] As a result of such direct and deliberate influence, especially in the days of David and Solomon, the great prose narrative was composed and compiled, and subsequently, the other literary strands, which together make up the Primary History of the Hebrew Bible (i.e., the Torah and Former Prophets). Our concern, however, is with the principal poems, which antedate these prose works and, we believe, escaped revision at the hands of monarchistic scribes.

[2]The latest treatment of the corpus by W. F. Albright is to be found in his *Yahweh and the Gods of Canaan* (New York: Doubleday, 1969), especially chap. 1. Other pertinent studies by him, his students, and other scholars are listed in the two papers mentioned above.

[3]The paper on "Early Israelite History" specifically addresses this problem.

[4]All the major literary strands of the Primary History (Genesis through Kings), come from the period after the formation of the monarchy and reflect its influence. For the significance of this basic change in Israel's experience and condition, see G. E. Mendenhall, *The Tenth Generation* (Baltimore: Johns Hopkins University, 1973) chap. 7.

While the poems have been incorporated into the larger literary complex, we contend that they are independent of it.[5]

On the basis of the work of many predecessors and contemporaries, chiefly that of my teacher W. F. Albright and my colleague and friend of long standing, F. M. Cross (including his independent studies and our collaborative efforts), certain basic conclusions may be drawn about this corpus of poetry. It consists of five major poems, along with a few small pieces and some fragments.[6] These are to be found in the Primary History as follows:

The Testament of Jacob	(Genesis 49)
The Song of the Sea	(Exodus 15)
The Oracles of Balaam	(Numbers 23-24)
The Testament of Moses	(Deuteronomy 33)
The Song of Deborah	(Judges 5)

This is a minimal list, but I think a reliable one. In agreement with a growing consensus among scholars, I hold that all of these poems are pre-monarchic in composition and may be dated in the 12th and 11th centuries B.C. with considerable confidence.[7] In general my views agree with those of Albright (which are elaborated in his volume, *Yahweh and the Gods of Canaan*), which will hardly come as a surprise, but there are some important differences. Thus Albright dated the Song of the Sea (Exodus 15) to the early part of the 13th century, while in my judgment it must be dated a century later, i.e., in the early 12th.[8] I may add, in passing, that his date depends upon a critical emendation, the only one he insists on in the poem, but all the more revealing (and unjustified) for that reason.[9] He included the Song of Moses (Deuteronomy 32) in this corpus, following Eissfeldt's original proposal concerning the relationship of Deuteronomy 32 to Psalm 78 and the dates of composition of these poems.[10] It seems to me that the Song of Moses cannot be earlier than the 10th-9th centuries, and therefore it should not be included in any pre-monarchic corpus.[11]

[5]The arguments and evidence for this conclusion are summarized in the two papers mentioned, which in turn cite books and articles by a sizable group of scholars.

[6]In addition to the major poems cited, mention may be made of Exod 17:16; Num 6:24-26; 10:35-36; 12:6-8; 21:17-18, 27-30; Deut 34:7b; Josh 10:12-13.

[7]See the discussion in "Divine Names and Titles."

[8]For Albright's latest view of the Song of the Sea, cf. *Yahweh and the Gods of Canaan*, 12-13. For mine and other views, see "Divine Names and Titles" and "Early Israelite History."

[9]Albright, *Yahweh and the Gods of Canaan*, 45-47. See his earlier comment in Cross and D. N. Freedman, "The Song of Miriam," *JNES* 14 (1955) 249; cf. our mediating remarks, p. 248, n. 44.

[10]Albright, *Yahweh and the Gods of Canaan*, 17-19; O. Eissfeldt, "Das Lied Moses Deuteronomium 32:1-43 und das Lehrgedicht Asaphs Psalm 78 samt einer Analyse der Umgebung des Mose-Liedes," *Verh. Sächs. Acad. Wiss. Leipzig, Phil.-hist. Kl.*, Vol. 104, No. 5 (Berlin, 1958) 26-41.

[11]See the discussion in "Divine Names and Titles" and references provided there, especially G. E. Wright, "The Lawsuit of God: A Form-Critical Study of Deuteronomy 32," in B. W. Anderson and W. Harrelson, eds., *Israel's Prophetic Heritage* (New York: Harper & Brothers, 1962) 26-67.

With regard to the corpus of poetry as defined, our next objectives are to organize them according to date of composition, i.e., to establish a sequence-dating, relative in terms of order, absolute in terms of external events and circumstances; and to classify their contents with relation to each other and in chronological order. At the end of this process we will offer a hypothetical outline of the principal events in the early history of Israel.

In the two earlier papers, I attempted to fix the dates of composition of a dozen poems (including the five in our corpus) about which there has been a good deal of discussion and more than a little controversy; and I also tried to reconstruct in a very partial way the history of Israel in the 12th century on the basis of an analysis of two of the poems in the list (Exodus 15 and Judges 5).

Briefly summarized, my conclusion about the dates was that the two earliest poems are the Song of the Sea and the Song of Deborah, both being composed in the 12th century. Of the two, the Song of the Sea is earlier, coming from the first half of the century, and the Song of Deborah is later, coming from the second half of the same century. The other three poems all belong to the 11th century, with the order of composition less easy to determine and not directly pertinent for our purposes. Perhaps Genesis 49 is somewhat earlier in the century and Deuteronomy 33 somewhat later, with Numbers 23-24 somewhere around the middle.

With respect to the contents of the poems and the historical situations presupposed or reflected in them, the chronological order is somewhat different. There is always some time lapse between an occurrence and the report of it — in the case of a poem composed chiefly to celebrate such an event the time-span may be very short indeed, a matter of days or weeks — and the gap may vary widely from poem to poem. On the basis of previous examination of the two 12th-century poems (Exodus 15 and Judges 5), and current investigation of the three remaining poems in our group (Genesis 49, Numbers 23-24, and Deuteronomy 33), I propose the following chronological order according to content (in contrast with composition):

1. Genesis 49. Pre-Mosaic, non-Yahwistic: late 14th-early 13th century.
2. Exodus 15. Mosaic, Yahwistic: around 1200, or early 12th century.
3. Numbers 23-24: 12th century, a little later than the situation in Exodus 15.
4. Deuteronomy 33: 12th century, roughly contemporary with Numbers 23-24.
5. Judges 5: 12th century, latter half.

This arrangement happens to agree with the order of the poems in the Bible, i.e., from Genesis to Judges. It shows that the editor or compiler of the biblical narrative had essentially the same insight into and appreciation of the historical background of the poems. The attributions of authorship cannot be defended, to be sure: e.g., in both Deuteronomy 33 and Judges 5 the assignment of authorship is based on the occurrence of the name of the principal figure in the poem (i.e., Moses in Deuteronomy 33 and Deborah in Judges 5) but involves a misinterpretation of his or her role in the poem. In neither case can the poem properly be attributed to the person named, in contrast with the Lament over Saul and Jonathan, which can safely be assigned to David himself. There is no reason, however, to question the validity of the reference or the proximate relation of the poem to the events described.

All this means is that the editor or compiler of the great prose work correctly understood the place of the poems in the developing history of Israel and put them in a plausible place in the narrative. The organization of the narrative also illustrates a major, if questionable, conviction on the part of the compiler of the biblical narrative, namely that the twelve-tribe confederation was already in being in the Wilderness Wanderings and that Moses was directly related to it. The assumption was part of a larger synthesis which combined patriarchal traditions with the narratives of the Exodus and Wanderings, Conquest, and Settlement, integrating everything around the themes of promise and fulfillment, and the migration from Mesopotamia to Canaan to Egypt and back by way of the wilderness to permanent settlement in the Holy Land.

A detailed examination of the poems produces a somewhat different picture of the sequence of events and of the relationship of the several narrative strands:

(1) The Song of the Sea links the tradition of the Exodus from Egypt with the crossing of the sea and the march through the wilderness to the holy habitation of Yahweh, the sacred mountain of the deity. There is nothing about a tribal confederation (the name Israel does not occur in the poem) and no connection with patriarchal traditions or promises about the land of Canaan. On the contrary, the horizon of the poem is limited to the southern wilderness, the traditional home of Yahweh.[12]

(2) The Oracles of Balaam share the same outlook and horizon as the Song of the Sea. Terror-stricken Moab of the Song of the Sea is the focus of attention, and its leader summons Balaam to counterpoise his magic to that of Yahweh. The results are predictable, but the exact location of Israel remains uncertain. While the prose narrative places Israel in the plains of Moab, and that is a possibility to be reckoned with, the description of Israel dwelling apart, presumably at an oasis, in its tents, reminds us of the description in Exodus 15 of the wilderness habitation. Egypt and the Exodus are the immediate past references, and Canaan remains beyond the concern of the poet. There is no substantial overlap in the names of peoples and places between the two poems (especially if we include the addenda to Numbers 24, vv 20-24). As the compiler correctly recognized, Israel is not yet settled in its permanent home.

[12]See the presentation of evidence in "Early Israelite History."

(3) The Song of Deborah is linked with Exodus 15 through Yahweh's march from Sinai to Canaan. Sinai is the point of departure (Egypt and the Exodus and the march through the wilderness are not included), and Canaan and the great struggle with the Canaanite city-states are the immediate target of the poet. Through the intervention of Yahweh the One of Sinai, his people Israel, organized into a confederation of tribes, is victorious in this life-or-death struggle. The tribal list in Deborah ties that poem to the two remaining poems in our group, the Testaments of Jacob (Genesis 49) and Moses (Deuteronomy 33). The order, relationships, and historical implications of these three early tribal lists are the next subjects of our inquiry.

As noted, the tribal group is identified as Israel in the Song of Deborah. An Israel, presumably not very different in composition is mentioned in the Marniptah stele of the latter part of the 13th century, so the presence of this community in the holy land at that time seems reasonably certain.[13] In fact, an earlier constitution of this community may be posited on the basis of information provided in the book of Genesis. The name itself is assigned to the patriarchal era as the alternate designation of Jacob, the last of the Fathers and the eponymous founder of the twelve-tribe league. It is reasonable to apply the statements in Gen 33:18-20 to the federation and observe that the God of the league is called El (i.e., the patriarchal deity) and that at one time its headquarters were at Shechem, whose well-known shrine was dedicated to El, *baᶜal bĕrît*.[14] The presumption is that the league traced its origins to the patriarchs, or at least to Jacob (the wandering Aramean), and that it was non-Yahwistic and pre-Mosaic in its initial stages. This view is supported by the tradition preserved in the Exodus narrative, that the twelve-tribe structure was already in existence before the departure from Egypt and in particular before the introduction of the name Yahweh to the Israelites by Moses. The narrator assumed that this development from individual to tribe took place by natural generation in Egypt, whereas the evidence suggests that the tribal league was organized in pre-Mosaic times in the land of Canaan, quite possibly under the aegis of Jacob himself, and dedicated to the worship and service of the patriarchal El, one of whose titles was *ᵓăbīr yaᶜăqōb*. It is worth noting that the name Israel does not occur in the Song of the Sea, that those who departed from Egypt, crossed the sea, and came to the mountain sanctuary are called the people whom Yahweh redeemed and purchased. But there is no tribal league there, and they are not called Israel. The combination: Israel, the people of Yahweh, occurs for the first time in the Song of Deborah; that expression is reflected in the statement that Yahweh came from Sinai to Canaan and presumably involved the conversion of the league (or the major part of it) to faith in the God of Moses.

[13]A convenient translation is given in *ANET*, pp. 376-78.

[14]See the discussion by Cross in *Canaanite Myth and Hebrew Epic* (Cambridge, MA: Harvard University, 1973) 39 and nn. 156-58; 47 and n. 16; 49 and n. 23.

Turning back to the tribal lists, there are six possible arrangements of the tribal groupings preserved in the three poems.[15] According to the previous analysis, the oldest of the three is Judges 5, which we date to the latter part of the 12th century, whereas both of the others, Genesis 49 and Deuteronomy 33 have been placed in the 11th century. If we were to assume that the chronological order of the lists was the same as the order of the composition of the poems, then we would start with Judges 5 and try to explain the development of the other two from the earlier grouping. We would posit a ten-tribe league (since only ten tribes were mentioned in Deborah) at the beginning of our series, which was expanded to eleven in Deuteronomy 33 (or possibly twelve if we do not accept the consolidation of two tribes, Ephraim and Manasseh [or Machir] into Joseph, mentioned earlier), and twelve in Genesis 49. Such developments are possible, though explanations are difficult to come by, especially since the two testaments are roughly comparable in date, and yet their lists are apparently incompatible. Some other hypothesis would seem to be required, and without running through all the remaining possibilities, I wish to suggest another approach to the relationships among the three lists. An incidental finding in the course of the sequence-dating analysis of the divine names and titles used in early poetry was that Genesis 49 is unique among the poems with divine names (n.b., David's Lament over Saul and Jonathan makes no reference to the deity, at least by name or title), in that the name Yahweh does not occur in any of the blessings (it appears once in v 18, commonly regarded as a liturgical aside).[16] The absence of the name Yahweh and the presence of the divine names derived from patriarchal times (e.g., El, Shadday, possibly ᶜAl, vv 25-26) suggests rather strongly that the tradition embodied in this material is pre-Mosaic or at the very least earlier than the time of Deborah and the confirmed association between Yahweh and the tribal league. The inference to be drawn is that the list in Genesis 49 is the earliest, with the others following. On further reflection it seems to me somewhat more likely that Deuteronomy 33 follows Genesis 49 and precedes Judges 5, but the case is hardly decisive. The critical points are those which involve changes from one list to the next, especially omissions or alterations in status. Since neither time nor space will permit a detailed examination of the three lists here, we will concentrate attention on the following entries (1) Joseph, including Ephraim and Manasseh (or Machir as in Judges 5); (2) Judah; (3) Simeon and Levi.

With respect to Joseph and its subdivisions, the order of development would seem to be from the single tribe Joseph (Genesis 49) to the two subtribes within the larger unit (Deuteronomy 33) and then the emergence of separate tribes, in this case Ephraim and Machir (from Manasseh). The reverse would be more difficult to rationalize, especially since the Joseph oracles in Genesis 49 and Deuteronomy 33 have very archaic features: e.g., the ABC // ABD pattern in Gen 49:22 (*ben pōrāt yōsēp // ben pōrāt ᶜălē-ᶜayin*),

[15]On the order of composition and the dating of the two testaments, see Albright, *Yahweh and the Gods of Canaan*, 17-20, and Addenda, 265-66.

[16]See the discussion in "Divine Names and Titles."

and the specification of Joseph's origin in Mesopotamia, or the identification of Yahweh as the bush-denizen in Deut 33:16, an allusion to the Sinai (*sĕnēh*-bush) tradition. The increase and expansion of the Joseph tribe is described in the book of Joshua, and in view of tribal losses elsewhere, the division into two sections makes sense.[17] In later formulations of the list of tribes, both traditions were preserved: in some lists Joseph occupies a single place, in others, Ephraim and Manasseh hold two spots, and in some instances, the three are grouped as in Deuteronomy 33.[18]

With regard to Judah, the evolution, or devolution, seems to proceed from Genesis 49, where Judah is accorded an exalted status, being promoted over the heads of three older but undeserving brothers, Reuben, Simeon, and Levi. It is tempting to associate this fulsome blessing with the emergence of David and the preeminent status of Judah at the time of the united monarchy.[19] There can be no doubt that the royal scribes were happy to preserve this piece of Judahite propaganda and to exploit its sentiments to the full in the support of the Davidic dynasty. But I think that Albright is correct in denying that there is any explicit connection with the monarchy in the material or that it is a subtle retrojection from the days of David and Solomon.[20] Typical monarchical terminology is lacking, and there is nothing in the blessing beyond what is said of Joseph in the same testament. The transition from Genesis 49 to Deuteronomy 33 is drastic and surely implies a very serious crisis in the fortunes of Judah. It appears that the tribe has been cut off from its fellows, and there is danger that the separation will be permanent.[21] By the time we reach Judges 5, Judah is no longer on the list; it is unavailable for service in the cause of Yahweh and Deborah and is not even summoned. Presumably the worst has happened, and Judah is no longer sufficiently independent or autonomous to be reckoned among the tribes of the confederation. May we interpret the situation in the light of the Samson story and presume that Judah is now under the control of the Philistines, in short part of a different political power structure?[22] The restoration of Judah and its reunion with the Israelite confederation would have been a major objective of the strategy of leaders like Samuel and Saul, but it would not be fully achieved until the Judahite David shattered the Philistine hegemony over Judah and much of Israel.

With respect to Simeon and Levi, these brother tribes are roundly condemned by the speaker in Gen 49:5-7. Whether this statement represents an intertribal judgment for misbehavior in violation of basic protocols,

[17] Josh 17:14-18; cf. Josh 14:4.

[18] See the discussion in "Early Israelite History."

[19] For older views, see the discussion in J. Skinner, *A Critical and Exegetical Commentary on Genesis* (The International Critical Commentary, rev. ed., New York: Scribner's, 1925) 518-25.

[20] *Yahweh and the Gods of Canaan*, 19, n. 49.

[21] For an earlier discussion of this point, see Cross and Freedman, "The Blessing of Moses," *JBL* 67 (1948) 193 and 203, esp. n. 27.

[22] Cf. Judg 15:11.

comparable to the internecine battle between the tribal confederation and Benjamin (reported in Judges 19-21) or a veiled reflection of some externally administered defeat, it is clear that the oracle forebodes disaster for these unholy brother tribes. That catastrophe is reflected in the lists of Deuteronomy 33 and Judges 5. Simeon has disappeared entirely from both lists, and we may suppose that some calamity engulfed it. There may be a faint echo of Simeon in the oracle addressed to Judah in Deut 33:7 (note the opening verb *šĕmaᶜ* which seems to play on the name Simeon: *šimᶜōn*); since Simeon's territory (after the calamity?) was located entirely inside of Judah, a single oracle may have encompassed both tribes.[23] Since there is no record of Simeon's subsequent revival as a geographic entity, we conclude that the sequence from life to death, from Genesis 49 to Deuteronomy 33 and Judges 5, is logically and chronologically correct and that the reverse is highly unlikely.

The history of Levi is more complicated, but at the beginning we may suppose it shared a common destiny with Simeon. At least Judges 5 gives them equal treatment — silence. Deuteronomy 33, however, offers a novelty. Levi has undergone a transformation, and the secular tribe, denounced and demolished for intransigent violence, has become the stalwart defender of the Mosaic faith in Yahweh.[24] This is the only tribal oracle with an explicit and necessary association with the wilderness wanderings. If the oracle may be trusted as both authentic and ancient, then we have here the transference of tribal status to a group which participated in the Exodus and Wanderings, without, however, a comparable territorial allocation. In Judges 5, there is no mention of Levi, so presumably it did not constitute a tribe for the purpose of the song and battle which is its main subject. Whether Levites were involved at all is not clear, but if they were, it was not on the same basis as the other groups. The status of Levi remained a problem for the biblical historians, and it is treated differently in different lists — generally in two ways reflecting the distinction between Genesis 49 (i.e., as a regular tribe among the twelve) and Deuteronomy 33 (i.e., as a special group, with unique responsibilities for the shrine and ark, but without territorial rights comparable to the other tribes). In any event, it would be much more difficult to explain the history of the tribe of Levi if we were to begin with Judges 5 (i.e., from non-existence to a schizoid split between piety and impious violence) or Deuteronomy 33 (i.e., from a sacral status as guardian of the ark and other holy things to a secular tribe condemned for its atrocities and a period of non-existence along the way). Since in this case we know that Levi officially constituted a sacral group associated with the tabernacle and temple, the status reflected in Deuteronomy 33 must be toward the end of the development rather than the beginning.[25]

[23]Josh 19:1-9.

[24]Deut 33:8-10.

[25]In the case of Levi, the most natural order would seem to be: Genesis 49 (a secular tribe); Judges 5 (no longer functional or in existence); Deuteronomy 33 (reconstituted as a sacral entity,

With respect to the other tribes, comparison of the oracles and comments on a cursory basis does not point to any clear chronological lines of development. Closer inspection may reveal otherwise, but we can profitably leave that for another presentation. It remains now to summarize the findings, draw some tentative conclusions, and pose a few questions to those in associated disciplines. Answers to the latter should dispose of the theories presented here in one way or another, but more importantly they may provide a solid basis on which to build a more attractive and convincing reconstruction of early Israelite history.

Our proposals concerning the history of Israel from the late patriarchal period to the end of the pre-monarchic era are as follows:

(1) The organization of a twelve-tribe league denominated Israel and occupying territory in the land of Canaan may be dated some time in the period between the end of the Amarna Age (ca. 1350) and the middle of the 13th century. Since the earliest non-biblical reference to this group is supplied by the Marniptah stele, with the indication that it was of recent origin, I would be inclined to date the emergence of the federation at the end of the 14th or beginning of the 13th century. The founding of the confederation was credited to an immediate ancestor, Jacob, who may well have been a figure of the Late Bronze Age. The origins of some of these groups in Mesopotamia are explicitly attested (e.g., the major group called Joseph) and may be presumed for all or most. The common God of this group is El (Shadday), the deity specifically associated with Abraham, Isaac, and Jacob. The central sanctuary may well have been at Shechem, and the formal relationship between league and deity may have been defined in terms of a covenant.[26]

(2) If we take seriously the statement of the Marniptah stele, an Egyptian punitive expedition around 1230 overran much of Palestine, devastated a number of cities, and put the Israelite league out of commission. While the language of the inscription is typically hyperbolic and we know that reports of the demise of Israel were exaggerated and premature to say the least, it would be reasonable to infer that the confederation suffered a damaging blow, which is reflected in the curtailed lists of Deuteronomy 33 and Judges 5. The apparent disappearance of the tribe of Simeon and somewhat similar fate of Levi suggest that the damage was real and that Israel was a long time in recovering from it. By the middle of the 12th century, Judah should be added

with special status). If, however, the connection between Levi and the wilderness experience is authentic, then the order we have posited is correct and the omission in the Song of Deborah is to be explained in another way (as in all likelihood the omission of Judah).

[26]In the light of convincing evidence for the destruction of Shechem in the late Bronze Age (ca. 1300 B.C.) presented by L. Toombs at the Symposium in Jerusalem, it is plausible and attractive to associate the event with the statement in Gen 48:22, to be rendered, following E. A. Speiser in *Genesis* ("The Anchor Bible"; New York: Doubleday & Co., 1964) 356: "As for me, I give you, as the one above your brothers, Shechem, which I captured from the Amorites with my sword and bow." Also deserving attention is the passage in Gen 33:20, "And he [Jacob] erected there [i.e., before Shechem] an altar, and he named it [i.e., dedicated it to] 'El, the God of Israel.'"

to the list of casualties, being cut off from the main group of tribes. Perhaps we find an echo of the tradition preserved in the Samson narratives in which we learn that Judah was subject to the power of the Philistines. The Song of Deborah describes a league of ten northern tribes, which coincides in all important respects with the secessionists at the time of the death of Solomon and accession of Rehoboam. There is a continuous tradition concerning this group from the time of Deborah until the formation of the northern kingdom, Israel — e.g., after the death of Saul, the northern group anoints Ishbaal to be king of Israel, while the southerners select David to be King of Judah (2 Sam 2:1-11). Later on the same distinction is made between northerners and southerners, when David returns to power following the death of Absalom (2 Sam 19:41-44).

(3) Around 1200, or shortly thereafter, the Exodus from Egypt occurred. According to the tradition, Moses led a congeries of people out of bondage to freedom, more specifically from Egypt, across the Reed Sea, to the mountain of God, there to constitute a new community, the people of Yahweh. It is altogether possible, in my opinion, that population elements of the Israelite confederation escaped to Egypt or were brought there as slaves and subsequently joined the Exodus group under Moses. It seems clear that the divine name Yahweh was learned by Moses during his sojourn in the southeastern wilderness, in the general region of Sinai, Paran, Seir, Midian, Edom, in accordance with a persistent tradition in the Bible (preserved in the early poems, including Exodus 15, Judges 5, Deuteronomy 33, and Psalm 68). This name was not known in Canaan or among the Israelite tribes in that area. It is the Mosaic group that brought the religion of Yahweh to Canaan and Israel, and it is only from the time of the Song of Deborah onward that Yahweh is identified as the God of Israel, then located in Canaan; the Song specifically asserts that Yahweh came from the southland, and this view is confirmed by the prologue to the Blessing of Moses (Deuteronomy 33). The date of the Exodus can be fixed from the reference in the Song of the Sea to the four nations which are described as observers of the crossing of the sea and the annihilation of the Egyptian chariot force (Exod 15:14-15). They are described as being struck dumb with terror by this spectacular display of Yahweh's might. These four — Philistia, Edom, Moab, and Canaan — can only have coexisted in their established territories during the 12th century B.C. The Philistines are not mentioned by name any earlier, while the Canaanites presumably did not survive as a national entity beyond the 12th century.[27] Edom and Moab are referred to in Egyptian sources of the 13th century, so their national presence at the time of the Exodus can hardly be questioned.[28] It seems to me as well that the Oracles of Balaam and the Blessing of Moses reflect a situation only slightly later than that of the Song of the Sea. The

[27]See the discussion in "Early Israelite History."

[28]See, e.g., a report from the reign of Marniptah mentioning Edom (*ANET*, 259) and a list of Rameses II which includes Moab (*ANET*, 243).

Exodus from Egypt is the point of departure (Num 23:22; 24:8), and the present idyllic existence of the people, isolated from other nations, suggests an oasis encampment in the wilderness (Num 24:5-6; Deut 33:28).

(4) From Sinai and its environs, the faith (and at least some of the faithful) spread northward through Transjordan and finally into Canaan, where it was adopted by the Israelite league, either to replace the older (and moribund) El faith, or conjointly with it. Since Yahweh's original name was probably *Yahweh-el* and a descriptive clause like *yahweh ṣĕbāʾōt* was attributed to El, there was an essential compatibility between the gods, which permitted an effective consolidation of aspects and attributes.[29] By the 11th century, Yahweh and El were accepted and worshipped as one God, the God of Mosaic faith, the God of the Fathers and of the Israelite confederation.

(5) Toward the end of the pre-monarchic period, if not before, deliberate efforts are made to restore the twelve-tribe league. Under the leadership of Samuel, Saul, and finally David, Judah (and Simeon) are reunited with Israel. Joseph is permanently divided into two tribes, Ephraim and Manasseh; and this leaves Levi in a somewhat anomalous position as a sacral unit without a territorial allotment. With the establishment of the united monarchy under David and Solomon, the tribal structure itself is replaced by a series of administrative districts in both kingdoms (Israel and Judah), only a few of which coincide with the old tribal names and areas.[30] The tribal lists pass from history into literature and become the stock in trade of nostalgic reminiscences of glories past and projections of future restorations. Essentially, they are of two types, reflecting both ends of the evolution of the tribal pattern from the Late Bronze Age (reflected in Genesis 49) until the end of the 11th century (reflected in various lists): the early list has twelve tribes corresponding to the twelve sons, including both Joseph and Levi. The more common cultic and administrative lists exclude Levi as a special group and divide Joseph between Ephraim and Manasseh.

Poem	*Content*	*Composition*
Genesis 49	14th-13th	11th
Exodus 15	13th-12th	12th
Numbers 23-24	12th	11th
Deuteronomy 33	12th	11th
Judges 5	12th	12th

[29]See my discussion of the name "Yahweh" in an appendix to "Divine Names and Titles" and in the forthcoming article on "Yahweh" in G. J. Botterweck and H. Ringgren, *Theologisches Wörterbuch zum Alten Testament* (Stuttgart: W. Kohlhammer, 1970-).

[30]See Cross and Wright, "The Boundary and Province Lists of the Kingdom of Judah," *JBL* 75 (1956) 202-26, esp. 224-26.

THE SONG OF THE SEA

This brief essay is a tribute to Professor James Muilenburg on two counts: 1) it is a token of appreciation and recognition of his impressive career and massive contribution to biblical studies, and 2) it is a response to his recent stimulating, provocative, and convincing article on the well-known poem in Exodus 15.[1] Professor Muilenburg's gifts are nowhere better demonstrated, nor his insights more original and valuable than in the area of literary appreciation and the use of rhetorical language. His comments on the "Song of the Sea" are brilliant and penetrating, and add much to the understanding of the movement of the poem from beginning to end, as well as its poetic structure. Professor Muilenburg's remarks about the latter mark a genuine advance in the analysis of the poem, and at the same time are an invitation to pursue the subject further, almost a demand to continue the investigation.

Starting from an extremely important and completely convincing observation of Professor Muilenburg, we can proceed at once to an examination of the strophic pattern of the poem. He points out that a special poetic device (of great antiquity since it is a common feature of pre-Mosaic Canaanite poetry) is used to separate the poetic units or stanzas of the composition. These dividers, or refrains (since they employ a repetitive pattern), are very much alike in structure or pattern but differ from the rest of the verses in the same respect. Thus the refrains consist of two (or three) lines of four words each in which the first two or three words are repeated at the beginning of each line: e.g.,

vs. 6: Your right hand, Yahweh
  majestic in power
Your right hand, Yahweh
  shatters the enemy.

vs. 11: Who is like you—
  among the gods, Yahweh?
Who is like you—
  Majestic, among the holy ones?
Awesome in praiseworthy deeds
  Worker of wonders.

vs. 16b: While your people pass through,
  Yahweh
While your people pass through,
  whom you created.

[1] "A Liturgy on the Triumphs of Yahweh," *Studia Biblica et Semitica (1966)*, pp. 233-51.

It is further to be noted that between vss. 5 and 16 the word "Yahweh" does not occur except in these refrains, although he is the central figure of the poem and is referred to or addressed directly throughout. Of the three refrains, the first and last have the same structure: They are couplets or bicola with the pattern, *abcd: abef.*[2] The middle refrain is more elaborate consisting of a three-line unit or tricolon, with the following patterns: *abcd: abef: GH*, in which the final colon consists of two participial phrases emphasizing the awesome features of the subject of the preceding couplet. These data indicate the pyramidal structure of the main part of the poem with the apex in the center of the poem. So far as the content is concerned, it coincides with the final destruction of Pharaoh's host in the turbulent waters.

The next step is to analyze the materials between the refrains. With regard to vss. 7-10, we find a definite dividing point at the end of vs. 8. Vss. 7-8 describe the violent commotion on the sea, while vs. 9 initiates a reprise of the action preceding the climactic disaster. We may speak then of two stanzas in this strophe. They are of approximately equal length, and each consists of five units, structurally divisible into a tricolon and a bicolon. The metrical analysis, according to the prevailing stress-pattern procedure, works out as follows:

IA	vs. 7	2:2/2:2
	vs. 8	2:2
		3:3

For reasons which appear to me to be sound, I prefer a syllable-counting technique, but there is no substantial difference in results:

vs. 7	12:12
vs. 8	10
	9:9

The second stanza, vss. 9-10, has the following pattern:

IB	vs. 9	2:2/2:2/2:2
	vs. 10	2:2/2:2

Or, analyzing it according to a syllable-counting technique we come up with:

vs. 9	8:10:9
vs. 10	11:11

If we now turn to the second strophe, vss. 12-16a, we find that it also falls into two parts of approximately equal length. The first stanza consists of vss.

[2]Vs. 6:	*yĕmīnkā*	*yhwh*	*neᵓdārī*	*bakkōaḥ*
	yĕmīnkā	*yhwh*	*tirᶜaṣ*	*ᵓōyēb*
Vs. 16b:	*ad-yaᶜăbōr*	*ammĕkā*	*yhwh*	
	ad-yaᶜăbōr	*am-zū*	*qānītā.*	

12-14, and is adequately described as a tricolon followed by a bicolon. Thus the metrical pattern is:

IIA	vss. 12-13	2:2/2:2/2:2
	vs. 14	3:3

Or, syllabically speaking:

vss. 12-13	11:12:13
vs. 14	8:8

The second stanza, vss. 15-16a, also consists of a tricolon and a bicolon, with the following metrical pattern:

IIB	vs. 15	2:2/2:2/2:2
	vs. 16a	2:2/2:2

The syllable count is as follows:

vs. 15	9:9:9
vs. 16a	11:11

A cursory comparison of the two strophes shows that the stanza structure and internal metrical arrangement are practically identical. Stanzas IA and IIA are virtually the same whether examined from a stress- or syllable-counting position, and the same is true of IB and IIB; while the difference between the A and B stanzas in each case is slight, it is noticeable, and carefully preserved in both cases.

On the basis of the preserved evidence, we may regard the supposed structure of the poem as validated. Thus we have the following for the torso of the composition:

Refrain 1	2:2/2:2	vs. 6
Strophe IA:	2:2/2:2/2:2	vss. 7-8
	3:3	
Strophe IB:	2:2/2:2/2:2	vs. 9
	2:2/2:2	vs. 10
Refrain 2	2:2/2:2/2:2	vs. 11
Strophe IIA:	2:2/2:2/2:2	vss. 12-13
	3:3	vs. 14
Strophe IIB:	2:2/2:2/2:2	vs. 15
	2:2/2:2	vs. 16a
Refrain 3	3:3 or 2:2/2:2(?)	vs. 16b

We may now turn to the material which precedes and follows the first and last refrains. The introductory lines, vss. 1-5, fall into three units according to content and grammatical structure. Thus vs. 1b is an independent unit, as shown by its use in vs. 21 apart from the body of the poem. There is this much truth in the common scholarly opinion that the couplet was the original composition, later elaborated into the long poem, vss. 2-18. Vs. 2 is properly the Exordium or introduction proper, using as it does first person singular forms throughout, and uniquely in the poem, with the exception of *ʾāšîrā* in vs. 1 (for which, however, we have the more suitable variant in the second person, *šîrū,* in vs. 21). Furthermore, the metrical pattern of vs. 2 differs markedly from that of the rest of the poem; and we may suggest that it constitutes a liturgical introduction reflecting temple usage and ceremonial practice.

The poem proper begins with vs. 3, in which the protagonist (Yahweh) and his main activity (warfare) are identified:

vs. 3 "Yahweh is a Warrior
Yahweh is his Name."

The metrical pattern is 2:2 (the syllabic count 10). This verse is balanced by the concluding line, vs. 18:

"Yahweh shall reign
forever and ever."

The divine Warrior, through his majestic victory at the Sea, and other mighty exploits, has confirmed his royal authority for all time. The metrical pattern is again 2:2 (syllable count 9).

While these lines open and close the poem proper, and thus stand somewhat apart, they nevertheless form constitutive elements of stanzas of the established five-unit length. These opening and closing stanzas (vss. 3-5, and 17-18) form a third strophe enclosing the poem. The rhetorical device known as *inclusio* is shown by the repetition of the name "Yahweh" in vss. 3 and 18—a continuity maintained in the refrains, as we have noted.

The opening stanza, then, has the following pattern:

vs. 3	2:2
vs. 4	2:2/2:2
vs. 5	3:3

The accent- or stress-counting system tends to falter somewhat since vs. 4a is really 3:2 as it stands, while vs. 5 is 2:3 in all likelihood. But in a syllable-counting system, we find a satisfactory symmetry. Thus:

10
8:4/6:6 or 12:12
8:10

The structure corresponds very closely to IA (vss. 7-8). Note that the last bicolon of vs. 8 is 3:3 or 9:9 (syllables); vs. 5 is a legitimate variant, 8:10 in which one syllable has been substracted from the first colon and added to the second.

If we turn to the closing stanza, vss. 17-18, we find the following pattern:

vs. 17 2:2
2:2/2:2
vs. 18 2:2

In syllabic terms, we have:

vs. 17 15
11:11
vs. 18 9

It will be noted that this stanza differs from all the others in that there are apparently only four units instead of the expected five. In both IB and IIB we have tricola followed by bicola, whereas here we seem to have three bicola followed by the closing line. If the normal pattern had been maintained, we would have expected something like this (recognizing the reordering necessitated by the closing line):

vs. 17 2:2/2:2
2:2/2:2
vs. 18 2:2

The last part of the pattern is visible in vs. 17b and c which are parallel structurally as well as in meaning, and vs. 18. The disturbance, if any, occurs in vs. 17a where the syllable count, if not the stress-analysis, indicates that something may have fallen out, presumably after *tĕbīēmō*, and parallel to *bĕhar naḥălātĕkā*.

The conclusion of the investigation into the strophic structure of the Song of the Sea is that it is a well-ordered poem, with a single inclusive design. The Song consists of an Exordium, followed by an opening stanza which is complemented by a parallel closing stanza, each one corresponding in length and pattern to the stanza-units of the body of the poem. There are three refrains of similar structure, which divide the poem into two major strophes each consisting of ten units, or two five-unit stanzas. Within each stanza the metrical pattern is uniform and closely followed with minimal variation.

To illustrate the strophic pattern of the Song of the Sea, we present it in its supposed formal structure:

INTRODUCTION: My mighty fortress is Yah(weh)
He is my Savior
This is my God—
whom I admire
My father's God—
whom I exalt.

---

3 Yahweh is a Warrior
Yahweh is his name.

4 Pharaoh's military chariots
He hurled into the sea
His choicest officers
were drowned in the Red Sea.

5 The abyss covered them
they sank into the depths like a stone.

R 1 6 Your right hand, Yahweh
is majestic in power
Your right hand, Yahweh
shatters the enemy.

I A 7 In your great pride,
you shattered your foes
You vented your wrath
it consumed them like stubble.

8 At the blast of your nostrils
the waters were heaped up
The waves stood like a wall
The deeps churned in the
midst of the sea.

I B 9 Said the enemy,
I will pursue, I will overtake
I will divide spoil
My appetite will be sated
I will bare my sword
My hand will conquer.

10 You blew with your breath
the sea covered them
They sank like lead
in the dreadful waters.

R 2 11 Who is like you—
among the gods, Yahweh?
Who is like you—
Majestic among the holy ones?
Awesome in praiseworthy deeds
Worker of wonders.

IIA 12 You stretched out your hand—
the underworld swallowed them.

13 You led by your kindness
the people whom you championed
You guided by your strength,
to your holy abode

14 When the peoples heard, they shuddered
Panic seized the inhabitants of Philistia.

IIB 15 Then they were dismayed—
the chieftains of Edom
The nobles of Moab—
trembling seized them.
They completely collapsed—
the kings of Canaan.

16a You brought down upon them
a numinous dread
By your sovereign power
they were struck dumb like a stone.

R 3 16b While your people pass through,
Yahweh
While your people pass through,
whom you created.

---

17 You will bring them
into.......[3]
You will plant them
in the mount of your heritage.
The dais of your throne
you have made, Yahweh
Your sanctuary, Yahweh,
your hands have established.

[3]It is possible to supply the "missing" words from a closely parallel verse, Ps. 78:54, which refers to the same experience. Vs. 54a reads, "And he brought them into his sacred district (territory)." The term is in parallel construction with "the mountain his right hand acquired." We could render Exod. 15:17a then:

You will bring them in [to your
sacred district]
You will plant them in the
mount of your heritage.

18 Yahweh will reign
forever and ever.

Strophe and Meter in Exodus 15

Continuing discovery and publication of Canaanite cuneiform tablets, current research into the language and forms of early Hebrew poetry, and recent contributions to the elucidation of the poem in Ex 15 have recommended further reflections on and reconsideration of certain aspects of this national victory song. We are primarily concerned with the strophic structure of the poem and the associated problem of metrical analysis. Other questions will be dealt with incidentally in the course of the discussion. Throughout, the presentation mentioned above will be assumed.[1]

In dealing with questions of strophe and meter, two opposing principles or assumptions must be reckoned with: 1) that in all likelihood the poem has not been transmitted to us precisely in the form in which it was composed, and that changes, some deliberate, some accidental have occurred in the course of transmission; 2) that strophic and metrical or rhythmic structures must be derived or established from the text as we have it, since it would be methodologically untenable to emend the text in the interests of a certain metrical or strophic structure or to base such a structure on an emended text.

In practice, then, if the results are to be at all convincing or persuasive, it is necessary to have a well-preserved text, with a minimum of difficulties in readings and meanings. It should be sufficiently long so that clear-cut patterns or structures can be determined. Then, presumably, if such patterns emerge from the analysis of the preserved materials, minor deviations, anomalies, or inconsistencies could be regarded as the result of accidental change in the process of copying and possibly corrected. At the same time, there must be compelling reasons for regarding the deviations as errors, and not as deliberate variations from the established scheme and therefore part of it. The following study is an attempt to analyze a representative piece of Hebrew poetry in a good state of preservation to determine whether strophic and/or metrical patterns exist, and to recover them so far as the evidence permits.

The existence of a strophic structure in this poem may be regarded as highly probable if not virtually certain. The single most important clue has been provided by Professor James Muilenburg in his recent study of Exodus 15.[2] He has correctly identified certain lines which serve a purpose similar to refrains and act as dividers or buffers between the strophes of the poem. They relate closely or loosely both with what precedes and what follows, but stand apart both in form and in content from the strophes themselves. They share certain formal characteristics which distinguish them from the rest of the poem, thus confirming the view that they are deliberately placed to serve as structural markers.

The lines to be considered are vss 6, 11, and the latter half of 16. All three follow a pattern of partial repetition familiar from Ugaritic poetry and a number of Biblical poems. This pattern is usually characterized as abc/abd, in which the first two elements of each colon are identical while the third is different. Variations occur, such as abcd/abef or abc/abd/efg, where the final colon repeats the thought of the preceding cola but uses different words. A well-known example of the last variety, based on a Ugaritic prototype, is to be found in Ps 92: 10:[3]

kī hinnē ʾōyᵉbēkā yahwē	For behold your enemies, Yahweh
kī hinnē ʾōyᵉbēkā yōʾbēdū	For behold, your enemies will perish
yitpārᵉdū kol - pōʿᵃlē ʾāwen	May all image makers be scattered

The Canaanite precursor goes as follows:

ht ibk bʿlm	Behold your enemies, Baal
ht ibk tmḫṣ	Behold, you shall smash your enemies
ht tṣmt ṣrtk	Behold, you shall destroy your foes

Other examples are scattered through the Psalter, especially Ps 29 (cf Ps 96: 1–2, 7–8); Ps 77: 17. The Song of Deborah, similar in many other respects to this victory ode, also contains numerous examples of this pattern: Judg 5: 3, 5, 6, 7, 12, 19, 21, 23, 24, 27, 30. The lines in Ex 15 follow:

6 ymynk yhwh	By your right hand, Yahweh[4]
n'dry bkḥ	resplendent among the powerful
ymynk yhwh	By your right hand, Yahweh
trʿṣ ʾwyb	you have shattered the enemy

11	my kmkh b'lym yhwh my kmkh n'dr bqdš nwr' thlt 'śh pl'	Who is like you among the gods, Yahweh? Who is like you resplendent among the holy ones Awesome in praises worker of wonders?
16^2	'd y'br 'mk yhwh 'd y'br 'm - zw qnyt	While your people pass over, Yahweh While your people, whom you purchased, pass over

It is to be noted that only these three lines have the repetitive pattern described. A possible exception is vs 3, with the repetition of *yhwh*, but the similarity is vague and limited, and the metrical structure is significantly different. Furthermore, in each of these refrains or dividers, the name Yahweh appears (twice in 6, once each in 11 and 16^2), whereas it appears nowhere in the material bounded by them (vss 7–10, 12–16^1). To complete the picture, it appears twice in vs 3 and twice in vss 17–18. It also occurs in vs 1 (and 21), which may have had a function similar to that of the dividers. The abbreviated form *Yah* occurs in vs 2, which, however, stands outside the strophic pattern, and requires special comment.

Returning to the repetitive lines (6, 11, 16^2), we observe that vss 6 and 16^2 are in couplet form, while vs 11 is more elaborate, having a third element in the form of participial phrases in apposition with *n'dr* and modifying *yhwh*. Thus the three refrains or dividers form the skeletal structure on which the poem is built.

It is in the shape of a triangle or pyramid, with the two regular refrains forming the base, and the more elaborate central refrain at the apex.

If we examine the material between Refrains A (vs 6) and B (vs 11), we find that it falls naturally into two parts, dividing at vs 9. This division is strictly in accordance with the content, though there is a corresponding shift in mood and rhythmic movement as well. Vss 7–8 deal with the violent storm and its effects both on the enemy (vs 7) and the sea (vs 8). With vs 9 we have a sharp break, since the poet goes back to an earlier stage of the story, picking up the action with the enemy's decision to pursue, overtake, and conquer. The fate of the enemy described in vs 10, which echoes vss 4–5 (and 1), stands in stark contrast to the glorious and greedy expectations expressed in the preceding verse.

If we turn to the material between Refrains B (vs 11) and C (vs 16^2), we find that it also falls structurally into two parts, though the disjuncture between the sections is not as sharp as in the preceding strophe. We find the break between vss 14 and 15; it is signalized by the particle *'az*, which introduces the second part of the strophe. Vss 15–16 pick up and elaborate the theme of vs 14, the terror of the nations at the demonstration of Yahweh's power.

According to this analysis, each strophe consists of two stanzas or half-strophes: vss 7–8 and 9–10; vss 12–14 and 15–16[1]. Closer inspection indicates that each of these stanzas consists of five units or bicola, organized in clusters of two or three units, forming couplets and triads. Thus Stanza B in the first strophe consists of a triad (vs 9) and a couplet (vs 10); Stanza B of the second strophe has the same structure—a triad (vs 15) and a couplet (vs 16[1]). Stanza A of Strophe II has a similar structure, with a triad (vss 12–13) and a couplet (vs 14). Although vs 12 stands somewhat apart, so far as content is concerned, it is structurally very similar to 13a and b. Turning to Stanza A in the first strophe, we find a more difficult situation. It is clear that vs 7 constitutes a couplet, its component units being parallel in content and structure. The same is true of 8b and c, which is a couplet containing parallel units. How does the unit 8a fit into the overall pattern? So far as content is concerned, it clearly belongs with 8b and c (cf *nʿrmw mym* / *nṣbw . . . nzlym* / *qp'w thmt*; the opening phrase, *wbrwḥ 'pyk*, applies to all three clauses). But structurally it is more closely related to 7a (and b): cf *wbrb g'wnk* / *wbrwḥ 'pyk*. Note also that the metrical pattern of vs 7 is 4:4 (or 2:2 / 2:2) and 8a is the same, while the pattern in 8b and c is, in all likelihood, 3:3.

It is to be observed, however, that the syllable count in vs 7 is 12:12 (or 6:6/6:6), while in 8a, it is 10 (6:4); 8b and c have a count of 9:9. In view of the fact that the other three stanzas have the triad first, followed by the couplet, we may conclude that the intended pattern in the first stanza was the same, but that content does not always follow form (as is true in a different sense in vs 12 and also, to some extent, with respect to the stanza division between vss 14 and 15).

On the basis of the foregoing discussion, we may represent the strophic structure of the central section of the Song of the Sea schematically as follows:

Refrain	A	(6)	4:4	or	(2:2/2:2)
Strophe	I	(7–10)			
	A	7	4:4		(2:2/2:2)
		8	4		(2:2)
			3:3		
	B	9	4:4:4		(2:2/2:2/2:2)
		10	4:4		(2:2/2:2)

Refrain	B	(11)	4:4:4	or	(2:2/2:2/2:2)
Strophe	II	(12–16[1])			
	A	12	4		(2:2)
		13	4:4		(2:2/2:2)
		14	3:3		
	B	15	4:4:4		(2:2/2:2/2:2)
		16[1]	4:4		(2:2/2:2)
Refrain	C	16[2]	3:3		

As already observed, the stanzas all have the same basic pattern, consisting of a triad followed by a couplet; the principal variation between Stanzas A and B (in both strophes) is that the concluding couplet in A is 3:3, while in B it is 4:4 (or 2:2/2:2). We note a similar pattern in the refrains: A and C are couplets, while B is a triad; A and B have the pattern 4:4(:4) or 2:2/2:2(/2:2), while C is 3:3. It may be added, however, that the analysis depends upon construing *mīkāmōkā* in vs 11 as 2, and *ʿad - yaʿabōr* in vs 16 as 1. In other words, the difference between 2:2 or 4 and 3 may not be significant. While on the subject of stress or accent counting, a comment may be in order concerning the controversy over whether the prevailing meter is 4 or 2:2. In my judgment, both characterizations are valid, but for different purposes. With respect to the content of the lines in question, there is rarely if ever any parallelism between the two cola; thus 4:4 (and 3:3) is the appropriate designation to indicate the parallelism in content between lines: for example, 7a/7b, 8b/8c, 9b/9c, 13a/13b, 15a/15b/15c.

To designate such 4 stress lines as 2:2 on the basis of content would be unwarranted. However, there is often a caesura in the middle of such a line, and some indication of it in notation would be appropriate, for example, 7a (after *gʾwnk*) and 7b (after *ḥrnk*), 9b (after *šll*) and 9c (after *ḥrby*). So long as the distinction is recognized, either or both sets of figures may be used: for example vs 15 can be designated 4:4:4 according to content, and 2:2/2:2/2:2 structurally; the last line (15c) poses a problem, since *kōl* is normally taken with *yšby knʿn* as part of a construct chain. While Masoretic punctuation encourages the division after *kōl*, we may remain hesitant. However, it may be better to take *kōl* adverbially and to compare *nāmōgū kōl* with *ʾāz nibhalū* as parallel constructions (i.e., verb plus emphatic adverb). Because of uncertainties in any stress-counting system and an inescapable element of subjectivity in deciding doubtful cases, and in order to reflect certain detailed poetic phenomena more precisely, I have opted for a syllable-counting system. Since there are many more syllables than accents in a line, the element of subjectivity is reduced (i.e., a disagreement over a count of nine or ten syllables is less important than one over two or three accents), and we have a more sensitive instrument for measuring the length of lines or cola.

There are additional complications since MT hardly reflects the actual pronunciation of words at the time of composition. The question of the length of syllables as well as the number of syllables can hardly be settled in the present state of our knowledge, and allowance must therefore be made for some variation in counting. Furthermore, the poet himself could take advantage of variations in current usage for metrical or rhythmic purposes, and syllables might be elided, or shortened, or lengthened in accordance with the exigencies of the verse. For example, we know that case and verbal endings which existed in older forms of the language were largely lost by the time of Moses and certainly by the time of composition of even very early Hebrew poetry. Nevertheless, case endings have been preserved in certain instances (cf vs 16, *ʾymth*), we believe for metrical reasons.[5] We may speculate further that in some instances such case endings, originally incorporated into the poem, have, in the process of transmission, been dropped or lost since their function was not recognized. We can document such developments with regard to other archaic features (like enclitic *mem*)[6] which were used deliberately by the poet for metrical and other stylistic reasons but which were edited out of the text by modernizers and revisers.

In attempting to determine the approximate time length of a line, it is necessary to consider not only the number of syllables but their length as well. Vowel quantity is a notoriously difficult question in the analysis of classical Hebrew, especially since the artificiality of the Masoretic vocalization is most apparent at this point. Nevertheless, a schematic representation on the basis of a hypothetical *Ursprache* would be equally bad or worse, since the language was already far along in the history of its development when biblical poetry was composed. Striking an appropriate balance is both the goal and the problem, since we do not have adequate controls for the period in question; and we must always recognize the liberty of the poet in using materials of different age and provenience to suit his purposes. The treatment of short vowels is a particularly thorny and difficult subject: some were lengthened, others reduced, still others elided, and a few remained as they were. MT illustrates all these changes, but when and under what conditions did they take place? Consider segolate nouns, which are regularly vocalized as having two syllables. Originally or at an earlier time, they were monosyllabic; but at a still earlier time, they had case endings; and in some words, it is difficult to see how they could have been pronounced as a single syllable. It may be that the process reflected in MT was a sort of compensation for the loss of the final syllables provided by case endings (note that the monosyllabic form is normally retained before pronominal suffixes). The same problem faces us with regard to diphthongs. For the most part, these were contracted in the north of Israel, and the syllable count is not thereby affected. But in the south, they were retained, and at some later date many of these were resolved into two syllables (e.g., *mayim* <*maym*). When? We know too that there were both long and short forms of the pronominal suffixes (e.g., *kā* and *-k* for 2 m.s.).[7] MT, for the most part, has standardized the long form, but is this true for the twelfth century B.C., or the tenth, or whenever the poem was written? My impression is that the poet was free to make choices among available forms, and did so according to the requirements of the poem, including metrical considerations. Individual problems will be considered as we work through the poem verse by verse.

With all these possible variations to consider, it may be said that the metrical pattern derived by syllable counting emerges with a regularity which matches that of the stress-counting system and, in some cases, improves upon it. On the whole, our poem is so well preserved that any metrical system will work and work well. In a third possible counting system, we attempt to take into account the difference between long and short vowels and between open and closed syllables. To apply this method, we simply count all the vocables in a colon, whether consonants or vowels, and then add one for each long vowel (taking a long vowel as having twice the value of a short vowel):

	Open Syllable	*Closed Syllable*
Short vowel	2	3
Long vowel	3	4

By using several systems simultaneously, we can check and confirm our results.

Proceeeding from the main body of the poem, with its strophes, stanzas, refrains, or dividers (vss 6–16), we turn to the immediately adjacent materials both before and after. The concluding stanza, vss 17–18, is balanced by a corresponding introduction, vss 3–5. More particularly, vs 18 forms an *inclusio* with vs 3. It is Yahweh the warrior, whose martial exploits are celebrated in the poem, who is also the eternal king. We may therefore recognize the parallel structure of these opening and closing stanzas (which together form an inclusive strophe like those in the body of the poem), but in reverse order. Thus vss 3 and 18 complement or balance each other. Similarly, vs 4ab is balanced by 17bc—4:4 (or 2:2 / 2:2) in both cases. That leaves 5 to match 17a. Neither seems to scan with any regularity, but they are roughly similar in length and make adequate sense as they are.

Leaving the details to later discussion, we may conclude that each stanza has five units distributed as follows:

vs 3	4 (2:2)	17	2:2(?)
4	4:4(2:2/2:2)		4:4(2:2/2:2)
5	3:3(?)	18	4(2:2)

Comparison with the stanzas of the main strophes indicates that these opening and closing stanzas belong to the same or a similar pattern, but with greater variation. Thus the introduction (vss 3–5) conforms to the A stanzas of Strophes I and II with a triad (the first element, vs 3, standing somewhat apart, as vs 12 in II A), 4:4:4 (or 2:2 / 2:2 / 2:2), followed by a couplet 3:3 (vs 5 could be taken as 2:3; the syllable count is 8:10, which may be a legitimate variant of the pattern reflected in vs 8bc, 9:9, or 14, 8:8). With regard to the final stanza, if we compare vss 17–18 with IB (9–10) and IIB (15–16), then we might identify vs 17 abc with the opening triad, and vs 18 as a truncated form of the closing couplet. But, in view of the connection between vs 18 and vs 3, we should perhaps look for a closing triad (to match the opening triad of vss 3–4), which we find in 17bc and 18 (the reign of Yahweh affirmed in 18 is predicated on the building of the divine throne and temple in 17). That leaves 17a, which ought to have come out as 3:3 to match vs 5 (or, on the analogy of I and IIB, 4:4). As the text stands, 17a looks like an anomalous and unbalanced 2:2, but it can hardly be anything else.[8] The syllable count is roughly 9:6, which balances rather cleverly with vs 5: 8/10 (but which could also be counted as 7/9). Thus we would have completely complementary stanzas forming an envelope for the body of the poem.

It remains to consider vss 1 and 2. Vs 2 may properly be regarded as an Exordium or personal introduction by the precentor, in this case, the "Moses" figure. It is only in vs 2 (cf discussion of *'šyrh* in vs 1; the suffix with *'dny* in vs 17 is purely formal) that the poet speaks in the first person; clearly this section stands by itself from a formal or structural viewpoint as well. It may have constituted the liturgical prologue to the singing of the Song of the Sea in the sanctuary or temple.

Finally, there is the opening line, which is repeated with slight variation as the Song of Miriam in vs 21. The form in vs 1 with *'šyrh* belongs to the same pattern as the Song of Deborah (Judg 5: 3), where the subject also is "I." The form in vs 21 with *šīrū* is a choral antiphon sung by Miriam and the women in response to the larger poem. Since the longer poem is already supplied with dividers, it would be difficult to position this refrain except at the beginning and end of the poem. It may well be that in liturgical performances the precentor began with vss 1–2 as the Exordium. Thus the opening and closing verses (1 and 21) form an *inclusio*, as indicated by the arrangement in MT, and with additional information as to how this device functioned in a liturgical setting: with precentor and chorus.

The form of this refrain is unlike those in the body of the poem, though the general metrical pattern is characteristic: 4:4 or 2:2 /2:2. Concerning the unity and overall symmetry of the poem, there should now be considerably less doubt than there has been. We suggest a date for the original poem in the twelfth century B.C., and attribute its final liturgical form to the worship in Jerusalem under David and Solomon.

Text and Translation

1	6	’aširā la yahwē	I will sing of Yahweh	2
	5	kī ga’ō ga’ā	that he is highly exalted	2
	5	sūs warōkibō	Horse and its charioteer	2
	4	ramā bəyām	he hurled into the sea	2
		Exordium (Proem)		
2	7	‘ozzī wazimrat(ī) yāh	My mighty fortress is Yah	3
	7	wayəhī lī līšū‘ā	He has become my Savior	3
	7	zē ’ēlī wa’anwēhū	This is my God whom I admire	3
	11	’elōhē ’abī wa’arōmimenhū	My father’s God whom I extol	3
		Opening		
3	6	yahwē ’īš milḥamā	Yahweh—that man of war	2
	4	yahwē šimō	Whose name is Yahweh	2
4	8	markabōt par‘ō waḥēlō	Pharaoh’s chariot army	3
	4	yarā bəyām	He cast into the sea	2
	6	wamibḥar šalīšēw	And his elite officers	2
	6	ṭubba‘ū bəyam sūp	Were drowned in the Reed Sea	2
5	8	tihōmōt yakassiyūmū	The Abyss covered them	2/3
	10	yaradū bəmaṣōlōt kəmō-’ābn	they went down into the depths like a stone	3
		Refrain (A)		
6	5	yamīnka yahwē ne’dōrī bəkōḥ	By your right hand, Yahweh resplendent among the mighty	2 / 2
	5	yamīnka yahwē	By your right hand, Yahweh	2
	4	tir‘aṣ ’ōyēb	you shattered the enemy	2
		Strophe I		
A				
7	6	wabərōb ga’ōnka	Through your great majesty	2
	6	tahar(r)ēs qāmēka	you destroyed your foes	2
	6	tašallaḥ ḥarōnka	You sent forth your anger	2
	6	yō’kilēmō kəqaš	it devoured them like stubble	2

8	6	wabərūḥ ʼappēka	By the blast of your nostrils	2
	4	neʻramū mēm	the waters were heaped up	2
	9	niṣṣabū kəmō-nēd nōzilīm	The waves mounted as a bank	3
	9	qapaʼū tihōmōt bəlib-yām	The depths churned in the heart of the sea	3

B

9	4	ʼamar ʼōyēb	The enemy boasted	2
	4	ʼerdop ʼaśśīg	"I'll pursue, I'll overtake	2
	5	ʼaḥallēq šalāl	"I'll seize the booty	2
	6	timlaʼēmō napšī	my gullet will be filled with them	2
	4	ʼarīq ḥarbī	"I'll bare my sword	2
	6	tōrīšēmō yadī	my hand will dispossess them"	2
10	6	nasăpta bərūḥka	You blew with your breath	2
	4	kissamō yām	the sea covered them	2
	6	ṣalalū kəʻopərt	They sank like lead	2
	5	bəmēm ʼaddīrīm	in the dreadful waters	2

Refrain (B)

11	4	mī-kamōka	Who is like you	2
	5	bəʼēlīm yahwē	among the gods, Yahweh?	2
	4	mī-kamōka	Who is like you	2
	4	neʼdār baqōdš	resplendent among the holy ones	2
	5	nōrāʼ təhillōt	Fearsome in praises	2
	3	ʻōśē pilʼ	worker of wonders?	2

Strophe II

A

12	6	naṭīta yamīnka	You stretched out your hand	2
	5	tiblaʻēmō ʼārṣ	the netherworld swallowed them	2
13	7	naḥīta bəḥasdika	You led in your kindness	2
	5	ʻam-zū gaʼālta	the people whom you redeemed	2
	7	nēhalta bəʻozzika	You guided them with your might	2
	6	ʼel nawē qodšeka	to your holy habitation	2
14	8	šamaʻū ʻammīm yirgazūn	The peoples trembled when they heard	3
	8	ḥīl ʼaḥaz yōšibē palāšt	Anguish seized the inhabitants of Philistia	3

B

15	4	ʼāz nibhalū	Indeed, the generals	2
	5	ʼallūpē ʼədōm	of Edom were unnerved	2
	4	ʼēlē mōʼāb	Shuddering gripped	2
	5	yōʼḥəzēmō rāʻd	the chiefs of Moab	2
	4	namōgū kōl	The kings of Canaan	2

	5	yōšibē kənāʿn	collapsed completely	2
16	5	tappīl ʿalēhem	You brought down on them	
	6	ʾēmāta wapaḥda	dreadful terror	
	6	bəgadōl zərōʿka	Through your great arm	2
	5	yiddammū kaʾābn	they were struck dumb	
			like a stone	2
			Refrain (C)	
	8	ʿad-yaʿbōr	While your people	2
		ʿamməka yahwē	passed over, Yahweh	2
	8	ʿad-yaʿbōr	While your people,	2
		ʿam-zū qanīta	whom you purchased,	
			passed over	2
			Ending	
17	4	tabīʾēmō	You brought them in	(3 or 4)
	(6)	[ʾel gəbūl qōdšəka]	(to your sacred territory)	
	5	watiṭṭaʿēmō	You planted them	3 or 4
	6	bəhar naḥlātəka	in your hereditary mountain	
	6	makōn ləšibtəka	The dais of your throne	2
	5	paʿalta yahwē	Yahweh, you made	2
	5	miqdāš ʾadōnay	Your sanctuary, Lord	2
	6	kōninū yadēka	your hands created	2
18	4	yahwē yimlōk	Yahweh has reigned	2
	5	ləʿōlām waʿed	from everlasting to eternity	2
		. . . .		
21		šīrū la yahwē	Sing of Yahweh	2
		kī gaʾō gaʾā	that he is highly exalted	2
		sūs warōkibō	Horse and its charioteer	2
		ramā bəyām	he hurled into the sea	2

General Comments

The received Hebrew text has been followed throughout the proposed reconstruction; the few very slight changes in readings adopted are almost all matters of vocalization, and are defended in the notes to the text. With regard to the vocalization, we have attempted, with more courage than prudence perhaps, to reproduce cultivated Hebrew speech of the twelfth to the tenth centuries B.C. The basis for this representation is inevitably MT, which remains our best source for Hebrew pronunciation in spite of its late date and artificial character. Next in order of importance are the Ugaritic tablets, which offer a partial vocalization of a closely related Canaanite dialect; their great value lies in their antiquity, since this material antedates the classical period of Hebrew poetry (fourteenth to the thirteenth centuries B.C.), and therefore offers an important corrective to MT. Then there are transcriptions of Canaanite words in a variety of languages, beginning with Egyptian texts of the second millennium, including the Amarna letters and other Akkadian transliterations, and extending to the LXX, the famous second column of the Hexapla, and other late sources.

In our transliterations we have endeavored to represent both long and short vowels. With regard to so-called tone-long vowels, we assume that in most cases short vowels under the accent were lengthened but that unaccented syllables were not (i.e., so-called pretonic lengthening). With regard to short vowels, we employ the symbol "ə" to indicate any short vowel concerning the quality of which we are uncertain (it may be *a*, *i*, *u*, or a variation of these: *o*, *e*). It often reflects MT vocal *shewa*, but we wish to leave open the question of which vowels were slurred over or elided in actual speech. We have accepted the Masoretic vocalization of 2 m.s. forms of the perfect form of the verb and the suffixes attached to nouns and verbs (with final *a*, except that we regard the vowel as short, not long), even though the consonantal text reflects a tradition in which these final vowels were not pronounced. We believe that the longer forms were preserved in cultivated literature, especially poetry of the classical period.

The vocalization of so-called segolate nouns poses a problem, since forms like *ʾereṣ* and *melek* are secondary, the earlier pronunciation being *ʾarṣ-* and *malk-*. Originally the nouns had case endings which facilitated pronunciation in some instances, so it may be that with the loss of case endings, the process which resulted in segolate forms was initiated. If this assumption is correct, then there would be no perceptible effect on the meter: for example, *ʾarṣu* → *ʾereṣ* (two syllables each). Nevertheless, the available evidence shows that the monosyllabic forms persisted for a long time and were recognized as such. The same considerations apply to the matter of diphthongs. In Ugaritic, Phoenician, and North Israelite, the diphthongs *ay* and *aw* were regularly contracted to *ê* and *ô*. In Southern Israelite (Judahite) as in Aramaic and classical Arabic, the diphthongs were preserved; in MT, they are often resolved into two syllables—for example *mayim* ← *maym* (→ *mēm* in the northern dialect). If we accept the vocalization of the northern dialect as normative, it is on the view that the earliest literature of Israel was composed and transmitted in northern circles, and that under the influence of Canaanite-Phoenician royal culture the court of David or Solomon adopted this mode of expression. There is no significant metrical difference between the northern and southern forms; even if we were to follow MT as is, instead of a reconstructed vocalization, we would secure essentially the same results. We wish to emphasize the flexibility of the language, the variety of forms (long and short) available to the poet, and his prerogative as a poet to vary his choices depending upon the requirements of a given line. We may add a note about the use of the definite article; the article as such does not occur in the poem, which is strictly in accord with the pattern of Ugaritic poetry (and presumably Canaanite poetry in general). It is presupposed here and there in the vocalization of MT (e.g., *bayyām*, vss 1, 4; *bakkōaḥ*, vs 6; *kaqqaš*, vs 7; *baqqōdeš*, vs 11), but the doubling of the initial consonant of the word is doubtless artificial, and can safely be disregarded. It is to be noted that neither *ʾēt* nor *ʾᵃšer*, which are elements of Hebrew prose usage, occurs in the poem—another indication that the text has been remarkably well preserved from contamination by prosaic additions or substitutions.

Notes on the Verses

Verse 1

ʾašīrā: Lit. "Let me sing." This form is to be compared with *šīrū*, "Sing!" in the parallel passage vs 21. Note the use of the same word *ʾāšīrā* in the Song of Deborah (Judg 5: 3) in a more elaborate construction. The verse in Judges supports the view that the preposition *l* before Yahweh is to be rendered "of, about" rather than "to." In Judg 5: 3, the poet is singing to the "kings/potentates" about Yahweh, the God of Israel. Cf also the opening line of the Aeneid: *arma virumque cano.*

sūs warōkibō. MT should be translated: "horse and its charioteer" rather than "horse and its rider." As Ex 15: 19 and 14: 9 (cf 14: 6, 7) make clear, the reference is to chariotry not cavalry. Vs 4 confirms that the poet had in mind the officers as well as the horse-drawn chariots.

The line is usually scanned as a couplet or double bicolon, and schematized as 4:4 or 2:2 / 2:2. Structurally, the main division occurs after *gaʾō gaʾā*, while there are secondary pauses after *yahwē* and *rkbw*, so that either or both analyses can be justified. But it is important to note that there is no parallelism of content either within half-lines or between them. The thought proceeds in consecutive fashion; the verse can be taken as a summary of the content of the poem which follows, especially the first part. The syllable count is as follows: 6:5 / 5:4. The parallel verse, 21, has 5:5 / 5:4. In accordance with the syllable-value system proposed above, we obtain these results: For vs 1, the first bicolon would have the following count: $13 + 3 = 16$ (or: $2 + 3 + 3$ / $2 + 3 + 3 = 16$) for the first colon (the parallel line, vs 21, would have a value of $11 + 3 = 14$, or $3 + 3$ / $2 + 3 + 3 = 14$). The second colon would be: $10 + 3 = 13$ (or 3 / $2 + 3$ / $2 + 3 = 13$). The second bicolon would have the following count: $11 + 3 = 14$ (or 4 / $2 + 3 + 2 + 3 = 14$) for the first colon; $9 + 2 = 11$ (or

2 + 3 / 2 + 4 = 11) for the second colon. The totals for vs 1 would be 16 + 13 = 29 and 14 + 11 = 25; for vs 21, 14 + 13 = 27 and 14 + 11 = 25. The general pattern is standard throughout the poem.

Verse 2

ʿozzī wazimrāt yāh, Lit. "My strength and fortress is Yah." The following points may be noted. The first person suffix is to be understood with *zmrt*; the text can be explained in one or more of several ways: the suffix of *ʿzy* is to be taken with *zmrt* as well (double-duty suffix); the *yod* at the beginning of "Yah" is to be understood as also representing the suffix at the end of *zmrt*. This was an epigraphic device which obviated the necessity of writing the same letter twice in succession. In early orthography, the *yod* of the first person suffix would not have been written. That the suffix was at least understood if not actually pronounced is demonstrated by the reading of the Samaritan Pentateuch (*zmrty*), along with some MSS of MT. The second proposal seems most attractive to us, and we have adopted it. Further, we take the two words as an example of hendiadys: "Yah is my mighty fortress."[9] Concerning the form *yāh*, it does not occur in other early poems and its usage here may be questioned; or else the whole verse may be regarded as late.

wayəhī lī lyšwʿh, Lit. "He belongs to me for salvation." The use of f.s. abstract nouns to represent concrete objects or persons is well attested in the Psalter; and in particular, *yšwʿh* is used often of Yahweh with the meaning, "Savior."[10]

wʾnwhw . . . wʾrmmnhw. The *waw* before the verb in each case is emphatic, not conjunctive.

With regard to the meter, the situation is not so clear. Normally vs 2a would be scanned as 3:3, but it is also possible to read it as 3:2, 2:3, or 2:2, depending on how the combination *zmrt yh* is construed in the first colon and *wyhy-ly* in the second. Syllable counting is similarly subject to differing interpretations, but the total is larger and the net variation therefore less important. Thus MT has 6 syllables for the first colon, while our preferred reconstruction comes to 7. The second colon, following MT, has 7 syllables (if we take the *shewa* in *wyhy* as vocal; if we regard the *shewa* as silent, then the total is 6). On the other hand, MT has elided a syllable in *līšūʿā* < *ləyəšūʿā*; the longer form may still have been in vogue when the poem was composed, or the poet may have preferred it here. In that case, the total could be 8. Averaging the differences, and assuming that the two cola were meant to balance, we emerge with a proposed 7:7 syllable count, acknowledging that it is approximate but insisting that it is not likely to be more than one syllable off:—that is, 6–7 / 6–8 represents the maximum range.

By following the vocable system already described, the first colon in MT would have a count of 16 vocables plus 3 long vowels = 19 (or by syllables, 3 + 3/ 2 + 3 + 4/ 4 = 19). However, according to our reconstruction, the total would be 17 + 3 = 20 (or 3 + 3 / 2 + 3 + 2 + 3 / 4 = 20). The second colon in MT would have a count of 14 + 5 = 19 (2 + 2 + 3 / 3 / 3 + 3 + 3 = 19). If we restore the elided syllable in *lyšwʿh*, the count would be 16 + 4 = 20 (or 2 + 2 + 3 / 3 / 2 + 2 + 3 + 3 = 20). If we regard the *shewa* in *wyhy* as silent, the total would be 18. The pattern can be described as follows 2a—19–20 / 18–20. The variation in each case is about the same, but its net importance has diminished. However we describe the mathematical ratios, we can say that the two cola balance—that is, they were meant to be said or sung in the same time.

Turning to vs 2b, we find a more complex situation. The meter would probably be regarded as 3:3, though the first colon could with much justice be counted as 2 by taking *zh ʾly* as one stress, while the second is so much longer that 4 would seem more appropriate (taking *ʾrmmnhw* as 2). Syllable counting serves to clarify the situation by pinpointing the discrepancy between the two cola; the first has 7 syllables, the second 11. Nevertheless, the cola balance; only in each case, the second term is considerably longer than the one it matches: *ʾlhy ʾby* // *ʾly* and *wʾrmmnhw* // *wʾnwhw*. Even the addition of *zh* to the first colon (it also serves the second: This is my God . . . / This is my father's God . . .) does not completely redress the imbalance. It would have been a simple matter to switch the verbs of the two cola and produce an exact syllabic balance (9:9); but presumably the poet preferred to overbalance the bicolon as in the preserved text, thus producing a sequence with 2a as follows: 7:7 / 7:11. Since this stanza is outside the body of the poem, and no other material conforms to it in content, it is impossible to say whether this is a deliberate pattern or not, or whether some corruption has occurred. Since the text makes good sense, and poetic parallelism is maintained, we should assume that the pattern is deliberate, and that the poet (presumably for melodic or rhythmic reasons) chose a 7:11 pattern against the normal or expected 9:9. That an unbalanced bicolon is a legitimate variation of the normal balanced variety can be established without difficulty from the corpus of early Israelite poetry. For example, in the Lament of David over Saul and Jonathan, 2 Sam 1: 20, we read:

20a	ʾl tgydw bgt	Do not announce it in Gath
	(w)ʾl tbśrw bḥwṣt ʾšqlwn	Do not proclaim in the streets of Ashkelon
20b	pn-tśmḥnh bnwt plštym	Lest the daughters of the Philistines rejoice
	pn-tʿlznh bnwt ()ʿrlym	Lest the daughters of the uncircumcised exult

The balance between the cola of 20b is clear and regular. It would normally be taken as 3:3; by syllable counting, we have 9:10 for MT, and if we drop the definite article before *ʿrlym* as a prosaic addition, we would have an exact equivalence at 9:9. In 20a, we have good parallelism in content but a serious imbalance in meter. It could be construed as 2:3 or 3:4, but hardly as 3:3, which would be expected on the basis of 20b. Syllable counting only serves to emphasize the imbalance. Following MT, we have 6:11 (or if we read the *waw* before *ʾl-tbśrw*, following the versions and some Hebrew MSS, the second colon would be 12). The ratio is approximately 1:2, though the poet could easily have achieved a more balanced bicolon by switching words or supplying a parallel term for *ḥwṣt* in the first colon.[11] Presumably he preferred to overbalance the line. The point we wish to make is that the total of the two cola of 20a, 6 + 11 (12) = 17 (18), is roughly the same as 20b, 9 + 9 (10) = 18 (19). Therefore we can say that an unbalanced bicolon, 6:11 (12), can legitimately be paired with a balanced one, 9:9 (10), or, more simply, that the unbalanced or overbalanced bicolon is a legitimate tool in the Israelite poet's arsenal.

Returning to Ex 15: 2b, if we use the vocable system of counting, we come out with 15 + 5 = 20 (or syllabically: 3 / 3 + 3 / 2 + 3 + 3 + 3 = 20) for the first colon, and 23 + 5 = 28 (or 2 + 3 + 3 / 2 + 3 / 2 + 2 + 3 + 2 + 3 + 3 = 28) for the second.

OPENING

Verse 3

This verse establishes the theme of the poem: Yahweh the invincible warrior. Throughout the poem, emphasis is placed on Yahweh's warlike prowess, his overwhelming power in nature and battle, and his enduring total sovereignty. With vs 18, it forms an *inclusio*, or envelope, within which the action of the poem develops. It may be noted that the form and order of the words are very similar to the Shema in Deut 6: 4, which is also deceptively simple and resists adequate analysis and interpretation:

Deut 6: 4	yhwh ʾlhynw /	yhwh ʾḥd	6:4
Ex 15: 3	yhwh ʾyš mlḥmh /	yhwh šmw	6:4

They share the same metrical structure, which is 2:2 (or 3:2), or 6:4 by syllable count. The vocable count is 18:11, apparently an unbalanced bicolon, but it is difficult to establish the pattern, since the expected parallelism is lacking. The balancing bicolon in vs 18 is also 2:2 (syllable count 4:5, vocable count 13:14) but without parallelism; it is a single continuous sentence.

Verse 4

There is widespread agreement among scholars that this verse is metrically unbalanced; and on the basis of metrical considerations, it is generally suggested that *wḥylw* be dropped from the first colon of 4a, since as it stands, the metrical pattern appears to be 3:2 / 2:2, which is not consistent with the prevailing 2:2 meter of the poem. The following considerations may be urged against such a conclusion, apart from the total lack of textual evidence for such an emendation: Assuming that the analysis is correct, would a variation in the prevailing pattern be automatic proof of later editorial tampering? Has the poet no freedom to vary his style deliberately? But in fact, the analysis is less than convincing. Thus it is to be noted that what parallelism in content there is in the verse is between the bicola 4a and 4b and not within them. Within the bicola, we have at most a caesura, the placement of which may vary somewhat from line to line. When the larger groupings are compared, there would still appear to be a discrepancy according to a stress system of analysis: 5/4. But in actuality, there is a very good formal balance as well as in content between the half-verses. Thus each has 5 content words and, perhaps more to the point, each consists of 12 syllables. The count by cola is as follows: 4a: 8/4; 4b: 6/6. In other words, the 8/4 division in the first bicolon is a perfectly legitimate variant of the "normal" 6/6 arrangement in the second bicolon. The conclusion therefore would be that *wḥylw*, far from being otiose, is necessary to the metrical balance. There would be a major imbalance if it were omitted. It should be added that the phrase at the beginning of 4 should be taken as hendiadys: Pharaoh's military chariots, or chariot force, rather than as a reference to both chariots and the rest of the army. The prose description in 14:7, 17, 28 sufficiently explains the situation. The vocable count is 19 + 4 = 23 (or: 3 + 2 + 4 / 3 + 3 / 2 + 3 + 3 = 23) for the first colon of 4a, and 9 + 2 = 11 (or: 2 + 3 / 2 + 4 = 11) for the second colon. For 4b, the count is as follows: 15 + 2 = 17 (or: 2 + 3 + 3 / 2 + 3 + 4 = 17) for the first colon, and 15 + 2 = 17 (or: 3 + 2 + 3 / 2 + 3 / 4 = 17) for the second colon. The total for 4a is 34, and for 4b is also 34. It may be said with some confidence that the verse as it has been transmitted divides into two half-verses of exactly equal length.

Verse 5

This verse also appears to be unbalanced, the metrical pattern being apparently 2:3, though 5a could be construed as 3 and 5b as 4. In any case, the second half-line is perceptibly longer than the first. Following MT, we have a syllable count of 3 + 4 or 5 (depending upon whether the *shewa* with *samek* is regarded as vocal or not) for 5a; 5b has 10 syllables in MT; a syllable has been elided in *bmṣwlt*, and so one syllable could be added to the total; on the other hand, the final word, *'āben*, was originally monosyllabic, so that one could be subtracted. The range could have been between 9 and 11; thus 10 is a satisfactory average. Our provisional conclusion is that we have an unbalanced bicolon of 18 syllables divided 8/10. It is to be compared with the bicolon 8bc, which also has 18 syllables, divided 9/9, or with vs 16cd, which in MT is a bicolon of 18 syllables, divided 9/9. It could also be compared with 2b, which totals 18 syllables, divided 7/11. The vocable count follows: 5a: 18 + 4 = 22 (2 + 3 + 4 / 2 + 3 + 2 + 3 + 3 = 22); 5b: 23 + 5 = 28 (2 + 2 + 3 / 2 + 2 + 3 + 4 / 2 + 3 / 5 = 28).

REFRAIN (A)

Verse 6

The metrical pattern is 2:2 / 2:2. From the syllabic point of view, there is some question about the proper count for *ymynk*, which may be considered 3 or 4 depending on whether the vowel after *nun* was elided or not. It is barely possible that the extra syllable was counted in one bicolon and not in the other, for metrical reasons. The preservation of the archaic infinitive form *ne'dōrī* may also have a metrical basis among other reasons. The syllable count would then be: 6a: 5:5, 5:4. The vocable count is: 6a: 12 + 2 = 14 (2 + 4 + 2 / 3 + 3 = 14) for the first colon, and 12 + 3 = 15 (3 + 3 + 3 / 2 + 4 = 15) for the second; 6b: 12 + 2 = 14 for the first colon, and 11 + 2 = 13 (3 + 3 / 3 + 4 = 13) for the second. The apparent discrepancy between $6a^2$ and $6b^2$ could be corrected, if desired, by reading the plural *'ōyᵉbīm* with LXX against MT *'ōyēb*. This would produce 5 syllables and 15 vocables in exact parallel with 6a; the inclusion of the archaic *ī* ending on *n'dr* seems to suggest that the poet required a fifth syllable in that colon. Other emendations in $6b^2$ are possible, such as adding the modal ending to the verb or the case ending to the noun. It must also be recognized that there may have been a slight shift in the rhythm corresponding to the shift in content from the first colon of each half-line to the second.

STROPHE I

Verse 7

The structure of vs 7 is fairly intricate, and deserves extended comment. The initial impression is that the second bicolon (7b) interprets and elaborates on the central element in the first—namely, the destruction of the foes. Further to be noted is the close parallel between $7a^1$ and b^1 in which the terms *g'wnk* and *ḥrnk* not only complement each other but rhyme; the means of destruction is the majestic anger of Yahweh. We must in fact combine these cola to get at the intention of the poet. The term *rb* applies as well to *ḥrn* as to *g'wn*; so also *tšlḥ* must extend to *g'wn*, since it governs *ḥrn*. These are symbolically the weapons or armed messengers whom Yahweh sends out to perform the act of punishment. The presentation here reflects two important themes of Canaanite myth: the messenger gods who perform the will of the sovereign deity, and the personified weapons of the god in his battle against the foe. The term *g'wn* may be the symbol of sovereignty of the king of the gods, the royal mace which is used to smash (cf Ps 58: 7, "Knock their teeth out of their mouths"), while *ḥrn* represents the sword which devours the foe as flames consume stubble. The association of anger with fire, and of both with the sword, is so standardized that the poet needs only to hint at the combination in his allusive statement to evoke all three images. It may be added that the verse is highly figurative in the context, since so far as we are aware there was no battle, no fire, no sword—only watery death. But these phrases point to the unique majesty of the king of the gods and his special prerogatives.

The meter of vs 7 is 2:2 / 2:2. The syllable count is as follows: 7a: 6 or 7 (depending on whether the original vowel after *n* in *g'wnk* was still pronounced or elided at the time of the poet; presumably he could have chosen either pronunciation. The initial *waw* is probably emphatic rather than conjunctive. / 6 (I suggest that we read **taharris* → *t^ehārēs* [Piel instead of Qal; cf Ex 23: 24], to match the emphatic *t^ešallaḥ* of the next bicolon. So far as MT is concerned, it does not affect the syllable count, which remains 3, though we may question whether the *ḥatef-pataḥ* was pronounced in forms such as *tah^arōs* in classical Hebrew.) 7b: 6 or 7 (*ḥrnk* presumably had the same vocalization as *g'wnk*, and could be taken as 3 or 4 syllables) / 6. We may conclude that the syllable count for this couplet was normalized at 12:12, as in vs 4. The vocable count is as follows: 7a: 14 + 2 = 16 (or: 2 + 2 + 4 / 2 + 4 + 2 = 16) for the first colon; 14 + 2 = 16 (2 + 3 + 3 / 3 + 3 + 2 = 16) for the second colon. 7b: 15 + 1 = 16 (2 + 3 + 3 / 2 + 4 + 2 = 16) for the first colon; 13 + 3 = 16 (3 + 2 + 3 + 3 / 2 + 3 = 16) for the second colon.

Verse 8

As already mentioned, 8a seems to belong structurally with vs 7: 8a is to be scanned as 2:2 or 4, like 7ab, while 8b and c are 3:3. At the same time, its content clearly connects with 8bc. The first colon of 8a, *wbrwḥ 'pyk*, while structurally similar to the first colon of 7, actually governs the whole of 8, thus serving a triple function. Clearly too, *n'rmw mym* is parallel to *nṣbw . . . nzlym* and *qp'w thmt*. Furthermore, 8a has 10 or, at the most, 11 syllables (depending on the count for *mym*), while 7 is consistently 12 in both parts, and 8b and c are 9. Thus we may say that 8a serves as a transition from 7 to 8bc sharing features with both preceding and succeeding couplets.

As indicated, the meter of 8a is 2:2; syllabically, the count is 6 (we do not count the *pataḥ* furtive in *rūaḥ*; it was either not pronounced or not considered significant) / 4 or 5 (we vocalize the verb *ne'ramū*, but this does not affect the count; with respect to *mym*, it is much more likely that the diphthong was preserved (*maym*) or contracted (*mēm*) rather than resolved, as in MT (*mayim*). The pattern is to be compared with vs 3. The vocable count is as follows: $8a^1$: 14 + 2 = 16 (2 + 2 + 4 / 3 + 3 + 2 = 16); $8a^2$: 10 + 2 = 12 (3 + 2 + 3 / 4 = 12); note that MT here has 12 + 1 = 13 (3 + 2 + 3 / 2 + 3 = 13). It will be observed that $8a^1$ conforms exactly to the pattern of the cola in 7 in all three systems, but that $8a^2$ does not. We may note a limited example of chiasm in 8bc. In 8b, we have after the verb a prepositional phrase followed by the subject; in 8c, the order of prepositional phrase and subject is reversed. Since this device became very popular in Hebrew poetry, it is interesting to observe its relatively modest role in this early poem.

The meter of 8bc is apparently 3:3, in contrast with the more common 2:2 / 2:2. The syllable count is 9:9; and the vocable count is 21 + 5 = 26 (or: 3 + 2 + 3 / 2 + 3 + 4 / 3 + 2 + 4 = 26) for 8b; and 21 + 4 = 25 (or: 2 + 2 + 3 / 2 + 3 + 4 / 2 + 3 + 4 = 25) for 8c.

STROPHE I B

Verse 9

Various poetic devices are employed in this verse. Notice should be taken of the alliterative pattern at the beginning of the verse (the first five words begin with *aleph*, perhaps as an onomatopoeic way of evoking the clatter of horses and chariots). Connected with this is the repetition of first person forms throughout the triad: four imperfect 1 s. forms of the verb, and three 1 s. pronominal suffixes attached to nouns, making 7 in all (cf Ps 74: 13 ff, in which the pronoun *'t* is repeated 7 times to symbolize the divine assault on the seven heads of the sea dragon).[12] In the balancing triad vss 12–13, 2 m.s. forms are used for God, by contrast with the enemy. There are four perfect forms of the verb, and four pronominal suffixes of the 2 m.s. attached to nouns, making 8 in all. Perhaps the sequence 7:8 familiar in Ugaritic and Hebrew poetry is deliberate in this case. The metrical scheme in vs 9 is 2:2 / 2:2 / 2:2. The syllable count produces 4/4 = 8; 5/6 = 11; and 4/6 = 10. With this should be compared the similar triad, vs 15: 9/ 9/ 9. The vocable count produces the following results: 9a: 10 + 2 = 12 (or: 2 + 3/ 3 + 4 = 12) for the first colon; 12 + 2 = 14 (3 + 4 / 3 + 4 = 14) for the second colon; 9b: 13 + 2 = 15 (2 + 3 + 4 / 2 + 4 = 15) for the first colon; 14 + 3 = 17 (3 + 2 + 3 + 3 / 3 + 3 = 17) for the second colon; 9c: 10 + 2 = 12 (2 + 4 / 3 + 3 = 12) for the first colon, and 12 + 5 = 17 (3 + 3 + 3 + 3 / 2 + 3 = 17) for the second colon.

In defense of MT, *tml'mw* and *twryšmw* with 3 m.pl. suffix, against LXX which apparently does not read them, it may be pointed out that the poet had a special interest in using the archaic form of the suffix. Including the cases under discussion, it occurs exactly seven times with imperfect forms of the verb, and in patterns which can hardly be the result of accident:

7 yō'k^{e}lēmō — 15 yō'ḥ^{a}zēmō
9 timlā'ēmō — 17 t^{e}bī'ēmō
9 tōrīšēmō — 17 tiṭṭā'ēmō
12 tiblā'ēmō

The single occurrences in vss 7, 12, and 15 all refer to actions against the Egyptians (7, 12) and the other nations (15). The forms in 7 and 15 match (Qal imperfect 3 m.s.) even with respect to vocalization (*pe aleph* verbs with initial *ō*). The subject in each case is an abstract noun; whereas the object varies from the Egyptians in the first case to the Moabites in the second: Yahweh's anger devours the former, while trembling seizes the latter.

The paired verbs in vss 9 and 17 have the Israelites as the object. In the former, it is the enemy who threatens them with conquest and annihilation: "my gullet will be filled with them, my hand will conquer them." In the latter, it is Yahweh who brings them into the land and plants them there. The first pair have 3 f.s. verbal prefixes, whereas the latter have 2 m.s. prefixes (the poet has taken advantage of the fact that these are homonymous forms—both represented by *t*). In each pair there is a Qal form and a Hiphil form, balanced chiastically.

9 (Q) tml'mw — tb'mw (H) 17
9 (H) twryšmw — tṭ'mw (Q) 17

Verse 10

In content, vs 10 is very similar to vs 5; in form and meter, 10a closely resembles 8a and 3, while 10b corresponds to the pattern of vss 4 and 7. The basic meter is 4:4 (or 2:2 / 2:2), but 10a is measurably shorter than 10b. Thus the syllable count in 10a is: 6 (reading *brwḥk* as three syllables): 4 (note that in *ksmw* the final *yōd* of the root has been elided, contrary to the practice in vs 5, where it has been preserved, *yksymw*; in our judgment, metrical considerations figure in the choice of the poet). In 10b, the count is: 6 (reading *kʿprt* as three syllables against MT, since the ending was originally monosyllabic—*part* or *pirt*): 5 (reading *mym* as *maym* or *mēm* instead of MT *mayim*). The syllable count is thus 10:11. The vocable count is 10a:14 + 1 = 15 (or: 2 + 3 + 2 / 2 + 4 + 2 = 15) for the first colon, and 10 + 2 = 12 (or: 3 + 2 + 3 / 4 = 12) for the second; 10b: 14 + 2 = 16 / (or: 2 + 2 + 3 / 2 + 3 + 4 = 16) for the first colon and 13 + 3 = 16 (or: 2 + 4 / 3 + 3 + 4 = 16) for the second.

REFRAIN (B)

Verse 11

Another instance of partial chiasm is to be noted (cf vs 8). After the initial interrogative expression, we have a prepositional phrase followed by the vocative form Yahweh in the first colon. In the second colon, however, the corresponding vocative, *nʾdr*, is followed by the prepositional phrase. With regard to the prepositional phrases, we may point to the m.pl. form *ʾlym* in the first colon, which is balanced by an abstract (or collective) singular form *qdš* in the second, a poetic device which occurs frequently in the Psalter. It may be added that in prose the two words would naturally be combined: "the holy gods," as in the Phoenician inscription of *Yḥymlk* from Byblus.[13] In similar fashion, *nʾdr* (here the Niphal participle m.s.) is linked to *yhwh*—that is, "Yahweh, the resplendent."

From the metrical point of view, the structure seems to be 4:4:4 (or 2:2 / 2:2 / 2:2) as was the case in vs 6. However, in each bicolon a case can be made for 3 stresses (depending on how we analyze *my-kmkh*, or whether we take *ʿśh plʾ* as a single unit in 11c), as is true presumably of vs 16cd, which also serves as a divider. The syllable count is somewhat easier to manage, though some variation is possible. Vs 11a: 4/5; 11b: 4/4 or 5 (depending on whether we read *bqdš* as 3 with MT, or 2 on the basis of an earlier monosyllabic pronunciation *qudš-*); 11c: 5/3 or 4 (if we read *plʾ* with MT we have 4 syllables for this colon, but 3 if we revert to an earlier monosyllabic form. In the latter case, however, it seems likely that the case ending would have been retained if the final *aleph* of the root was to be pronounced at all—that is, *pilʾi* or *pilʾa*). Our judgment is that the triad consisted of bicola of 9, 8, and 8 or 9 syllables. The vocable count is as follows: 11a: 8 + 2 = 10 (3 + 2 + 3 + 2 = 10) for the first colon, and 12 + 3 = 15 (or: 2 + 3 + 4 / 3 + 3 = 15) for the second; 11b: 10 for the first colon, and 12 + 2 = 14 (3 + 4 / 2 + 5 = 14) for the second; 11c: 12 + 3 (omitting the *aleph* at the end of *nwrʾ* from the count) = 15 (or: 3 + 3 / 2 + 3 + 4 = 15) for the first colon, and 8 + 2 (counting either the final *segol* or the final *aleph* of *plʾ* but not both) = 10 (or: 3 + 3 / 4 = 10).

As has been pointed out, the refrain in vs 11 is longer and more elaborate than the ones in vss 6 and 16 which follow a similar pattern. In the present case, the third bicolon picks up the participle in 11b (*n'dr*), and expands on the theme of the fear-inspiring, wonder-working Deity. Thus *nwr'* is parallel to *n'dr*, and *'śh pl'* partakes of the same numinous quality. By thus concentrating on the unique splendor of Yahweh, in contrast with other divine beings, and his mighty works, the poet here reaches the climactic point in his composition. Standing at the center and apex of the poem, it relates equally to both strophes: the God described in vs 11 is equally responsible for the victory at the sea and for the triumphant march to the Holy Land. By being less specific than the other refrains, which relate directly to the theme of their respective strophes (i.e., vs 6 focuses on the powerful right hand of Yahweh by which he wreaked destruction on the enemy; vs 16 speaks of the passage of the people of Yahweh into the promised land), vs 11 serves them both as center and fulcrum.

STROPHE II

Verses 12–14

Vss 12–13 form a triad of bicola, in which the first (vs 12) recapitulates the content of the first half of the poem, while the latter two carry the story from that point. The destruction of the Egyptian host is the necessary condition and presupposition of the march through the wilderness, so that the association of these ideas in a single unit is entirely in order. If that were insufficient to convince, then the word patterns in the three bicola provide additional evidence of their purposeful combination in the plan of the poet: thus each bicolon begins with a perfect form of the verb (2 m.s.); the verbs form an alliterative sequence—*naṭīta, naḥīta, nēhalta*—and each verb is followed by a noun with the 2 m.s. suffix: *ymynk, bḥsdk, b'zk.* While 13ab are more closely related in content, 12 clearly belongs to the same scheme.

The structure of Strophe II is essentially the same as that of Strophe I, though there are some minor variations. That structure has already been discussed and defended. At the same time, there is a contrasting movement in the two strophes, toward and away from the central point in vs 11. Thus we may expect to find certain points of contact between Part A of Strophe I and Part B of Strophe II, and similarly between Part B of Strophe I and Part A of Strophe II, reflecting a certain chiasm in the whole pattern of the poem and cutting across the purely structural lines.

Vs 12 serves as a connecting link between the two strophes, and constitutes an admirable parallel to 10a, providing a sequence of synonymous terms in the same order:

10a	nšpt brwḥk ksmw ym	You blew with your breath The sea covered them
12	nṭyt ymynk tbl'mw 'rṣ	You stretched out your hand The netherworld swallowed them

Vs 13, however, correlates well with the opening couplet of Strophe I, vs 7. Just as the theme of vs 7 is the destructive violence of Yahweh against his enemies, so in vs 13 emphasis is placed on the constructive care and guidance of his own people. The twin instruments of military punishment in vs 7, *g'wnk* and *ḥrnk*, are balanced by Yahweh's protective agents in vs 13, *ḥsdk* and *'zk*. The imperfect verbs *thrs* and *tšlḥ* are matched by the perfect forms *nḥyt* and *nhlt*, while in the subordinate clauses we have *y'klmw* balanced by *zw g'lt*. It is not yet clear what distinction, if any, is to be drawn between perfect and imperfect forms in early Hebrew poetry; it is clear that they are interchangeable so far as tense is concerned, and it may be that the poet's choice is purely stylistic. (Note the alternations between perfect and imperfect, or vice versa, in vss 5, 12, 14, 15, 17.) From the point of view of the poet, it can be argued that all the action of the poem (vss 4–17) is in the past, or at least that there is no warrant for supposing that any of the verbs are necessarily in the future tense.

There is also a correlation between vss 12–13 and vs 9. In vs 9, the enemy boasted, and his boasting was made emphatic by the repetition of the first person singular forms no fewer than seven times. Now in vss 12–13, we have the counter to man's boasting—namely, God's action. In this triad, the second person singular used of Yahweh is repeated eight times, thus confirming the old adage that man proposes but God disposes.

Metrically, the structure of vss 12–13 is 4:4:4 (or 2:2 / 2:2 / 2:2). The syllable count has some slight uncertainties but is fairly regular: 12: 6 or 7 (depending on whether we vocalize the shewa after *n* in *ymynk*; originally there was a connecting vowel here, but it ultimately was elided) / 5 or 6 (if we follow MT in the pronunciation of *'rṣ*, then the count is 6; if we read it as a monosyllable, it is 5). The minimum total for the verse is 11. The count in 13 is as follows: 13a: 7 (in this case we cannot avoid reading some vowel after *d* in *bḥsdk*) / 5; 13b: 7 (we also need a vowel after *'z* in *b'zk*) / 6. The vocable count is as follows: 12: 13 + 2 = 15 (or: 2 + 3 + 2 / 2 +4 + 2 = 15) for the first colon, and 13 + 3 = 16 (or: 3 + 2 + 3 + 3 / 5 = 16) for the second. Vs 13a: 15 + 1 = 16 (or: 2 + 3 + 2 / 2 + 3 + 2 + 2 = 16) for the first colon, and 12 + 2 = 14 (or: 3 + 3 / 2 + 4 + 2 = 14) for the second. Vs 13b: 16 + 1 = 17 (or: 3 + 3 + 2 / 2 + 3 + 2 + 2 = 17) for the first colon, and 14 + 1 = 15 (or: 3 / 2 + 3 / 3 + 2 + 2 = 15) for the second. On this method of reckoning, the triad of bicola balances out satisfactorily, with the total for 13a and b (30 + 32) coming out exactly double that of 12 (31).

With regard to the two bicola of vs 13, we wish to point to an interesting example of combination or enjambment. To begin with, we have closely parallel first cola: *nḥyt bḥsdk* / *nhlt b'zk*, though, strictly speaking, *ḥsd* and *'z* complement rather than duplicate each other. A form of hendiadys is indicated here: "your mighty *ḥesed*" or "your merciful strength." For the rest, we have two separate objects—one direct, the other indirect—which are not parallel at all but are in sequence. They are meant to be taken together as the objects of the verbs, which are themselves synonymous. If we were to write the verse as prose, we could bring out the intended sense as follows: "You led / guided in your powerful kindness the people whom you redeemed, to your holy habitation." Thus we have in vs 13 three types of material distributed between the cola: synonyms, *nḥyt* // *nhlt*; complements or combinations which belong together but are often divided between cola in poetry: *bḥsdk—b'zk*, cf *b'lym—bqdš* in vs 11; supplements or sequences, *'m-zw g'lt* and *'l-nwh qdšk*. Vs 14 concludes Part A of Strophe II. Part B is then an elaboration of this verse; in a similar way, Part B of Strophe I is an elaboration of vs 7 in Part A. The metrical pattern is presumably 3:3, though 4 is a possibility for the second colon (it depends on how the first two words, *ḥyl 'ḥz*, are treated). The syllable count is 8/8 (counting *plšt* as 2 syllables rather than 3 with MT). The vocable count is as follows: 14a: 20 + 3 = 23 (or: 2 + 2 + 3 / 3 + 4 / 3 + 2 + 4 = 23), and 14b: 20 + 4 = 24 (or: 4 / 2 + 3 / 3 + 2 + 3 / 2 + 5 = 24).

STROPHE II B

Verse 15–16ab

While structurally parallel to vss 9–10 (Part B of Strophe I), which also consist of a triad and couplet in that order, this stanza has very interesting affinities with Part A of Strophe I, thus reflecting the contrasting movement toward and away from the central point of the poem. In this case, in a chiastic arrangement, vs 15 corresponds to the triad 8abc, while 16ab corresponds to vs 7, thus providing a closing sequence to match the opening sequence in vss 7–8. While the subject matter of vs 15 corresponds more closely to that of vs 9 (i.e., the enemy or foreign nations) and there is a striking contrast between the boastful words of the "enemy" in 9 and the horror-struck silence of the "foreigners" in vs 15 as a result of the intervening action of Yahweh, there are other factors which link 15 and 8. Thus we have three synonymous nouns, the subject of the action in each triad: *mym, nzlym, thmt* in 8, and the compounds *'lwpy 'dwm, 'yly mw'b, yšby kn'n* in 15. Then there are two Niphal perfect forms of the verb in each triad, along with one *Qal* form. There are partial chiasms in both triads: *kmw-nd nzlym* // *thmt blb-ym* in 8 and *nbhlw 'lwpy 'dwm* // *'yly mw'b y'ḥzmw . . . nmgw . . . yšby kn'n* in 15. Both triads express Yahweh's complete control over nature (8) and nations (15), which serve as instruments in the achievement of his purpose.

Vs 16ab is structurally parallel to vs 10, and there is a certain similarity of content. Both describe the completion of Yahweh's work with respect to the "enemy" (10) and the "nations" (16). There are also resemblances to vs 7, but this is not surprising in view of the similarity in content and form of 7 and 10. Thus the reference to *'ymth wpḥd* reminds us of *g'wn* and *ḥrn* in vs 7 as well as the *mym 'dyrym* of vs 10, while in 16b *bgdl zrw'k* evokes *brb g'wnk* of 7 as well as *brwḥk* of 10; *ydmw k'bn* is reminiscent of *y'klmw kqš* structurally if not strictly according to content, and *ṣllw k'prt* of vs 10; cf also *yrdw . . . k'bn* in vs 5.

Metrically the stanza scans as a triad (vs 15) 4:4:4 (or 2:2 / 2:2 / 2:2) and a couplet (16ab) 4:4 (or 2:2 / 2:2). The problem of 15c has been discussed; in all likelihood we should read *kl* as an adverb modifying *nmgw* rather than as a pronoun in the construct chain with *yšby kn'n* (note the parallels *'lwpy 'dwm* and *'yly mw'b* with two words each). The syllable count is as follows: 4:5 / 4:5 vocalizing *r'd* as monosyllabic (rather than as bisyllabic as in MT) / 4:5 counting *kn'n* as two syllables against three in MT. The parallel triad, vs 9, does not offer much help in deciding the question, since its bicola range from 8 to 11. Presumably the normal figure would be 27 for the triad and 9 for each member. The vocable count follows: 15a: $10 + 2 = 12$ (or: $4 / 3 + 2 + 3 = 12$) for the first colon, and $12 + 3 = 15$ (or: $3 + 3 + 3 / 2 + 4 = 15$) for the second; 15b: $9 + 4 = 13$ (or: $3 + 3 / 3 + 4 = 13$) for the first colon, and $12 + 4 = 16$ (or: $3 + 2 + 3 + 3 / 5 = 16$) for the second colon (MT would be $13 + 4 = 17$); 15c: $9 + 3 = 12$ (or: $2 + 3 + 3 / 4 = 12$) for the first colon, and $12 + 3 = 15$ (or: $3 + 2 + 3 / 2 + 5 = 15$) for the second (MT would be $13 + 3 = 16$).

The syllable count in 16ab is as follows: 16ab: 5/6 (depending upon how we read *pḥd*; if we follow MT or read *paḥda*, with the accusative case ending to match *'ymth*, then the total would be 6; if we reduce *pḥd* to its monosyllabic state, the figure would be 5); 16b: 6/5 (with regard to the first colon, the figure can be as low as 5 or as high as 7, giving an adequate mean of 6). MT *bigdōl* reflects the elision of a syllable in the phrase which more originally read *bəgadōl*; on the other hand we should elide the *ḥatef pataḥ* after *'ayin* in *zrw'k*. Eliminating both vowels, we would have 5 syllables; counting both, we would have 7. In the second colon, we vocalize *'bn* as a monosyllable in accordance with the older pronunciation. We parse *ydmw* as Niphal imperfect of *dmm* reading *yiddammū*.

The vocable count is as follows: 16a: 13 + 2 = 15 (or: 3 + 4 / 2 + 3 + 3 = 15) for the first colon, and 13 + 2 = 15 (or: 3 + 3 + 2 / 2 + 2 + 3 = 15) for the second; 16b: 14 + 2 = 16 (or: 2 + 2 + 4 / 2 + 4 + 2 = 16) for the first colon (MT would be 17); and 14 + 2 = 16 (or: 3 + 3 + 3 / 2 + 5 = 16) for the second (MT would be 17).

REFRAIN (C)

Vs 16cd is the third refrain or divider, and closes off the main part of the poem with an explicit reference to the passage of Israel into the Holy Land, thus recapitulating the second strophe (cf vs 13 especially).

The meter is apparently 3:3. The syllable count is as follows: 16c: 8, since we do not read the *ḥatef pataḥ* in *y'br*, against MT 16d: 8. The vocable count is as follows: 16c: 21 + 2 = 23 (or: 3 / 3 + 4 / 3 + 2 + 2 / 3 + 3 = 23; MT would be 24); and 16d: 20 + 3 = 23 (or: 3 / 3 + 4 / 3 / 3 / 2 + 3 + 2 = 23; MT would be 24). These totals may be compared with those for vss 14, 11, 8bc, and 5.

THE CLOSING

Vss 17–18 constitute the closing section, comparable in structure with vss 3–5, which constitute the opening. The two together form a strophe comparable to the regular strophes in the body of the poem, and thus enclose the main part of the poem. Each consists of five units. For the opening, vs 3 is the initial unit, while the corresponding unit in the closing is the final bicolon, vs 18. In similar fashion, vs 4 constitutes the "long" couplet following the initial unit (4:4 or 2:2 / 2:2); and vs 17bc in the closing, following in reverse order, corresponds to this unit in the opening. It also is 4:4 (or 2:2 / 2:2). That leaves vs 5 to match 17a. Since 5 is somewhat irregular, it should not surprise us to find 17a also a bit abnormal. The latter appears to be 2:2 (though unbalanced), while 5 seems to be 2:3 (though 3:3 or 3:4 is also possible). The syllable count for 17a would be 9/6 (counting *nḥltk* as 4 syllables in place of MT *naḥᵃlātᵉkā* which has 5, or a possible *naḥlatka* with 3. Vs 5, on the other hand, was unbalanced in the other direction, and is now counted 8/10. It is possible to reduce each colon by one and produce 7/9, which would counterbalance approximately vs 17a 9/6. The vocable count for 17a is as follows: 19 + 5 = 24 (or 2 + 3 + 3 + 3 / 2 + 3 + 2 + 3 + 3 = 24) for the first colon, and 14 + 1 = 15 (or: 2 + 3 / 3 + 3 + 2 + 2 = 15) for the seond colon. At the same time, the minimum count for vs 5 would be 20 and 26, showing that there is still a considerable discrepancy.

The real question is whether we are entitled to divide 17a after *wṭṭ'mw*, thus placing the two verbs in the first colon and the prepositional phrase in the second. There is no other division like it elsewhere in the poem (9a hardly qualifies), and normally we would read the colon as follows:

wtṭ'mw bhr nḥltk	Indeed you have planted them in the mountain you possess

This would provide us with the 3-stress colon indicated by comparison with 5b, while the syllable count of approximately 11 corresponds well with the 10 or 11 of 5b. That leaves the first colon somewhat short with only *tb'mw*, and we must suppose then that something has fallen out. If 5a is to serve as a guide, then only one word (plus preposition) is to be supplied (e.g., *'el 'ereṣ* or the like). However, if we disregard such precise indications, we may be helped by having recourse to Ps 78: 54, where the same verb is used in a closely parallel context:

wyby'm 'l-gbwl qdšw	And he brought them into his holy territory
hr-zh qnth ymynw	The mountain which his right arm created.

We would therefore be inclined to add *'el gəbūl qōdšeka* to the first colon of 17a, thus balancing the bicolon and producing a 3:3 meter to correspond to the strophic structure of the poem as a whole, and the opening stanza in particular. The syllable count would be 10 for the first colon, and 11 for the second. The vocable count would be 23 + 4 = 27 (2 + 3 + 3 + 3 / 3 / 2 + 4 / 3 + 2 + 2 = 27) for the first colon, and 25 + 3 = 28 (2 + 3 + 2 + 3 + 3 / 2 + 3 / 3 + 3 + 2 + 2 = 28) for the second. The second colon of 17a corresponds exactly to 5b (also 28), while the first is somewhat longer than 5a.

However we deal with vs 17a, there can be no question that the "mount of inheritance"—that is, Yahweh's own portion—is the promised land of Canaan, which is the earthly counterpart of the heavenly mountain on which Yahweh dwells. Whether any particular mountain or range is meant is dubious though doubtless after the establishment of the temple in Jerusalem, Mount Zion was understood to be the point of reference. In the light of 17a, the meaning of 17b and c can be clarified: the "dais of your throne" (17b) and "your sanctuary" (17c) refer to the same "mount of inheritance," and specify the divine palace and throne which Yahweh himself has fashioned. These are, in the first place, the heavenly prototypes in which Yahweh dwells, and, second, describe the sacred territory which Yahweh has claimed for himself. The language is mythopoeic and therefore inexact, but it cannot refer to any existing earthly sanctuary, since all these have been made by human hands not God's. Both tabernacle and temple were regarded as human achievements, albeit based on plans provided by God and in imitation of the heavenly abode of the Deity. But what is described here is a work of God, his heavenly palace-sanctuary. His corresponding earthly abode is the Holy Land, into which he has now brought his people. There, as in heaven, he shall reign eternally.

The metrical pattern of 17bc is 4:4 (or: 2:2 / 2:2), while the syllable count is for 17b: 6/5, and for 17c: 4 or 5 (the reading *yhwh* has strong textual support, and is most likely more original than *'dny*) / 6. The vocable count is as follows: 17b: 14 + 1 = 15 (or 2 + 4 / 2 + 3 + 2 + 2 = 15) for the first colon, and 12 + 1 = 13 (or: 2 + 3 + 2 / 3 + 3 = 13) for the second; 17c: 13 + 2 = 15 (or: 3 + 4 / 2 + 3 + 3 = 15) for the first colon (if we read *yhwh* instead of *'dny*, then the count is reduced to 13); and 12 + 3 = 15 (or: 3 + 2 + 3 / 2 + 3 + 2 = 15) for the second.

Vs 18 closes the poem, forming an *inclusio* with vs 3 as already mentioned. It is a single bicolon of 4 beats or 2:2 meter. The syllable count is 4/5, and the vocable count is as follows: 18a: 11 + 2 = 13 (or: 3 + 3 / 3 + 4 = 13) for the first colon, and 12 + 2 = 14 (or: 2 + 3 + 4 / 2 + 3 = 14) for the second.

On the basis of the transmitted text, we believe that a strong case can be made for the essential unity of the poem in Exodus 15. A repeated pattern of strophes and stanzas, marked off by refrains, in a determinate metrical structure has been demonstrated for the main part of the poem vss 3–18. The Exordium, vs 2, may have been attached in order to provide the proper liturgical framework for presentation of the poem in public worship (by a prophetic or royal representative). Concerning vss 1 and 21, we suggest that they constituted an opening and closing refrain similar to the other dividers which set off the major sections of the poem. Structurally vss 1 and 21 are very much like vs 6 (2:2 / 2:2; syllable count 10:9, which is the same as vs 21); and they share the practice of the dividers in using the name Yahweh.

The main body of the poem falls into two parts (vss 3–10, and vss 12–18). The principal theme of the first part is the victory of Yahweh over the Egyptians at the Reed Sea. The principal theme of the second part is Israel's march through the wilderness and passage into the promised land under the guidance of the same Yahweh. Thus Yahweh the warrior, who annihilates his foes, is identified with Yahweh the redeemer, who saves his people and establishes them in their new homeland. The themes are linked causally. It is the victory at the sea which permits the people of God to escape from bondage; and it is through his devastating display of power that Yahweh overawes the other nations who might otherwise block the passage of the Israelites. Thus the one mighty action produces two notable results: the destruction of the enemy; and the intimidation of the other nations, who are paralyzed by fear and cannot obstruct the victorious march of the Israelites or their successful entry into the Holy Land. At one stroke therefore the Egyptians "went down into the depths *like a stone*" and the other nations "were struck dumb *like a stone*." Neither could interfere with the realization of the divine plan—to release the slaves and establish them in a new land.

The refrains carry the same content as the opening and closing. The first of these (vs 6) emphasizes the mighty hand of Yahweh in dealing death to the enemy, while the third (vs 16) speaks of the passage of Yahweh's people into the Holy Land. The victory at the sea is Yahweh's alone, and it makes possible the passage of the people. The second refrain stands at the center of the poem, and is an elaborate apostrophe on the incomparability of Yahweh. It serves to link not only the two major parts of the poem but also the thematic statements at the beginning and end: vs 3, Yahweh the warrior, and vs 18, Yahweh the king who will reign over his people.

The strophes develop in detail the thematic statements concerning the victory at the sea and the passage of the people. Thus Strophe I deals with specific aspects of the victory over the Egyptians. Part I (vss 7–8) treats of Yahweh's overwhelming rage and the violent storm with which he stirs up the sea. The stage is set for the appearance of the antagonist. Part II (vss 9–10) shows the enemy in all his boastful folly (vs 9). He is already gloating over the spoils, gorging himself on his prey, when the raging sea breaks over his head, and he sinks like lead in the dreadful waters (vs 10). Act one has ended.

The second strophe presents the aftermath, Israel's march through the wilderness and entry into the promised land. The theme is mentioned in the first part (vs 13), to be repeated and expanded in the closing section of the poem. This part closes with a reference to the effect of the victory at the sea on the other nations: When they heard, they trembled; terror seized them (vs 14). The second part of the strophe (vss 15–16) develops this interest in detail: Overwhelmed by divine fear and dread, they are benumbed, and watch helplessly as the people cross over into the promised land, Yahweh's own possession.

While we do not expect a poem, especially in the mythopoeic tradition, to record historical experience soberly and in sequence, we can use it, with caution, to recover a historical tradition. Since the poem comes from the twelfth century in all likelihood, its relative proximity to the events which it celebrates makes it a prime witness, if not to the events themselves, then at least to the effect produced on the people of Israel by them. In this connection, both what is said and what is omitted (in contrast with the prose traditions concerning the victory at the sea and the entry into the land) are of special interest. With regard to the episode at the Reed Sea, the poet focuses on the storm at sea and the drowning of the Egyptian chariot force. By contrast, nothing is said of the passage of Israel on dry ground, or in fact of Israel at all in connection with the event. The only passage of which the poet is conscious or that he mentions is the crossing into Canaan (vs 16cd).

With regard to the entry into the promised land, the poet speaks of Yahweh's guidance and protection and at some length of the total paralysis of the nations, which enabled Israel to enter without opposition. Nothing at all is said of the battles with those peoples or of the victories by Moses and Joshua over them which are described in detail in the prose narratives. According to the poet, only one battle counted, and one victory, at the sea; that was enough to permanently disable Egypt and at the same time terrify the other nations into complete passivity. The victory was total—and totally Yahweh's. Israel contributed nothing then or later, except to march under divine guidance. While the poet's view is essentially the same as that of the bulk of biblical writers, historians, and prophets, it is radically stated, and suggests a certain background or orientation on the part of the poet, to which the views of Isaiah or Hosea may be compared. But perhaps we should not press a poet too far in any particular direction.

One fairly certain result of the analysis of this poem is the establishment of a strophic structure. The poem has been organized into a regular pattern of strophes and stanzas, with divisions marked by refrains. Opening and closing stanzas form an envelope in which the body of the poem is encased. An Exordium or Proem introduces the whole. We have also suggested a role for vss 1 and 21.

Within this larger framework, an attempt has been made to describe the internal metrical pattern of the stanzas and strophes. Following the commonly accepted stress- or accent-counting system, we arrive at the following scheme:

Introduction (vs 1b):	2:2	______	2:2
Exordium (vs 2):	3:3	______	3:3
Opening (vss 3–5):			
3	2:2		
4	3:2		2:2
5		3:3	
Refrain (A) (vs 6):	2:2		2:2

Strophe I (vss 7–10):			
A (7–8)			
7	2:2		2:2
8		2:2	
		3:3	
B (9–10)			
9	2:2	2:2	2:2
10		2:2 2:2	
Refrain (B) (vs 11):	2:2	2:2	2:2
Strophe II (vss 12–16ab):			
A (12–14)			
12		2:2	
13	2:2		2:2
14		3:3	
B (15–16ab)			
15	2:2	2:2	2:2
16ab		2:2 2:2	
Refrain (C) (vs 16cd):		3:3	
Closing (vss 17–18):			
17		2:2 (or 3:3)	
	2:2		2:2
18		2:2	
Conclusion (vs 21b):	2:2		2:2

According to this scheme, the prevailing metrical pattern is a bicolon 2:2 (or simply a colon of 4). It occurs separately as a unit, as well as in couplets and triads: Units: vss 3, 8a, 12, 17a, 18; Couplets: 1b, 4, 6, 7, 10, 13, 16ab, 17bc; Triads: 9, 11, 15. A variant pattern is 3:3, which occurs in vss 5, 8bc, 14, 16cd. We have the apparently anomalous 3:2 in 4a, and a possible 2:3 in 5, as well as a peculiar situation in 17a, but each of these is susceptible of explanation (see Notes).

The Strophes consist of two stanzas each, while the stanzas are made up of several units. IA (7–8) consists of two couplets with a transition link between them: the first couplet has bicola of 2:2, and the link is a bicolon with the same pattern. The closing bicolon is 3:3. The parallel stanza, Strophe IIA (12–14), has the same units in different order: an opening bicolon 2:2, followed by a couple of bicola 2:2, and a closing bicolon 3:3. The B stanzas, on the other hand, have a slightly different structure. They consist of a triad 2:2 / 2:2 / 2:2 followed by a couplet 2:2 / 2:2.

The refrains show some variation: vss 1 and 21, as well as vs 6, are couplets: 2:2 / 2:2; vs 16cd is a bicolon 3:3; vs 11 is a triad 2:2 / 2:2 / 2:2. Each of these types is attested in the Strophes.

The opening and closing stanzas have a structure similar to that of the Strophe stanzas: the opening (vss 3–5) begins with a bicolon, followed by two couplets, the first 2:2 / 2:2, the second 3:3 (similar to IIA). The closing (vss 17–18) begins with a bicolon 2:2, continues with a couplet 2:2 / 2:2, and ends with another bicolon 2:2. As it stands, it is somewhat anomalous, since it does not conform to any of the patterns so far noted. The difficulties in the analysis of 17a have been discussed, and we have proposed an emendation which results in a 3:3 pattern.

The Exordium (vs 2) consists of a quatrain 3:3 / 3:3, but its structure is by no means symmetrical. This pattern is otherwise unattested in the poem.

On the face of it, the patterns exhibited in this schematic presentation are sufficiently regular to show that some metrical structure is inherent in the poem. Its precise nature remains elusive, however, because the analysis is rather flexible, not to say loose. The categories tend to be broad and indefinite, and the terms rather vague, referring to a number of diverse items. In other words, such a scheme conceals more than it reveals, and the image of symmetry and regularity it presents may be inexact, indicating more consistency than is actually present. At the same time, it may fail to indicate more intricate patterns that may be present.

In the search for a more precise method of reflecting the actual meter of Hebrew poems, we have turned to syllable counting and even vocable counting (in order to make allowance for open and closed syllables, as well as the length of vowels). Not that we imagine that the Hebrew poets used such a method or were even aware of numerical ratios and equivalences in their poetic composition, but we are convinced that a strong sense of rhythm permeated poetry that was composed to be sung, and that men and women marched and danced to these songs. In fact, Ex 15 is a victory march, as both the contents and the prevailing 2:2 or 4:4 meter indicate. In marching rhythms especially, unaccented syllables must be reckoned with as well as accented ones. It is in an effort to deal with more of the phenomena and more accurately reflect the actual state of affairs that we have employed these methods alongside the more familiar stress system. It may be that such effort is wasted because of our lack of controls (of vocalization of the words and ignorance of ancient Israelite musical patterns) or because the poetry is simply not amenable to such detailed analysis. But it is worthwhile to set the evidence down and then to draw conclusions, if any. On the whole, the two proposed systems agree with each other very well and generally with the stress system, only adding detail and occasionally clarifying a hazy or erroneous impression of the actual meter before us.

Turning to the material at hand, we find the following in Strophe IA:

	A	*S*	*V*
7a	2:2	6:6	16:16
b	2:2	6:6	16:16

8a	2:2	6:4	16:12
b	3	9	26
c	3	9	25

The corresponding stanza in Strophe IIA:

	A	*S*	*V*
12	2:2	6:5	15:16
13a	2:2	7:5	16:14
b	2:2	7:6	17:15
14a	3	8	23
b	3	8	24

While the accent scheme shows no variations between the stanzas, both the syllable and vocable count do, and thus reflect the attested differences in the structure of the stanzas as well as their resemblances. The initial couplet of IA (vs 7) is shown to be absolutely symmetrical in both S and V. At the same time, 8a is shown to vary distinctly from the pattern of 7 although also designated 2:2. It is clearly shorter, and in fact close to 8bc with which it belongs, though the latter are 3:3. The balance between 8b and c is strongly attested in S and V.

In IIA, the initial bicolon (vs 12), which differs in content from the couplet in vs 13, is nevertheless structurally very similar. Both S and V bear this out, so that we have a triad in pattern if not in content. The symmetry of the concluding couplet (3:3) is borne out in S and V. Taking the stanzas as a whole, we have: for IA: 12:12 / 10 / 9:9; a total of 52 syllables; for IIA:11 / 12:13 / 8:8, also a total of 52 syllables, thus demonstrating that the stanzas are of equal length. The V count shows: IA, 32:32 / 28 / 26:25, for a total of 143; IIA, 31 / 30:32 / 23:24, for a total of 140. The discrepancy is well within the margin we must allow for possible variations in vowel length and pronunciation at the option of the poet, to say nothing of our limited knowledge of the state of the language at the time of composition.

The second stanzas of Strophes I and II may be described as follows:

Strophe IB	*A*	*S*	*V*
9a	2:2	4:4	12:14
b	2:2	5:6	15:17
c	2:2	4:6	12:17
10a	2:2	6:4	15:13
b	2:2	6:5	16:16
Strophe IIB			
15a	2:2	4:5	12:15
b	2:2	4:5	13:16
c	2:2	4:5	12:15
16a	2:2	5:6	15:15
b	2:2	6:5	16:16

While the A system shows an unbroken line of 2:2 bicolon, both S and V point to a break between the triad (vss 9 and 15) and the following couplet (vss 10 and 16ab). The former are shorter, averaging 9 syllables; the latter are longer, averaging 11 syllables. The pattern for the stanzas as a whole is: IB: 8: 11:10 / 10:11, for a total of 50; IIB: 9:9:9 / 11:11 = 49. The vocable count shows for IB: 26:32:29 / 28:32 = 147; for IIB: 27:29:27 / 30:32 = 145. Taking the Strophes as a whole, we have for I : S = 102, V = 290; for II: S = 101, V = 285.

Turning to the opening and closing stanzas, we find:

	A	*S*	*V*
Opening			
Vs 3	2:2	6:4	18:11
4a	3:2	8:4	23:11
b	2:2	6:6	17:17
5a	3(?)	8	22
b	3	10	28
		52	147
Closing			
Vs 17a	2:2	9:6	24:16
b	2:2	6:5	15:13
c	2:2	5:6	15:15
18	2:2	4:5	13:14
		46	125

The peculiarities and difficulties of both the opening and closing have already been discussed. With regard to the opening, the irregularities in the metrical count under A are resolved in S and V. As a whole, the opening conforms to the pattern of IA and IIA. The syllable count is 10 / 12:12 / 8:10 = 52; the vocable count is 29 / 34:34 / 22:28 = 147.

For the closing, if we accept 17a (2:2) as a legitimate variant of the expected 3:3, we have the following totals: S: 15 / 11:11 / 9 = 46; V: 40 / 28:30 / 27 = 125. If, however, we restore 17a, as suggested above, the totals become:

	A	*S*	*V*
Vs $17a^1$	(3)	(10)	(28)
$17a^2$	3	11	28

The revised count would be: S: 10:11 / 11:11: 9 = 52; V: 28:28 / 28:30 / 27 = 141.

The totals for the group would be:

	S	*V*
Opening	52	147
Closing	46 (52)	125 (141)
Total	98 (104)	272 (288)

The Refrains present the following pattern:

		A	*S*	*V*
	(1b)	2:2	6:5	16:13
		2:2	5:4	14:11
A	(6a)	2:2	5:5	14:15
	(6b)	2:2	5:4	14:13
B	(11a)	2:2	4:5	11:15
	(11b)	2:2	4:4	11:14
	(11c)	2:2	5:4	15:10
C	(16c)	3	8	23
	(16d)	3	8	23
	(21b)	2:2	5:5	14:13
		2:2	5:4	14:11

Taking the Refrains together as a structural unit, we have the following totals:

	S	*V*
Vs 1b	11:9 = 20	29:25 = 54
6	10:9 = 19	29:27 = 56
11	9:8:9 = 26	26:25:25 = 76
16cd	8:8 = 16	23:23 = 46
21b	10:9 = 19	27:25 = 52
Total	100	284

It is interesting to note that the total is equivalent to that of the other strophes:

	S	*V*
I	102	290
II	101	285
Opening and closing	98 (104)	272 (288)
Refrains	100	284

The Exordium (vs 2) presents the following pattern:

	A	*S*	*V*
Vs 2a	2	7	20
2b	2	7	19
2c	3	7	20
2d	3	11	28
Total		32	87

We may combine vss 1 and 2, as was done at some point in the history of the poem, to form a preliminary stanza: the various counts would be: S:32 +

20 = 52; V:87 + 54 = 141. S is thus approximately the same as S for the opening, Strophes IA, IIA, and our reconstructed closing stanza. The similarity is superficial, however, and the pattern of vss 1–2 remains uncertain. Possibly we should construe it as a couplet 2:2 / 2:2 followed by a transitional line 2:2, which leads into the closing bicolon, 3:3. The pattern would resemble that of Strophe IA, in which we have an opening couplet 2:2 / 2:2 followed by a transitional line, 2:2, which connects with a closing couplet, 3:3. The unbalanced final line of vs 2 (S, 7:11) can be compared with vs 5 (S, 8:10), also read as 3:3.

As a check on our statistical analysis, and to test the view that almost any syllable counting system will produce the same comparative results providing that it is applied consistently, we can substitute the figures derived from rigorous adherence to MT, both text and vocalization. The results show no significant change from the patterns already observed.

	S	*V*
Introductory Refrain (1b)	6:5	17:15
	5:4	14:13
Exordium (2)	6:7	19:19
	7:11	20:29
Total	51	146
Opening (3–5)		
3	6:4	19:11
4a	8:4	23:13
b	6:6	18:17
5a	7	20
b	10	29
Total	51	150
Refrain (A) (6)	6:5	16:16
	6:4	16:13
Total	21	61
Strophe IA		
Vs 7a	6:6	17:17
b	6:6	17:17
8a	6:5	17:13
b	9	26
c	9	26
Total	53	150
Strophe IB		
9a	4:4	13:14
b	5:6	16:18
c	4:6	13:18
10a	7:4	19:13
b	7:6	18:17
Total	53	159

Refrain (B)		
11a	4:5	12:16
b	4:5	12:16
c	5:4	15:11
Total	27	82
Strophe IIA		
12	6:6	18:18
13a	7:5	19:16
b	7:6	19:16
14a	8	25
b	9	26
Total	54	157
Strophe IIB		
15a	4:5	12:15
b	4:6	13:17
c	4:6	13:16
16a	5:6	15:17
b	6:6	17:17
Total	52	152
Refrain (C)		
16c	4:5	11:14
d	4:5	11:15
Total	18	51
Closing		
17a	9:7 (10) (12)	25:17 (28) (31)
b	6:5	17:15
c	5:6	16:17
18	4:5	13:15
Total	47 (53)	135 (152)
Concluding Refrain		
21b	5:5	14:15
	5:4	14:13
Total	19	56

Summary and Comparison

	S		*V*	
	MT	Prop.	MT	Prop.
Exordium (1–2)	51	52	146	140
Opening and Closing	98 (104)	98 (104)	285 (302)	272 (288)
Strophe I	106	102	309	290
Strophe II	106	101	309	285
Refrains	105	100	309	284

It is apparent that the variations introduced into MT with respect to pronunciation aad vocalization tend to cancel each other out, and that the ratios and proportions tend to remain constant. Thus all the stanzas fall within the range of 51–54 syllables in MT, which is precisely the theoretical range postulated by the possible sequences of long and short lines: that is, 3 short lines with 27 syllables, and 2 long ones with 24 syllables, making a total of 51; or 3 long lines with 36 syllables, and 2 short ones with 18, making a total of 54. The Strophes total S = 106, and V = 309, while the sum of the opening and closing stanzas is S = 104 and V = 302 (as reconstructed; as the text stands, the totals are S = 98 and V = 285). The Exordium also comes within the limits indicated at S = 51 and V = 146.

To summarize, we suggest that the poem exhibits two basic line lengths: one of approximately 12 syllables (sometimes 11, rarely 13) normally construed as 2:2; the other usually of 8 or 9 syllables (occasionally 10) and construed as 2:2 or 3. These are the basic building blocks used by the poet and ingeniously arranged in pairs or triads to produce a dramatic work of art. Designating the lines S and L, we can diagram the poet's structural pattern for the poem as follows:

Opening Refrain (1b)	S : S
Exordium (2)	S : S
	S : L
Opening (3–5)	S
	L : L
	S : S
Refrain (A) (6)	S : S
Strophe IA (7–8)	L : L
	S
	S : S
IB (9–10)	S : S : S
	L : L
Refrain (B) (11)	S : S : S
Strophe IIA (12–14)	L
	L : L
	S : S
IIB (15–16b)	S : S : S
	L : L
Refrain (C) (16cd)	S : S
Closing (17–18)	(S : S) ?
	L : L
	S
Closing refrain (21b)	S : S

In our opinion, all three systems of analysis (A = accent; S = syllable counting; V = vocables) contribute to an appreciation of the metrical patterns; of the three, S seems to be the most useful and flexible.

A few words about the date of the poem may be in order. The standpoint of the author is some time after the settlement in the Holy Land, when it would be possible to speak of a general occupation of the country. Hence the earliest date of composition would be the twelfth century B.C. Very likely the period of the United Monarchy would provide us with an adequate *terminus ad quem*. Certain details may help us to fix the date more exactly. The omission of the Ammonites from the list of nations in vss 14–15 (if it is not a happenstance owing to the exigencies of stanza construction) reflects an accurate knowledge of the political situation in the thirteenth and twelfth centuries, when only Moabites and Edomites were in that region. Later traditions, as reflected in the Deuteronomic writings, were confused on this point. Such a datum would tend to support an earlier date for the poem, or at least indicate that the author had access to reliable, presumably early historical traditions. On the other hand, the inclusion of Philistia in the list points in another direction. If the word is part of the original composition, then it reflects the hegemony established by the Philistines in the Holy Land beginning in the twelfth century. The author imagines that the Philistines were already settled in the land and, in fact, in control of much of it at the time of the wilderness wandering. He has apparently telescoped events and reversed the sequence of Israelite and Philistine entry into the land of Canaan. We must place the poem subsequent to the Philistine invasion and conquest. All the data suggest that the poem in its original form was composed in the twelfth century. Its nearest companion in form and style is the Song of Deborah, universally recognized to be a product of the same period.

We may add that the evidence of vocabulary, grammar, usage, poetic structures, and poetic devices is all inconclusive. There are numerous archaic features, correctly used, in the poem; they are certainly not inconsistent with an early date, but they do not prove it. The knowledge of many archaic elements of the language persisted in Israel, and some of them show up even in comparatively late materials. Until more refined methods are developed, and more exact information concerning poetry writing in Israel is acquired, we must rely on impressions and the few historical references and details which appear.

Notes

1 This paper is intended a a supplement to and revision of the joint article, "The Song of Miriam," *JNES* 14 (1955), 237–50, by Frank M. Cross, Jr., and me. Among recent articles on the subject, the following may be noted: B. S. Childs, "A Traditio-Historical Study of the Reed Sea Tradition," *VT* 20 (1970), 406–18; G. W. Coats, "The Traditio-Historical Character of the Reed Sea Motif," *VT* 17 (1967), 253–65; and "The Song of the Sea," *CBQ* (1969), 1–17; Cross, "The Song of the Sea and Canaanite Myth," *JTC* 5 (1968), 1–25; N. Lohfink, "Das Siegeslied am Schilfmeer," *Das Siegeslied am Schilf-*

meer (1965), pp. 103–28; J. Muilenburg, "A Liturgy on the Triumphs of Yahweh," *Studia Biblica et Semitica* (1966), pp. 233–51; D. A. Robertson, *Linguistic Evidence in Dating Early Hebrew Poetry* (University Microfilms, 1970; Yale University dissertation, 1966); P. C. Craigie, "An Egyptian Expression in the Song of the Sea (Exodus XV 4)," *VT* 20 (1970), 83–86; "Psalm XXIX in the Hebrew Poetic Tradition," *VT* 22 (1972), 143–51.

[2] *Studia Biblica et Semitica*, pp. 237 ff.

[3] M. Dahood, *Psalms II*, *AB* (1968), pp. 335, 337.

[4] While the verb *trʿṣ* may be interpreted as either a 3 f.s. or 2 m.s. form, I think it preferable to take Yahweh as the subject; *ymynk* would then be a dative of means.

[5] D. N. Freedman, "Archaic Forms in Early Hebrew Poetry," *ZAW* 62 (1960), 101–7. See also my "Prolegomenon" in G. B. Gray, *The Forms of Hebrew Poetry* (1972), pp. vii–lvi.

[6] Cross and Freedman, "A Royal Song of Thanksgiving—II Sam 22 = Psalm 18," *JBL* 72 (1953), 26 and fn. 41 for discussion of the parallel texts, II Sam 22: 16 = Ps 18: 16.

[7] See the discussion of these and similar forms in Cross and Freedman, *Early Hebrew Orthography* (1952), pp. 65–68.

[8] The problem is discussed in some detail and a solution proposed at a later point in this paper.

[9] E. M. Good, "Exodus XV 2," *VT* 20 (1970), 358–59.

[10] Dahood, *Psalms III*, *AB* (1970), pp. 411–12; examples occur in Pss 28: 8, 68: 20, and 88: 2.

[11] Cross and Freedman, *Studies in Ancient Yahwistic Poetry* (1950), pp. 45, 48 fn. *a*, for the suggested emendation. Since then it has been proposed independently by S. Gevirtz, *Patterns in the Early Poetry of Israel* (1963), pp. 83–84. A similar emendation has also been adopted by W. Holladay, "Form and Word-Play in David's Lament over Saul and Jonathan" *VT* 20 (1970), 157–59.

[12] Dahood, *Psalms II*, p. 205.

[13] W. F. Albright, "The Phoenician Inscriptions of the Tenth Century B.C. from Byblus," *JAOS* 67 (1947), 156–57.

The Aaronic Benediction (Numbers 6:24-26)

The Aaronic Benediction has come down to us through the traditions of early Israel. The setting (Num 6:22-23) explains both its preservation intact, and its function unchanged. It has the ultimate sanction of the deity, and was transmitted through Moses for use by Aaron and his priestly descendants in blessing the community of Israel. The poetic form and transparent simplicity of the piece have insured its faithful transmission through oral and written media, while its universal liturgical usefulness has guaranteed its persistence in the cult of Israel and its inheritors, the synagogue and the church.[1]

The soundness of the text has never been questioned seriously, nor can there be much doubt about the meaning or interpretation of the passage. Chief interest has lain in the word-associations, theological values, homiletical expansions and applications, as well as form-critical considerations. Little has been said about metrical pattern or structure, and apparently for a good reason. Nevertheless, just because the text is intact, and the meaning of the parts quite clear, it makes an ideal subject for metrical analysis. An inductive assembly and assessment of the data should provide us with a clear picture of this poem, the nature and relationship of its component parts, and its structure.[2]

In the following analysis, I will attempt to vocalize the text as it was spoken or chanted in the classic period of biblical Hebrew (around the 10th century B.C.). In this way it may be possible to fix the syllable count more accurately than if we simply followed the Massoretic vocalization. While the latter is generally satisfactory (and often we have no better information about pronunciation), and the results are comparable to those derived from more sophisticated methods of vocalization and syllable-counting, for a poem as brief and beautiful as this one, greater precision is both desirable and necessary.[3] It need not be added that in any metrical analysis the preserved text must be treated as given, and not subject to casual emendation, as otherwise the value of the exercise, which is to determine meter inductively, is diminished to the extent of the alterations, and is in continuous danger of becoming a self-serving expression of scholarly ingenuity and expediency. The vocalization generally follows the MT, but where there is compelling evidence for an earlier and more correct pronunciation, that is given instead.

24) *y*^{e}*bārek*^{e}*kā yahweh*	7	(a)	May Yahweh bless you
w^{e}*yišm*^{e}*rekā*	5	(b)	And may he keep you
25) *yā'ēr yahweh pānāw 'ēlekā*	9	(c)	May Yahweh make his face shine upon you
w^{e}*yaḥunnekkā*	5	(d)	And may he treat you graciously
26) *yiśśā' yahweh pānāw 'ēlekā*	9	(e)	May Yahweh lift up his face upon you
w^{e}*yāśēm l*^{e}*kā šālōm*	7	(f)	And may he grant you peace

a) That the first word (*ybrkk*) originally had five syllables (and even the vocalization of the MT supports this view) may be shown in the following manner. The original form of the Piel of the verb with the 2nd m. s. suffix was probably vocalized as follows: **yabarrikika*. The reduction of the doubled middle consonant of the root does not affect the syllable count. The original vowel connecting the pronominal suffix to the verb was *-u*, *-i*, or *-a*, depending upon the mood of the verb. The Massoretic vocalization or indication by *shewa* is ambiguous: i.e., it could be interpreted as silent, though the vocal form is more likely. But the Massoretic pointing is not determinative in this case, since the spelling of the word with two *kaph*'s shows that there must have been in intervening vowel. Otherwise the consonant would have been written only once. Therefore there can be no doubt that in classic usage, the expression had five syllables, not four.

b) According to Massoretic vocalization, the expression *wīḥunnekkā* has only four syllables; but this form reflects the elision of the *yodh* of the pronominal prefix, and the consequent reduction from an original five syllables. The classic reading would have been something like this: *wayaḥunnikkā* (the doubled *kaph* reflects the assimilation of the so-called energic *nun* at the end of the verbal component). That the five-syllable pronunciation persisted into late times is shown by the preservation of the *yodh*, which might otherwise have been dropped from the spelling once the consonant had been elided in pronunciation.

The metrical pattern of the poem may be described in the following way:

24) $5 + 2 = 7$; 5 ; 12
25) $2 + 2 + 2 + 3 = 9$; 5 ; 14
26) $2 + 2 + 2 + 3 = 9$; $3 + 2 + 2 = 7$; 16

There may be a question about the vocalization of the pronominal suffix *-kā*. In very early times, as in very late times (i.e., the vocalization reflected in the MT), the pronunciation was *-kā* (or *-ka*), and at those times, the syllable would be counted. There was a period during which two forms were distinguished: the long form was spelled *-kh* and pronounced *-kā*; the short form was written *-k* and pronounced without the final vowel, e.g., *-āk*. In view of the fact that only the short form is preserved in the MT in this passage, the short pronunciation should be reckoned as a possibility if not a probability in this case. It is plausible that at some point in the transmission of the text, the short form and pronunciation prevailed.[4] Since the pronominal suffix occurs in each colon of the poem, each shoud then be reduced by one syllable, producing the following pattern:

24) 4 + 2 = 6 ; 4 ; 10
25) 2 + 2 + 2 + 2 = 8 ; 4 ; 12
26) 2 + 2 + 2 + 2 = 8 ; 3 + 1 + 2 = 6 ; 14

The ratios and correlations among the cola are scarcely affected by the reduction, and the resulting patterns will be the same, or nearly so, whichever enumeration we adopt.

It will be observed immediately that in the form in which we have the blessing there is a stair-like progression from shorter to longer bicola: 10/12: 12/14: 14/16 (giving both shorter and longer syllable counts). Whether or not such a structure is considered symmetrical depends upon one's view of the term "symmetry"; but in any case, it is a balanced pattern, and was consciously constructed by the poet. Further examination exposes other possibilities in analysis and organization of the material, and these may turn out to be more artistically persuasive and satisfying. Thus, for example, there is a striking correlation between the first and last cola of the poem: they are exactly the same length, 6 or 7 syllables, and they form an excellent frame or envelope around the body of the poem:

ybrkk yhwh	May Yahweh bless you
wyśm lk šlwm	and grant you peace.

The association of "blessing" and "peace" is a frequent one in the hymnody of the Hebrew bible, so we may regard the collocation and separation as intentional on the part of the poet. Comparison with Ps 29:11 is instructive:[5]

yhwh ybrk 't-ʿmw bšlwm	May Yahweh bless his people with peace!

It may also be noted that one combination does not exclude others, and that the more skillful the poet, the more complex his structures, the more diverse his objectives, and the more subtle his connections. In this case, reading the poem consecutively makes perfectly good sense, but it is equally possible, and possibly more satisfying to recognize other arrangements of the parts.

Once the association of the opening and closing cola (*a* and *f*) is acknowledged, then it is a matter of sorting out and combining the remaining cola (*b*,*c*,*d*,*e*). Since *a* and *f* together make a bicolon of 14 syllables (12 on the short count), the remaining units can and should be combined to produce the same total: 5 + 9 = 14, and 5 + 9 = 14. The symmetry of the bicola is even more impressive if we adopt the lower numbers: (a = 6 + f = 6 for a total of 12; b = 8 + c = 4 for a total of 12; d = 8 + e = 4 for a total of 12).[6]

If we regard the combination of *a* and *f* as both plausible and logical, then we must consider the proper order of the remaining cola: *b*,*c*,*d*,*e*. The natural sequence is possible, to be sure, but the presence of the conjunction *waw* before *b* and *d* (as also before *f*) suggests that they should be balancing (i.e., second cola) rather than initiating elements; and that we must begin such combinations with the other heavier units, *c* and *e*. Following the initial leap from *a* to *f*, it would be natural to proceed then to *e*, rather than *b* or *c*; the contents of the blessing support this supposition: the raising of the face precedes its shining, i.e., it is only after the face is raised, that its beams can shine upon the worshipper, or to change the image back to the original idea behind the blessing: it is only after the sun has risen that it shines upon the world. If *e* follows *a*-*f*, then we have a choice between a simple retrogression, *e*,*d*,*c*,*b*, or a more serpentine arrangement, *e*,*b*,*c*,*d*. While the former is straight-backward, the latter seems to me slightly more artistic, and in keeping with the initial pattern: a-f, e-b, c-d. Structured in this fashion, the poem would read:

> May Yahweh bless you
>   and may he grant you peace!
> May Yahweh raise his face upon you
>   and may he protect you!
> May Yahweh make his face shine upon you
>   and may he be gracious to you!

These arrangements are not mutually exclusive; the poet has achieved multiple effects by using interchangeable parts. In each case, the verb and its pronominal complement (whether attached directly to the verb as a suffix or indirectly as a prepositional phrase) have five syllables: there are three cases with the pronominal suffix (*a*, *b*, *d*), and three with the prepositional phrase (*c*, *e*, *f*). Thus each unit has a verb of five syllables (with complement). There are also six nouns (each of two syllables) to go with the six verbs: *a* and *f* have one noun each, while *c* and *e* have two; *b* and *d* have none. Three of the nouns are subjects (Yahweh in every case: *a, c, e*); three are objects (*pānāw* twice, *c* and *e*; and *šālōm* once, *f*). Taking the bicola as units, in each pair we have two verbs and their complements, five syllables each, and two nouns, one subject and one object, two syllables each: making a total in all cases of 14 syllables. The parts are all metrically interchangeable, thus guaranteeing the symmetry of the poetic structure. For the pair, *a-f*, the two cola are evenly matched with verb and complement in each colon, and the subject noun in the first, and the object noun in the other; in the case of *eb* and *cd*, or *ed* and *cb* the nouns are bunched in the first unit, thus dividing the bicolon unevenly (the dividing point comes roughly at 2/3 and 1/3, and would be exactly there if we used the shorter count: 6/6 and 8/4; 8/4).

The content of the blessing has become so familiar through repetition in liturgical usage that its unusual character is hardly noticed. The emphasis on the "face" of Yahweh brings us back to the earliest period of Israelite religion, and ultimately to the experience of Moses himself. In the oldest references to the annual feasts, the obligation of all Israelites to present themselves before Yahweh three times a year is emphasized. Comparison of the relevant passages (Exod 23:14-17 and Exod 34:20-24) shows that the specific objective was "to see the face of Yahweh," although the Massoretes tried to avoid the plain statement by revocalizing the verbs.[7] If the Aaronic Blessing had its original setting in these annual feasts, then it expressed the confidence or hope that when the worshipers assembled in the sanctuary, Yahweh would raise his face as an act of grace, so that the rays of his countenance (like the sun in its splendor) would shine upon them.

I suggest that in the background of the Blessing lies the experience of Moses, recorded in the tradition, concerning the "face" of Yahweh, and the extended discussion or debate about whether Moses would be granted the beatific vision. There is a persistent tradition in the bible that human beings cannot see the face of God and survive the experience. It is not implied that the experience is impossible, only that it is likely to be fatal. Hence the wonder expressed when having seen the face of God, the beholder survives: e.g., Gen 32:31, "And Jacob called the name of the place, 'Peniel: for I have seen God face to face, and I have escaped with my life' " (cf. Judg 13:2-23). The same point is made in connection with Moses' request that he be allowed to see "the glory" of God (Exod 33:18, "And he said, 'Show me your glory' "). The response is that, "You cannot see my face, for human beings (*hā'ādām*) cannot see me and live" (Exod 33:20). A compromise solution is reached: "It shall be, when my glory passes by — I shall have set you in the cleft of the rock, and covered you with my hand until I pass by — then I will remove my hand, and you shall see my back, but my face shall not be seen" (Exod 33:22-23).

While this tradition reflects the deep concern to affirm that Moses saw the person of God, and at the same time deny that he saw the divine face, there is another tradition, which implies if it does not flatly assert that Moses was granted the beatific vision, and therefore that Moses was the exception to the rule: "And Yahweh would speak to Moses face to face, as a man talks to his companion" (Exod 33:11); "And there has not arisen a prophet in Israel like Moses whom Yahweh knew face to face" (Deut 34:10). While the verb "to see" is not used in these "face to face" confrontations, it must be assumed as the parallel passage in Gen 32:31 indicates (cf. Judg 13:22). Also pertinent is the account in Exod 34:27-35 of Moses' conferences with Yahweh (a parallel or complement to the story in Exod 24:12-18; note especially the 40 days and 40 nights). The glory of God is present at the mountain (Exod 24:16-17), and Moses spends the time at the top of the mountain in conference with the deity. When Moses comes down from the mountain to confer with Aaron and the others, they observe that his face is shining (Exod 34:29, 30, 35). After he speaks with the people he covers his face with a veil, but when he approaches the deity, he uncovers his face. The inference is that he sees the radiant face of God, and that his own face shines with the reflected glory of the divine countenance.

Moses' experience as the recipient and beneficiary of the beatific vision of God is clearly linked to his vocation as the unique prophet to whom Yahweh spoke directly, face to face, rather than in dreams as he does with other prophets.[8] The Aaronic Benediction seems to reflect the experience of Moses, and to express the hope that the worshiper may have a share in it, and see the refulgent glory of God's face. The general idea of sharing or democratizing the privileged experience of the Chosen One or Few is found, for example, in the story in Num 11:25-30, in which the spirit of God comes upon the 70 elders, and also moves the two men in the camp, Eldad and Medad, to prophesy. Far from being disturbed at this untoward development, Moses is quoted as saying on that occasion: "Would that all Yahweh's people were prophets, and that Yahweh might put his spirit upon them" (Num 11:29).

The conclusion is that the Aaronic Benediction is a product of that early period of Israel's history when the people went up three times a year to present themselves to Yahweh and "to see his face." The blessing itself, more specifically, is rooted in the experience of Moses, the unique prophet, who spoke to Yahweh face to face, and whose own face shone with the reflected glory of Yahweh's countenance. It expresses the confident hope that Yahweh will raise his face, and let it shine upon the worshipers gathered in his presence.

I further suggest that the poem — a gem of metrical symmetry and artistic simplicity — belongs to the same period, Phase I, as the Song of the Sea, Psalm 29, and the Song of Deborah. In style and manner, in the use of the divine name, it has the characteristic features of that period (12th century B.C.). With it, we may associate other poetic pieces, now scattered through the books of the Pentateuch, especially Numbers and Deuteronomy. We may speculate that at one time they formed part of Moses saga, an early poetic treatment of the life and achievement of Yahweh's first prophet, and leader of his people. On a provisional basis, we can identify the following items as belonging to the saga of Moses:

Numbers 10:35

qûmāh yahweh	2 + 2 = 4	Arise Yahweh
*w*ᵉ*yāpūṣū 'ōy*ᵉ*bēkā*	4 + 4 = 8	and let your enemies be scattered
*w*ᵉ*yānūsū m*ᵉ*śan'ēkā*	4 + 4 = 8	and let those who hate you flee
mippānēkā	4 = 4	from your presence

mśn'k. The original pronunciation was something like: *maśanni'ika*, which has five syllables. The contraction may have occurred at an early date, and would then have been available to the poet. In view of the regularity of the lines otherwise, and the close correlation between the second and third cola, the four-syllable count seems preferable.

Numbers 10:36

šûbāh yahweh	2 + 2 = 4	Return Yahweh
*rîb*ᵉ*bōt 'alpē yiśrā'ēl*	3 + 2 + 3 = 8	Myriads of the troops of Israel

The second utterance relating to the ark seems to be truncated, and we would expect another 12-syllable bicolon to match the first. Since the second line as it stands is not entirely comprehensible, the missing parts may have fallen out at various points. The passage is to be compared with Ps 68:18 and Deut 33:2, and seems to combine the heavenly hosts of Yahweh (*rbbwt*) with the earthly armies of Israel.

šûbāh. The word is naturally interpreted as an imperative form of the root *šûb* I "turn, return." The root may be *šûb* II, a biform of *yšb*, with the meaning "rest, sit."[9] The pairing of *qûm* and *yšb* in a number of passages supports this interpretation.[10] As between *š*ᵉ*bāh* and *šûbāh*, there is not a great deal to choose, and it may be that the original form was the former (from *yšb*). However, there is good reason to suppose otherwise, and to defend the MT in the reading *šūbāh*, since it corresponds exactly to *qūmāh*. In other words, the poet deliberately chose a rarer biform rather than a common form, in order to preserve a stylistic pattern (assonance and rhyme): the meaning is more likely to have been "rest" than "return," but it cannot be proved. A similar usage occurs in Ps 23:6, where *wšbty* (vocalized in the MT as *wešabtī*) must be rendered "and I will dwell."[11] The MT requires the derivation from the root *šūb* rather than *yšb*, so in order to retain the rendering (which is not really in question), we must appeal to *šub* II as the root.

Numbers 12:6-8:

6)	*šimᶜū - nā' debāräy*	2 + 1 + 3 = 6
	'im - yihyeh nebî'akem yahweh[a]	1 + 2 + 4 + 2 = 9
	bammar'āh 'ēlāw 'etwaddāᶜ	3 + 2 + 3 = 8
	baḥalōm 'adabber - bō	3 + 3 + 1 = 7
7)	*lō'- kēn ᶜabdî mōšeh*	1 + 1 + 2 + 2 = 6
	bekol - bētî ne'mān[b] *hū'*	2 + 2 + 2 + 1 = 7
8)	*peh 'el - peh 'adabber - bō*	1 + 1 + 1 + 3 + 1 = 7
	ūmar'eh[c] *welō' beḥīdōt*	3 + 2 + 3 = 8
	ūtemūnat yahweh yabbīṭ	4 + 2 + 2 = 8
	ūmaddūᶜ[d] *lō' yerē'tem*	3 + 1 + 3 = 7
	ledabbēr beᶜabdī bemōšeh	3 + 3 + 3 = 9

Listen intently to my words
If any of you is Yahweh's prophet
In a vision I may make myself known to him
In a dream I may speak with him.

Not so is Moses my servant
In my whole house, he is the most loyal

Mouth to mouth I speak with him
Not in a vision or in riddles
And the form of Yahweh he beholds.

And why were you not afraid
to speak against Moses my servant?

a) The sequence *nby'km yhwh* is peculiar, but no emendation is required. The broken construct chain is a recognized phenomenon in Hebrew poetry.[12] The terms *nby'* and *yhwh* form a natural construct chain: "the prophet of Yahweh." The pronominal suffix *-km* is connected more loosely but clearly refers back to the subject of *šm'w* (vs. 6) and ahead to the subject of *yr'tm* (vs. 8). The sense may be expressed as follows: "If there is among you a prophet of Yahweh," or more pointedly: "If either of you [Aaron and Miriam are the ostensible subjects] is or claims to be Yahweh's prophet [i.e., as a rival to Moses, who is], in a vision, I will [or may] make myself known to him, in a dream I will [or may] speak to him."

b) In the MT, the vocalization is *ne'ᵉmān*, three syllables. However, the compound shewa is secondary, and should not be counted.

c) *ūmar'eh* is ambiguous. Apparently the Massoretes wished to distinguish the word from *mar'āh* above (vs. 6), and there may be reason then to interpret this word as meaning "visible appearance" rather than "vision." If the latter is true, then the word should be taken as a parallel to *tmwnt* and analyzed as the direct object of *ybyṭ*: ". . . and the appearance and the actual form of Yahweh he observes." The phrase, *wl' bḥydt*, however, must be taken with the verb *'dbr-bw*: "Mouth to mouth I speak with him, . . . and not in riddles." While in poetry there can be a great deal more flexibility in the order and arrangement of terms, there is a plausible alternative which does not require such adjustments. The term *mr'h* would be interpreted as equivalent to *bmr'h* above, and linked with *bḥydt* and the expression *wl' b-* (the latter would apply to *mr'h* as well as *ḥydt*).[13] This arrangement, with the meaning: "And neither in visions nor in riddles," would correspond more closely to the pairing of equivalent terms in vs. 6: *bmr'h* and *bḥlwm* // *mr'h* and *bḥydt*. It may be added that there is important textual support for the reading *bmr'h* instead of *wmr'h* (vs. 8). If an error is involved (either way), it would be due to the confusion of bilabial sounds in the course of oral transmission, or dictation to scribes. In view of the occurrence of the preposition before the other three terms, it may well be original here; in that case, it would tip the scales in favor of our second interpretation. The metrical count would be not affected in any case.

d) The vocalization of *wmdwᶜ* in the MT is *ūmaddūaᶜ*, four syllables. However, the *pataḥ* furtive is secondary and should not be included in the syllable count.

The opening unit, vs. 6, consists of two bicola with 15 syllables each, making a total of 30 syllables. It is balanced by another unit, including vss. 7 (6 + 7 = 13) and 8de (7 + 9 = 16), which also consists of a pair of bicola, with a total of 29 syllables. The latter (vss. 7 and 8de) serves as an envelope for a tricolon (8abc: 7 + 8 + 8 = 23) which is the core of the poem, and expresses the main theme of the poet: Moses' unique status as Yahweh's prophet. The links and echoes of terms and forms confirm the analysis: thus 2nd m. pl. forms are used in 6ab and again in 8de (*šmᶜw* and *nby'km* in 6, and *yr'tm* in 8); 7a and 8e form an inclusion with the repetition of the terms *ᶜbdy* and *mōšeh*. Vs. 6cd finds an echo in 8ab (note the repetition of the expression *'dbr-bw*, and the association of *bmr'h* and *wmr'h*). The third colon of the tricolon (8abc) is expansionary and emphasizes the unique aspect of Moses' prophetic vocation: he alone sees the actual form, the person of Yahweh.

Numbers 21:17-18 — The Song of the Well

While there is no explicit connection with Moses, this bit of verse has an archaic ring to it and is linked by vocabulary with the Song of Deborah: note the terms *śārīm*, *nᵉdībē (hā) ᶜām*, and *mᵉḥōqēq* in the Song of the Well, and the corresponding terms in Judg 5:2, 9, 14, 15.

ᶜᵃlī bᵉ'ēr[a]	2 + 1/2 = 3/4
ᶜᵉnū lāh (a)[b]	2 + 1/2 = 3/4
bᵉ'ēr ḥᵃpārūhā śārīm[c]	1/2 + 3/4 + 2 = 6/8
kārūhā nᵉdībē (hā)ᶜām[d]	2/3 + 3 + 1/2 = 6/8
bimḥōqēq[e]	3/4
bᵉmišᶜᵃnōtām[f]	5

"Spring up, O well!"
Sing to it.
Well which the princes dug
which the leaders of the people hollowed out
with their staff
with their sticks

a) *bᵉ'ēr*. The vocalization of the MT is artificial. The original form of the noun was *bi'ru*; with the loss of the case ending, it became *bi'r*, and then in due course, with the quiescence (or assimilation and later reduction of the doubled consonant) of the 'aleph, *bēr*. The MT *bᵉ'ēr* is a back-formation, designed to restore or preserve the 'aleph as a consonant.[14] The minimum count for the colon would be 2 + 1 = 3.

b) The form *lāh* is pausal; the more original form would have been *laha* or *liha*, with an additional syllable. In my view, the treatment of the 3rd f. s. suffix would have been the same throughout the poem in all positions: the final *-a* would have been preserved as a long vowel *-ā* or dropped entirely. I assume that in the very early period of which we are speaking (12th-11th centuries), the longer form was more common, if not regular. During the same period (at least until the 10th century final vowels were not indicated in the spelling), there would have been no difference in the orthography. The minimum count for this colon would have been three syllables; more likely we should count four.

c) The minimum count would be 1 + 3 + 2 = 6. The 3rd f. s. suffix should probably be counted, in which case the total would be 7.

d) Here the minimum count would be 2 + 3 + 1 = 6. The definite article with *ᶜām* probably should not be counted, since it is very rare in early Hebrew poetry; however, its occasional occurrence may be deliberate on the part of the poet, and care should be exercised in dealing with the phenomenon. Since the article is relatively rare in poetry in general, and is standard usage in prose, scribal inadvertence in copying (especially since little if any distinction was made in copying practice between prose and poetry) is to be expected, and there are doubtless many cases in which the article has been added in Hebrew poetry. At the same time the fact that the distinction has been preserved to a statistically significant extent (the use of the article is much more common in prose books of the bible, in contrast with its relative paucity in poetic books), suggests that its occasional presence in poetry may be deliberate and not accidental. Hence caution should be exercised in making a decision. It is important to note that the corresponding term *śārīm* is just as definite as *hāᶜām*, but there would be no warrant for adding the article to the former word, though the *he* could be regarded as a double-duty particle.[15] It would be very difficult to make any distinction between the parallel terms on the basis of the presence or absence of the article. The minimum count is 6 syllables, but if we added the 3rd f. s. suffix to the verb, the total would be 7.

e) The minimum count, following the MT, would be 3. An earlier form of the expression would have had an additional syllable, i.e., *bimaḥōqēq*. The elision, which takes place in accordance with Massoretic rules, may have taken place at almost any time. Whether it was available to the poet, and whether he exercised his right to use it must remain matters of speculation. The syllable count must have been either 3 or 4.

f) The syllable count on the basis of the MT would be 5. It has been suggested that the final *mem* is enclitic rather than pronominal, but this would not affect the syllable count; in any case there is no reason to question the traditional analysis or interpretation. The antecedent is clearly understood as the plural nouns in the preceding cola (*śrym*, and *ndyby hᶜm*). The suffix would then serve double duty with *bmḥqq*. The only remaining question is whether the noun is to be taken as plural (as vocalized by the MT), or singular as implied by the singular *mḥqq*. The preserved orthography would be equally valid for either form into late post-Exilic times (only then would a *waw* have been inserted before the *taw* to signify the plural ending, and then not consistently in these suffixed forms). The singular form, if correct, would have been vocalized as follows: *bᵉmišᶜantām*, or four syllables against the MT five. The minimum count for the bicolon would be 3 + 4 = 7. The vocalization of the MT gives us 3 + 5 = 8, while the maximum possible would be 4 + 5 = 9.

The minimum and maximum syllable counts for the four units are as follows:

1)	6 - 8	(7)
2)	6 - 8	(7)
3)	6 - 8	(7)
4)	7 - 9	(8)

I have indicated the most likely count in each case (the number in parentheses).

Numbers 21:27-29

This poem is a unique example of a non-Israelite composition of early date, and deserves detailed treatment beyond the limits of this paper. For the present see the studies of Paul Hanson and John Van Seters.[16] I hope to bring out a study of this work in the near future.

All together these poetic bits and pieces contribute significantly to the picture of the early period in the wilderness, and especially to the Moses tradition. The Aaronic Blessing fits with the other poems as an archaic composition. It has the characteristic features of Phase I poetry (12th century), and there are specific affinities with early poems like Psalm 29. Its central interest is in the "face of Yahweh" and the gracious, protective light which radiates from it. Just as in the oldest traditions of the annual festal pilgrimages, the Israelites are enjoined to present themyelves before Yahweh, and to see his face; so here the complementary benediction of the divine presence is offered: they will see his face, and his face will shine upon them. Behind it all are the traditions concerning Moses, and his unique status as the servant of God, who spoke with him, mouth to mouth, and saw him in person. The narrative in Exod 34:27-35 describes the specific effects of the face-to-face confrontation: the face of Moses shines with the reflected glory of Yahweh's radiant countenance, because Yahweh first raised his face, and graciously made it shine upon Moses.

1. The most recent study is by P. D. Miller, Jr., "The Blessing of God: An Interpretation of Numbers 6:22-27," *Int* 29 (1975) 240-51.

2. Ibid., esp. 243, n. 11: "It has been pointed out that there is no metrical symmetry to these lines." While the present study was planned and worked out before the appearance of Miller's article, a primary objective of it is to challenge the common opinion, and to show that there is metrical symmetry, and to explain its nature and structure.

3. I have discussed the theory and method of syllable-counting in a number of articles, and hope to give a comprehensive and detailed account in a proposed volume on Hebrew poetry. For the present, see my "Prolegomenon" to G. B. Gray, *The Forms of Hebrew Poetry* (reprint; New York: Ktav, 1972), vii-lvi; "Strophe and Meter in Exodus 15," *A Light Unto My Path: Old Testament Studies in Honor of Jacob M. Myers* (eds. H. N. Bream, R. D. Heim, and C. A. Moore; Philadelphia: Temple University, 1974) 163-202; "Acrostics and Metrics in Hebrew Poetry," *HTR* 65 (1972) 367-92; "The Refrain in David's Lament over Saul and Jonathan," *Ex Orbe Religionum: Studia Geo Widengren* (eds. C. J. Bleeker, S. G. F. Brandon, and M. Simon; Supplements to *Numen* 21-22; Leiden: Brill, 1972) vol. 1, 115-26.

4. See the discussion in F. M. Cross and D. N. Freedman, *Early Hebrew Orthography* (Philadelphia: American Oriental Society, 1952) 65-70.

5. See the study by D. N. Freedman and C. Frank-Hyland, "Psalm 29: A Structural Analysis," *HTR* 66 (1973) 237-56.

6. The same pattern appears in Exod 15:4 (8 + 4 = 12 syllables; 6 + 6 = 12 syllables). Failure to observe this larger balance has led to unwarranted emendation of the first colon; see the discussion in "Strophe and Meter in Exodus 15," 179; see also "Prolegomenon," xxxiv-xxxvii.

7. In Exod 23:15 and 34:20 we read: *wᵉlōʾ - yērāʾū pānay rēqām*, "And my face shall not be seen empty-handed." The meaning, however, must be: "They must not present themselves before me (i.e., see my face) empty-handed (i.e., without suitable offerings)." In Exod 23:17, the reading is: *yērāʾeh kol - zᵉkūrkā ʾel pᵉnē hāʾādōn* "Every one of your males must appear (present himself) before the Lord." But Exod 34:23 has *ʾet - pᵉnē YHWH*, which makes the Niphal form of the verb more difficult to accommodate. The original meaning must have been: "Every male among you shall present himself before Yahweh (i.e., shall see the face of Yahweh)." The same interpretation must be given to Exod 34:24, *lērāʾōt et* pᵉ*nē YHWH ʾᵉlōhēkā* "to see the face of your God" (reading the Qal inf. *lirʾōt* for the Niphal).

8. Num 12:6-8, a poetic piece, preserves the same tradition, but articulates it in slightly different terms: "Mouth to mouth, I speak with him / and the figure of Yahweh he beholds."

9. On the occurrence of this root, *šūb* II, see M. Dahood, *Psalms I* (AB 16; Garden City: Doubleday, 1966) 44, 148, 213; *Psalms II* (AB 17; Garden City: Doubleday, 1968) 69.

10. Cf. Ps 127:2, 139:2, Lam 3:63, Gen 27:19, Isa 52:2, Deut 6:7, 11:19.

11. See my forthcoming study of "Psalm 23" in the Festschrift in honor of Prof. George Cameron, University of Michigan.

12. See my article, "The Broken Construct Chain," *Bib* 53 (1972) 534-36. See the recent discussion of the entire unit by F. M. Cross, *Canaanite Myth and Hebrew Epic* (Cambridge: Harvard University, 1973) 203-4.

13. The same treatment was suggested by W. F. Albright (*Yahweh and the Gods of Canaan* [Garden City: Doubleday, 1968] 42) and has recently been seconded by E. F. Campbell ("Moses and the Foundations of Israel," *Int* 29 [1975] 146).

14. On this formation see GKC, §23f. But see also §93t.

15. On double-duty particles, see Dahood, *Psalms III* (AB 17A; Garden City: Doubleday, 1970) 437-39.

16. See the recent studies by P. Hanson, "The Song of Heshbon and David's *'Nir'*," *HTR* 61 (1968) 297-320, and J. Van Seters, "The Conquest of Sihon's Kingdom," *JBL* 91 (1972) 182-97. In my opinion the poem ends with vs. 29; the travelogue is resumed in vs. 30. It is instructive that neither Yahweh nor any other sanctioned name of the God of Israel appears in the poem, only Chemosh the god of Moab; the role assigned to Chemosh is very much like that assigned to Yahweh in Israelite poems. It seems clearly to be a non-Israelite composition, which makes it all the more interesting.

PSALM 113 AND THE SONG OF HANNAH*

The purpose of this paper, which is dedicated to a master craftsman in the art of poetic analysis and interpretation, is to examine the structure of the Song of Hannah in comparison with Psalm 113, a poem to which it is closely related. It will be argued that Psalm 113 is the more archaic of the two, and belongs to an earlier phase of Israelite prosody, while the Song of Hannah, constructed along similar lines, has been adapted and elaborated in the interests of the monarchy.[1] As they stand, they are independent compositions, and it is neither possible nor profitable to reconstruct a common original from which both derive. Nevertheless, they share both formal and literary features, and comparison is helpful in determining the process of development and change.

Psalm 113

I

hallĕlû ʿabdê yahweh	(1a)	Praise, O servants of Yahweh,
hallĕlû ʾet-šēm yahweh	(1b)	Praise the name of Yahweh.
yĕhî šēm yahweh mĕbōrāk	(2a)	May the name of Yahweh be blessed
mēʿattâ wĕʿad ʿôlām	(2b)	from now even until eternity;
mimmizraḥ-šamš ʿad mĕbôʾô	(3a)	from the sun's rising until its setting
mĕhullāl šēm yahweh	(3b)	May Yahweh's name be praised.

II

rām ʿal-kol-gôyīm yahweh	(4a)	High above all nations is Yahweh,
ʿal haššāmaym kĕbôdô	(4b)	(High) above the heavens is His Excellency.

*I wish to thank my student Clayton Libolt for his generous and unstinted assistance in the preparation of this manuscript. He contributed many of the ideas which are incorporated in the article, but the final product is the responsibility of the author.

[1] On the sequence dating of early Hebrew poetry, see W. F. Albright, *Yahweh and the Gods of Canaan* (Garden City, N.Y., 1968), Ch. 1; also D. N. Freedman, 'Divine Names and Titles in Early Hebrew Poetry', *Magnalia Dei: The Mighty Acts of God*, eds. F. M. Cross, W. E. Lemke, P. D. Miller, Jr. (New York, 1976), pp. 55-107. Psalm 113 makes use of the divine name Yahweh only (six occurrences), which is typical of poetry of Phase I (12th century B.C.). In the Song of Hannah, however, there are several other divine names which are typical of later phases, especially *ṣûr* 'mountain' which is characteristic of Phase III, belonging to the period of the monarchy (10th century, or possibly later). The Psalm has other archaic features: various verbal forms with an ending in *-ī*. The corresponding forms in the Song are normal which may indicate a somewhat later date: e.g., *mašpîlî* (Ps.) and *mašpîl* (Song); *mĕqîmî* (Ps.) and *mēqîm* (S.); *lĕhôšîbî* (Ps.) and *lĕhôšîb* (S.). While there are various theories about the significance of the endings, they seem to be archaic survivals of case endings, or other peculiar elements.

mî kayahweh ᵓĕlōhênû	(5a)	Who is like our God, Yahweh—
hammagbîhî lāšibt	(5b)	who sets up on a high seat,
hammašpîlî lirᵓôt	(6a)	who sets down in full view—
baššāmaym wĕbāᵓārṣ	(6b)	in heaven or in earth?
	III	
mĕqîmî mēᶜāpār dāl	(7a)	Who raises from the dirt the poor,
mēᵓašpōt yārîm ᵓebyôn	(7b)	from the ash-heaps he lifts up the destitute.
lĕhôšîbî ᶜim-nĕdîbîm	(8a)	Indeed he makes (him) sit with nobles,
ᶜim nĕdîbê ᶜammô	(8b)	with the nobles of his people.
môšîbî ᶜaqirt habbayt	(9a)	Who settles the barren one in her household,
ᵓēm habbānîm śĕmēḥâ	(9b)	a mother who rejoices in her sons.

The metrical pattern of the poem may be described as follows:[2]

Stanza I

1a)	3 + 2 + 2 = 7		14	43
1b)	3 + 1 + 1 + 2 = 7			
2a)	2 + 1 + 2 + 3 = 8		+	
2b)	3 + 2 + 2 = 7	15 +	14	
3a)	3 + 1 + 1 + 3 = 8			
3b)	3 + 1 + 2 = 6			

Stanza II

4a)	1 + 1 + 1 + 2 + 2 = 7		14	40
4b)	1 + 3 + 3 = 7			
5a)	1 + 3 + 4 = 8		+	
5b)	4 + 2 = 6	12 +	14	
6a)	4 + 2 = 6			
6b)	3 + 3 = 6			

Stanza III

7a)	3 + 3 + 1 = 7	14	42
7b)	3 + 2 + 2 = 7		
8a)	4 + 1 + 3 = 8	14	
8b)	1 + 3 + 2 = 6		
9a)	3 + 2 + 2 = 7	14	
9b)	1 + 3 + 3 = 7		

It is assumed that the opening and closing expressions (*hallĕlû-yāh*) constitute a liturgical frame, which was supplied when the poem was incorporated

[2]For a detailed discussion of the subject of syllable counting, see D. N. Freedman, 'Prolegomenon', in G. B. Gray, *The Forms of Hebrew Poetry* (Ktav reprint, New York, 1972), pp. xxxii-xxxv. For a description of operating principles and actual examples, see D. N. Freedman, 'Acrostics and Metrics in Hebrew Poetry', *HTR* 65 (1972), 368-9; *idem* 'Strophe and Meter in Exodus 15', in *A Light unto my Path: Old Testament Studies in Honor of Jacob M. Myers*, eds. H. N. Bream, R. D. Heim, C. A. Moore (Philadelphia, 1974), 167-70.

into the Hallel portion of the Psalter. The poem proper consists of three stanzas of six lines each, which are practically identical in structure. The basic metrical unit, defined by a simple syllable-counting system, is a bicolon of 14 syllables, divided in the middle, 7:7. This is the form of the opening bicolon of each stanza (vv. 1, 4, 7), and of the closing bicolon (v. 9). A slight modification of this pattern, involving the same bicolon of 14 syllables, but divided 8:6 instead of 7:7, occurs three times (vv. 3, 5, 8). The remaining lines vary a little more: v. 2 is a bicolon of 15 syllables, divided 8:7; and v. 6 is a bicolon of 12 syllables, 6:6. These latter fall well within a modest range of poetic freedom on the one hand, and scholarly uncertainty about morphology and vocalization on the other.

The count offered is minimal, and other possibilities exist. Massoretic vocalization results in a slightly higher count, but the general pattern would not be affected significantly. The only real requirement of an adequate methodology is to be consistent, though we have also made a serious effort to conform to known practices and conventions of classical Hebrew. Thus segolate formations are treated as monosyllables, and auxiliary vowels with laryngeals and *pataḥ* furtive are treated as secondary developments. Where a more ancient pronunciation is attested firmly (as in the case of resolved diphthongs), it is adopted in preference to MT. At the outside, the differences are very small, and whatever system may be used, the underlying patterns of distribution should emerge quite clearly.

Within the basic general pattern, some subtleties and intricacies may be observed. There is an interlocking or envelope construction in vv. 2-3, which is duplicated in vv. 5-6. In the first stanza, vv. 2a and 3b are parallel expressions, as are vv. 2b and 3a. In vv. 5-6, the effect is even more pronounced, since vv. 5a and 6b form a sentence, while vv. 5b and 6a match each other exactly. Recognizing these associations does not affect the numerical description of the stanzas, because the lines involved are metrically interchangeable: 2a) 8 + 3b) 6 = 14; 2b) 7 + 3a) 8 = 15; 5a) 8 + 6b) 6 + 14; 5b) 6 + 6a) 6 = 12. The metrical model or basic pattern adopted by the poet, and then adapted by him, is as follows: for Stanzas I and II—

1ab) 7 + 7 = 14
2a & 3b) 8 + 6 = 14
2b & 3a) 7 + 7 = 14

and for Stanza III—

1ab) 7 + 7 = 14
2ab) 8 + 6 = 14
3ab) 7 + 7 = 14

The first two stanzas vary slightly from the presumed norm, and then only with respect to the interior pair within the envelope (vv. 2b & 3a, and 5b & 6a), but not more than would be true of the average hymn sung in synagogues or churches. The third stanza, which does not employ the envelope pattern, conforms exactly to the standard. The metrical regularity of the poem as it has survived is impressive.

Comments

Stanza I:

There are no significant textual or linguistic difficulties, and as already noted, the metrical pattern is quite regular, with a single slight deviation from the norm (i.e., v. 2a has eight syllables instead of an expected seven). Poetic devices abound. There is an example of repetitive parallelism in v. 1: abc // adc (an unusual type). A major chiasm occurs in vv. 2-3: 2a) *šm yhwh mbrk* // 3b) *mhll šm yhwh*. There is a neat inversion in vv. 2b and 3a, where the daily round of the sun (3a) logically precedes the indefinite extension of time (2b): all day and every day. The theme of the stanza is expressed amply by the repetition of the phrase *šēm yhwh* in conjunction with various words for praise and blessing: *hllw*, *mhll*, and *mbrk*. This usage may be compared with the very effective repetition of the phrase *qwl yhwh* in Psalm 29, an early poem.[3] The initial repetition of *hllw* (v. 1) is echoed in *mhll* (v. 3b), which together define the boundaries of the unit.

Stanza II:

Again the text appears to be unassailable, while the content is an elaboration of the first stanza: the theme is the exaltation of Yahweh. Structurally the second stanza is practically the same as the first, with only the slightest deviation from a metrical norm: vv. 5b & 6a are counted as six syllables each instead of an expected seven. Since our calculation is minimal, we must reckon with the possibility, if not probability, that the poet exercised an available option indicating a higher count: the words *lšbt* and *lrʾwt* may well have been pronounced with three syllables (e.g., MT *lāšābet* and *lir*[*ĕ*]*ʾôt*).

Verse 4 resembles vv. 2-3 in its syntactical structure: the verb *rām* governs the two phrases beginning with *ʿal*, just as *yĕhî* controls the two participles *mbrk* and *mhll*. The verse celebrates Yahweh's exaltation over the nations (which are on earth), and over the heavens (which should be understood as an ellipsis for the more explicit and familiar 'hosts of heaven'). The divine supremacy here is political rather than spatial; it is Yahweh's authority that is emphasized rather than his location above the skies. Verse 6b echoes the phrases in v. 4 in chiastic order: the word 'heavens' is repeated, while 'earth' complements 'all nations'. As for *kbwdw* at the end of v. 4, we interpret the term as an honorific, or title of address, rather than as an attribute of the deity. Hence the rendering, 'His Excellency', which goes

[3]For a discussion of the date of Psalm 29 (around 1100 B.C. in my opinion) see Freedman, 'Divine Names and Titles in Early Hebrew Poetry', pp. 60-61.

directly with 'Yahweh'. The difference is slight, and the original meaning is the same, but the parallelism of the terms suggests the added nuance of the breakup of a stereotyped expression: 'His Excellency, Yahweh'.[4]

Verses 5-6 exhibit the same kind of envelope construction already observed in vv. 2-3. Verses 5a & 6b, however, form a single sentence: 'Who is like our God, Yahweh . . . in heaven or in earth?'[5] As in the parallel passage, Exod. 15:11, the required response is, 'No one.' Verses 5b & 6a form a balanced unit, with contrasting descriptions of the deity, constituting a merism: he elevates and he abases, i.e., he controls the destinies of men. The participles *mgbyhy* and *mšpyly* are Hiphil causatives rather than elatives, and describe activities of Yahweh rather than states of being. The same terms are used elsewhere to reflect God's authority and power in elevating some and abasing others, e.g., Ps. 75:8, Ezek. 17:24 and 21:31. Synonymous terms express the same thought elsewhere, particularly in the parallel passages in the Song. The third stanza of the present poem elaborates on the theme of divine power, adducing other instances of God's action in deciding the circumstances and fate of men and women. The meaning of this passage can hardly be other than that Yahweh raises up some and sets down others. The exact force of the infinitives *lšbt* and *lrʾwt* is less easy to determine. That each is directly associated with the preceding participle seems certain in view of the parallelistic structure (and is reinforced in the case of *lrʾwt* by the Massoretic punctuation). Viewed in this light, the verbal noun *lšbt* refers to the status of the person elevated, namely his place of honor or seat of dignity. The same point is made in greater detail in v. 8, while the seat itself is defined as a throne in the parallel passage in the Song, 1 Sam. 2:8. In a similar way, the infinitive construct *lrʾwt* describes the circumstances of the one who suffers degradation. An essential feature of this experience is that it happens in full view. The disgraced individual is the object of the derision and gloating of his erstwhile enemies, and of the public generally. The verb *rʾh* is used repeatedly in the Bible to express this idea: e.g., Judg. 16:27; Mic. 7:10; Ezek. 28:17; Obad. 11, 12, 13; Pss. 22:18, 112:8, 118:7; cf. Ps. 59:11, and the Mesha Stone, 1.7. Publicity only aggravates the shame, as Job's experience makes clear. One may compare also the explicit condemnation of David's behavior by Nathan in 2 Sam. 12:11-12, and the public nature of the retribution to be inflicted. The sense of the passage may therefore be rendered: 'Who elevates some to a seat of honor/Who abases others in the sight of all.'

[4]On *kābôd* as a divine title, cf. Ps. 29:9; see M. Dahood, *Psalms I (1-50)* in 'The Anchor Bible' (Garden City, N.Y., 1966), p. 179, and p. 18 (Ps. 3:4); other references in the Index, p. 321. See also Dahood, *Psalms II* (1968), 92, and *Psalms III* (1970), 357.

[5]On this phenomenon as an extension of the familiar envelope construction, see Freedman, 'Prolegomenon', xxxvi-xxxvii; D. N. Freedman and C. F. Hyland, 'Psalm 29: A Structural Analysis', *HTR* 66 (1973), 243-6; and D. N. Freedman, 'The Structure of Job 3', *Biblica* 49 (1968), 503.

Stanza III:

Verse 7 is identical with 1 Sam. 2:8ab, with the exception of the anomalous *-y* at the end of *mqym*. It may be a fossilized survival of the old genitive case ending (cf. *hmgbyhy* and *hmšpyly* in vv. 5-6, and *mwšyby* in v. 9), or some other archaic remnant. In v. 8a there is another anomalous *-y* at the end of *lhwšyb* (cf. 1 Sam. 2:8c which has the normal form). We take the *lamed* at the beginning of the word to be an emphatic particle before the Hiphil perfect form of the verb.[6] In 1 Sam 2:8cd, the perfect form is balanced by the imperfect form, *ynḥlm*, whereas in this passage we must make do with the preceding *yrym*. The alternation of perfect and imperfect forms in archaic Hebrew poetry, as also in Ugaritic poetry, is a characteristic feature; there is no change in tense or aspect, it being simply a belletristic device. M. Dahood identifies the final *yod* of *lhwšyby* as the third masculine singular suffix, in support of which contention he has assembled an impressive number of examples.[7] The presence of the suffix is attested by the versions. Verse 8b is entirely different from the corresponding colon in 1 Sam. 2:8d. Neither is derived from the other; they are independent units, each related to its complement, and serving its poetic purpose in its context. In the Psalm we have an instance of repetitive parallelism: abc // bc′d; in the other there is an example of the alternation of perfect and imperfect forms of the verb, and chiasm. If we follow Albright, the occurrence of repetitive parallelism is a sign of earlier composition; we may take that along with other signs, such as the preservation of archaic forms, as an indication that the Psalm is older than the Song.[8]

Verse 9 is echoed in 1 Sam. 2:5cd. Each bicolon is adapted to the prevailing pattern of the poem. In Psalm, the complementary cola repeat or emphasize the initial affirmation, whereas in Song this is the case only in v. 8 (on the elevation of the poor). In vv. 4-5, the poet presents a series of contrasts: e.g., the barren woman bears many, while the fertile woman is bereaved of those she has borne. In Psalm nothing is said of the prolific mother, while attention is focused on the formerly barren woman, who becomes a fruitful parent. The general sense of Psalm v. 9 is clear; the specific force of the terms and their syntactic and semantic relationships remain uncertain. A literal rendering would be: ‘Who makes the barren one of the house sit, the mother of sons rejoices.’ The pairings of constructs and absolutes reflect a more varied and subtle relationship than the normal possessive, while the verbs serve to link the two.[9] We would paraphrase as

[6]On emphatic *lamed*, see Dahood, *Psalms III*, 406.

[7]On the occurrence of the third masculine singular pronominal suffix in *yod*, see Dahood, *Psalms III*, 376.

[8]Albright, *Yahweh and the Gods of Canaan*, Ch. 1.

[9]For examples of this phenomenon, see Freedman, ‘Prolegomenon’, xxix-xxx.

follows: 'Who makes the barren woman mistress of a household, a mother rejoicing in her sons.' Since the emphasis is upon the transformation of the barren woman into the mother of children and the mistress of a household, it is tempting to see in the participle *mwšyby* a biform of the Hiphil of the root *šwb* rather than the root *yšb* "to dwell", and to read, 'Who transforms the barren one into the mistress of a household. . . .'[10]

Verse 9 introduces a theme parallel to what we have in vv. 7-8, and one would expect further elaboration, as is the case in Song. The Psalm ends rather abruptly; in view of the extended introduction (vv. 1-3), one would be led to expect a comparable conclusion, but there is none here. We seem to have only half a poem in Psalm, with stanzas missing to match II and III, along with an appropriate conclusion. Comparison with Song suggests that there was originally a poem of six stanzas, of which only the first three have been preserved. There is no point, however, in attempting to restore the presumed original, since to do so would reflect either excessive originality and ingenuity on the part of the scholar, or slavish conformity to existing models, or a mixture of both. None of these would be edifying. But it is wise to bear this consideration in mind (that the Psalm apparently is incomplete) when we look at the Song.

1 Samuel 2:1-10

Opening: 1a-3b

ʿālaṣ libbî bayahweh	(1a)	My heart exults in Yahweh,
rāmâ qarnî bēʾlōhāy	(1b)	My horn is raised by my God,
rāḥab pî ʿal-ʾôyĕbay	(1c)	My mouth is enlarged over my enemies,
śāmaḥtî bîšûʿātî	(1d)	I rejoice in my victory.
kî ʾên qādôš kayahweh	(2a)	For none is holy like Yahweh,
wĕʾên ṣûr kēʾlōhênû	(2b)	and there is no Rock like our God.
ʾal tĕdabbĕrû gĕbōhâ	(3a)	Don't speak haughtily
yēṣēʾ ʿātāq mippîkem	(3b)	or let insolence issue from your mouth.

Divider I: 3cd

kî ʾēl dēʿôt yahweh	(3c)	For the God of wisdom is Yahweh,
wĕlēʾ nitkĕnû ʿălîlôt	(3d)	even the Powerful One by whom deeds are tested.

Stanza I: 4-5

qašt gibbōrîm ḥattâ	(4a)	The bow of the warriors is shattered,
wĕnikšālîm ʾāzĕrû ḥayl	(4b)	but the stumblers gird on strength.
śĕbēʿîm belaḥm niśkārû	(5a)	The well-fed sell themselves for food
warĕʿēbîm ḥadēllû ʿad	(5b)	while the hungry gorge themselves on prey.

[10]In Ps. 23:6 we have the opposite phenomenon; the form *wĕšabtî* derives apparently from the root *šwb*; but this must be a by-form of *yšb* since the required meaning is, 'And I will dwell. . . .'

ᶜăqārâ yālĕdâ šibᶜâ	(5c)	The barren woman bears seven
wĕrabbat bānîm ᵓumlālâ	(5d)	while the one with many children languishes.

Main Divider: 6-7

yahweh mēmît wamĕḥayyeh	(6a)	Yahweh it is who puts to death and restores to life,
môrîd šĕᵓôl weyaᶜleh	(6b)	who brings down to Sheol and raises up (from there).
yahweh môrîš wemaᶜšîr	(7a)	Yahweh it is who makes poor and makes rich,
mašpîl ᵓap-mĕrômēm	(7b)	who abases and exalts.

Stanza II: 8a-f

mēqîm mēᶜāpār dāl	(8a)	Who raises the needy from the dirt,
mēᵓašpōt yārîm ᵓebyôn	(8b)	from ash-heaps he lifts up the poor;
lĕhôšîb ᶜim-nĕdîbîm	(8c)	indeed he makes them sit with nobles,
wĕkissēᵓ kābôd yanḥīlēm	(8d)	and a splendid throne he gives them as a possession.
nōtēn nidr lannōdēr	(8e)	Who grants to the vower his vow,
wayĕbārek šānôt ṣaddîq	(8f)	and he blesses the righteous with years.

Divider III: 8gh

kî layahweh mĕṣūqê ᵓarṣ	(8g)	For to Yahweh belong the pillars of the netherworld;
wayāšet ᶜălêhem tēbēl	(8h)	indeed he set the world upon them.

Closing: 9-10

raglê ḥăsîdāw yišmōr	(9a)	The feet of his faithful ones he guards,
warĕšāᶜîm baḥušk yiddāmmû	(9b)	but the wicked perish in the darkness,
kî lōᵓ bĕkōḥ yigbar-ᵓîš	(9c)	for no man prevails by his own strength—
yahweh yēḥattû mĕrîbāw	(10a)	Yahweh—those who oppose him are shattered.
ᶜalû baššāmaym yarᶜēm	(10b)	The Exalted One thunders from the heavens,
yahweh yādîn ᵓapsê ᵓarṣ	(10c)	Yahweh judges the ends of the earth.
wĕyitten-ᶜōz lĕmalkô	(10d)	Now let him give strength to his king,
wĕyārēm qarn mĕšîḥô	(10e)	and let him raise the horn of his anointed.

In comparing Song with Psalm, we note a structural correlation precisely at the point where the content of the two poems is the same. 1 Sam. 2:4-5 constitute a six-line unit structurally comparable to v. 8a-f. These in turn have the same shape as the basic stanza form of Psalm; notice especially Stanza III of the latter (vv. 7-9) which has lines almost identical with Song, vv. 8a-d, and 5cd, although the order is different. Essentially these units consist of three bicola of approximately 14 syllables each, divided at the center, or close to it. In Song the two stanzas (vv. 4-5, and 8a-f) are set in a framework consisting of vv. 3cd, 6-7, and 8gh. The first and last serve as dividers between the body of the poem and the opening (vv. 1-3ab) and the closing (vv. 9-10), while the central couplet constitutes a climactic assertion of the power and authority of God, the central theme of the poem.

The text of the poem has been reconstructed on the basis of the best available readings of MT, LXX, and 4QSam[a].[11] Deviations from MT are justified by a variety of considerations, including the poetic structure of the piece as a whole. Chiasm and symmetry of a sophisticated kind are dominant factors in the composition of biblical poems, and their presence in Song indicates the lines which the analysis should follow. The opening and closing are linked by key words and belong to a uniform structure. The same is true of the body of the poem with its interlocking arrangement of dividers and stanzas. A critical element is the distribution of the divine names and titles, especially that of Yahweh, which dominates the poem. There are eight occurrences; we must subtract one from the nine in MT by substituting *bʾlhy* in v. 1b on the basis of LXX for MT and 4QSam[a] *byhwh*.[12] In the opening it occurs twice with the preposition (vv. 1a, 2a), while in the corresponding places in the closing, it serves as the subject of a verb (v. 10a, c).[13] The prepositional use in v. 8g (*lyhwh*) is balanced by the predicate nominative in v. 3c (*yhwh*). In vv. 6-7, *yhwh* is in the initial emphatic position as the subject of a participle. As may be seen in the accompanying table, the occurrences with and without prepositions are carefully balanced in the two halves of the poem, while special prominence is given to the name of God in the centerpiece:

byhwh (1a)		yhwh (10c)
kyhwh (2a)		yhwh (10a)
yhwh (3c)		lyhwh (8g)
	yhwh (6a)	
	yhwh (7a)	

The metrical pattern of the poem may be described as follows:

[11]For the text of 4QSam[a], we have a preliminary publication by F. M. Cross, 'A New Qumran Biblical Fragment Related to the Original Hebrew Underlying the Septuagint', *BASOR* 132 (1953), 15-26; the translation of the Books of Samuel in the *New American Bible* (Paterson, N.J., 1969/1970) is based on an eclectic text which incorporates additional readings from 4QSam[a], and some of the data may be found in the end-notes, pp. 342ff. (Second Part).

[12]Albright defends MT here, but stylistic considerations support the reading of LXX (*Yahweh and the Gods of Canaan*, 21).

[13]In v. 10a, 'Yahweh' is grammatically independent of the following clause, though it is usually connected with the following words, and occasionally the verb is emended to agree with Yahweh as subject. None of this is necessary when it is recognized that Yahweh is the subject of the verb *yšmr* in v. 9a; this completes the envelope construction.

The Opening (1a-3b)

(without *waw*)

1a)	2 + 2 + 3 = 7 ⎫ 14	2 + 2 + 3 = 7 ⎫ 14	
1b)	2 + 2 + 3 = 7 ⎭ ⎫ 28	2 + 2 + 3 = 7 ⎭ ⎫ 28	
1c)	2 + 1 + 1 + 3 = 7 ⎫ 14 ⎭	2 + 1 + 1 + 3 = 7 ⎫ 14 ⎭	
1d)	3 + 4 = 7 ⎭ ⎫ 57	3 + 4 = 7 ⎭ ⎫ 56	
2a)	1 + 1 + 2 + 3 = 7 ⎫ 14	1 + 1 + 2 + 3 = 7 ⎫ 13	
2b)	2 + 1 + 4 = 7 ⎭ ⎫ 29	*1 + 1 + 4 = 6 ⎭ ⎫ 28	
3a)	1 + 4 + 3 = 8 ⎫ 15 ⎭	1 + 4 + 3 = 8 ⎫ 15 ⎭	
3b)	2 + 2 + 3 = 7 ⎭	2 + 2 + 3 = 7 ⎭	

Divider I (3cd)

3c)	1 + 1 + 2 + 2 = 6 ⎫ 14	1 + 1 + 2 + 2 = 6 ⎫ 13	
3d)	2 + 3 + 3 = 8 ⎭	*1 + 3 + 3 = 7 ⎭	

Stanza I (4-5)

4a)	1 + 3 + 2 = 6 ⎫ 14	1 + 3 + 2 = 6 ⎫ 13	
4b)	4 + 3 + 1 = 8 ⎭	*3 + 3 + 1 = 7 ⎭	
5a)	3 + 2 + 3 = 8 ⎫ 16 ⎫ 46	3 + 2 + 3 = 8 ⎫ 15 ⎫ 43	
5b)	4 + 3 + 1 = 8 ⎭	*3 + 3 + 1 = 7 ⎭	
5c)	3 + 3 + 2 = 8 ⎫ 16	3 + 3 + 2 = 8 ⎫ 15	
5d)	3 + 2 + 3 = 8 ⎭	*2 + 2 + 3 = 7 ⎭	

Centerpiece (6-7)

6a)	2 + 2 + 4 = 8 ⎫ 15	2 + 2 + 4 = 8 ⎫ 15	
6b)	2 + 2 + 3 = 7 ⎭ ⎫ 28	2 + 2 + 3 = 7 ⎭ ⎫ 28	
7a)	2 + 2 + 3 = 7 ⎫ 13	2 + 2 + 3 = 7 ⎫ 13	
7b)	2 + 1 + 3 = 6 ⎭	2 + 1 + 3 = 6 ⎭	

Stanza II (8a-f)

8a)	2 + 3 + 1 = 6 ⎫ 13	2 + 3 + 1 = 6 ⎫ 13	
8b)	3 + 2 + 2 = 7 ⎭	3 + 2 + 2 = 7 ⎭	
8c)	3 + 1 + 3 = 7 ⎫ 15 ⎫ 42	3 + 1 + 3 = 7 ⎫ 14 ⎫ 40	
8d)	3 + 2 + 3 = 8 ⎭	*2 + 2 + 3 = 7 ⎭	
8e)	2 + 1 + 3 = 6 ⎫ 14	2 + 1 + 3 = 6 ⎫ 13	
8f)	4 + 2 + 2 = 8 ⎭	*3 + 2 + 2 = 7 ⎭	

Divider II (8gh)

8g)	1 + 3 + 3 + 1 = 8 ⎫ 16	1 + 3 + 3 + 1 = 8 ⎫ 15	
8h)	3 + 3 + 2 = 8 ⎭	*2 + 3 + 2 = 7 ⎭	

The Closing (9a-10e)

9a) $2 + 3 + 2 = 7$ $\Big\}$ 16		$2 + 3 + 2 = 7$ $\Big\}$ 15	
9b) $4 + 2 + 3 = 9$ $\Big\}$ $\Big\}$ 31		$*3 + 2 + 3 = 8$ $\Big\}$ $\Big\}$ 30	
9c) $1 + 1 + 2 + 2 + 1 = 7$ $\Big\}$ 15		$1 + 1 + 2 + 2 + 1 = 7$ $\Big\}$ 15	
10a) $2 + 3 + 3 = 8$ $\Big\}$ 59		$2 + 3 + 3 = 8$ $\Big\}$ 56	
10b) $2 + 3 + 2 = 7$ $\Big\}$ 14		$2 + 3 + 2 = 7$ $\Big\}$ 14	
10c) $2 + 2 + 2 + 1 = 7$ $\Big\}$ $\Big\}$ 28		$2 + 2 + 2 + 1 = 7$ $\Big\}$ $\Big\}$ 26	
10d) $3 + 1 + 3 = 7$ $\Big\}$ 14		$*2 + 1 + 3 = 6$ $\Big\}$ 12	
10e) $3 + 1 + 3 = 7$		$*2 + 1 + 3 = 6$	

The numerical distribution of the bicola and cola is as follows:

Number of Syllables	Number of Bicola	(Without waw)
12	0	2
13	2	5
14	8	3
15	4	8
16	4	0

Number of Syllables	Number of Cola	(Without waw)
6	5	9
7	17	19
8	13	8
9	1	0

In both cases the data for the revised version of the poem (omitting all waw's at the beginning of cola) are closer to a presumed norm; with regard to single cola (second table), the distribution pattern is an almost perfect bell-shaped curve.

The basic metrical unit of the Song, as also of the Psalm, is a bicolon of 14 syllables, divided at the center or close to it. Of the 18 bicola in the poem, eight have 14 syllables, of which five are divided 7:7 (vv. 1a, 10bc, 10de), and three are divided 6:8 (vv. 3cd, 4ab, 8ef). Six other bicola are within one syllable of the norm: four have 15 syllables, divided 7:8 (vv. 8cd, 9c-10a) or 8:7 (vv. 3ab, 6ab); two have 13 syllables, divided 6:7 (v. 8ab), or 7:6 (7ab). The four remaining bicola all have 16 syllables, divided 8:8 (vv. 5ab, 5cd, 8gh) or 7:9 (v. 9ab). The underlying pattern may be described schematically as follows: the opening and closing consist of two pairs of bicola of 14 syllables each, making a total of 56 syllables for each unit. The boundary markers (dividers) consist of one bicolon each, whereas the central unit contains a pair of bicola, also of 14 syllables each. The dividers taken together add up to 56 syllables. The two stanzas each have three bicola of 14 syllables each making a total of 42 syllables. When each is combined with its boundary marker, the total is 56, while if the two stanzas are linked with the centerpiece, forming the central mass of the poem, the total is 112, the same as the opening and closing together. There are different ways to view the parts in relation to one another, but the symmetry is palpable in all possible arrangements. The actual syllable counts vary slightly from the norm, and the total of 262 is somewhat above the target score of 252. At this point, if we were to take the admittedly drastic step of eliminating the conjunction (represented by *waw*) wherever it occurs at the beginning of cola, the total would be reduced to 251, which is practically identical with the optimum score (252). The conjunction occurs in the following cola in the initial position: vv. 2b, 3d, 4b, 5b, 5d, 8d, 8f, 8h, 9b, 10d, 10e. It has been observed that the early poems of the Pentateuch and the Historical Books make very sparing use of the conjunction at the beginning of cola, and that there is a tendency to increase their number in the course of transmission.[14] We may add that there is not a single instance of the conjunction at the beginning of cola in Psalm 113.

The metrical data for the Song may be summarized as follows:

	Actual Count	Without *waw*	*Model*
Opening (1a-3b)	57	56	56
Divider I (3cd)	14	13	14
Stanza I (4-5)	46	43	42
Centerpiece (6-7)	28	28	28
Stanza II (8a-f)	42	40	42
Divider II (8gh)	16	15	14
Closing (9-10)	59	56	56
Total	262	251	252

The evidence shows that the original metrical scheme has been preserved almost intact in the existing texts. The minor deviations from the norm are to be expected, and in most cases can be attributed to the poet himself. The two instances requiring significant emendation (v. 3a) reflect a rare conflation in MT. In another instance a whole line, which fell out of MT, has been restored on the basis of LXX and presumably 4QSam[a] (v. 8ef).

When comparing the Song with the Psalm, it is clear that they share a common metrical unit: a 14-syllable bicolon divided at or near the middle. There is also a common stanza form, the triad of 42 syllables. From this point, the Song exhibits considerable elaboration and adaptation in contrast with the Psalm which has a very simple structure. With suitable disclaimers and reservations, it may nevertheless be argued that the evolution from the Psalm, with its sequence of identical stanzas, to the Song, with its much more

[14]Cf. F. M. Cross and D. N. Freedman, 'A Royal Song of Thanksgiving: 2 Samuel 22 = Psalm 18', *JBL* 72 (1953), 17-20.

complex patterning, reflects the transition from tribal league to central monarchy, and the progressive acculturation of the State, along with the literary forms used to express its religious faith.

Comments

The parallel structure of the four cola in v. 1 is quite evident. With respect to the first pair (v. 1ab), each element in the first colon is matched by the corresponding element in the second: a Qal perfect third masculine singular verb followed by a noun subject with a first person singular pronominal suffix, and a prepositional phrase introduced by *b* and containing a divine name or title. The corresponding terms have the same number of syllables, so the two cola match precisely: 2 + 2 + 3 = 7 // 2 + 2 + 3 = 7. The first two words in each colon form synonymous or complementary pairs: *ᶜālaṣ libbî // rāmâ qarnî*, while the remaining words represent the breakup of a stereotyped expression: *yhwh ᵓlhy*; here we follow the reading of LXX against MT and 4QSam[a]. Verse 1cd exhibits the same type of parallelism in structure, though with somewhat more variation in detail: the two-word sequence *rḥb py*, which continues the pattern of 1ab, is here matched by the single verb form *śmḥty*; this single term, however, has the same number of syllables as the two-word phrase, and the same vowels in the same order. In each colon of 1cd there is a prepositional phrase, and these also have the same number of syllables: 4. We follow LXX (which is supported in part at least by 4QSam[a]) in omitting *ky* before *śmḥty*, but in reading it before *ᵓyn* at the beginning of v. 2. The suffix attached to the last word of v. 1, *byšwᶜtk*, is a problem, since it is the only second singular pronominal form in the whole poem. The reading is supported by both MT and LXX (with the exception of a few MSS which have the third masculine singular suffix, *autoũ*) and would be difficult to challenge. Nevertheless, a reading with the third masculine singular suffix ('his victory') or the first singular suffix ('my victory' following NAB) would be preferable.[15] The *kap* at the end of the word would be the surviving remnant of the original *kî* which may well have been written defectively at the time of the composition of the poem. Similarly the *waw* or *yod* of the third or first person pronominal suffix would not have appeared either. The metrical pattern of the restored text would be symmetrical:

1c) 2 + 1 + 1 + 3 = 7
1d) 3 + 4 = 7

Verse 2 poses a special problem. As observed by many scholars, both MT and LXX appear to be conflate texts, but containing different doublets; 4QSam[a] seems to diverge from both.[16] While in principle there should be no objection to the appearance of a tricolon among a group of bicola, in this

[15]Compare Cross's implied reconstruction, 'A New Qumran Biblical Fragment . . .', 26, with the reading and explanation of the *New American Bible*, 342 (Second Part).

[16]Cf. Cross, 'A New Qumran Biblical Fragment . . .', 20.

instance preference is all but universally expressed in favor of an original bicolon, and the choice of cola is made on the basis of parallel structure and maximum variety. The best result is: *ky ʾyn qdwš kyhwh // wʾyn ṣwr kʾlhynw*, which produces a balanced bicolon:

2a) 1 + 1 + 2 + 3 = 7 2b) 2 + 1 + 4 = 7

Verse 3 poses several difficulties. Compared with all the other cola in the poem, v. 3a is seriously overloaded: 13 syllables as compared with a normal colon of seven syllables, and a maximum range from six to eight or nine. Since it cannot satisfactorily be divided into two cola, it is reasonable to regard the colon as conflate, with one component reading *ʾl tdbrw gbhh* and the other *ʾl trbw gbhh*. Of the two, the former is preferable, as it provides a more exact parallel to the second colon, v. 3b: *yṣʾ ʿtq mpykm.*[17] It is to be noted that LXX omits one occurrence of *gbhh*, and the sequence *trbw tdbrw* is anomalous at best. Needless to say, the negative particle *ʾl* serves double or triple duty, and governs *yṣʾ* as well as the verbs in the first colon, *trbw* and *tdbrw*.

Verse 3cd marks the first major division in the poem; it separates the introduction from the main section of the poem, but also connects them. This bicolon describes the nature of Yahweh as the supreme judge, just as the corresponding divider (v. 8gh) depicts the unlimited dominion and power of Yahweh as creator of the inhabitable world (*tbl*) and controller of the mysterious netherworld (*ʾrṣ*) on which the former rests. Together these bicola frame the central message of the poem, which is that the God of wisdom and authority controls the affairs and destinies of men, regardless of their ambitions and actions. His overriding interest is reflected in a series of reversals of the ordinary and expected in human experience (vv. 4-5 and 8a-f). The God of v. 3cd is one who weighs human actions, as is expected, but not on the basis of appearances or superficial consideration of the facts; he it is who examines the heart of man, and understands motivation and intention, and evaluates them along with the deeds in deciding cases and rendering judgments.[18] The second colon, v. 3d, is problematic because of the initial term, *wlʾ*; it can hardly be interpreted as the familiar negative particle in view of the context, which requires a positive assessment of the divine role: actions indeed are weighed by God. There are several proposed solutions to the problem, which was recognized early in the course of transmission. Against the Kethib, the Qere reads *wělô*, interpreting the expression as instrumental: 'By him deeds are weighed.' This is a possible but unusual meaning of the preposition *l*. Another procedure is to adopt the presumed reading of LXX, *ʾēl tōkēn*

[17]Cf. Ps. 75:6 and the surrounding verses. There is a literary relationship between the Psalm and the Song of Hannah, but it is considerably more remote than the connection between Psalm 113 and the Song.

[18]Cf. 1 Sam. 16:7.

(= *theós hetoimázōn*).[19] On the whole, however, LXX is less attractive than MT even with its difficulties: *nitkĕnû* (Niphal perfect) is preferable to *tōkēn* especially with *ᶜălīlôt* as a plural subject. Two other proposals of more recent vintage deserve consideration. We may have here an instance of the emphatic or asseverative *lᵓ* instead of the negative particle: i.e., 'For Yahweh is a God of knowledge, and indeed actions are weighed (by him).'[20] Alternatively, following a suggestion of M. Dahood, we may vocalize the word *lēᵓ*, and recognize the divine title, 'the Mighty One', from a root extant in Ugaritic and Phoenician.[21] Whichever of these options is chosen, the meaning remains unaffected, and the metrical pattern is unchanged.

In vv. 4-5, we have a series of role reversals which attest to the supreme authority of God and his control of human affairs. He decides and disposes, regardless of man's plans and proposals. In each pairing, therefore, dramatic effect is achieved by transferring the subject from a normal to an abnormal setting, or shifting from an accustomed to an unexpected experience. In every case the result is the contrary of what one would expect. In the first pair (v. 4), *gibbōrîm* 'warriors', are contrasted with *nikšālîm* 'stumblebums'. Under normal circumstances, the panels would show the warriors girding on their battle gear in anticipation of fighting and winning, while the stumblers are already defeated, their broken bows symbolic either of their ineptness in arming themselves before or during the battle, or of defeat and surrender. In this passage, however, it is the stumblers rather than the warriors who gird on their weapons, while it is the latter, not the former, whose bows are broken, leaving them helpless. The relationship of the words in v. 4a has been the subject of much discussion. In MT, *ḥattîm* is the adjective agreeing with *gibbōrîm*; hence we should translate, 'The warriors are dismayed (or: shattered)', leaving the syntax of *qešet*, 'bow' to be explained. While it could be interpreted as an instrumental dative, 'by the bow', the association of the same three terms (*ḥtt*, *qšt*, and *gbwr*) in Jer. 51:56, shows that the action involved is the shattering of the bows, not the warriors. More in line with this interpretation is the reading of 4QSam[a]: *ḥattâ* (supported effectively by LXX) which is to be construed with *qešet*, i.e., 'The warriors' bow is broken.' This reading preserves the sense, conserves the ambiguity as to when and how the bow of warriors is broken (i.e., by accident or design, before, during, or after the battle), and fits the context. Still the reading of MT is not merely more difficult, but in keeping with the general pattern of role reversals. In the other five sentences in vv. 4-5, the subject is always a person or group of persons, not a thing related to them: *nkšlym*, *śbᶜym*, *rᶜbym*, *ᶜqrh*, and *rbt bnym*. The concern in every case is with the person or group, and what happens to them, or what they do. If the first

[19]See the end note in the *New American Bible*, 342 (Second Part).

[20]Cf. M. Dahood, 'Hebrew-Ugaritic Lexicography I', *Biblica* 44 (1963), 293-4; D. N. Freedman, 'The Burning Bush', *Biblica* 50 (1969), 245-6.

[21]Dahood redivides MT to produce a text closer to LXX: *wĕlēᵓōn tōkēn* (*Psalms I*, 144).

colon conforms to this pattern, we would have to interpret MT to mean, 'The warriors break their bows'; or if we followed 4QSam[a]: 'The warriors—their bow is broken.' The difficulty with the proposed interpretation of MT is that *ḥtym* never has the active force required here, but is always stative or passive. Curiously, the verb occurs in the Piel perfect with transitive force in the related passage, Jer. 51:56, which unfortunately bristles with difficulties. If we translate literally, we get the following: 'For a destroyer has come against her, against Babylon; and her warriors will be captured—she shattered their bows. . . .' While the intention of the author is not clear, and various explanations and emendations have been offered, the syntax of the sentence indicates that the breaking of the bows precedes the capture of the warriors (who may have broken and discarded them as a sign of surrender). This seems also to be the picture in the Song (1 Sam. 2:4): The stumblers gird themselves for battle like warriors, while the warriors suffer the ignominy of being rendered weaponless and helpless.

In v. 5, the pattern of role reversal persists. Under ordinary circumstances, it is the hungry who must sell themselves into slavery for food to eat, while the well-to-do gorge themselves on the spoils of victory. The poet, however, visualizes a radically changed order in which the well-fed must sell themselves for bare necessities, while the starving grow plump on plunder. The phrase *ḥdlw ᶜd* also occurs in the Song of Deborah (Judg. 5:7), and thanks to the combined efforts of several scholars, a satisfactory interpretation of the expression has been attained.[22] It brings out vividly the contrast in the fortunes of the well-fed and the hungry. In v. 5cd the pattern continues, though the order of terms is reversed. Whereas in vv. 4-5ab the strong and the plump come first, followed by the weak and the starved, here the barren woman precedes the fertile one, though the same principle of role reversal is maintained. In this case, the sterile becomes fertile and bears seven, while the prolific woman becomes barren and bears no more. While the text does not say so explicitly, the term *ᵓmllh* probably involves the further implication that the woman with many children loses those she has, so that the exchange of roles or conditions is complete: the barren one has seven, but the one with many children is bereaved.[23]

The central theme of the poem is expressed in vv. 6-7. The basic idea that Yahweh is creator and lord of the universe, that he controls the lives and destinies of human beings, is a commonplace of Scripture and need not be elaborated. There is, however, a special emphasis in this poem and this passage: Yahweh is cast in a revolutionary role; he upsets the normal and expected order of things, and demonstrates his political concerns, as well as his unique power, by reversing the natural process and achieving results contrary to ordinary

[22] D. W. Thomas, 'Some Observations on the Hebrew Root חדל', *Supplements to Vetus Testamentum* 4 (1956), 8-16; J. Calderone, 'ḤDL II', *CBQ* 23 (1961), 451ff. A more detailed discussion of the passage in Judg. 5:7 in relation to the passage here is to be found in the doctoral dissertation of M. L. Chaney (Harvard).

[23] Cf. Jer. 15:9.

experience. Yahweh's authority and activity are defined in a series of contrasts which exemplify the range of human circumstances and conditions, and the way in which Yahweh controls and decides them. There are four pairs of contrasting actions relating to death and life, poverty and wealth, and abasement and exaltation.[24] The sequence within the pairs, in our opinion, is important as it reverses the normal pattern and brings out the special emphasis noted above. Thus the first two pairs of modifiers deal with the same theme: life and death, only the order is, 'Yahweh is the one who puts to death, and the one who brings to life.' It is customary to regard this as an expression of the standard doctrine of Yahweh's power over the life and death of man, that he decides who lives and who dies, and when; such a general view is reflected in Job's statements: 'Yahweh has given and Yahweh has taken . . .' (1:21), and , 'If we receive good things from God, should we not also receive bad things?' (2:10). The order of the verbal forms in the Song (1 Sam. 2:6) shows that the contrast is not between life and death, but rather between 'putting to death' and 'restoring to life'. That the interest of the poet is in the power of God to bring the dead back to life is confirmed by the parallel colon with its contrasting pair of terms: 'He brings down to Sheol, and he brings up (from Sheol).'[25] Here there can be no question of the sequence of the actions, or of the meaning of the poet. Ordinary birth and the commencement of life are not described in terms of emergence from Sheol, whereas the sequence of dying and rising from death to life is naturally so described. Whether the poet had in mind literal dying and literal rising, and whether he was thinking in terms of the individual or the community, are questions which need not detain us at this point, so long as the image itself is understood clearly: what is stressed is Yahweh's ability to exert sovereign control even with regard to processes normally regarded as fixed and immutable, e.g., to raise the dead to life. In the light of v. 6, the contrasting pairs in v. 7 may also be understood as illustrating a reversal of fortunes, as well as being equivalent and complementary (i.e., the rich and exalted belong to the same class, as do the poor and abased). Not only does Yahweh impoverish the rich, but he enriches the poor; he brings down those on high, and he elevates those who have been brought low. In both cases we seem to be dealing with a sequence of actions involving the same person or group, though the terminology is not decisive.

Verse 8a-c is virtually identical with Ps. 113:7-8a. The partial chiasm in 1 Sam. 2:8ab has been noted: *mqym m*ᶜ*pr* // *m*ʾ*špt yrym*. The fourth colon in the couplet, however, is different in the two poems: the Psalm has ᶜ*im nĕdîbê*

[24]The poet combines seven participles with one imperfect form of the verb, thus achieving symmetry, required by the structure of the poem, and also making use of the number seven with respect to attributes of the deity; cf. Psalm 29, where the phrase *qwl yhwh* occurs seven times.

[25]We vocalize the verb as *wĕya*ᶜ*lē*, the imperfect indicative, rather than the apocopated form after the *waw* consecutive in MT. In the period to which we assign the poem, there would have been no difference in the spelling.

ᶜammô 'with the nobles of his people', to balance *lĕhôšîbî ᶜim nĕdîbîm* 'to make him sit with nobles', whereas the Song diverges with *wĕkissēᵓ kābôd yanḥīlēm* 'and a glorious throne he gives them as a possession'. The third person plural pronominal suffix is retrospective and serves as the object also of *lhwšyb*. After v. 8cd in Song, LXX and 4QSam[a] supply a bicolon (8ef), which apparently fell out of MT. It can be reconstructed on the basis of the Greek: *didous euchēn tō euchomenō // kai eulogēsen etē dikaiou* as *nōtēn neder lannōdēr // wayĕbārek šĕnôt ṣaddîq.*[26] There are legitimate arguments as to whether this line is a plus in LXX (and 4QSam[a]) or a minus in MT. What tips the balance in favor of including it in the poem, in our opinion, is the fact that it has not been copied from any other poem in the Bible; and if structural considerations can be adduced, then it provides a needed line to balance the corresponding triad in vv. 5-6. If it is contended that this line, v. 8ef, diverges from the content of v. 8a-d, then it can be pointed out that v. 5cd also has the most tenuous connections with vv. 4-5ab. In a similarly inconclusive way it can be argued that v. 8ef is a deliberate addition to tie the poem to the story of Hannah (i.e., the vow she made, and the gift of the child by way of divine response), but this could be argued as well for v. 5cd. More likely such bicola provided clues (wrongly as it turns out) for the editor who placed the poem in the context of the story of the birth of Samuel. The restoration of the second triad (v. 8a-f) in parallel construction with the first (vv. 4-5) is supported also by the pattern of Psalm, which consists of a series of triads with the same metrical structure.

The next bicolon, v. 8gh, is a divider corresponding to v. 3cd; together they form an envelope around the main part of the poem (vv. 4-8f). They also have links in both directions, contributing a theological framework to the central section and forming a bridge from the introduction to the conclusion, which identify the benefactor and the beneficiary in the transaction.

Verses 9-10 constitute the closing, and are structurally parallel to vv. 1-2, the opening. Contrary to the division of the verses in the Hebrew Bible, there are two couplets: the first unit includes vv. 9a-c and 10a, while the second consists of v. 10b-e. Verses 9a and 10a form an inclusion in which *ḥăsîdāw* 'his faithful ones', is balanced by *mĕrîbāw* 'his contenders (enemies)'. The Niphal imperfect third masculine plural form *yēḥattû* (v. 10a) matches the same Niphal form *yiddāmmû* (v. 9b). The subject of *yšmr* (v. 9a) must be *yhwh* (v. 10a). Comparing vv. 9-10 with vv. 1-2, we note the position of *yhwh* at the beginning of each stanza of the opening (vv. la and 2a), whereas *yhwh* is in the complementary or end position in the closing (v. 10a, the fourth colon of stanza 1, and v. 10c, the second colon of stanza 2). The two-word inclusion

[26]The emendation proposed in the *New American Bible* from *šĕnôt* to *šĕnat* 'sleep', is gratuitous. We take the phrase *šnwt ṣdyq* 'the years of the righteous', as a double accusative, not as a construct chain; regardless of the syntax the sense should be, 'and he blesses the righteous with years (i.e., long life)'. This brings the sentiment into line with a standard biblical image of blessing: 'length of days'.

or echo: *rmh qrny* (v. 1b) and *wyrm qrn* (v. 10e) defines the boundaries of the poem, confirming its unity, and also identifies unmistakably the first person subject of the opening as the anointed king of the closing. The pairing *yhwh* / *ṣwr* in v. 2ab is matched by the pair *ᶜlw* / *yhwh* in v. 10bc. The four perfect forms of the verbs in v. 1 are balanced by the four imperfects in v. 10b-e; we note also that the subject of the opening stanza is the psalmist (first person or equivalent), while in the closing stanza it is Yahweh (third person).

The text of MT for vv. 9-10 seems to be in order (LXX departs notably, and has been contaminated by a long extract from Jer. 9:22-23), and few comments are needed. Verse 9c seems loosely connected with the context, but is consistent with the passage from Jeremiah cited in LXX (and may be the reason LXX continued as it did). The sense is that no man can prevail by his own strength, which is the failing of the wicked, whereas the pious rely on the strength of God. The same sentiment is expressed vigorously in the Deuteronomic sermons of Moses, especially Deut. 8:17-18 (where the same word *kōaḥ* is used). In v. 10b, the peculiar form *ᶜlw* clearly is not the preposition plus pronominal suffix; it has been identified, correctly in our judgment, with Ugaritic *ᶜly* an epithet of Baal, and with the theophorous element *ᶜly* in Phoenician names (cf. also the name of the high priest Eli). It is equivalent in meaning to *ᶜelyōn* 'Most High', and in this passage can be vocalized *ᶜalû* a contraction from an older *ᶜalīyû* or *ᶜēlīyû*.[27] The colon may be compared with 2 Sam. 22:14 = Ps. 18:14, a poem of approximately the same period (10th-9th century). The Song of Hannah in its present form cannot date earlier than the monarchy, but its roots lay in a more distant past. Thanks to the preservation of Psalm 113, we have been able to trace part of this poetic tradition to an older source.[28]

According to our analysis, the Psalm reflects the earliest phase of Yahwistic poetry. The concentrated use of the name Yahweh (six times in the first two stanzas), to the exclusion of other titles (the use of participles and adjectives is noteworthy but thus far inconclusive for dating purposes), is evidence in support of this view. A date in the 12th century B.C. would be consistent with this and other features of the poem noted earlier. In any case it must be assigned to the pre-monarchic period. The Song, on the other hand, cannot be earlier than our Phase III in the evolution of early Israelite poetry, or the monarchic period. In addition to the explicit mention of 'the king, the anointed one', there are divine titles typical of the later periods.[29]

[27]See M. Dahood, 'The Divine Name *ᶜELI* in the Psalms', *TS* 14 (1953), 452-7; cf. the *New American Bible*, 342 (Second Part).

[28]Compare the more elaborate treatment of Psalm 29 and related poems by H. L. Ginsberg, 'A Strand in the Cord of Hebraic Hymnody', *Eretz Israel* 9 (1969), 49-50. For an independent treatment of the two poems, with similar conclusions, see J. T. Willis, "The Song of Hannah and Psalm 113", *CBQ* 35 (1973), 139-54.

[29]Cf. Freedman, 'Divine Names and Titles in Early Hebrew Poetry'.

THE REFRAIN IN DAVID'S LAMENT OVER SAUL AND JONATHAN

In David's Lament over Saul and Jonathan (II Sam. 1 : 19-27) we find the following refrain :

ʾēk nāpelū gibbōrīm	How have the heroes fallen !

It occurs both at the beginning and end of the poem, which would be expected. It also occurs once in the body of the poem, but not anywhere near the midpoint. On two occasions, it is accompanied by the phrase *ʿal-bāmōtēkā ḥālāl*, once before the refrain (vs. 19), once after (vs. 25, but not immediately). Other expressions associated with the refrain are *betōk hammilḥāmāh* (vs. 25), and *wayyōʾbedū kelē milḥāmāh* (vs. 27).

The occurrence of the refrain at the beginning and end of the poem is entirely in order. This device, usually called an Inclusion (Lat. *inclusio*) occurs frequently in Hebrew poetry, with the same or similar expressions, from a word to a sentence, used to open and close a composition.[1] In David's Lament the question is whether the third occurrence of the refrain (vs. 25) has a structural function, and if it does, whether we must supply it elsewhere in the interests of sense and symmetry. In the attempt to arrive at a conclusion, it would defeat the purpose of the investigation if changes of a metrical nature were made, or emendations in the text which had the same effect. The result might be the creation of a new metrical scheme, but we could hardly claim to have recovered the original. We therefore present the text and a translation, along with a metrical analysis and such comments as may be necessary to explain or defend a reading : [2]

---

[1] For discussion and examples, see M. Dahood, *Psalms I* in *The Anchor Bible* (New York, 1966), Index of Subjects, p. 327, under "*inclusio*", and *Psalms II* (1968), Index of Subjects, p. 393, under "*Inclusio*".

[2] For an earlier provisional study of the poem, see Cross and Freedman, *Studies in Ancient Yahwistic Poetry* (hereafter *AYP*; Baltimore, 1950), pp. 43-50. *Cf*. also. S. Gevirtz, *Patterns in the Early Poetry of Israel* (Chicago, 1963), pp. 72-96, and W. Holladay,

Opening

haṣṣ^{e}bī Yiśrā'ēl	(19)	The Gazelle, O Israel
'al - bāmōtēkā ḥālāl		is slain upon thy ridges.
'ēk nāp^{e}lū gibbōrīm		How have the heroes fallen!
'al-taggīdū b^{e}Gat	(20)	Do not announce (it) in Gath
'al - t^{e}baśś^{e}rū b^{e}ḥūṣōt 'Ašq^{e}lōn		Do not proclaim (it) in the streets of Ashkelon
pen - tiśmaḥnāh b^{e}nōt P^{e}lištīm		lest the daughters of the Philistines rejoice
pen - ta'lōznāh b^{e}nōt hā'^{a}rēlīm		lest the daughters of the uncircumcized exult.

I

hārē bagGilbō'	(21)	O mountains in Gilboa —
'al - ṭal w^{e}'al - māṭār '^{a}lēkēm		let there be neither dew nor rain upon you —
ūś^{e}dē t^{e}rūmōt		O lofty fields.
kī šām nig'al		For there was disfigured
māgēn gibbōrīm		the warrior chieftain
māgēn Šā'ūl		Saul the chieftain
b^{e}lī māšīḥ baššāmn		duly anointed with oil.

II

middam ḥ^{a}lālīm	(22)	From the blood of the slain
mēḥelb gibbōrīm		from the fat of the warriors
qašt Yahunātan		Jonathan's bow
lō' nāśōg 'āḥōr		never turned back
w^{e}ḥarb Šā'ūl		and Saul's sword
lō' tāšūb rēqām		never returned empty.

III

Šā'ūl w^{e}Yahunātan	(23)	Saul and Jonathan
hanne'hābīm w^{e}hann^{e}'īmīm		who were beloved and graceful
b^{e}ḥayyēhem ūb^{e}mōtām lō' niprādū		in their lives and in their deaths they were not separated
minn^{e}šārīm qallū		They were swifter than eagles
mē'^{a}rāyōt gābērū		they were stronger than lions.
b^{e}nōt Yiśrā'ēl	(24)	O daughters of Israel
'el - Šā'ūl b^{e}kēnāh		weep for Saul

"Form and Word Play in David's Lament over Saul and Jonathan", *VT*, XX (1970), pp. 153-89.

hammalbiškem šānī ʻim - ʻ^{a}dānīm hammaʻleh ʻ^{a}dī zāhāb ʻal l^{e}būšken	who clothed you in scarlet set with jewels who put gold ornaments on your clothing.

Closing

ʼēk nāp^{e}lū gibbōrīm b^{e}tōk hammilḥāmāh Yahunātan ʻal - bāmōtēkā ḥālāl	(25) How have the heroes fallen in the midst of the battle! O Jonathan slain upon thy ridges.
ṣar - lī ʻālēkā ʼāḥī Yahunātan nāʻamtā lī m^{e}ʼōd niplāʼ ʼattāh ʼahbāt^{e}kā lī mēʼahbat nāšīm ʼēk nāp^{e}lū gibbōrīm wayyōʼb^{e}dū k^{e}lē milḥāmāh	(26) I grieve for you Jonathan my brother You delighted me greatly you were extraordinary Loving you, for me, was better than loving women. (27) How have the heroes fallen and perished with (their) weapons.

Notes

Vocalization and Syllable-counting:

Since we base our metrical analysis on an exact enumeration of syllables, it is important to establish the principles by which this is done. Our primary concern is with the total number of syllables, not the quality or quantity of the vowels. The latter are doubtless a significant factor in determining the precise length of lines, and their metrical relationship to each other; but in the present state of our knowledge, it is hazardous to try to trace the history of vowel change in Biblical Hebrew, and to pin down the situation for given words at different periods. Add to this our lack of certainty about the date of composition of most poems in the Hebrew Bible, and it is clear that we must settle for considerably less in the way of precision than we would like. For the present, we will assume that lines with the same number of syllables are equal in length; and that in a large sample, the distribution of long and short vowels will balance out.[1]

In determining the number of syllables, we follow the vocalization

[1] An effort has been made to reconstruct the actual vocalization of early Hebrew, and to give due weight to differences in vowel length, in the detailed study of Exod. 15 to be published in the *J. M. Myers Festschrift*. In general, the results bear out the statement made in the text; there is no significant change in the overall picture.

of MT generally, even though it is late and somewhat artificial. Where there is compelling evidence to the contrary, chiefly from transcriptions, we adopt an earlier pronunciation. Since our concern is with the number of syllables, we take into consideration only the relatively infrequent gains or losses (e.g., resolutions or elisions), not the numerous and complicated vowel changes. Thus we treat as secondary developments, not reflecting classical Hebrew, such items as *pataḥ* furtive, and auxiliary vowels (*ḥatef*'s) used in conjunction with laryngeals (e.g., *ya'aleh* for earlier *ya'leh*). We also consider segolate formations as secondary, and prefer the more original monosyllabic pronunciation (e.g., *malk* for *melek*); the same is true of resolved diphthongs in the absolute forms of certain nouns (e.g., we read *maym* or *mēm* for MT *mayim*). We recognize the existence of both long and short forms of many particles (e.g., *hinnēh* and *hēn*). In general we follow the specific form used in MT. In the case of the 2nd m. s. pronominal suffixes (*-k* and *kh*, both vocalized *kā*; and *-t* and *th*, both vocalized *tā*), there has been a levelling through of the long pronunciation, whereas the short spelling is predominant, thus making the choice more difficult.[1] From the inscriptional evidence, it seems clear that by the early 6th century B.C.E., the short form was standard, though we would expect that in literary texts and especially in poetry, the long form would be retained or restored.[2] For the Lament of David, presumably an 11th-10th century composition we assume the long form throughout, regardless of the spelling in MT.

The vocalization of the name Jonathan poses a special problem. The original form seems to have been **Yahunatan*. With the syncope of intervocalic *he* it became **Yawnatan*, and then with the contraction of the diphthong *-aw*, *Yōnatan*. The LXX regularly reads *Iōnathan*, which confirms the three-syllable form of the name. The short form is further supported by the spelling in the oldest extant MS of Samuel (4Q Sam b from the early 3rd century B.C.E.: *Ywntn*). Both forms of the name occur in MT, but the more archaic spelling, *Yhwntn*, predominates in the books of Samuel.[3] Our judgment is that MT preserves

---

1 See the discussion of this problem in Cross and Freedman, *Early Hebrew Orthography* (*American Oriental Series*, Vol. 36; New Haven, 1952), pp. 65-68.

2 *Ibid.*, p. 53.

3 The ratio is roughly 2 : 1. In I and II Samuel, the actual count for the different spellings of the name of Saul's son Jonathan is : *Yhwntn* 62; *Ywntn* 29. All but one of the instances of the short spelling ooccur in chaps. 13 and 14 (the exception is in I Sam. 19 : 1). With two exceptions (I Sam. 14 : 6, 8), the longer spelling is confined to the material

an authentic tradition and that the original four-syllable pronunciation was correct for the time of David, and was used in the poem.

It should be added that we count vocal *shewa* as a syllable, but not the *shewa* associated with so-called half-open syllables. We accept minor contractions in MT (e.g., the coalescence of two very short vowels into a single vowel : *w^e y^e- > wi-*), though in particular instances the poet may have preferred the long form of such combinations. To summarize, the vocalization presented above follows MT generally, with the exceptions noted. In questionable cases, a defense is offered for the choice made. The approach is inductive throughout, since the purpose was to uncover metrical patterns if any existed, not to create or impose them.[1]

Vs. 19. While there are difficulties in the verse, and a variety of improvements have been proposed, the received text is satisfactory and can be defended.[2] The first word, *hṣby*, has been the subject of considerable discussion, but no emendation is necessary. It is usually rendered "beauty" (KJV) or "glory" (RVS), but is indistinguishable from *ṣby* 'gazelle', which is to be preferred here. The terms may well have a common etymology, since the gazelle is characterized by its beauty and grace, as well as its speed. Which meaning is original would be difficult to determine, but both literal and figurative uses are well attested in the Bible. The occurrence of *ṣby* 'beauty, glory' as a description or title of places and nations, on the one hand, and of *ṣby* 'gazelle' as a term of comparison with human beings (cf. Song of Songs 2 : 9, 17, etc.) and warriors (*cf.* II Sam. 2 : 18, I Chron. 12 : 9), on the other, offer ample substantiation for its appearance here in reference to one of the heroes, Saul or Jonathan, or possibly both of them. It is only a small step from simile to metaphor; the use of animal terms to represent

---

from I Sam. 18 on. In the later books, especially the Chronicler's Work, the shorter spelling is more common.

[1] While many lines could be counted differently, the possible range is not great. The percentage of variation in a poem of any length is small enough to be ignored. What is remarkable, given our ignorance of the fine points of vocalization in the history of the language, and the long period of transmission from the original composition to our extant texts, is the degree of regularity and symmetry exhibited by the text.

[2] In our judgment, the difficulties are exaggerated by both Gevirtz, *Patterns in the Early Poetry of Israel*, pp. 77-82, and Holladay, *VT*, XX (1970), pp. 162-68; their proposed solutions are far too drastic to be acceptable.

human figures is common both in biblical and Ugaritic literature.[1] In view of the comparisons in vs. 23, the term "gazelle" would be equally appropriate for either hero, and the poet may have been deliberately ambiguous. The explicit reference, however, to Jonathan in vs. 25, which is parallel to vs. 19, suggests that "gazelle" was a nickname or sobriquet for the prince rather than the king. It would also serve to express the more intimate relationship of the brothers-in-law and brothers-in-arms.

Verses 19, 25, and 27 have several elements in common, and are linked by themes as well as key words. The pattern of relationships may be illustrated in the following diagram :

19	25	27
hṣby Yśr'l	'yk nplw gbwrym	'yk nplw gbwrym
ʿl - bmwtyk ḥll	btwk hmlḥmh	wy'bdw kly mlḥmh
'yk nplw gbwrym	Yhwntn ʿl - bmwtyk ḥll	

The basic structural element, the refrain (*'yk nplw gbwrym*) occurs three times; it is twice balanced by the phrase *ʿl - bmwtyk ḥll*. The middle element in vs. 25, *btwk hmlḥmh*, is linked to the second element in vs. 27 by the key word *mlḥmh* (cf. *wy'bdw kly mlḥmh*). The three passages are closely related and tightly interwoven. *Yśr'l* serves as the antecedent of the pronominal suffix attached to *bmwtyk* not only in vs. 19, but also in vs. 25. In our opinion, "Jonathan" in vs. 25 explicates "the gazelle" in vs. 19. The poet, using the same basic theme, has rearranged the key elements, and modified or adapted them in the several contexts to suit his purposes. The structural function of these passages will be dealt with subsequently.

Vs. 20. There is an obvious imbalance between the cola of vs. 20a. Reckoning stressed syllables only, the count is either 2 : 3 or 3 : 4 depending upon whether the negative particle is to receive an accent or not. The syllable count confirms the disparity, 6 : 11, and shows that the second colon is almost twice the length of the first. A number of scholars, noticing the lack of a term parallel to *ḥwṣt* in the first colon, and wishing to restore the presumed balance of the lines, have proposed the insertion of *r^{e}ḥōbōt* before *Gat* (cf. Amos 5 : 16 where the terms are in parallel construction.[2] The proposal is plausible and

---

[1] *Cf.* Exod. 15 : 15, and comments thereto by Cross and Freedman, "The Song of Miriam", *JNES*, XIV (1955), p. 248, fn. 6. On *ẓby* 'gazelle' in Ugaritic, see Gordon, *Ugaritic Textbook* (Rome, 1965), Glossary, No. 1045 (p. 407).

[2] *Cf. AYP*, pp. 45, 48, fn. *a*. Since then the emendation has been proposed by S. Gevirtz, *Patterns in the Early Poetry of Israel*, pp. 83-84. Holladay has also adopted it in

may be correct. Nevertheless, a case can be made for the present text on the basis of the total-syllable count, which is 6 : 11 for vs. 20a, and 9 : 10 for vs. 20b. While the correspondence is not exact, there is a general balance between 20a and 20b (17 : 19). The main difference is that the first bicolon is divided unevenly at *bGt* (6 : 11), whereas the second is divided in the middle at *Plštym* (9 : 10). The general pattern is very close to that of Exod. 15 : 4, where the first bicolon is divided unevenly (8 : 4), and the second in the middle (6 : 6). Greater precision in II Sam. 1 : 20 could be achieved if we read *wᵉ* before *'l - tbśrw* with a number of MSS and the Versions, which would produce a syllable pattern of 6 : 12 in 20a; and if we omitted the definite article before *'rlym* in 20b, we would obtain a perfectly parallel structure for the bicolon, 9 : 9. The overall structure of the verse would then be 18 : 18.[1]

The apparent imbalance in the first line is the result, in our opinion, of a deliberate displacement of the caesura producing a 6 : 11 (12) pattern instead of the more normal 9 : 10 (9), which we find in the second line of vs. 20. We remain to be convinced that any addition to the first colon (*'l - tgydw bGt*) is necessary or desirable for metrical or stylistic reasons.

Vs. 21. Against the widely accepted emendation of MT *wśdy trwmt*, first proposed by Professor H. L. Ginsberg, i.e., *wšr'y thwmwt* 'nor upsurging of the deep',[2] we prefer the received text, though not with the traditional rendering. The poet's specific concern is with the battlefield on which his compatriots were slain, and his prayer is that it should remain barren and receive no fructifying water from heaven. The nearest parallel is Elijah's oath concerning the drought, in which the same expression, *ṭal ūmāṭār*, occurs.[3] What the context in II Sam. 1 requires, then, is an expression parallel to, and consistent with

---

modified form, *VT*, XX (1970), pp. 168-89. If the emendation were accepted, the syllable count for vs. 20 would be : 8 + 11 = 19 / 9 + 10 = 19. See comments below on the strophic structure of the poem as a whole.

[1] *AYP*, pp. 45, 48, fn. *b*. There is good reason to believe that the use of the definite article was very limited in early Hebrew poetry. We do not find it at all in Exod. 15, for example. Apart from the present instance, it occurs four times in David's Lament, vss. 23-24. In all of these cases, however, it functions as a relative pronoun with the participle.

[2] "A Ugaritic Parallel to II Sam. 1 : 21", *JBL*, LVII (1938), pp. 209-13. The reading was adopted in the RSV, and has been accepted by Gevirtz, pp. 85-86, and Holladay pp. 170-73.

[3] I Kings 17 : 1.

*hry bGlb*ʿ 'O mountains in Gilboa'. We render *wśdy trwmt* 'Even you lofty fields', i.e., "fields of the heights", the plateau in the Gilboa range where the battle actually took place. We call attention to the related expression in the Song of Deborah, *m^{e}rōmē śādēh,* usually rendered "heights of the field" but clearly referring to an elevated plain, or plateau. The passage (Judg. 5 : 18) also comes out of a battle context, and is semantically equivalent to *ś^{e}dē t^{e}rūmōt.* Since *trwmt* and *mrwmy* are derived from the same root (*rwm* meaning "high, raised"), the equation is justified. While the common use of *t^{e}rūmōt* in the Bible is restricted to the sacrificial system, there is reason to suppose that the term had other applications, especially in early times. We may point out also that the singular *t^{e}rūmāh* is used repeatedly by Ezekiel as a description of the sacred area in the center of the New Israel where the new Temple was to stand (chaps. 45, 48). While it is not explicitly so stated, it is altogether probable, on the basis of the term itself, and prevailing practice in the siting of temples both in Israel and neighboring countries, that the *trwmh* was a mound or plateau.[1] Following M. Dahood, we take the *waw* before *śdy* as an emphatic particle, here with vocative force.

We interpret the term *mgn* as "benefactor, suzerain, chieftain" rather than "shield". The word, perhaps *magan,* is a cognate of Phoenician - Punic *magon,* which is rendered in Latin by "imperator". Its occurrence in Biblical Hebrew has been demonstrated effectively by Dahood and others.[2] The association of *mgn* and *mšyḥ* ('anointed one') is strikingly illustrated in Ps. 84 : 10 where we read :

māginnēnū r^{e}'ēh '^{e}lōhīm	Look favorably upon our suzerain, O God!
w^{e}habbēṭ p^{e}nē m^{e}šīḥekā	Have regard for the countenance of your anointed one.

In view of the chiastic structure of the verse, and the use of synonymous verbs, it seems clear that *mgnnw* is the object of *r'h* as *mšyḥk* is the object of *hbṭ*; hence both refer to the same person. The juxtaposition of "our sovereign" and "your anointed" accurately depicts the role of the king as chieftain of his people, and anointed vassal of the deity.[3] So in II Sam. 1 : 21, Saul as the anointed vassal of Yahweh

1 *Cf.* Ezek. 40 : 2, "In visions of God, he brought me to the land of Israel, and set me at a high mountain; and upon it was something like the structure of a city".

2 *Cf. Psalms I,* Index, p. 321; and *Psalms II,* Index, p. 384.

3 Against Dahood (*Psalms II,* pp. 278-82), we equate *mgnnw* and *mšyḥk*; both refer to the king.

is at the same time the sovereign of his people, more specifically the commander-in-chief of the warriors. In the context we think it more appropriate to take the verse as a reference to the fate of Saul himself, rather than of his shield: "For there was dishonored the chieftain of warriors". The final phrase *bly mšyḥ bšmn* equally applies to Saul. The usual rendition, "not anointed with oil", is in flat contradiction not only with the facts, but with the repeated emphasis on Saul's legitimacy as the "anointed of Yahweh". It seems clear that we have here an instance of the asseverative use of *bl/bly* instead of the negative use;[1] other particles usually regarded as negative, like *lō'* and *'al*, also have emphatic and asseverative functions.[2] An example of *bal* used asseveratively is to be found in Isa. 40 : 24, where we have the combination *'ap bal* with the apparent meaning: "Surely, firmly, duly" but not "scarcely" or the like. Thus we translate II Sam. 1 : 21. "Saul the chieftain, who was duly anointed with oil".

Vs. 26. We read MT *npl'th* as two words *niplā' 'attāh*, "You were extraordinary".[3] The Hebrew term is anomalous. What is required by the context is a 2nd person singular expression, and a phrase parallel to *n'mt ly m'd*. The proposed reading *npl' 'th* meets both requirements. The omission of an *aleph*, which led to the telescoping of two words into one, may have been the result of accidental haplography. More likely the omission was deliberate, an example of a substantiated spelling practice whereby a repeated consonant (at the end of one word, and at the beginning of the next word) was written only once.[4]

Vs. 27. In view of the parallelism between *nplw* 'have fallen' and *y'bdw* 'have perished', it is probable that *gbwrym* is the common subject of both. If so, then *kly mlḥmh* is to be taken as the indirect object

---

[1] On the asseverative use of *bl* / *blt* in Ugaritic, see Gordon, *Ugaritic Textbook*, Glossary, No. 466 (p. 372), and references there. *Cf.* Dahood, *Psalms* I, Index, p. 319.

[2] *Cf.* Gordon, *Ugaritic Textbook*, Glossary, No. 162 (p. 357), and No. 1339 (p. 425); Dahood, "Hebrew-Ugaritic Lexicography I", *Biblica*, 44 (1963), pp. 293-94; and Freedman, "The Burning Bush", *Biblica*, 50 (1969), pp. 245-46.

[3] *AYP*, pp. 47 and 50, fn. *k*.

[4] See Dahood, *Psalms II*, p. 81; other examples are listed in the Index, p. 397, under "Single writing of consonant where morphology requires two". *Cf.* I. O. Lehman, "A Forgotten Principle of Biblical Textual Criticism Rediscovered", *JNES*, XXVI (1967), pp. 93-101; W. Watson, "Shared Consonants in Northwest Semitic", *Biblica*, 50 (1969), pp. 525-33. A contrary position is presented by A. R. Millard in " 'Scriptio Continua' in Early Hebrew: Ancient Practice or Modern Surmise?" *JSS*, XV (1970), pp. 2-15.

of *y'bdw*, i.e., "with (their) weapons", or with instrumental force: "How have the heroes fallen//perished by the instruments of war". One is reminded of the New Testament expression, "They that take the sword will perish by the sword" (Matt. 26 : 52).

The metrical structure of the poem may be described as follows:

Vs. 19 :	3+3 = 6	1+4+2 = 7	1+3+3=7	Total : 20 (20)
Vs. 20 :	1+3+2 = 6	1+4+3+3 =11		Total : 17
	1+3+2+3 = 9	1+3+2+4 =10		Total : 19 (36)
Vs. 21 :	2+3 = 5	1+1+2+2+3= 9	3+3 =6	Total : 20
	1+1+2+2+3= 9	2+2+2+2+2=10		Total : 19 (39)
Vs. 22 :	2+3 = 5	2+3 = 5		Total : 10
	1+4 = 5	1+2+2 = 5		Total : 10
	2+2 = 4	1+2+2 = 5		Total : 9 (29)
Vs. 23 :	2+5 = 7	4+5 = 9		Total : 16
	4+4+1+3 =12			Total : 12
	4+2 = 6	4+3 = 7		Total : 13 (41)
Vs. 24 :	2+3 = 5	1+2+3 = 6		Total : 11
	4+2+1+3 =10			Total : 10
	3+2+2+1+3=11			Total : 11 (32)
Vs. 25 :	1+3+3 = 7	2+4 = 6		Total : 13
	4+1+4+2 =11			Total : 11 (24)
Vs. 26 :	1+1+3 = 5	2+4 = 6		Total : 11
	3+1+2 = 6	2+2 = 4		Total : 10
	4+1 = 5	3+2 = 5		Total : 10 (31)
Vs. 27 :	1+3+3 = 7	4+2+3 = 9		Total : 16

The strophic structure of the poem may be analyzed in the following manner:

1. The opening, vs. 19, forms an inclusion with vs. 25. Not only is the refrain *'yk nplw gbwrym* repeated, but the associated phrase *'l - bmwtyk ḥll* as well. It is to be noted that these occur in chiastic order, which reinforces the conclusion.

Vs. 19 : (ḥṣby Yśr'l)	'l - bmwtyk ḥll	'yk nplw gbwrym
Vs. 25 : 'yk nplw gbrym	(btwk mlḥmh Yhwntn)	'l - bmwtyk ḥll

2. Vss. 20 and 24 form a structural unit in which the threatened rejoicing of the "daughters of the Philistines" (vs. 20) is set off against the necessary weeping of the "daughters of Israel" (vs. 24). Taking vss. 19 and 20 together and vss. 24 and 25, we then have two double units in a chiastic construction which balance each other exactly:

Vs. 19 :	20 syllables	Vs. 24 :	32 syllables
Vs. 20 :	36 syllables	Vs. 25 :	24 syllables
Total	56		56

3. Vs. 21, which is devoted entirely to Saul, is matched by vs. 26, which is devoted entirely to Jonathan. These verses enclose two units in which both heroes are named, and dealt with together : vss. 22-23. Once again a chiastic pattern emerges in the alternation of the names Saul and Jonathan :

Vs. 21 (Saul) :	39		Vs. 22 : (J & S) :	29
Vs. 26 (Jonathan) :	31		Vs. 23 : (S & J) :	41
Total	70	=		70

4. We are now ready to assemble the different units into larger strophes :

I		II	
Vs. 19 (Refrain)	20	Vs. 21 (Saul)	39
Vs. 20 (Daughters of the Philistines)	36	Vs. 24 (Daughters of Israel)	32
Vs. 22 (Jonathan & Saul)	29	Vs. 25 (Refrain)	24
Vs. 23 (Saul & Jonathan)	41	Vs. 26 (Jonathan)	31
Total	126	=	126

It is to be noted that the names Saul and Jonathan occur twice in each strophe, that the Daughters of the Philistines are balanced by the Daughters of Israel, and that the refrain (with its accompanying phrase) occurs in each strophe.[1] We need only add that the Closing (vs. 27), also contains the refrain, which links it with both strophes. With vs. 19, it forms a major inclusion encompassing the whole poem, and with vs. 25, a minor inclusion framing the personal and poignant lament over Jonathan.

The complex, interlocking, but at the same time carefully balanced structure of the whole poem may be diagrammed as follows :

---

[1] The units can also be combined in a slightly different, possibly simpler fashion :

I		II	
Vs. 19)	20	Vs. 22)	29
20)	36	23)	41
21)	39	24)	32
26)	31	25)	24
Totals :	126		126

Other arrangements might be considered as well, e.g. :

I				II			
Vs. 19)	20	Vs. 21)	39	Vs. 22)	29	Vs. 25)	24
20)	36	24)	32	23)	41	26)	31
(27)	16					27)	16
Totals :	72		71		70		71

Vs. 19 (20)⌉
Vs. 20 (36)⌋ -56
Vs. 21 (39)⌉
Vs. 22 (29)⌉
Vs. 23 (41)⌋ -70
Vs. 24 (32)⌉
Vs. 25 (24)⌋ -56
-70
Vs. 26 (31)⌋
Vs. 27 (16)

The individual units vary in length but when combined in accordance with their distinctive characteristics (key words or phrases), the larger groupings are evenly matched. A principle of compensation may be observed in these combinations : thus the short refrain (vs. 19) is linked with the long unit on the Daughters of the Philistines (vs. 20); on the other hand the short unit on the Daughters of Israel (vs. 24) is connected to the long refrain (vs. 25). Similarly the long unit on Saul (vs. 21) is combined with the short unit on Jonathan (vs. 26). These match the combination of short (vs. 22) and long units (vs. 23) on Saul and Jonathan together.

THE TWENTY-THIRD PSALM

Psalm 23 is commonly classified as a personal psalm of trust, expressing confidence in the Divine Shepherd.[1] As such it has been accepted by countless millions of worshippers, who have committed it to memory and repeated it in their devotions. It is a matter of some interest that this most popular and best loved Psalm continues to puzzle scholars. This brief poem does not pose the usual problems of textual corruption or linguistic obscurity. There are no significant textual difficulties; the vocabulary while unusual is quite comprehensible, and the grammar and syntax are well within the range of classical Hebrew style. Difficulties arise when one considers the cohesion of the parts, or the interpretation of the poem as a whole. Thus, while the figure of the Divine Shepherd dominates the first half of the poem (through vs. 4), there is a shift to the figure of the Divine Host in vs. 5. The unity and integrity of the Psalm seem to be insured by its brevity and its structure, yet its meaning and proper interpretation remain in doubt.[2]

In my view there is an underlying theme which integrates the disparate elements of the poem and provides a framework for the variety of bold and striking images used by the poet. That unifying factor is the central theme of the Old Testament, the Exodus from Egypt, and its accompanying phenomena: the wandering through the wilderness, and the settlement in the domain of God. The key clause, according to this understanding of the Psalm, is vs. 5a: "You set before me a table," a difficult clause which is in jarring contrast to the shepherd imagery of the preceding verses. Nevertheless, it is consistent with the Exodus pattern, as the

[1] See A. Weiser, *The Psalms* (trans. from the German by H. Hartwell; Philadelphia, 1962), pp. 226 ff.; H.-J. Kraus, *Psalmen* (*"Biblischer Kommentar,"* Vol. 15; Neukirchen, 1960), pp. 186 ff.; M. Dahood, *Psalms I* ("The Anchor Bible," Vol. 16; New York, 1966), pp. 145 ff.

[2] See Kraus, *Psalmen,* Vol. I, pp. 186-88.

corresponding expression in Ps. 78:19 confirms:[3] "And they spoke against God. They said, 'Is El able to set a table in the wilderness?' "

The context shows that the poet has in mind the miraculous provision of food for the Israelites (vss. 20-29, cf. vss. 15-16). Since the poem also includes the picture of Yahweh as shepherd of his people, leading them out of Egypt and through the wilderness (vss. 52-53), the juxtaposition of the two images—Shepherd and Host—is fully in keeping with the ancient tradition.

If the central content and much of the imagery of Psalm 23 are rooted in the Exodus tradition, nevertheless there are distinctive aspects of the Psalm which rule out a simple identification of the poem with the historical experience, or as an epitome of Israel's past, such as we have in a number of canonical Psalms (e.g., Pss. 78, 105, 106). In the present instance, the Psalmist both personalizes and universalizes the experience. Thus the expression *yahweh rō'ī* 'Yahweh is my shepherd,' stressing the personal relationship between God and the worshipper, is unique in the Bible, although the figure of God as shepherd of his people is well known, especially in relation to the Exodus, and to the Restoration from Exile.[4] Furthermore, although the connection with the wilderness in one way or another is inescapable, there are no explicit references to it in the Psalm. It seems to suggest that everyone may share the experience of the Mosaic generation, its impressions and effects, without actually marching across the same terrain. Finally, there is an idyllic tone about the experience of the Psalmist and his relationship with Yahweh, which is not completely consistent with the inherited tradition, but reflects rather the idealized picture presented by Hosea and Jeremiah.[5] For example, there is the unique phrase: *'al mē m^e^nūhōt* 'beside the waters of

[3]On the date of Ps. 78, see my forthcoming article, "Divine Names and Titles in Early Hebrew Poetry," to appear in the *Magnalia Dei: The Mighty Acts of God,* ed. F. M. Cross *et al.* (New York, 1976); also the following: O. Eissfeldt, *Das Lied Moses Deuteronomium 32:1-43 und Das Lehrgedicht Asaphs Psalm 78; samt einer Analyse der Umgebung des Mose-Liedes* ("Verhandlungen der Sächsischen Akademie der Wissenschaften zu Leipzig, phil.-hist. Klasse, Vol. 104, Part 5; Berlin, 1958), pp. 26-41; D. A. Robertson, "Linguistic Evidence in Dating Early Hebrew Poetry," Ph.D. Dissertation for Yale University, 1966, pp. 223-28; W. F. Albright, *Yahweh and the Gods of Canaan* (New York, 1968), pp. 17, 155.

[4]For the exilic period, note especially Ezek. 34 and Isa. 40:11.

[5]Cf. Hosea 11:1-4; Jer. 2:1-3.

repose' in vs. 2, which conveys fully the prevailing mood of serenity and tranquillity. While it has no obvious counterpart in the narrative or poetic tradition of the wanderings, it is very nearly the exact opposite of the phrase: *'al mē m^{e}rībāh* 'by the waters of Meribah (= strife, contention).' The latter figures prominently in those traditions: cf. Pss. 81:8; 106:32, and Num. 20:13.[6]

Briefly put, the poet has adapted the main elements in the Exodus tradition to encourage and enhance personal piety. It is his conviction that every faithful follower of Yahweh does or can experience deliverance, protection, tranquillity, and permanent peace, even beyond the achievements of the early Israelites in the decisive events of their time. The individual relives, as in the festivals of Passover and Tabernacles, the experience of his ancestors as they proceed from bondage to freedom, from danger to security, recipients of amazing grace and abundant blessing. They follow a path from the house of slaves in Egypt through the wilderness to settle at last and forever in the sacred territory of Yahweh, where the heavenly palace and its earthly counterpart (originally the Tabernacle) are conjoined in a mythic yet historic space-time continuum.[7]

The following analysis of the structure of the poem, both metrical and syntactic, and study of its distinctive vocabulary are intended to support the thesis proposed above. Some of the pertinent details are offered in the transcription and translation of the text, and the comments on it. The transcription has been prepared in accordance with the vocalization of classical Biblical Hebrew (roughly 10th to 6th centuries B.C.) as currently understood among scholars.[8] Deviations from the Massoretic Text are explained and defined in the notes, as are departures from traditional arrangements, renderings, and interpretations. In the translation I have

[6] The full story is given in Num. 20:2-13; cf. Deut. 33:8-9.

[7] See my article: "Divine Names and Titles in Early Hebrew Poetry" in *Magnalia Dei*; and "Early Israelite History in the Light of Early Israelite Poetry," in *Unity and Diversity: Essays in the History, Literature, and Religion of the Ancient Near East.* ed. H. Goedicke (Baltimore, 1975), pp. 3-35. For an earlier analysis, now partly inoperative, see my "Strophe and Meter in Exodus 15," *A Light unto My Path: Old Testament Studies in Honor of Jacob M. Myers* (Philadelphia, 1974), pp. 190-93.

[8] My basic approach is explained in a number of articles: e.g., "Strophe and Meter in Exodus 15," pp. 173-75; "The Structure of Psalm 137," *Near Eastern Studies in Honor of William Foxwell Albright* (Baltimore, 1971), pp. 188-90; "Acrostics and Metrics in Hebrew Poetry," *Harvard Theological Review*, 65 (1972), 368-69.

adopted a “timeless present” tense as a rough equivalent of the Hebrew: neither the verb forms nor their context offer any decisive indication of the time scheme intended by the poet.

Psalm 23[9]

1) *yahweh rō‘ī lō’ ’eḥsār*	7	Yahweh is my shepherd, I lack nothing.
2) *bin’ōt daš’ yarbīṣēnī*	7	In grassy meadows, he makes me lie down.
‘al mē m^{e}nūḥōt y^{e}nah^{a}lēnī	10	Beside tranquil waters, he guides me.

3) *napšī y^{e}šōbēb*	5	He restores my spirit–
yanḥēnī b^{e}ma‘g^{e}lē ṣidq	8	He leads me in the tracks of righteousness
l^{e}ma‘n š^{e}mō	4	For his name’s sake–
4) *gam kī ’ēlēk b^{e}gē’ ṣalmūt*	8	Even when I walk in the valley of deep shadow.

lō’ ’īrā’ rā‘ kī ’attāh ‘immādī	10	I fear no evil, for you are with me.
šibṭ^{e}kā wamiš‘antekā	8	Your rod and your staff–
hēmmāh y^{e}naḥ^{a}mūnī	7	Indeed! they vindicate me.

5) *ta‘rōk l^{e}pānay šulḥān*	7	You arrange a banquet for me–
nagd ṣōr^{e}ray	4	In front of my foes
diššantā bišamn rō’šī	7	You anoint my head with oil–
kōsī r^{e}wāyāh	5	My cup overflows.

6) *’ak ṭōb waḥasd yird^{e}pūnī*	8	Surely goodness and kindness will accompany me
kol-y^{e}mē ḥayyāy	5	All the days of my life.
wāšabtī b^{e}bēt yahweh	7	I will dwell in the house of Yahweh
l^{e}’ōrk yāmīm	4	For the length of (my) days.

[9] In the presentation which follows, the transcription of the Hebrew text, arranged in metrical units, is on the left, and the English translation is on the right. The translation is intended to be literal rather than artistic, but not painful. On the left hand margin are the verse numbers according to the Hebrew text (the numbering in the Hebrew Bible is followed throughout the paper); in the center column I have indicated the syllable count of the Hebrew line to the left.

Metrical and Strophic Structure:

The poem divides naturally into five stanzas of approximately equal length, as indicated in the arrangement above. Each stanza consists of about 24 syllables, distributed among lines of uneven length. The major divisions or strophes of the poem can be determined on the basis of grammatical shifts in vs. 4, and at the end of vs. 5. While the whole poem is narrated in the first person by the Psalmist, Yahweh is described in the third person in vss. 1-3, and again in vs. 6, while in vss. 4-5 he is addressed directly in the second person. As against the traditional and commonly accepted division at the end of vs. 3, I believe that the first clause of vs. 4 (ending with *bgy' ṣlmwt*) belongs with vs. 3, and closes the strophe.[10] The second strophe, which extends through vs. 5, is controlled by the opening clause: *l' 'yr' r'* 'I fear nothing evil,' just as the first strophe is dominated by the clause: *l' 'ḥsr* 'I lack nothing.' The correlation is enhanced by the play on the words *rō'ī* 'my shepherd' in vs. 1, and *rā'* 'the evil (one)' in vs. 4. Yahweh the protective shepherd is contrasted with the nameless evil person or thing which threatens the poet.[11]

The major strophes each consist of two stanzas of practically equal length (I: A. vss. 1-2; B. vss. 3-4a; II: A. vs. 4 [the remainder]; B. vs. 5), while the concluding unit, vs. 6, comprises a single stanza equivalent in form to the second or "B" stanza of the strophes. Following the same syllable-counting system I have used in the analysis of other biblical poems, I have calculated the metrical structure of Ps. 23 on a word-by-word basis as follows (the total for each line is given, along with that of the Massoretic Text; MT is generally somewhat higher but the overall pattern is unaffected by such slight differences):[12]

[10]Thus the phrase *bgy' ṣlmwt* forms a contrasting pair with *bm'gly ṣdq* in vs. 3; it is also linked with *bn'wt dš'* which is paired with *'l my mnḥwt* (vs. 2).

[11]Perhaps *rā'* should be rendered "the evil one"; cf. Dahood, *Psalms III* ("The Anchor Bible," Vol. 17A; New York, 1970), pp. XLVIII ff. Instead of the mythic figure of Death, the poet may have had in mind the historic figure of the Pharaoh, who is the archetypal human antagonist of Yahweh and his people. See Dahood's remarks in *Psalms III*, p. 81, in which he identifies the "oppressor" in Ps. 107:2 with Pharaoh.

[12]The vocalization of the Massoretic Text is accepted generally, with certain modifications: secondary vowels (including *pataḥ* furtive) added in relation to laryngeals in MT are not counted, and segolate formations are treated as monosyllabic, all in accordance with available evidence for the morphology of the classical language. Vocal

Strophe I

			Stanza A	Massoretic Text
1)	2 + 2 + 1 + 2	=	7	7
2)	2 + 1 + 4	=	7	8
	1 + 1 + 3 + 5	=	10	10
			24	25

Stanza B

					MT
3)	2 + 3	=	5		5
	3 + 4 + 1	=		8	9
	2 + 2	=		4	5
4)	1 + 1 + 2 + 2 + 2	=	8		9
			13 + 12 = 25		28
	I: A + B		24 + 25 = 49		25 + 28 = 53

Strophe II

			Stanza A	MT
4)	1 + 2 + 1 + 1 + 2 + 3	=	10	10
	3 + 5	=	8	8
	2 + 5	=	7	7
			25	25

shewa, however, is counted, since it regularly represents an original full vowel. MT is not a reliable guide in the choice between long and short forms of pronominal suffixes and other particles. We cannot be certain about contractions, e.g., *bin'ōt* (vs. 2: two syllables) for older _*b^{e}nā'ōt_ (three syllables). Doubtless the poet could exercise discretion, if not license, in such matters. Except in rare instances such variations have been smothered by Massoretic uniformity, though occasional differences between the written form of the word and its vocalization offer us a glimpse at some of the available options.

		Stanza B		Massoretic Text
5)	2 + 3 + 2	= 7		8
	1 + 3	=	4	5
	3 + 2 + 2	=	7	8
	2 + 3	= 5		5
		12 + 11 = 23		26
	II: A + B	25 + 23 = 48		25 + 26 = 51

		Close		
6)	1 + 1 + 2 + 4	= 8		9
	1 + 2 + 2	=	5	5
	3 + 2 + 2	=	7	7
	2 + 2	= 4		5
		12 + 12 = 24		26

In both Strophes, Stanza A consists of a triad totalling 24 or 25 syllables (25 in MT). A long line of 10 syllables is balanced by two shorter ones of approximately the same length (7 or 8 syllables). Stanza B, on the other hand, consists of two lines averaging out at 12 syllables (the range is from 11 to 13; in MT it is 13-14). The totals are 25 and 23 syllables, making an average of 24. The closing stanza (vs. 6) conforms to the "B" pattern, having lines of 13 and 11 syllables, making a total of 24 (in MT the lines are 14 and 12 syllables for a total of 26). The two Strophes balance out at 49 and 48 syllables, while the Close is half as long at 24 syllables. (For MT, the totals are 53 and 51, averaging 52, while the Close is half of that at 26 syllables.)

In the "B" stanzas and the Close, the lines are marked by a caesura which occurs at the end of the first or second third of the line. In Strophe I, Stanza B, the short colon precedes the long one: 5 + 8; 4 + 8, whereas in Strophe II, Stanza B, the long colon precedes the short one: 7 + 4; 7 + 5. The Close follows the second of these patterns: 8 + 5; 7 + 4. In my opinion, however, the actual pattern is more complex, and involves an envelope construction:

we must combine the first and fourth cola, and the second and third cola, to produce the following patterns:

I:B.	5 + 8;	8 + 4
II:B.	7 + 5;	4 + 7
Close	8 + 4;	5 + 7

Such structures are observable in a number of poems in the Bible, e.g., Ps. 29:7-9.[13] In I:B, the link between the second and third cola is unmistakable, and while it has never been suggested before, cola one and four combine nicely to form an intelligible line. With respect to II:B, the parts are substantially interchangeable, so any arrangement would be satisfactory. The same would apply to the Close, but note that Ps. 27:4b, which is practically identical with Ps. 23:6, nevertheless combines *šbty bbyt yhwh* with *kl ymy ḥyy* (although the order is opposite from that in Ps. 23). We may claim this datum as indirect evidence in support of the suggestion that cola two and three of Ps. 23:6 be linked.

A model structure for the Psalm may, therefore, be posited:

				MT
Strophe I:		48		52
Stanza A:	7 + 7 + 10 = 24		8 + 8 + 10 = 26	
Stanza B:	12 + 12 = 24		13 + 13 = 26	
Strophe II:		48		52
Stanza A:	10 + 7 + 7 = 24		10 + 8 + 8 = 26	
Stanza B:	12 + 12 = 24		13 + 13 = 26	
Close:		24		26
	12 + 12 = 24		13 + 13 = 26	
	TOTAL	120		130

[13] The pattern is slightly different, but the principle is the same; see D. N. Freedman and C. Franke Hyland, "Psalm 29: A Structural Analysis," *Harvard Theological Review,* 66 (1973), 251-52. An example of interlocking lines is found in Lam. 3:56; see "Acrostics and Metrics in Hebrew Poetry," pp. 383-84. For examples of a larger inclusion, involving Ps. 29:2b and 9c, and Hosea 8:9 and 13, see the article on Ps. 29 mentioned earlier in this footnote, pp. 243-46, and my "Prolegomenon" to G. B. Gray, *The Forms of Hebrew Poetry* (New York, 1972), pp. XXXVI-XXXVII.

The poem conforms very closely in practice to the suggested norm. As to the minor deviations from the standard, some of these may be the result of scribal slips, or editorial alterations, but some should be regarded as deliberate on the part of the poet.

The case for metrical regularity and strophic symmetry hinges on the proposed division between Strophes I and II at the end of the first clause of vs. 4, which is certainly contestable. It will be noted, however, that the syntactic and structural arguments advanced earlier for this division are independent of the metrical analysis, and the two sets tend to support each other against the traditional view. There is no debate that vs. 4a serves as a connecting link between the two Strophes. Whether it belongs formally with the first or the second would have to be decided by other factors.

The initial conclusion is that the poem is a unity and complete as it stands. Reinforcing this view is the use of an envelope construction or *inclusio,* which binds the opening and closing lines together. This familiar device involves the repetition of the name Yahweh in the first and last verses; what sharpens this feature is that the name Yahweh occurs nowhere else in the poem, and in fact no other divine name is used. The opening and closing lines can be tied to each other semantically and syntactically. The same is true of the other two key clauses (in vss. 1 and 4). The four taken together reveal the basic structure of the poem, as well as its force and direction:

yahweh rō'ī	(vs. 1)	Yahweh is my shepherd
lō' 'eḥsār	(vs. 1)	I lack nothing
lō' 'īrā' rā'	(vs. 4)	I fear nothing evil
wāšabtī bᵉbēt yahweh	(vs. 6)	I dwell in Yahweh's house

As already indicated, I believe that the poem has its roots in the Exodus events and draws on the national tradition in depicting the pilgrimage of the individual believer, under the guidance of the Divine Shepherd, through the valley of deep darkness and its dangers, to the land of Yahweh himself, with its ultimate security and tranquillity. In the nature of the case, it is not possible to make a positive demonstration of the poet's intentions, but it can be shown that the imagery and movement of the poem are compatible with the Exodus theme, and that it serves to unify otherwise disparate elements in the composition.

Commentary:

Vs. 1

yahweh rō'ī, 'Yahweh is my shepherd': It has already been observed that the name Yahweh occurs only at the beginning and ending of the poem, and that no other divine name is used. The Psalm therefore satisfies the principal criterion I have devised to identify the earliest poems in the Hebrew Bible: Phase I which is to be dated to the 12th century B.C.[14] It would be rash to attempt to fix the date of composition on the basis of such meager evidence, and in view of the brevity of the poem. Such an archaic feature is worth noting, however, especially since there are others in the poem.

With respect to the second word, it has been pointed out that the traditional theme of Yahweh as shepherd of his people (cf. Ps. 80:2 *rō'ēh yiśrā'ēl*, 'the shepherd of Israel'; Pss. 95:7; 100:3) has been adapted to the individual, the Psalmist. Even if the "I" of the Psalm is a collective, or more likely a representative figure for the people or congregation, the usage is different, and symbolically important. There is also a positive link between Yahweh as shepherd of his people and the Exodus theme: cf. Pss. 77:20; 78:52-53; 95:7-11; 100. Even more striking is the association of the image of the Divine Shepherd with the New Exodus and restoration of the people in Exile, as described by Ezekiel and II Isaiah. In Ezek. 34, the prophet rings the changes on the theme of the return of the people, and the role of Yahweh as their shepherd. He will bring them back from the lands of their captivity, and also watch over them henceforth in their own land. Among the numerous points of contact between Ezek. 34 and Ps. 23, note especially Ezek. 34:11-16, and 25-31. The same combination of ideas is found in the oracles of II Isaiah, explicitly in Isa. 40:11; 49:10 (cf. chaps. 35; 41:17 ff.; 42:14 ff.; 43; 45.13; 48:21; 51:9 ff.;

[14]See my article on "Divine Names and Titles in Early Hebrew Poetry" for a discussion of this point.

52; 55:12 ff.; 56:7 - 57:13; 63:10-14).[15] It is clear that the image of Yahweh as shepherd is closely linked with the Exodus tradition, and that the 7th-6th century prophets, especially Ezekiel and II Isaiah, combine them in forecasting the return of the exiles and the restoration of Israel.

lōʾ ʾeḥsār 'I lack nothing': The verb *ḥsr* is relatively uncommon in Biblical Hebrew, occurring about 22 times in all. Several instances, however, relate directly to the Exodus experience: e.g., Deut. 2:7 "For Yahweh your God has blessed you in all the work of your hands; he knows your going through this great wilderness; these forty years Yahweh your God has been with you; you have lacked nothing [= *lōʾ ḥāsartā dābār*]." The same sentiment is expressed in Neh. 9:21 "Forty years you sustained them in the wilderness, and they lacked nothing [= *lōʾ ḥāsērū*]." The absolute construction, without any object, is the same as in Ps. 23. In Deut. 8:9, the expression is similar, but the reference is to life in the promised land, rather than the wilderness: ". . . a land in which you will eat food without scarcity, in which you will lack nothing [= *lōʾ teḥsar kōl bāh*]."

Vs. 2

binʾōt dešeʾ, 'in grassy meadows': The combination of terms in this precise form is unique in the Bible, though equivalent and comparable expressions occur: e.g., Joel 2:22 *kī dāšᵉʾū nᵉʾōt midbār* 'For the pastures of the wilderness are green.' The construct chain, *nᵉʾōt midbār*, appears repeatedly (cf. Jer. 9:9, 23:10; Joel 1:19, 20; Ps. 65:13), so the association of *nʾwt* with the wilderness would be a natural one. The use of the term might be expected to evoke in the mind of the hearer or reader some thought of the wilderness, and the traditions connected with it. The apparently related term *nāweh* has similar literary associations with the wilderness and the pasturage of flocks. It occurs in two passages of special interest: Exod. 15:13, which describes the

[15] I use the designation "II Isaiah" loosely to cover all the material in Isa. 40-66 (and chaps. 34-35 as well), but do not mean by this that a single author was responsible for the whole work (any more than I Isaiah, the 8th century prophet, was the author of everything in chaps. 1-33). The dividing line between II and III Isaiah is not clear to me, and there may well be other contributors to the corpus. At the same time, I believe that everything in II Isaiah can be dated in the latter half of the 6th century B.C.

march through the wilderness after the victory at the Reed Sea, and Ezek. 34:14, which describes the restoration of Israel by the Divine Shepherd.

yarbîṣēnî, 'he makes me lie down': The verb is used with animals, both wild and domestic, literally and in figures of speech for human beings. Specific references to a flock occur in Ezek. 34:14, 15; Jer. 33:12; Zeph. 2:14. In several instances the act of lying down is a symbol of peace and tranquillity: cf. Isa. 11:6-7, 14:30; Jer. 33:12 (in the context of the messianic age), and Ezek. 34:14-15 (already cited in another connection). Of special interest is the association with the phrase *wᵉʾēn maḥᵃrîd* 'and none shall frighten (them)': Job 11:19; Isa. 17:2; Zeph. 3:13–a succinct statement of the central theme of Ps. 23.

ʿal mê mᵉnūḥôt, 'beside tranquil waters': The phrase is unique in the Bible. The word *mᵉnūḥôt* (a plural of emphasis in all likelihood) itself occurs only one other time, in Isa. 32:18. The passage, Isa. 32:15-18, is pertinent to our discussion since it speaks of the future peace, security, and contentment of the people of Yahweh, and reflects the tradition of the wilderness wanderings and settlement in the land, using such key terms as *nᵉwēh šālôm* 'peaceable habitation,' *miškᵉnôt mibṭaḥîm* 'secure dwellings,' and *mᵉnūḥôt šaʾᵃnannôt* 'quiet resting-places.' The singular form of the noun, *mᵉnūḥāh,* occurs repeatedly in contexts relating to the Exodus and the wanderings, identifying the resting-place of the people and its palladium, the Ark of the Covenant: e.g., Num. 10:33 and 36; cf. Ps. 132:8, 14 (in which the Ark and its traditions have been transferred to Zion); see also Deut. 12:9 and I Kings 8:56. More pertinent for our purposes is Ps. 95, especially the latter part, vss. 6-11, which focusses attention on the wilderness experience and the divine decision to punish the rebellious generation of the Exodus (vss. 10-11): "For forty years I loathed that generation . . . and I swore in my anger that they should not enter my rest [= *mᵉnūḥātî*] ." Earlier the poet has established the link between the theme of the wanderings and Yahweh's role as shepherd of his flock. He has also pointed to the episode at Meribah/Massah in the wilderness (Ps. 95:8) as the precipitating factor in the decision against the generation which came out of Egypt, but proved unworthy in the trials of the wilderness.

By contrast, the author of Ps. 23 expresses confidence that no such disaster will befall him. Unlike the generation of the

Exodus which came to grief beside the waters of Contention (= *'al mē m^{e}rībāh,* cf. Pss. 81:8 and 106:32),[16] he comes peacefully to the waters of permanent security and repose (*'al mē m^{e}nūḥōt*). The congruence in form and the contrast in force are striking and suggest a deliberate reworking of the wilderness tradition in the interest of a present concern and future expectation, as well as a possible reinterpretation of the past experience of the people. Regardless of the value of this particular proposal, there can be little question of the association of this phrase with the central theme of the Exodus and wanderings.

y^{e}nah^{a}lēnī, 'he guides me': The verb *nhl* is quite rare, occurring only 10 times in the Bible. From the beginning the term was associated with the wilderness wanderings, as the key passage, Exod. 15:13, makes clear:[17]

> You led *(nāḥītā)* in your kindness the people whom
> you redeemed
> You guided *(nēhaltā)* in your might to your holy
> habitation.

The pairing of the verbs *nḥh* and *nhl* is also attested in Ps. 31:4, and here in Ps. 23 (vss. 2-3, though in reverse order). Since the verb *nḥh* occurs more frequently in the Bible (38 times), it should be regarded as the A-word in this poetic pattern, and the verb *nhl* as the corresponding B-word.[18] The normal sequence is found in Exod. 15 and Ps. 31, while the arrangement in Ps. 23 would be unusual. The verb also occurs in Isa. 40:11, which as previously noted combines the image of Yahweh as shepherd of his flock with the theme of a new Exodus from bondage to liberty, the march through the wilderness and settlement in Yahweh's domain:

[16] Cf. footnote 6.

[17] On the date of the poem, see F. M. Cross, Jr. and D. N. Freedman, "The Song of Miriam," *Journal of Near Eastern Studies,* 14 (1955), 239-40; also my "Strophe and Meter in Exodus 15," pp. 201-2, and "Divine Names and Titles in Early Hebrew Poetry" (all supporting a 12th century date); cf. Robertson, "Linguistic Evidence in Dating Early Hebrew Poetry," p. 231. For an earlier date see Albright, *Yahweh and the Gods of Canaan,* pp. 12 and 33.

[18] See R. G. Boling, " 'Synonymous' Parallelism in the Psalms," *Journal of Semitic Studies,* 5 (1960), 221-55; cf. Albright, *Yahweh and the Gods of Canaan,* pp. 31-32.

He will feed his flock like a shepherd
He will gather the lambs in his arms
He will carry them in his bosom
And lead *(= y^e^nahēl)* the nursing ewes.

Another passage embodying the same idea is Isa. 49:10–

They shall not hunger or thirst
Neither scorching wind nor sun shall smite them
For the one who loves them will lead them *(y^e^nah^a^gēm)*
And by springs of water he will guide them
(w^e^ 'al mabbū'ē mayim y^e^nah^a^lēm).

Vs. 3

napšī y^e^šōbēb, 'he restores my spirit': While the root *šūb* is one of the most common in the Bible, the Polel form is rare (10 occurrences). The closest parallel to the usage in Ps. 23 is to be found in Ps. 60:3, where the verb occurs in the generic sense of restoring well-being or good feelings (cf. Ps. 19:8). Among the other passages in which the Polel form of *šūb* occurs, several are of special interest because they deal with the theme of the second Exodus and the reestablishment of Israel in its land: e.g., Jer. 50:19 "I will restore Israel to his habitation [= *w^e^šōbabtī 'et - yiśrā'ēl 'el-nāwēhū*], and he shall feed [= *w^e^rā'āh*] at Carmel and Bashan, and in Mt. Ephraim and Gilead his desires [= *napšō*] shall be satisfied."[19] Ezek. 39:27 speaks of the restoration of the exiles, who will be gathered from the lands and peoples among whom they were scattered. There is also the well-known servant passage in Isa. 49:5-6. In vs. 5 we read: "And now Yahweh has said, who formed me from the womb to be his servant, to bring back [= *l^e^šōbēb*] Jacob to him, and that Israel might be gathered to him. . . ." In vs. 6, however, a different form of the same verb is used: "It is too light a thing–your being my servant–to raise up the tribes of Jacob, to restore [= *l^e^hāšīb*] those preserved in Israel. . . ." The emphasis in the three exilic passages cited is on the return and restoration of the people of Yahweh, whereas in Ps. 23:3, the primary concern is the well-being of the Psalmist.

[19]The context for this statement is provided in Jer. 50:17-20.

Nevertheless the close association with the image of the flock and Yahweh's protective care and guidance justifies the broader interpretation of the term *y^{e}šōbēb*. Nor should it be forgotten that the original Exodus and wilderness march were understood to involve a return and restoration to the land of the Patriarchs on the part of their descendants.

yanḥēnī, 'he leads me': As already noted, this verb is used repeatedly in contexts relating to the Exodus, wanderings, and settlement, with reference both to the old Mosaic tradition and to the new Exodus and restoration. The root occurs in both the Qal and Hiphil stems, but without noticeable difference in meaning or force. It is curious that whereas perfect forms of the verb are attested in both the Qal and Hiphil, all of the imperfect forms are vocalized as belonging to the Hiphil stem. It may be wondered whether some of these were originally Qal forms, especially as there would have been no distinction in the pronunciation of the Qal and Hiphil in classical Hebrew: Qal **yinḥeh* < **yanḥeh* = Hiph. **yanḥeh*. Its use in connection with the Exodus and wanderings is attested in early poems: Exod. 15:13 (with an echo in Ps. 77:21 "You led [= *nāḥītā*] your people like a flock. . . ."); Deut. 32:12 "Yahweh alone led him [= *yanḥennū*], and there was no foreign god with him." The verb also occurs in Ps. 78, to which reference has already been made concerning the combination of themes and images of Yahweh as shepherd and the Exodus and wanderings, in a passage of interest to us, vs. 14:

> And he led them *(wayyanḥēm)* by a cloud in the
> daytime
> And every night with a fiery light.

Cf. also vs. 53:

> And he led them *(wayyanḥēm)* to a safe (place), so
> that they were not afraid
> But the sea covered their enemies.

The same usage is found in prose passages dealing with the Exodus: e.g., Exod. 13:17, 21; 32:34 (where Moses is to lead the people; cf. Ps. 78:72 where David fills this role); Neh. 9:12, 19.

The closest verbal parallel to Ps. 23:3 is Ps. 31:4, which links the verbs *nḥh* and *nhl* along with the phrase *l^{e}ma'an šimkā* 'for your name's sake.' Another parallel is to be found in Ps. 143:10 (-11): "Let your good spirit lead me [= *tanḥēnī*] into the level land" (cf. Ps. 139:24 for a similar sentiment). The first words of the next verse (Ps. 143:11) are *l*[e]*maʿan šimkā*, which may belong with the preceding line, as in Ps. 31:4 and our passage. The same verb form as in Ps. 23:3 occurs in the Oracles of Balaam, Num. 23:7, but there is no connection with the Exodus theme. Another passage expressing the general idea of divine guidance and protection, but not related directly to the central theme, is Ps. 107:30. "Then they were glad because they had quiet, since he brought them [= *wayyanḥēm*] to their desired haven." Finally, notice should be taken of Ps. 43:3, in which the verb *nḥh* occurs. The verse itself is structurally very much like Ps. 23:4

š[e]*laḥ ʾōrkā waʾ*[a]*mitt*[e]*kā*	Send forth your light and your truth
hēmmāh yanḥūnī	Behold! they will guide me.
y[e]*bīʾūnī ʾel - har - qodš*[e]*kā*	They will bring me to your holy mountain.
w[e]*ʾel - mišk*[e]*nōtēkā*	Even to your Dwelling.

There is some manuscript support (and the Syriac) for the reading *y*[e]*naḥ*[a]*mūnī* instead of *yanḥūnī*, but the parallel verb *ybyʾwny* supports the reading in the Massoretic Text, and the context confirms it.[20] On the basis of this passage, M. Dahood interprets *y*[e]*naḥ*[a]*mūnī* in Ps. 23:4 as a form of the root *nḥh* rather than *nḥm*, with enclitic *mem* (used here, however, to link the verb with the pronominal suffix). He renders the clause in Ps. 23 as follows: "Behold! they will lead me."[21] While the proposed reading is perfectly plausible and suits the context, nevertheless I believe that MT is correct as vocalized, and that the verb is derived from the root *nḥm*. The principal argument against Dahood's view, in my opinion, is that every verb in the poem is different from every other (i.e., no two are derived from the same root). It is questionable whether a reinterpretation which results in having two verbs from the same root (in vss. 3 and 4) should be supported. I believe that MT in vs. 4 can be defended, as also in Ps. 43:3. This is not to deny that the passages are related and share a parallel structure. They also share an unusual interjection, *hmh*. Since, however, the

[20]For the textual evidence see *Biblia Hebraica*^{3}, *ad loc.*

[21]*Psalms I*, pp. 145, 147.

nouns which form the subject of the sentence are quite different, there is no reason to insist that the verbs in the two passages must be the same. In addition, Ps. 43:3 echoes the theme of the Exodus and wanderings, and speaks directly about the holy mountain of God (cf. Exod. 15:13 *nwh qdšk*, and 15:17 *hr nḥltk*), and his Dwelling.[22]

bᵉmaʿgᵉlē ṣedeq 'in the tracks of righteousness': The precise phrase is unique in the Bible, but there is a close parallel in Prov. 4:11

> I have taught you the way of wisdom
> I have led you in the paths of uprightness.
> *(hidraktīkā bᵉmaʿgᵉlē - yōšer)*

There is only one other occurrence of the m. pl. form of the noun *mʿgl,* Ps. 65:12, where *maʿgālēkā* is in synonymous parallelism with *nᵉʾōt midbār*; a similar relationship may be posited for *binʾōt deše'* and *bᵉmaʿgᵉlē ṣedeq* in Ps. 23, confirming the wilderness association of these terms. Other words and roots are common to both Psalms, marking out an area of overlapping interest: e.g., *rwh* (23:5 and 65:11), *dšn* (23:5 and 65:12).

lᵉmaʿan šᵉmō, 'for his name's sake': This expression in its various forms is far too common in the Bible to deal with exhaustively, but we have indicated two occurrences in passages which are related on other grounds to Ps. 23:3, namely Pss. 31:4 and 143:11. A few other instances are of interest because of the context in which the phrase occurs. Ezek. 20 is a recapitulation and interpretation of Israel's experience in the Exodus and wanderings, with special emphasis on Yahweh's decision to act "for my name's sake": Ezek. 20:9, 14, 22; God will also bring back the exiles "for my name's sake" (vs. 44). The same sentiment with respect to the Exodus is expressed in Ps. 106:8. The remaining passages show the following distribution: I Kings 8:41 = II Chron. 6:32; Jer. 14:7, 21; Isa. 48:9; 66:5; Pss. 25:11; 79:9; 109:21. The clearly datable materials all come from the 7th-6th centuries: Jeremiah, Ezekiel, the Deuteronomic Historian, II and III Isaiah. In Ps. 79 there are explicit references to the Fall of Jerusalem, while the other Psalms do not provide specific data.

[22] *Psalms I,* pp. 261-62, on the singular translation of the plural form.

Vs. 4

gam kī 'ēlēk b^e gē' ṣalmūt, 'even when I walk in the valley of deep shadow': The phrase *bgy' ṣlmwt* also is unique, and clues to the location of this "valley of deep gloom" are hard to come by. Neither term is very common (*gy'* occurs 14 times in the singular, and *ṣlmwt* appears 18 times, 10 of them in Job). The only pertinent passage for our purposes is Jer. 2:6, which links "the land of deep gloom" with the wilderness wanderings:

> They did not say, "Where is Yahweh
> Who brought us up from the land of Egypt
> Who led us *(hammōlīk)* in the wilderness
> In a land of deserts and pits
> In a land of drought and deep darkness *(ṣlmwt)*
> In a land that none passes through
> Where no man dwells?"

In view of the words *'ēlēk* and *ṣlmwt* in Ps. 23:4, the possibility of a link with the Exodus theme exists, not more. Also to be considered are the references in Ps. 107: 10 and 14 to the "gloomy darkness" to which prisoners are condemned. There may be a distinct echo of Israel's bondage in Egypt, but it is more likely that the poet has in mind some contemporary predicament like the Babylonian Captivity (cf. Isa. 61:1-2).[23] In Job a specific connection is made between the term *ṣlmwt* and the land (Job 10:21-22) or city of death (38:17); these items may support the traditional interpretation of *ṣalmāwet* as a compound expression, "shadow of death."[24]

lō' 'īrā' rā', 'I fear no evil': While the individual terms are common enough, the precise form and combination in Ps. 23:4 are distinctive. The words *yr'* and *r'* are combined in Ps. 49:6 where the reference is to "evil days" or "the days of the evil one." They also occur in Zeph. 3:15-16, where we read:

[23] See the comment by Dahood, *Psalms III,* pp. 83-84; on the date of the poem as a whole, see p. 81.

[24] Dahood, *Psalms I,* p. 147.

The King of Israel, Yahweh is in your midst
You shall not fear evil any more *(lō' tîr^e'î rā' 'ōd).*

The subject is *bat - ṣiyyōn* 'the girl Zion' // *bat - y^{e}rûšālāyim* 'the girl Jerusalem.' The same underlying sentiment is expressed in the following Psalms: 3:5; 27:1; 56:5, 12; 118:6.

In relation to the Exodus experience, there is repeated emphasis in the tradition, especially in Deuteronomy, on the necessity of "fearing Yahweh," and in view of his continuing presence and powerful support, on the obligation not to fear anything or anyone else. Behind the abstraction *rā'* in Ps. 23:4, there may lurk the figure of Pharaoh, the epitome of human evil, and the persistent opposition to the will of God, which the prose narrators exploited so effectively in their story of the conflict between Yahweh and the Egyptian god-king.

kî 'attāh 'immādî, 'for you are with me': Once again the individual words are very common, but the precise combination is very rare. The only other instance in the Bible of the combination *'attāh 'immādî* is in I Sam. 22:23, where David addresses these words to Abiathar. However, the underlying sentiment expressed in Ps. 23:4 is well attested elsewhere, in the form of affirmation of the presence of God with him by the worshipper, or of assurance on the part of God of his presence with the petitioner. The basic conviction is a constant in Israelite religion, and though it may be shaken in times of trouble and calamity, it persists throughout all periods and experiences of Israel. It could reflect the time of Exodus and wandering, or of renewed hope of a return from exile and restoration.

šibṭ^{e}kā umiš'antekā hēmmāh y^{e}naḥ^{a}mūnî, 'your rod and your staff–indeed! they vindicate me': The two nouns are well suited for use in Hebrew poetry, with its characteristic parallelism, but this is the only case in the Bible in which they are paired. In Num. 21:18, in the Song of the Well, there is a slightly different pair of words, but the meaning is similar: *m^{e}ḥōqēq* and *miš'^{a}nōtām* are in parallel construction. The word *šēbeṭ* normally is paired with *maṭṭeh* (cf. Isa. 10:15; 28:27; 30:31).

As indicated in the translation, I take the word *hmh* to be the interjection, "Behold!" rather than the independent pronoun, 3rd

m. pl.[25] I also adopt the traditional analysis of the verb as the Piel imperfect, 3rd m. pl., with the 1st person singular pronominal suffix, and derive the form from the root *nḥm* which usually is rendered (in the Piel): "console" or "comfort." In my opinion, it is the translation which is at fault, rather than the formal analysis or derivation. It is not necessary therefore to assign the verb to a different root, namely *nḥh,* in order to achieve a satisfactory interpretation, but it is necessary to examine the semantic field and range of meaning of the root *nḥm.* Needless to say, its meaning is inadequately represented or covered by the words "comfort" or "console" though these are appropriate in certain instances. An idea of the range of meaning, and also the difficulty in rendering this elusive term, can be gained by a consideration of the variety of parallel verbs with which *nḥm* is paired: e.g., *rḥm* (Isa. 49:13); *g'l* (Isa. 52:9); *'zr* (Ps. 86:17); *śmḥ* (Jer. 31:13). If the root idea is "to console," then we must add to it elements of compassion, redemption, protection or assistance, and rejoicing. We may suggest the meaning: "to protect" or "defend." In the Niphal and Hithpael, there is a usage which takes us into the area of military deliverance or judicial vindication. In Isa. 1:24, the verb in the Niphal is paired with *nqm,* which has the basic meaning suggested for *nḥm,* and is the key to this analysis. The verse is rendered in RSV as follows:

> Ah, I will vent my wrath *('ennāḥēm)* on my enemies
> and avenge myself *(wᵉ'innāqᵉmāh)* on my foes.

In view of G. Mendenhall's analysis of the root *nqm* the translation of the second line ought to be: "I will deliver myself from my enemies."[26] In parallel with that line, the first line should then be rendered: "Ah, I will protect [or: defend] myself from my

[25] Cf. Dahood, *Psalms I,* p. 147. Other examples of this interjection may be found in Deut. 33:17 *(hm),* and Hosea 8:9 and 13 *(hmh)*; cf. my "Prolegomenon," pp. XXXVI-XXXVII, and n. 17 on p. LVI. A new example occurs in Ruth 1:22, where *hmh* can hardly be analyzed as the independent pronoun, 3rd m. pl. (the subjects of the verb are feminine plural), but would serve admirably as the interjection: "Indeed! they came to Bethlehem at the beginning of the barley harvest."

[26] Mendenhall's rendering of the line is: ". . . and obtain redress from my foes"; *The Tenth Generation* (Baltimore, 1973), p. 95. He accepts the standard reading for the first line, hence failing to carry through the needed correction to achieve proper balance in the couplet, and thus reflect the purpose of the prophet.

adversaries. There is no basis for the translation of *'nḥm* offered by RSV. In Deut. 32:36, the verb *nḥm* is paired with *dyn.* RSV renders as follows.

> For the Lord will vindicate *(yādīn)* his people
> and have compassion *(yitneḥām)* on his servants.

While the rendering of the second line is possible, it is more likely that the verb describes some protective or defensive action on the part of Yahweh in behalf of his servants. The same line occurs in Ps. 135:14. An even stronger sentiment is expressed in Gen. 27:42. Again RSV renders: "Behold your brother Esau comforts himself [= *mitnaḥēm*] by planning to kill you." The Anchor Bible reads: "Your brother Esau is hoping for redress by killing you." I suggest the following: "Behold your brother Esau will avenge himself on you by killing you." Our conclusion about Ps. 23:4 is that the purpose of the club and staff is to protect and defend the Psalmist, or vindicate and deliver him from the enemies (see vs. 5) in whose midst he finds himself.

Vs. 5

ta'ᵃrōk lᵉpānay šulḥān, 'you arrange a banquet for me': This enigmatic passage has occasioned lengthy and continuing scholarly debate.[27] In spite of its apparent difficulty, especially in the context of a pastoral psalm, the soundness of the text is not in question, and all attempts to solve the problem by emendation must be rejected. The combination of the verb *'rk* with the noun *šlḥn* is attested in four other passages, widely separated (Isa. 21:5, 65:11; Ezek. 23:41; and Ps. 78:19). In one case we also have the preposition *lpny* with the pronominal suffix: Ezek. 23:41 "You sat upon a stately couch, with a table spread before it [= *wᵉšulḥān 'ārūk lᵉpānēhā*]. . . ." Of these passages, only one sheds direct light on the meaning of the line in Ps. 23, and that is Ps. 78:19, which reads: "And they spoke against God saying 'Is El able to arrange a table in the wilderness [*la'ᵃrōk šulḥān bammidbār*]?' " The Psalm has already been cited as a striking example of the fusion of the imagery of the divine shepherd (vs. 52) and the theme of the

[27] Cf. Kraus, *Psalmen I,* pp. 186-87, 190-91.

Exodus and wanderings. In Ps. 78, the setting of the table is located in the wilderness, belongs to the story of the wanderings, and is symbolic of the miraculous provision of water and food for the thirsty and starving people. The following verses supply the details of the water and the food including both manna and quails (vss. 20-31). This was the banquet provided by the divine shepherd for his flock: the transition from shepherd to host and from sheep to people becomes quite understandable in the context of the Exodus and wilderness sojourn. The passage in Ps. 23 is to be understood in the same way. The poet evokes the memory of the bountiful provision in the wilderness in expressing his utter confidence in Yahweh to provide for him and those like him in similar circumstances. While the two passages are rooted in the same tradition, there is a difference between them. In Ps. 78, the historical context is specified, and the occasion and circumstances of the feasting in the wilderness are spelled out in considerable detail. In Ps. 23, the key term *midbār* 'wilderness,' is omitted, or not used, as elsewhere in the poem. Where Ps. 78 is historical and specific in the matter of detail, Ps. 23 remains allusive and vague as to details. By now we must conclude that the procedure is deliberate, and that the poet wishes to evoke the past, especially the wilderness experience, but not to dwell on it. His main interest is elsewhere, to use the past as a key to the present and future, and to express his conviction that the God who was shepherd to his people in the ancient past, and led them through the wilderness to freedom, and security, and peace, would and will do the same and more for his people now and in the future. The message is conveyed by an individual to other individuals: each member of the community is a bearer of the tradition, a recipient of the blessing and the promise which inhere in it.

neged ṣor^{e}*rāy,* 'in front of my foes': The phrase in this precise form does not occur elsewhere. In Ps. 69:20 we read *negd*^{e}*kā kol - ṣōr*^{e}*rāy* which is quite similar, but not entirely intelligible. The participle *ṣōrēr* 'enemy, adversary' is fairly frequent in the Psalter, occurring 12 times (out of a total of 24 in the Bible). The only passage in which the term occurs which relates directly to the Exodus experience is Num. 25:17-18. It is incorporated in a hostile comment on the Midianites in the wake of the disastrous encounter with the Baal of Peor. The Midianites are hardly typical of Israel's enemies, but there were others who lay in wait to harm the people of Yahweh (the Amalekites), or who blocked their path

3) Omit the initial *waw* as secondary, and read *šabtī.* Since there is no other instance in the poem in which a verb is preceded by a conjunction, there is good reason to believe that there was no conjunction preceding this verb either. Additional support for this view is to be found in the closely parallel passage in Ps. 27:4, where the text reads:

šibtī b^{e}bēt yhwh	My dwelling will be in the house of
kol - y^{e}mē ḥayyay	Yahweh all the days of my life.

Instead of the infinitive construct, *šibtī,* it is better to read *šabtī,* as in Ps. 23, and interpret the verb as the precative perfect: "May I dwell. . . ." In Ps. 23, the same form can be rendered as a simple future, in view of the alternation of imperfect and perfect forms in vss. 5 and 6.

4) The initial *waw* of *wšbty* is to be interpreted as the initial root consonant of the verb, rather than as the conjunction. The original form of the root was *wšb,* which later became *yšb.* While the change from initial *waw* to *yod* was practically universal, there is a striking exception in Gen. 11:30, where in place of the normal and expected *yeled* 'child, offspring' we have *wālād* with the same meaning.[30] The anomalous spelling can be regarded as a scribal error, the substitution of *waw* for *yod.* During the Herodian period, in the square script *waw* and *yod* were practically identical, and were often interchanged in the course of copying. It is not often that a scribal slip will produce a morphologically correct, if archaic or dialectal form, and therefore we ought not to dismiss the readings at Gen. 11:30 and Ps. 23:6 out of hand. It may be added that this solution removes the unwanted conjunction preceding the verb without resorting to the surgery proposed in the third suggestion. The alternation of imperfect and perfect forms corresponds to the practice of archaic Hebrew poetry, as shown by D. Robertson.[31]

[30]At II Sam. 6:23, there is some manuscript support for a variant reading, *wld* instead of MT *yld.* The passage is very much like Gen. 11:30, and we may be dealing with a generic term signifying "offspring" (the suggestion comes from F. I. Andersen in a private communication).

[31]"Linguistic Evidence in Dating Early Hebrew Poetry," Chap. Two, 'Syntax,' pp. 12-80, esp. 42-65.

It is noteworthy that while the individual terms used in this colon are quite common, the specific sequence of *yšb* + *b*^{e} before the phrase *byt yhwh* occurs only here and in the related passage Ps. 27:4. Apparently it was not customary to speak of people dwelling on a permanent basis in the house of Yahweh. There is one instance, in Ezek. 8:14, where women are described as sitting in the temple mourning for Tammuz, but that is hardly a model to be emulated. It has been suggested that the phrase *byt yhwh* in the two Psalms does not refer to the temple in Jerusalem, or in fact to any historical shrine (e.g., Shiloh, I Sam. 1:7, 24, etc.), but rather to Yahweh's domain, i.e., the land of Yahweh.[32] A passage in Hosea may offer support for this view. It has long been recognized that the expression *byt yhwh* in Hosea 8:1 and 9:4 does not refer to the temple in Jerusalem, and probably not to any particular temple in Israel either, but rather to the whole land of Ephraim (= Israel, the northern kingdom or what was left of it in Hosea's time), regarded as Yahweh's territory. Pertinent to this discussion is Hosea 9:3, which reads: "They shall not dwell in the land of Yahweh [= *lō' yēšᵉbū bᵉ'ereṣ yahweh*]." It is parallel to Hosea 9.4, which reads: "They shall not enter the house of Yahweh [= *lō' yābō' bēt yahweh*]."

If the analysis of the verse in Ps. 23 is correct, then the Psalmist is affirming that he will dwell in Yahweh's holy land for the rest of his life. The original abode of Yahweh was in the Sinai region, as is made clear by the Song of Deborah (Judg. 5:4-5 = Ps. 68:8-9) and the Blessing of Moses (Deut. 33:2).[33] Just as Hosea has adapted the concept of the land of Israel, so the Psalmist may well have in mind the traditional holy land, which was staked out by the Patriarchs and possessed by their descendants. It is that land to which the exiles will be brought back in a new Exodus, promised by the prophets of the 7th-6th centuries.

lᵉ'ōrek yāmīm, 'for the length of (my) days': The last phrase in the Psalm is to be interpreted by the parallel in vs. 6a: *kl ymy ḥyy* 'all the days of my life.' If we understand the pronominal

[32]This suggestion also comes from F. I. Andersen.

[33]See my discussion in "Early Israelite History in the Light of Early Israelite Poetry." My present view is in marked contrast with an earlier position concerning the location of the "mount of inheritance" in Exod. 15:17, reflected in "The Song of Miriam," pp. 239-40, 249-50, and also in "Strophe and Meter in Exodus 15," pp. 190-91, and 193.

suffix of the 1st person as serving double duty, then we should interpret *l'rk ymym* as meaning, "for the length of my days." In Ps. 21:5, *'rk ymym* is associated with *ḥayyīm* 'life' and *'ōlām wā'ed* 'for eternity and everlasting'; cf. Ps. 91:16, and 93:5. In 30:20, it is parallel with *ḥayyīm* 'life.' In every case the term *'rk ymym* has historical and chronological connotations (just as *kl ymy ḥayy-* does). For the king (Pss. 21:5; 91:16) it signifies long life, and for the dynasty continuity and permanence. For the individual (Ps. 23:6, and cf. Deut. 30:20), it signifies a long, full life, and for the people he represents and symbolizes, it means survival and persistence into the indefinite future.

Concerning the essential nature of the Psalm, and its date of composition, I wish to suggest the following:

1) The Psalm has its roots in the central tradition of Israelite faith: the Exodus from Egypt, the wanderings in the wilderness, and the settlement in Yahweh's domain. The principal emphasis of the poem is on Yahweh as the shepherd of his people, leading his flock through difficulties and dangers to the promised land of peace, security, and contentment.

2) There are genuinely archaic features in the Psalm: e.g., the limitation of divine names to Yahweh alone, the tense system of the verbs, involving the alternation of imperfect and perfect forms, with no distinction of time or aspect.

3) The language of the Psalm nevertheless bears marked resemblances to the distinctive vocabulary and ideas of the exilic period, with special interest in a new Exodus, a new march through the wilderness, and a new settlement in the promised land. In addition, the wilderness experience has been idealized with respect to past history, and projected into the future: e.g., the "waters of contention" have become the "waters of repose."

My conclusion is that the Psalm is a product of the 6th century B.C., that its closest affinities are with the prophecies of the return and restoration of the exiles in Babylon. The poet is confident that for him there will be a new Exodus: a miraculous deliverance and a safe march through the verdant plains to the permanent abode of Yahweh. He speaks as an individual, but one who is representative of his people. The Psalm may well have been used in connection with one or another of the great feasts which celebrates the Exodus (Passover) and the march through the wilderness (Tabernacles).

The Structure of Psalm 137

PSALM 137 is one of the few poems in the Bible concerning the date and provenience of which there is general scholarly agreement. It is reasonably certain that it was composed in Babylon during the first half of the sixth century B.C.E. It echoes vividly the experience and emotions of those who were taken captive, and may, therefore, be assigned to the first generation of the Exiles. It is roughly contemporary with the bulk, if not the whole, of Lamentations, with which it shares both contents and mood. Likewise, it belongs to the time of Ezekiel, bridging the period from Jeremiah to Second Isaiah. From these and other biblical literature it is clear that there was a major revival of Hebrew poetry during this period. The national catastrophe imposed a burden on Judah's prophets and poets no less than on its political and ecclesiastical leaders. The mingled despair and hope of the people evoked an appropriate literary response.

A study of the Psalm, with particular regard for its stylistic devices and metrical structure, should provide us with some insight into the state of the art in the sixth century, during the last great period of classic Hebrew poetry. So far as the text is concerned, there is little choice but to follow *MT*. Regrettably, almost nothing of Ps. 137 has survived in the Psalm Scroll from Cave 11 of Qumran;[1] nevertheless, one variant has been preserved in

1. The official edition is by J. A. Sanders, *The Psalms Scroll of Qumran Cave 11*, vol. IV in *Discoveries in the Judaean Desert of Jordan* (Oxford, 1965). Only parts of vss. 1 and 9 have been preserved: Columns XX and XXI (Plate XIII), pp. 41, 42.

vs. 1 which we regard as more original than, and superior to, *MT*.[2] In general *LXX* and the other versions follow *MT*, and where they diverge, the readings do not inspire confidence or materially improve the picture. Furthermore, in view of its impressive metrical symmetry we believe that the poem is complete as it stands, and that we have it as it was composed without significant subsequent alteration. If in fact the end product is the work of a later editor, we can only marvel at his skill in erasing all the usual signs of such activity.

The principal observation about the poem is that it has a unified structure, in spite of abrupt shifts in content and tone (e.g., at vs. 7 and again at vs. 8). The over-all pattern is at once chiastic and symmetrical or balanced. Thus the Introduction (vss. 1–2) is linked with and balanced by the Conclusion (vss. 8–9). An effective stylistic device (*inclusio*) is used to bring out both points: Babylon is explicitly mentioned at the beginning and end of the Psalm (vss. 1 and 8). The impression of symmetry is strengthened by a more detailed strophic analysis which shows that both sections consist of five units of approximately equal length. The body of the poem (vss. 3–7) consists of three parts: an opening (vs. 3) and a closing (vs. 7) forming a frame around the central section (vss. 4–6). Once again detailed analysis confirms the initial impression of structural symmetry: the opening and closing comprise four units each of equal total length, and these together exactly match in length the central section (vss. 4–6). The central part has a similar envelope structure, with the outer elements (vss. 4 and 6b) enclosing the nucleus (vss. 5–6a), which is a perfect chiasm, and the heart of the whole poem.

Before proceeding to a verse-by-verse analysis of the Psalm, some discussion of Hebrew meter is in order. After using several stress or accent systems in the investigation of Hebrew metrics, I am satisfied that such systems are too vague in principle and too flexible in application to produce adequate results. The widespread variation among scholars illustrates both points and exposes a substantial degree of subjectivity on the part of those working on these materials. On the other hand, weighted quantitative systems, concerned with syllable length as well as number, have proved too complicated to apply effectively; there is no reason to suppose that such methods were employed by the poets themselves. In place of either type we have chosen a relatively objective and simple syllable-counting system, designed to describe accurately the metrical structure of the poem under consideration. The purpose is to provide a widely applicable and acceptable, as well as a neutral, procedure for describing the phenomena and, thus, establish a

2. The reading is in vs. 1: *bbbl* for MT *bbl*. See discussion ad loc.

framework within which scholars can test their theories of poetic composition and debate the relevant issues. Without insisting that the Hebrew poets consciously or deliberately counted syllables in composing their works, we observe that their poems exhibit patterns with a degree of regularity and repetition which is best captured by a syllable-counting process.

Admittedly there is some difference of opinion among scholars as to the exact number of syllables in a given line, or even word. At one extreme are those who follow Massoretic vocalization slavishly, and count secondary vowels of late origin, as in segolate nouns and words containing laryngeals, or even *pataḥ* furtive, which can hardly be justified. At the other extreme are those who attempt to reconstitute the full vocalization as they imagine it to have been at the time of composition. Such an effort is certainly laudable and, to the extent that the objective can be achieved, very worthwhile. But it must be recognized that there are significant gaps in our knowledge of the historical morphology and phonology of Hebrew, and as yet a reliable reconstruction is beyond us.

In the analysis of Psalm 137 we have adopted a compromise position, following Massoretic vocalization generally. However, where there is compelling evidence for a vocalization involving a different number of syllables for a given word, we accept that against *MT*. The only significant departures from *MT* in the Psalm have to do with secondary vowels: e.g., $^{\supset}e^{c}leh$ (vs. 6) instead of *MT* $^{\supset}a^{ca}leh$ (on the change from Hiphil to Qal, see comments on the verse); segolates, which were monosyllabic in the classical period and are so treated here: e.g., *hassāl*^{c} for *MT* *hassāla*^{c}; the name Jerusalem which was pronounced y^{e}*rūšālēm*, or the like, in the biblical period, with four syllables in accordance with the Kethib, as against the Qere *perpetuum*, y^{e}*rūšālayim*, which is clearly secondary and not attested until the Dead Sea scrolls of the second and first centuries B.C.E. The correctness of the four-syllable pronunciation in the sixth century B.C.E. is confirmed by the inscription in a burial cave, not far from Lachish, containing the name Jerusalem, spelled *yršlm*.[3] The inscription, which is the oldest preserving the name Jerusalem, can be dated paleographically to the sixth century or, roughly, the same time as the poem.[4] The same spelling occurs in the pentagram stamps of the late fourth century B.C.E., to which the Greek transcription Ιερουσαλημ in the LXX corresponds.

3. J. Naveh, "Old Hebrew Inscriptions in a Burial Cave," *IEJ*, XIII (1963): 74-92, especially 84–85.

4. In the article, Naveh expressed a preference for a date in the late eighth century (pp. 87–92); he has since shifted to the early sixth century, in agreement with other leading paleographers. This information is based on a private conversation.

We accept Massoretic contractions, e.g., *dibrē* (vs. 3), and *libnē* (vs. 7), and ignore so-called half-open syllables on the grounds that such syllables were never pronounced, but serve as a grammarian's device to explain certain linguistic phenomena. On the other hand, syllables with vocal shewa are counted, unless of secondary origin. No formal notice is taken of vowel-length in syllable counting because of the acknowledged difficulty in distinguishing between tone-long and pure-long, and short and very short. Even the distinction between short and long is not always clear because of pre-tonic lengthening and shortening. It is quite likely that the poet recognized and made use of the different vowel lengths, but we do not find the evidence adequate to make decisions in borderline cases. As with accents or stresses, there are too many variables, though the matter is worthy of further investigation. We suppose, perhaps optimistically, that the differences tend to cancel out, and that it is a sufficient indication of metrical symmetry and balance to count the syllables without regard to their length.

We assume that the poet, while bound by the usual conventions of his craft, also had considerable freedom in the choice of archaic and exotic words and forms and could adjust the pronunciation of words to suit his purposes. We believe that he exercised such options to achieve metrical objectives. For the most part, we will refrain from exercising the same options in recreating a hypothetical original text and will limit ourselves to those features which have been preserved in the text, having survived all the natural efforts to eliminate oddities in the course of transmission. It is reasonable to suppose that the original was even more symmetrical and structured, but our purpose will be to show those aspects in what has survived in the existing text. We do this in order to avoid charges of manipulation or circular reasoning, i.e., to create what we wish to demonstrate, and because we believe that, in spite of editorial and scribal changes in the course of transmission, the metrical patterns used by the poet have been sufficiently preserved to make a convincing case.

Metrical and stylistic details are examined in the following stanza-by-stanza analysis of the Psalm.[5]

I

ᶜal nᵉhārōt [bᵉ]Bābel	(1a)	By the rivers in Babylon
šām yāšabnū / gam bākīnū	(1b)	there we sat down / loudly we wept

5. In the translation, for which we make no other claim, we have attempted to preserve the rhythm, or at least the syllable count, of the original. This inevitably creates a certain awkwardness, since English on the whole tends to run longer than Hebrew. By exercising some of the privileges assumed by English language poets, however, we have generally succeeded in matching the number of syllables.

bᵉzokrēnū ʾet-Ṣiyyōn	(1c)	—when we remembered Zion—
ʿal ʿᵃrābīm bᵉtōkāh	(2a)	By the laurels in its midst
tālīnū kinnōrōtēnū	(2b)	we hung up our many-stringed lyres.

1a) We read *bbbl* with 11QPs[a] against *MT bbl*, and vocalize *ʿal nᵉhārōt bᵉbābēl*.[6] The preference is based upon the following considerations: (a) Accidental haplography in copying an original sequence of three successive *b*'s is more likely than the deliberate addition of a *bēt*, or the accidental dittography which would produce at the same time an acceptable result: (b) The parallelism with vs. 2a *ʿal ʿᵃrābīm bᵉtōkāh* is more precise, and such precision is characteristic of this poet's work. Compare, e.g., the exact repetition of *'ašrē še-* in vss. 8,9, which complement and correspond to vss. 1,2. (c) The resultant meter (7 syllables instead of 6) is more in keeping with the rest of the stanza. The pattern 7:8 for vs. 1ab matches exactly the parallel vs. 2ab (also 7:8).

1b) We read *gm* as the cognate of Ugaritic *g* = voice, plus the adverbial *m*, with the meaning "loudly," following M. Dahood; see most recently his article, "The Independent Personal Pronoun in the Oblique Case in Hebrew," *CBQ*, XXXII:1 (January, 1970): 86–90, specifically p. 86, fn. 4 with references cited there.

As already indicated, the Introduction (vss. 1–2) consists of five units of 7 or 8 syllables each, or more exactly of two double-units (1ab and 2ab) connected by a single element (1c) with the following pattern: 7–8:7:7–8. While 1c is clearly linked with the preceding unit it is also connected with the following one; it specifies the occasion or reason for the related actions in 1ab and 2.

To be noted as well is the extensive use of alliteration, assonance, and similar sound effects to produce a mournful tone in keeping with the content of the Psalm. The effect is achieved by the repeated occurrence of the labials *b* and *m*: e.g., the sequence *bbbl šm yšbnw gm bkynw bzkrnw*, and *ʿrbym btwkh*, simulates the sound of the wind in the willows, resonating over the waters; while the keening note of the pronominal ending *-nū* is sounded again and again in these verses: *yšbnw, bkynw, bzkrnw, tlynw, knrwtynw*.

II

kī šām šᵉʾēlūnū	(3a)	For there they asked of us—
šōbēnū dibrē-šīr	(3b)	our captors words of a song
wᵉtōlālēnū śimḥā	(3c)	those who mocked us rejoicing—
šīrū lānū miššīr Ṣiyyōn	(3d)	"Sing to us from Zion's songbook."

6. Sanders, *The Psalms Scroll of Qumran Cave 11*, p. 41, and *The Dead Sea Psalms Scroll* (Ithaca, New York, 1967), p. 73.

The second unit (vs. 3) continues the content and maintains the tone of the Introduction; it serves as a transition to the central statement of the lament (vs. 4, beginning with *ʾêk*). There is an added note of poignancy in the reference to the mockery (if our interpretation of the unique term *tôlālênû* is correct) of their captors. The sadness and despair of the exiles articulated in vss. 1–2 are aggravated by the derisive demand that they sing one of the joyous songs of Zion (the Songs of Ascents would be particularly appropriate in view of vs. 6; see the comments below). This demand leads in turn to the agonizing protest of vs. 4, and an entirely different kind of song about Jerusalem: the terrible oath of remembrance and return, as well as the prayer for divine vindication against the enemies of his people.

Verse 3 has a number of points of lexical and syntactic interest. The main clause, 3a, *kî šām šᵉʾēlûnû*, is modified by two phrases in paratactic construction, each supplying a subject (or nominative appositive) and a second object for the verb. Thus *šôbênû* and *tôlālênû* have the same function in the sentence and should be interpreted as parallel or complementary terms. Since *šwbynw* is the Qal active participle m. pl. with a 1st person pl. suffix, we might expect *twllynw* to have the same form and derive it from the root *tll* = to mock, taunt. The slightly anomalous vocalization (i.e., the second syllable *lā* instead of the expected *lᵉ*) may be explained in a variety of ways, including uncertainty about the form on the part of the Massoretes. Behind the secondary root *tll* lies the primary root *hll*, which means "to boast" both in the Qal and the Hithpael conjugations. In fact, the latter may provide the connecting link to the root *tll*. Attention may also be drawn to the root *htl*, with a similar meaning, "to mock." Whatever the precise derivation and form of the term in this Psalm, we can hardly be wrong in placing it in the semantic and morphological field represented by the several related roots; we can therefore translate: "boastful ones, mockers." In the light of this analysis we should interpret the terms *šwbynw* and *twllynw* in complementary or combinatory fashion, i.e., "our boastful captors" or more likely "those who captured us—those who mocked us"; "our captors, who mocked us."

In similar fashion, the expressions *dibrê-šîr* and *śimḥā* serve as objects of the main verb *šᵉʾēlûnû*. The terms may be regarded as parallel in meaning, since *šîr* often denotes a happy song suitable for festive occasions, as indicated by the Psalms and other hymns to which the title *šîr* is attached. Note as well the contrast between *šîr* and *qînā* in Amos 8:10. At the same time, the terms are complementary and should be combined as their association in other contexts suggests: cf. Gen. 31:27, Isa. 30:29. Reading them together, we arrive at the following sense: "words of a song of joy, i.e., joyous lyrics."

Our contention is that the poet has constructed a sophisticated, stylized quatrain by skilfully rearranging the elements of a straightforward declarative sentence, which ran approximately as follows: "For there our mocking captors demanded of us the lyrics of a happy song."

The last clause of vs. 3 is also dependent on the main verb *š*ᵓ*lwnw*; it further specifies the demand voiced in vs. 3a, and described in general terms in 3b and 3c. Here, in the form of a direct quotation, the joyous lyrics are identified with "Zion's song." If the preceding preposition is to be understood partitively or selectively, then the construct form *šīr* must be interpreted as a collective: i.e., the song-book or hymnal of Zion. We may render the request as follows: "Sing for us out of Zion's hymnal," i.e., one or more of the songs of Zion.

As previously observed, vs. 3 continues both the theme and tone of vss. 1–2. The plaintive personal note is stressed in the repeated occurrence of the 1st person plural pronominal suffix (*-nū*), four times in vs. 3, making a total of nine for the first three verses. There is only one other occurrence of this suffix in the poem (vs. 8), making a sum of ten for the Psalm as a whole. The grammatical distribution of these forms is as follows: three occurrences as pronoun subject of a perfect form of the verb: *yšbnw*, *bkynw*, *tlynw*; three as pronoun object of the verb: *š*ᵓ*lwnw*, *šyrw lnw*, *šgmlt lnw*; three as pronoun suffix attached to nominal forms: *knrwtynw*, *šwbynw*, *twllynw*; the remaining form is as pronoun subject of an infinitive in a prepositional phrase: *bzkrnw*. The pronominal prefix (*nā-*) occurs in vs. 4, but the morphologic and phonemic differences separate this use from the others.

To balance the repeated use of voiced labials (*b* and *m*) in vss. 1–2, we have persistent repetition of sibilants in vs. 3, especially *šin*, perhaps to reflect the stubborn silence of the exiles in the presence of their masters. Note the sequence: *šm š*ᵓ*lwnw šwbynw* . . . *šyr* . . . *šyrw* . . . *mšyr*; cf. *śmḥh* and *ṣywn*.

III

ᵓēk nāšīr ᵓet-šīr-Yahwē	(4a)	How can we sing Yahweh's song
ᶜal ᵓadmat nēkār	(4b)	on alien soil?
ᵓim ᵓeškᵉḥēk(ī) Yᵉrūšālēm	(5a)	If I forget thee, Jerusalem,
tiškaḥ yᵉmīnī	(5b)	may my right arm wither
tidbaq lᵉšōnī	(6a)	may my tongue stick
lᵉḥikkī ᵓim lōᵓ ᵓezkᵉrēkī	(6b)	to my palate, if I remember thee not!
ᵓim lōᵓ ᵓeᶜlē ᵓet-Yᵉrūšālēm	(6c)	Surely, I will ascend Jerusalem
ᶜal rōᵓš śimḥātī	(6d)	with joy on my head.

Verses 4–6 constitute the core of the Psalm. Out of the despair of their present situation and in response to the taunts and demands of their captors

the exiles make their response. It is impossible to sing Yahweh's song on foreign ground. At the same time, it is not only possible but necessary to swear, in a dreadful oath, undying devotion to Jerusalem and to affirm in the face of geo-political reality the certainty of a return in joy to the Holy City. In place of the collective lament: "How can we sing Yahweh's song on alien soil?" the psalmist shifts to the intensely individual oath which each exile must invoke upon himself with all its terrible consequences.

Vs. 4a. The use of the construct chain (*šîr-Yhwh* = Yahweh's song) reinforced by *ʾet*, the sign of the definite direct object, indicates that a specific composition is meant. We would normally think of the anthology of sacred songs, the Hymnal of the Temple, more explicitly perhaps the Songs of Ascents (Pss. 120–134) or the Songs of Zion (e.g., Pss. 48, 74, 87, 125, 126, 149). If a particular hymn was intended, however, we may speculate that it was the Song of the Sea (Exod. 15:1–18), which, as we have argued elsewhere, has a reasonable claim to be regarded as Israel's national anthem.[7] It also serves as the model for the "new song" (cf. Isa. 42:10, Pss. 33:3, 40:4, 96:1, 98:1, 144:9, 149:1) which will celebrate the "new Exodus" from exile in Babylonia.

The use of *ʾet*, while rare and perhaps questionable in the earliest Hebrew poetry (e.g., it does not occur at all in the Song of Deborah, Judg. 5:1–31, or in the Song of the Sea), can hardly be denied as deliberate on the part of the poet in later compositions. It occurs six times in Ps. 137, twice with proper nouns (*ʾet-Ṣiyyōn* vs. 1, and *ʾet-Yᵉrūšālēm* vs. 6), twice in construct chains, also involving proper nouns (*ʾet-šîr-Yhwh* vs. 4, and *ʾēt yōm Yᵉrūšālēm* vs. 7), and twice with nouns defined by possessive pronominal suffixes (*ʾet-gᵉmūlēk* vs. 8, and *ʾet-ʿōlālayk* vs. 9). The pairing of parallel constructions suggests a deliberate pattern, with *ʾet* performing a double function: for emphasis and to fill out the meter. Dahood's proposal that *ʾt* in vss. 1 and 6 (our first pair) is to be read as *ʾatt*, the independent pronoun 2nd person feminine singular, is attractive,[8] but in view of the other unquestioned occurrences of *ʾet* as the sign of the definite direct object it is preferable to interpret these instances as well in accordance with the tradition.

The closing phrase of vs. 4, *ʿal ʾadmat nēkār*, evokes the similar *ʿal* phrases of the opening unit (vss. 1,2) and summarizes them. For the exiles, Babylon is the alien territory referred to, where no song of Yahweh can be sung or even attempted. At the same time, vs. 4 is structurally parallel to vs. 6cd.

7. F. M. Cross, Jr., and D. N. Freedman, "The Song of Miriam," *JNES*, XIV (1955): 237–55, esp. 237, fn. f.
8. Dahood, *CBQ*, XXXII (1970): 86–87.

The sentence structure and sequence of parts of speech are almost identical: introductory particle (*ʾyk* and *ʾm lʾ*), verb in the 1st person imperfect (*nšyr* and *ʾʿlh*), *ʾt* plus the direct object (*ʾt-šyr-Yhwh* and *ʾt-Yrwšlm*, and closing phrase with *ʿl* followed by two nouns, one of which is feminine singular the other masculine singular.

Vss. 5–6ab also exhibit structural balance, but it is chiastic in nature. Thus we have *ʾm ʾškḥk* paralleled by *ʾm-lʾ ʾzkrky* (5a and 6b), while *tškḥ ymyny* is matched exactly by *tdbq lšwny* (5b and 6a): the compact interlocking pattern is accentuated by the use of alliteration, assonance, and even internal rhyme. The striking double chiasm at the very center of the poem is the major clue to its basic structure: a series of concentric shells with an *X* at the center.

In view of the exact parallelism between the members of the chiastic pair: *tiškaḥ yᵉmīnī* and *tidbaq lᵉšōnī* (in addition to the initial alliteration and closing rhyme, we have precise matching of vowels both as to quality and length, with the single exception of *ō* for *ī* in the second syllable of the second word of each element), we suggest that there was a similar precision in the balance between the members of the other chiastic pair: hence read *ʾeškᵉḥēkī* (5a) for *ʾeškāḥēk* (MT) to match *ʾezkᵉrēkī* (6b). The use of the archaic form of the pronominal suffix in 6b is apparently deliberate, and it is reasonable to suppose that the poet intended to use the same suffix in the parallel expression. It may be added that no revision of the written text (i.e., the Kethib: consonants and vowel letters) is necessary if we accept the proposal that the *yōd* at the beginning of the following word, *Yᵉrūšālēm*, could also serve to mark the end of the preceding word, *ʾeškᵉḥēkī*. In a number of cases where sense and other considerations require the same letter both at the end of one word and at the beginning of the next word, the letter is actually written only once.[9] Whether such a practice originated in and perpetuates simple scribal haplography, or was deliberately adopted at some point in the transmission of texts, the result is much the same. Applied with due caution, it is a useful device for resolving certain difficulties in the text and in this case for discovering a refinement in style which might otherwise have escaped detection.

The interpretation of the word *tiškaḥ* (5b) "wither" as a homonym of the common root "to forget" was first proposed by W. F. Albright in 1941, and has been widely adopted.[10] Other examples in the Bible, derived from the

9. Dahood, ibid., p. 88, fn. 7.

10. W. F. Albright, "Anath and the Dragon," *BASOR*, No. 84 (1941): 14–17, esp. p. 15, fn. 3. Cf. also J. H. Patton, *Canaanite Parallels in the Book of Psalms* (Baltimore, 1944), pp. 26–27.

same root (which has a cognate in Ugaritic) have been identified.[11] In spite of certain reservations, this seems the best solution to an otherwise difficult problem. It is in the nature of such oaths to refer to a physical calamity of major proportions (cf. Job 31:22, with reference to the "shoulder" and "arm"), and the common root *škḥ* can hardly sustain such a meaning. On the other hand, there is no evidence of any textual corruption; word-play or paronomasia is a common device in such contexts and particularly appropriate here (i.e., to match the consequence with the dereliction, at least by sound and form).[12] It may be added that *yāmīn*, like *yād*, designates the forearm including the hand.

Looking now at the metrical pattern of vss. 5–6ab, we observe that vs. 5 has 14 syllables according to our revised interpretation (i.e., reading *ʾešk^{e}ḥēkī* and *Y^{e}rūšālēm* in place of *ʾeškāḥēk* and *Y^{e}rūšālayim* [Qere]; these changes balance out so the total remains the same). The natural break in vs. 5 comes after *Yrwšlm*, giving the syllabic division as 9:5. Vs. 6ab also has 14 syllables. The sense break comes after *l^{e}ḥikkī*, which produces the following pattern: 8:6. This division is sufficiently close to the prevailing structure in the section under consideration (vss. 4–6) to merit acceptance as it stands. Nevertheless, closer inspection suggests a different arrangement which more clearly reflects the evident chiasm of the couplet. The rigorously balanced pair: *tiškaḥ y^{e}mīnī // tidbaq l^{e}šōnī* are matching parts in this symmetrical structure. The implication is that the term *l^{e}ḥikkī*, while belonging with *tidbaq l^{e}šōnī* so far as sense is concerned, should be taken with the following *ʾim lōʾ ʾezk^{e}rēkī* so far as the meter is concerned. Such a procedure would produce the following stanza form:

ʾim ʾešk^{e}ḥēkī Y^{e}rūšālēm	9
tiškaḥ y^{e}mīnī	5
tidbaq l^{e}šōnī	5
l^{e}ḥikkī ʾim lōʾ ʾezk^{e}rēkī	9

The metrical pattern 9:5 // 5:9 sharply defines the chiastic structure. The opening and closing clauses neatly balance, as do the two central units. The unmatched terms (*Yrwšlm* and *lḥky*), which break the monotony of repetition, fill out the meter in both instances.

This passage is important in the continuing discussion of the nature of Hebrew prosody and, in particular, the widely asserted claim that sense and

11. Dahood, *Psalms I*, vol. 16 in *The Anchor Bible* (New York, 1966), p. 190; *Psalms II*, vol. 17 in *The Anchor Bible* (1968), pp. 72, 78, 228–29.

12. For comparable usage, cf. Isa. 5:7.

structure are congruent, i.e., that all lines are end-stopped. While we are concerned here with a minor division within a line, there is a strong implication that form and sense do not always coincide and that content and meter are not necessarily commensurate.

With regard to the chiastic pattern proposed here, there is an excellent parallel in Ps. 101:7. In that verse we have a clear case of double chiasm which may be diagrammed as follows:

lōʾ-yēšēb b^{e}qereb bētī	(7a)	Shall not dwell within my house
ʿōśē r^{e}miyyā	(7b)	the doer of deceit,
dōbēr š^{e}qārīm	(7c)	the speaker of lies
lōʾ-yikkōn b^{e}neged ʿēnāy	(7d)	shall not abide before my eyes.

The parallelism is precise throughout, including the order of the words and the parts of speech employed. The longer clause in each case begins with the same negative particle (*lōʾ*) and continues with a verb in the imperfect 3rd m. s. form (*yēšēb* // *yikkōn*); there follow compound prepositions of identical form (*b^{e}qereb* // *l^{e}neged*), and nouns with the 1st person singular suffix (*bētī* // *ʿēnāy*). The shorter phrase in each case consists of a Qal active participle, m. s., followed by a noun (*ʿōśē r^{e}miyyā* // *dōbēr š^{e}qārīm*). The syllable count for each pair of parallel terms is exactly the same, as inevitably are the total numbers (8:5 / 5:8; or 7 instead of 8 if we count the segolate forms as monosyllabic). The quatrain in Ps. 137:5–6ab is slightly less rigorous in structure, but derives from essentially the same metrical pattern.

Vs. 6cd is remarkable in a number of ways, not least because the traditional translation and interpretation have rarely if ever been challenged. The RSV reflects the common view: "if I do not set Jerusalem above my highest joy." However, the proposed interpretation of the verb *ʿlh* in the Hiphil is otherwise unattested in the Bible, and it is never used, figuratively or literally, with a city or other demographic entity. The Qal form of *ʿlh* is often used with geographic locations, on the other hand, and we suggest that it should be substituted for the Hiphil in this verse. No change in the written text is involved and only a very slight one in the vocalization of the first syllable, according to Massoretic rules (i.e., *ʾe-* for *ʾa-*; in classical times the forms were probably indistinguishable, as is true of most imperfect forms in *lamed he* verbs). While *ʿlh* is generally followed by a preposition before the place or place-name, there are many examples where no preposition is used. A close parallel to the reading we propose is to be found in II Sam. 19:35, . . . *kī ʾe^{ʿe}lē* . . . *Y^{e}rūšālayim*, "that I should go up . . . to Jerusalem." There is one example in which the verb is followed by the sign of the definite direct object, as we suppose the case to be here: Num. 13:17, . . . *wa*ᶜ*ᵃlītem* ᵓ*et-hāhār*, "and you shall ascend the mountain."[13]

While vs. 6cd continues the 1st person singular affirmations of vss. 5–6ab, there is a shift away from the direct address to Jerusalem, unless we accept Dahood's proposal that ᵓ*t* is to be read ᵓ*att*, the 2nd f. s. pronoun, and construed as the object of the verb.[14] In view of the structural parallels with vs. 4, however, including specifically the occurrence of ᵓ*et* as the sign of the definite direct object after the verb, it is preferable to interpret ᵓ*t* in vs. 6 in the same fashion. We must acknowledge the shift in person as a deliberate device of the poet. The use of ᵓ*im lō*ᵓ at the beginning of the line shows that the force of the oath is still felt, but the clause is less tightly bound to the preceding couplet (5–6ab). The rendering as a strong asseverative: "Surely I will ascend Jerusalem . . ." is therefore justified.

The final phrase of the verse (6d) ᶜ*al rō*ᵓ*š śimḥātī*, usually understood as a construct chain and rendered "above my highest joy," is also without attestation in the Hebrew Bible, or convincing parallel. A better rendering would be "upon my festive head," following Dahood.[15] But the meaning of such a phrase is not at all clear, and the sentence as a whole is less than convincing. Fortunately, there is a striking parallel to the expression in the Psalm, the syntactic structure and meaning of which are not in doubt. In Isaiah 35:10 = 51:11,[16] the composition of which must be dated within a generation of that of the Psalm, we read:

ūpᵉdūyē Yhwh yᵉšūbūn	And Yahweh's redeemed shall return
ūbāᵓū Ṣiyyōn bᵉrinnā	and they shall enter Zion with a shout,
wᵉśimḥat ᶜ*ōlām* ᶜ*al-rō*ᵓ*šām*	with eternal joy upon their heads.

Our immediate concern is with the third unit of the passage, which provides the decisive clue to the correct interpretation of the enigmatic phrase in Ps. 137:6. Except for the changes in word order, the position and person of the pronominal suffix, and the addition of the term ᶜ*ōlām*, the expressions are the same. It becomes clear, then, that the Psalm passage is not to be analyzed as a single construct chain, but rather as a prepositional phrase plus another noun. It may then be rendered: "upon (my) head (is) my joy" or "with my joy upon (my) head." It should be noted that the pronominal suffix is often omitted with parts of the body, especially when there is no doubt about the

13. Cf. also II Kings 16:5 (Jerusalem); Jer. 31:6 (Zion); II Kings 19:14; 20:5,8; 23:2; Jer. 26:10 (the house of Yahweh).
14. Dahood, *CBQ*, XXXII (1970): 87.
15. Ibid.
16. Cf. Isa. 61:7.

reference. Alternatively, the suffix attached to *śimḥā* may serve in a dual capacity and also define *rōʾš*.

There are other affinities between the two passages which deserve consideration. According to Isa. 35:10, it is when the redeemed of Yahweh return to Zion that everlasting joy will be upon their heads. According to our interpretation of Ps. 137:6cd, the setting would be the same: when the Psalmist (also an exile) ascends Jerusalem, his joy will be upon his head. Exactly what the expression *śimḥā ʿal rōʾš* denotes is not explained, but it is reasonable to suppose that some visible object or physical action was originally involved, though the use here may be figurative. Hence, we may have here an allusion to the well-known practice of anointing the head on festive occasions, and *śimḥā* may be the semantic equivalent of *šemen śāśōn* (cf. Isa. 61:3, Ps. 45:8, Prov. 27:9, and not least Ps. 23:6).

IV

z^{e}kōr Yahwē libnē ʾEdōm	(7a)	Yahweh, recall to Edom's sons
ʾēt yōm Y^{e}rūšālēm	(7b)	the day of Jerusalem!
hāʾōm^{e}rīm ʿārū	(7c)	Who were saying, "Strip bare!
ʿārū ʿad hay^{e}sōd bāh	(7d)	Strip bare to its foundation."

Vs. 7 introduces the final section of the poem (vss. 7–9), which corresponds to the opening unit (vss. 1–3). There is a logical connection between this verse and the preceding block of material, as the poet proceeds from his oath of loyalty to Yahweh to the demand that Yahweh vindicate his justice by dealing in the same measure with those who had invaded Judah and destroyed Jerusalem. There is, nevertheless, a sharp grammatical break as Yahweh is addressed directly for the first time. With respect to content as well, a new element is introduced by the reference to the sons of Edom. Dahood's proposal to take "Yahweh" as the direct object of the verb "remember," and "the sons of Edom" as the subject (with the *lamed* construed as a vocative particle) is novel and ingenious, but the evidence, grammatical and syntactic, in this verse and elsewhere in the Bible is against his interpretation.[17] The use of *zkr* in the imperative, with God as subject, is frequent in the Psalter; it also occurs with the preposition *l^e* attached to the personal object (cf. Exod. 32:13; Deut. 9:27). Furthermore, *ʾēt yōm Y^{e}rūšālēm* is the direct object of the verb. The traditional analysis and interpretation are therefore inevitable and correct: "Yahweh, remember Jerusalem's day (of catastrophe) in respect of the Edomites. . . ."

17. Dahood, *CBQ*, XXXII (1970): 87, fn. 6.

The second clause of vs. 7 (cd) yields a satisfactory sense as it stands. We may render literally: "Who were saying: 'Lay bare! lay bare as far as the foundation in it (Jerusalem).'" The implied object of the verbs may be secured from the 3rd f. s. suffix attached to the preposition b^e: "lay it bare." It is also possible to take the prepositional phrase as the object of the verb, even though the use of the verb with b^e is otherwise unattested in the Bible; i.e., "Strip it to the foundation." There is no substantial difference in meaning, however.

The nearest parallel to the clause is to be found in Hab. 3:13, in its present form a product of the same age.[18] The latter passage, which is difficult and possibly corrupt, may be rendered as follows:

māḥaṣtā rōʾš mibbayit rāšāʿ	(13c)	You crushed inward the head of the Evil One
ʿārōt y^{e}sōd ʿad-ṣawwāʾr	(13d)	Laying him open backside to neck.

We take *mbyt* as the adverb *mibbayit* meaning "within, on the inside, inwards," and modifying the construct chain *rōʾš rāšāʿ*, into which it has been inserted.[19] In the second clause, we take *ʿārōt* as an unusual form of the infinitive absolute, which is parallel to the perfect form *māḥaṣtā* in the first clause.[20] The movement described, from fundament to neck, is the reverse of that in Ps. 137, in which the walls are demolished from top to bottom, laying bare the foundations.

With respect to the meter, vs. 7 consists of two lines with 14 and 13 syllables each, making a total of 27. This is the same total as vs. 3, with which vs. 7 corresponds in the structure of the poem. While there is no parallelism in vs. 7 and both lines are continuous, it is nevertheless possible to find a natural pause or break in each line. In the first line there is a caesura after *libnē ʾEdōm*, producing the following division: $8 + 6 = 14$. In the second line

18. The best treatment of Hab. 3 remains that of W. F. Albright, "The Psalm of Habakkuk," *Studies in Old Testament Prophecy*, ed. by H. H. Rowley (Edinburgh, 1950), pp. 1–18. For his view of vs. 13, see pp. 11, 13, 16–17, fns. nn through qq.

19. For a possible parallel to this use of *mibbayit* in relation to the body, cf. II Kings 6:30, *ʿal b^{e}śārō mibbayit*. There is increasing evidence for the deliberate insertion of particles and words between the construct and absolute in construct chains. A paper on the subject is in preparation, but consider, in addition to the familiar occurrence of prepositions in construct chains (e.g., *hry bGlbʿ*, II Sam. 1:21), and enclitic *mem* (e.g., Deut. 33:11 *mtny-m qmyw*; Ps. 18:16 *ʾpyqy-m ym* // *ʾpyqy ym* II Sam. 22:16), the following cases: Ezek. 39:11 *mqwm-šm qbr* (I owe this example to Prof. Nahum Sarna), and these instances from Hosea 14:3 *kl-tśʾ ʿwn*; 8:2 *ʾlhy ydʿnwk Yśrʾl*, which must be read, "O God of Israel, we know you"; and 6:9 *drk yrṣḥw-škmh*.

20. Cf. G-K, #75n. Albright's comment is pertinent, "The Psalm of Habakkuk," p. 17 fn. pp.

there are various possibilities. From the point of view of sense, the break should come after *hāʾōmᵉrīm*, but this produces a strongly unbalanced division: 4 + 9 = 13. Also plausible is a pause after the second verb (*ʿārū*), which was favored by the Massoretes. The resulting division is 8 + 5 = 13. Comparison with vs. 3, however, suggests a third possibility. Vs. 3 consists of four units with the following syllable count: 6, 6, 7, 8 making a total of 27. As we have already pointed out, 3b and c naturally belong together, while 3a and d form an envelope around them. Metrically, then, 3a and d can be counted as 6 + 8 = 14, which corresponds to vs. 7a, 8 + 6 = 14. Likewise 3b and c may be counted as 6 + 7 = 13, to match 7b, which is also 13. If the correlation is to be pursued further, then the break in vs. 7b should come before the second *ʿārū*, giving a count of 6 + 7 = 13, the same as 3bc. The rendering would be: "Lay it bare! Lay it bare to its foundation!"

It may be added that the reference to the Edomites, while unexpected in a poem about Babylon, is entirely appropriate in the immediate context, corresponding closely to other sixth century oracles about the Edomites and their role in the destruction of Jerusalem: cf. Obadiah, Ezekiel 35, etc.

bat-Bābel haššᵉdūdā	(8a)	Daughter Babylon the doomed
ʾašrē šeyᵉšallem-lāk	(8b)	Happy he who renders you
ʾet-gᵉmūlēk šeggāmalt lānū	(8c)	the payment which you paid out to us.
ʾašrē šeyyōʾḥēz wᵉnippēṣ	(9a)	Happy he who grasps and shatters
ʾet-ʿōlālayk ʾel-hassālʿ	(9b)	your children upon the cliff.

The poem closes as it opens, with an explicit reference to Babylon (cf. *Bābel* in vs. 1 and *bat-Bābel* in vs. 8), thus forming a characteristic *inclusio*. But the correlations between the two sections (vss. 1–2 and 8–9) extend beyond this rather simple device to other considerations of structure and style. Thus the Introduction and Conclusion are materially longer than the standard units making up the body of the poem (vss. 3–7). The latter are characteristically in couplet (vss. 3 and 7) or quatrain (i.e., double-couplet, vss. 4–6) form, with syllable counts of 27 and 54, comprising a symmetrical whole. The opening and closing sections fall into a different pattern, each consisting of a pair of matching lines modifying a pivotal phrase or clause. The result in each case is a longer section of 37 or 38 syllables in contrast with the pattern in the body of the poem. In vss. 1–2, the parallel clauses are introduced by the preposition *ʿal*, whereas in vss. 8–9 the common introductory expression is *ʾašrē še-*. In the opening section, the additional unit comes in the middle, between the balancing couplets:

Beside the rivers in Babylon
  there we sat down, loudly we wept—
    when we remembered Zion—
Beside the poplars in its midst
  we hanged up our lyres.

The pivotal clause, "when we remembered Zion," which gives point and cohesion to the section and links it with the body of the poem, goes naturally with the preceding line, but it can also be taken with what follows, since both actions were occasioned by the remembrance of Zion.

In the closing section, the additional unit comes at the beginning, but it is structurally linked with both of the following clauses:

O daughter Babylon, destined for destruction—
Happy shall he be who renders to you
  your payment which you paid to us—
Happy shall he be who seizes and smashes
  your children against the cliffs.

The metrical count is as follows:

Vs. 1)	7 + 8			7	(Vs. 8
	7	= 37 //	38 =	7 + 9	
Vs. 2)	7 + 8			8 + 7	(Vs. 9

The patterns are remarkably similar. Each of the couplets has 15 syllables, except for one which has 16 (vs. 8c), while the added unit has 7. The longer lines break down into subdivisions of 7 and 8 syllables, again with a single exception where we have 7 and 9.

In vs. 8a, *MT hašš*^{e}*dūdā*, literally, "the destroyed," is often emended to *haššōdēdā* or *haššādōdā* on the basis of limited versional evidence, with the meaning, "the destroyer." While the proposed emendation is superficially more plausible, especially when associated with world-conquering Babylon, the more difficult reading in *MT*, the passive participle, can be defended, both on the basis of the immediate context (i.e., the poet's intention) and a series of remarkable parallels in contemporary or nearly contemporary biblical literature, specifically Jer. 51:47–57. In the Jeremiah passage, as in the Psalm, emphasis is placed on the doctrine of divine retribution in relation to the impending destruction of Babylon. In Jeremiah there is repeated reference to the destroyer(s) whom Yahweh will bring against Babylon. While it is clear that Babylon will be destroyed because it has destroyed others, the words derived from the root *šdd* are used exclusively of the action to be taken against Babylon, never by Babylon. In other words, Babylon is destined for and doomed to destruction.[21] Since the literary and verbal similarities between the two passages are considerable, it is better to accept *MT* here and interpret the reference as a proleptic statement of the irreversible fate already determined and soon to be accomplished. It is precisely the imminent destruction of Babylon that is described picturesquely in the following clauses in vss. 8–9 of the Psalm. The destruction of Babylon will conform to the standard of divine retribution: payment will be in kind and in equal measure. As Babylon did to others, so it shall be done to her.[22] A vivid example of such retribution, which at the same time illustrates prevailing practice all over the ancient world, including the Babylonians themselves, suffices to complete the case. The appalling procedure is fully attested.[23]

STRUCTURAL ANALYSIS

Psalm 137 is characterized by an envelope construction in which the outer sections fold around the inner ones producing a cohesive and integrated whole. Thus the opening and closing sections (vss. 1–2 and 8–9) form an *inclusio* which is keyed on the word *Bābel.* The body of the poem, likewise, consists of an outer shell, vss. 3 and 7, and an inner core, vss. 4–6. Even this core follows the same pattern, with vss. 4 and 6cd forming a frame around the nucleus at the very center of the poem. This nucleus is an artfully designed chiastic couplet which is at once the dramatic high point or apex of the poem and the axis linking the parts and exhibiting the essential structure of the whole (vss. 5–6ab).

It may be noted that vs. 3 in itself is an example of a complicated form of the envelope construction. The center section (3bc), while dependent on the main verb *š*$^{e\text{ʾ}}$*ēlūnū*, is a tightly knit unit in which the parallel components interlock: e.g., "our captors" // "our mockers"; "words of a song (lyrics)" // "joy." In our view, the sense or intention of the poet can be expressed as follows: "Our mocking captors (demanded of us) happy songs." The last unit (3d) expresses directly the demand mentioned at the beginning. Thus

21. Typical are vss. 55–56 (cf. also vss. 48, 53), which may be rendered as follows: For Yahweh will destroy (*šōdēd*) Babylon. . . . For a destroyer has come against her, against Babylon. Her warriors have been captured, and their bows broken. For Yahweh is a God of retribution (*g*^{e}*mūlōt*); he will pay back in full (*šallēm y*^{e}*šallēm*).

22. Cf. Jer. 51: 49.

23. Cf. II Kings 8:12; Isa. 13:16; Hosea 14:1; Nahum 3:10.

we are justified in grouping 3a with 3d and 3b with 3c, producing a metrical pattern 6 + 8 = 14 and 6 + 7 = 13, making a total of 27, matching the structurally comparable verse 7, which breaks down as follows: 7ab, 8 + 6 = 14; and 7cd, 6 + 7 = 13, making the same total of 27. A schematic representation of the Psalm follows:[24]

	I						V	
Vs. 1a)	7						7	(8a
1b)	8						7	(8b
1c)	7		37		38		9	(8c
2a)	7						8	(9a
2b)	8						7	(9b
	II						IV	
Vs. 3a)	6						8	(7a
3b)	6						6	(7b
3c)	7		27		27		6	(7c
3d)	8						7	(7d
				III				
Vs. 4a)	7	12		54		14	9	(6c
4b)	5						5	(6d
			5a)	9				
			5b)	5	28			
			6a)	5				
			6b)	9				

In order to make the case for an intentional and fairly precise metrical structure we have dealt with the text of the poem as it has come down to us. No changes have been made in the consonantal text and only a few minor

24. For the sake of comparison, we offer an analysis of the Psalm according to the common stress/accent system:

Vs. 1)	2:2:2	2:2:3	(8
2)	2:2	3:2	(9
Vs. 3)	2:2:2	3:2	(7
	4	3:2	
Vs. 4)	2:2	3:2	(6cd
5)		2:2	
6ab)		3:2	

The pattern is roughly the same as that exhibited by the syllable-counting method. Variations are possible, and a somewhat more rigorous pattern can be reconstructed. But, given both the vagueness and flexibility of the system, it is hard to see what is gained by such an approach.

ones in the vocalization. Even if we were to follow *MT* slavishly, the general pattern would still be quite visible. However, by attempting to recover earlier forms of pronunciation and to recognize special stylistic features, we hope to reproduce more exactly the original structure as created by the poet. The Massoretes can hardly have been aware of such details.

THE STRUCTURE OF JOB 3

The opening speech of the Dialogue consists of three major units (as indicated in the RSV and the Jerusalem Bible): 1. vss. 3-10; 2. vss. 11-19; 3. vss. 20-26.[1]

The first unit, vss. 3-10, is devoted entirely to the "day", i.e. day/night of Job's birth. The opening pair of cola vs. 3, are neatly balanced and completed by the closing pair, vs. 10:

3) Perish the day on which I was born
  and the night when it was said,
    "A man-child has been delivered",

10) Because it did not close the doors
  of my (mother's) womb
and failed to hide trouble from my eyes.

The antecedent for the subject of the verbs of vs. 10 seems to be the day/night of vs. 3 (echoed in the intervening verses as well).[2] Within the framework provided by vss. 3 and 10, there are two subdivisions, one dealing with the day (vss. 4-5) and the other with the night (vss. 6-9). In spite of the apparent imbalance, and the questionable consistency of the poet in his use of imagery, the present text and its arrangement seem correct.[3]

For the analysis of the structure of the unit as a whole, the number and distribution of the tricola and bicola are both helpful and instructive. It should be noted that the tricolon in vs. 4 beginning *hayyōm hahūʾ* is balanced by the tricolon in vs. 6 beginning *hallaylāh hahūʾ*. Furthermore the second and third cola of vs. 4 are both *ʾal* clauses, followed by jussive forms of the verb. The same pattern is followed in vs. 6, except that the expression *ʾal* + verb comes at the end of the third colon instead of at the beginning (as in vs.

[1]Patrick W. Skehan, "Strophic Patterns in the Book of Job", *CBQ* 23 (1961) 125-42, divides the speech into seven strophes of approximately equal length (pp. 128-29), but in order to achieve this result certain rearrangements and emendations are made which this writer regards as unnecessary and unwarranted. We recognize subdivisions within the larger units, and these coincide at several points with Skehan's. At the same time the divisions at vss. 11 and 20 (note the use of *lāmmāh* at the beginning of each of these verses) are universally recognized and thus constitute an excellent point of departure.

[2]It is difficult to see why the *kī* clause must refer only to the night (so Skehan, op. cit. p. 129) when in fact day and night are used interchangeably in the specification of the event.

[3]Skehan's change of "night" to "day" in vs. 6 is too drastic, and results in a different imbalance.

4). This is a stylistically attested variation, producing a chiasm in vs. 6bc.[4] In vs. 5, which is a tricolon as well, the curse on the day is continued and concluded. The balancing verse, however, is 9 which is also a tricolon, and elaborates the curse on the night. While the structural parallels are not as exact as in the case of vss. 4 and 6, they are nevertheless sufficient to demonstrate the case. Thus, the verses begin with plural imperfect verbs (cf. also *ḥōšek* in vs. 5, and *yeḥšĕkū* in vs. 9); both have three clauses, and close with similarly patterned and unusual phrases: *kimrīrē yōm* (vs. 5) and *bēᶜapᶜappē šāḥar* (vs. 9). Essentially then there is a basic pattern for the specific condemnations of the day and the night: two tricola which are sufficiently unusual in Job to indicate that this was a deliberate construction on the part of the poet. However, the curse on the night has been further elaborated by the insertion of a couplet of bicola (vss. 7-8) in the framework of the two tricola.

The structural pattern which emerges from this analysis is as follows:

1. Introduction, vs. 3.
2. "That day", vss. 4-5
3. "That night", vss. 6-9
   a) Major theme, vs. 6
   b) Parenthesis on "that night" vss. 7-8
   c) Completion of major theme, vs. 9
4. Conclusion, vs. 10.

In the second major unit, vss. 11-19, there is only one structural problem of significance, the proper location of vs. 16. It is generally agreed that vss. 13-15 form a unified group, and the same is true of vss. 17-19. So far as sense is concerned, vs. 16 clearly belongs with vs. 11, and therefore the rearrangement: *a*) vss. 11, 16, 12; *b*) 13-15; *c*) 17-19 has been widely adopted.[5] We would agree that the proposed rearrangement is both rational and plausible, but these are not necessarily constant or even normal features of Hebrew poetry. The displacement of vs. 16 may have been a deliberate device of the poet, both to enclose the section vss. 13-15 within the statement of the main theme, and to serve as a reminder to the hearer of that main theme. Thus the opening lines (vss. 11-12) are an introduction to the hypothetical statements in vss. 13-15, while vs. 16 resumes the earlier contention and introduces the parallel set of anticipated conditions in the realm of death (vss. 17-19).

The resulting pattern is:

A. Vss. 11-15: 1) vss. 11-12; 2) vss. 13-15.
B. Vss. 16-19: 1) vs. 16; 2) vss. 17-19.

[4]We heartily concur with Skehan's observation about the authenticity of the tricola in this unit. It is worth noting that there are four tricola, two each for the day and the night.

[5]So Skehan, op. cit. p. 129; cf. Marvin H. Pope, *Job* in AB (New York 1965) 26 and 31.

Vs. 16 serves as a divider between the two main sections of this unit (vss. 13-15 and 17-19), evoking the opening lines (vss. 11-12), and resuming the theme expressed in them.

In the third major unit (vss. 20-26), we find a pattern similar to that of the second unit. There are two main sections, vss. 20-22 and 24-26 which balance each other, while vs. 23 stands in essentially the same relationship to vs. 20 as vs. 16 does to vs. 11 (*lĕgeber* in vs. 23 is parallel to *lĕ*^{c}*āmēl* in vs. 20, and depends upon the preceding *lāmmāh yittēn* in vs. 20; in similar fashion vs. 16 presupposes the *lāmmāh* of vs. 11). A second instance of the same kind of displacement in the same poem strongly implies that the peculiarity is no accident, but a deliberate device on the part of the poet, and that the present order of the lines should be retained. According to our analysis of the first unit, vs. 9 stands in a similar relationship to vs. 6 (regarding vss. 7-8 as parenthetical), further illustrating the stylistic device mentioned and strengthening the case for the unity and integrity of the poem. Returning to the third unit, we note that vs. 23 while echoing vs. 20 and resuming the theme of that line, at the same time serves as an introduction or transition to the concluding section (i.e., the "man" in vs. 23 is Job himself and this makes the shift to the first person in vss. 24-26 quite natural).

The resulting pattern for the third unit is:

a) vss. 20-22; *b*) vs. 23; *c*) vss. 24-26.

Summarizing the structural analysis of the whole speech, we have the following pattern:

I. Vss. 3-10
- *a*) Introduction vs. 3
- *b*) That day: vss. 4-5
- *c*) That night: vss. 6-9
  - 1) vs. 6
  - 2) vss. 7-8
  - 3) vs. 9
- *d*) Conclusion vs. 10

II. Vss. 11-19
- *a*) Introduction vss. 11-12
- *b*) vss. 13-15
- *c*) Resumption vs. 16 Divider
- *d*) vss. 17-19

III. Vss. 20-26
- *a*) vss. 20-22
- *b*) Divider vs. 23
- *c*) vss. 24-26

The first unit has eight lines with a total of twenty cola (there are four tricola). The second unit has nine lines and eighteen cola; and the third unit has seven lines and fourteen cola. The totals are twenty-four lines and fifty-two cola. Regarding the overall structure of the poem, there is a curious affinity between the last line, vs. 26, and the middle line, vs. 13. Not only is there a thematic contrast between the tranquillity and peace Job might have enjoyed had he died at birth, and the present disturbed situation, but the actual words are repeated: *ʾešqōṭ* and *šāqaṭtī*; *yānūăḥ lī* and *nāḥtī*. It is perhaps worthy of note that vs. 13 marks the midpoint of the poem: vss. 3-13, eleven lines, twenty-six cola; vss. 14-26, thirteen lines, twenty-six cola.

We append a final note on the feasibility of syllable-counting in determining metrical structure. Marvin Pope has analyzed Jb 3,3-10 to "illustrate the character of the poetry of Job and lack of rigid metrical pattern".[6] At first sight the variations in syllable-counting seem to support his contention, but closer inspection reveals an impressive symmetry which is at least suggestive, if not convincing. To avoid controversy and maintain objectivity we shall accept Pope's syllable count for the verses in question, though in fact there are uncertainties in vocalization and syllable-counting, and legitimate differences of opinion as to the results. Following the analysis of the passage offered above, we arrive at the following figures.

vs. 3	7 + 10 = 17		
vs. 4		8 + 10 + 8 = 26	51
vs. 5		9 + 7 + 9 = 25	
vs. 6		11 + 7 + 9 = 27	
vs. 7	11 + 7 = 18		
vs. 8	8 + 9 = 17		52
vs. 9		8 + 7 +10 = 25	
vs. 10	8 + 8 = 16		

It will be noted that vs. 3(17) matches vs. 10(16), and vss. 4-5(51) match vss. 6 and 9(52). The slight differences can easily be accounted for by the legitimate variation in counting systems. Further, the total for vss. 3-5(68) exactly balances the total for vss. 6, 9-10(68). In addition, vss. 7-8(35) nicely balance vss. 3 and 10(33) to which they are structurally related. And if, with Skehan, we regard the initial *hinnēh* in vs. 7 as extra-metrical, then the count is precisely equal, 33 syllables (vs. 7 = 16, vs. 8 = 17, matching vs. 3 = 17, and vs. 10 = 16).

With regard to syllable-counting, the following variables must be taken into account: 1) reduction of syllables in MT through elision of vowels in earlier forms of the language, e.g. *bīmē* < **biyāmē*; 2) resolution of diphthongs in MT, e.g. *layĕlāh* < *laylāh*, or *ʾayin* < *ʾayn*; 3) resolution of segolates, producing bisyllabic forms from original monosyllables: e.g., *ḥōšek* < **ḥušk*, *šāḥar* < **šaḥr*, *ʾōpel* < **ʾupl*, etc.; 4) insertion of *pataḥ* furtive in MT; 5) apparent mispointings such as *ṣalmāwet* for *ṣalmūt*; 6) introduction of

[6]Pope, op. cit. pp. xlviii-xlix.

prosaic elements such as *wĕ*, *ʾēt* and *ʾăšer* (though these may be authentic usage in certain cases). In the table which follows we offer minimum and maximum counts for vss. 3-10, as well as the actual count of MT:

	Min.	Max.	MT	Pope
vs. 3a	7	7	7	7
b	9	11	11	10
	16	18	18	17
4a	7	8	8	8
b	9	11	11	10
c	9	9	9	8
	25	28	28	26
5a	8	10	10	9
b	7	7	7	7
c	9	10	10	9
	24	27	27	25
6a	10	12	12	11
b	7	8	7	7
c	9	9	9	9
	26	29	28	27
7a	11	12	12	11
b	7	7	7	7
	18	19	19	18
8a	8	8	8	8
b	9	9	9	9
	17	17	17	17
9a	8	8	8	8
b	6	7	7	7
c	9	10	10	10
	23	25	25	25
10a	8	8	8	8
b	8	8	8	8
	16	16	16	16

The variations do not affect the general results, though it is possible to achieve more precise patterns by judicious approximation. Lest such procedure be regarded as tampering it need only be pointed out that minor variations in pronunciation and therefore in syllable valuation are both necessary and permissible in all metrical systems and the variations suggested here fall well within normally allowable divergences. Our composite results are as follows:

	Range	*Average*	*MT*	*Pope*
vs. 3	16-18	17	18	17
vs. 10	16	16	16	16
	32-34	33	34	33
vs. 4	25-28	26.5	28	26
5	24-27	25.5	27	25
	49-55	52	55	51
vs. 6	26-29	27.5	28	27
9	23-25	24	25	25
	49-54	51.5	53	52
vs. 7	18-19	18.5	19	18
8	17	17	17	17
	35-36	35.5	36	35

The only possible disturbance in an otherwise impressively symmetrical pattern is to be found in vs. 7 where the initial *hinnēh* seems to overload the line.[7] We may regard the word as extra-metrical rather than secondary, and thus preserve the intention of the poet, the integrity of the text, and its metrical uniformity.

[7]Cf. Skehan, op. cit. p. 129, n. 8.

NOTES AND OBSERVATIONS

THE ELIHU SPEECHES IN THE BOOK OF JOB

A Hypothetical Episode in the Literary History of the Work

It is generally agreed by scholars that the Elihu speeches in the book of Job (chaps. 32–37) did not belong to the original draft of the work, but constitute an addition to it. As evidence in support of this view, it is pointed out that Elihu appears nowhere else in the book, not even in the Epilogue where he ought to have been noticed along with the other participants. Further, his speeches interrupt the continuity of the Dialogue (between Job's final challenge to God in chap. 31, and the divine response in chap. 38). Finally the speeches contribute little if anything to the content or movement of the book. Without inquiring further into this question we may accept the general view for the purposes of this paper.

A second, related question concerns the authorship of this block of material. Again the preponderant view favors diversity of authorship, though there are staunch defenders of the view that the same author is responsible for the Dialogue, and the Speech from the Whirlwind, as well as the Elihu speeches. This disagreement among scholars reflects different evaluations of the pertinent data: 1) that the Elihu speeches are intrusive in the book as we have it, and exhibit divergences in style and treatment; at the same time 2) there are many points of contact in vocabulary and style, as compared, for example, with other books of the Bible. We may say that, at the very least, the author of the Elihu speeches was not only well acquainted with the content of the book of Job, but was thoroughly steeped in its thought patterns and modes of expression. For our purposes it is not necessary to decide the question of authorship, but it will suffice to keep in mind the alternative proposals.

Our concern is with a subordinate datum, namely the number of the Elihu speeches. Following the rubrics of the Massoretic Text, scholars count four speeches (1: chaps. 32–33; 2: chap. 34; 3: chap. 35; 4: chaps. 36–37). The obvious question is: Why is this monologue broken into a series of speeches? and why are there four of them? It may be a trivial matter, and any proposed solution must remain hypothetical, but the investigation of the question may shed incidental light on some of the more important issues concerning Elihu's speeches and their relationship to the Dialogue on the one hand, and the Voice from the Whirlwind on the other.

The simplest answer to the question is that it is unreal: there is no answer because there is no question. Actually there is only one speech by Elihu, which has been broken up into shorter units by the device of reintroduction or resumption. Perhaps this is so, but it is an odd way to achieve an objective: to interrupt a speech by not interrupting it. It may be noted in passing that the long speech of Yahweh (chaps. 38ff.) is divided into two speeches by the insertion of a brief statement on the part of Job (chap. 40:3–5), thus maintaining the normal pattern of dialogue. Had it been the author's intention simply to break a long speech into manageable units, he could have employed a similar device. The puzzling feature of the Elihu speeches is precisely the lack of dialogue, even though three of them are fitted out with more or less elaborate introductory remarks. Thus, the first, second, and fourth speeches have their own introductions, which suggests that they were conceived and composed as separate entities. The third, on the other hand, lacks its own introduction, and except for the rubric in vs. 1 (chap. 35) could be regarded as a continuation of the second speech. Compare, for example, Job 27:1, which is a similar rubric, though it links two apparently consecutive speeches by Job. It is only fair to add, however, that many scholars assign the latter part of chap. 26 to one of the friends, since its contents conform more readily to their viewpoint than to that of Job. In our judgment, then, there were either three or four separate speeches composed for Elihu, and intended to be inserted at strategic points in the Dialogue between Job and his friends. More specifically, each of Elihu's speeches was intended to refute or counterbalance a speech or assertion of Job, and to be placed in juxtaposition with it.

The next question to be asked is where in the Dialogue these speeches of Elihu were meant to be inserted, or where do they most logically fit. At first glance, one might assign them at random throughout the Dialogue, since the general themes are repeated with little substantial change from one cycle to the next, and the speeches often have only loose connections with the preceding or following ones. Nevertheless, some effort is made to maintain the integrity of the Dialogue. Thus, Job and his friends respond directly to each other on occasion; the personal references tend to become more vituperative as the Dialogue proceeds. In the case of Elihu we have more explicit connections. In certain instances he quotes Job directly in order to refute him, and in other cases he paraphrases or summarizes.

In his first speech, Elihu quotes Job at chap. 33:9–11 (cf. vs. 8: "Surely you said it in my hearing / I heard the words themselves"). The latter part of the quotation, vss. 10b–11, is taken almost verbatim from chap. 13: 24b and 27ab:

33:10b —	*yaḥš^{e}bēnī l^{e}'ōyēb lō*	He reckons me as his enemy
13:24b —	*w^{e}taḥš^{e}bēnī l^{e}'ōyēb lāk*	And you reckon me as your enemy
33:11 —	*yāśēm bassad raglāy*	He sets in the stocks my feet
	yišmōr kol-'orḥōtāy	He watches all my steps
13:27a —	*w^{e}tāśēm bassad raglāy*	And you set in the stocks my feet
	w^{e}tišmōr kol-'orḥōtāy	And you watch all my steps

There is no exact equivalent to 33:9, though the idea is reflected in a number of Job's statements: cf. 9:21, 10:7, 13:18(n.b.), 16:17, 23:10, 27:5–6, and chap. 31. Just from the evidence presented, it would appear logical to place Elihu's first speech after Job's speech in chaps. 12–14.

In his second speech, Elihu again quotes Job (34:5–6) in order to refute him. Of these lines, only 34:5b is a direct quotation, being taken from 27:2a:

27:2a	*ḥay-ēl hēsīr mišpāṭī*	For El has taken away my right
34:5b	*w^{e}'ēl hēsīr mišpātī*	As El lives (who) has taken away my right

On the basis of this datum we would suggest that Elihu's second speech was intended to follow Job's speech in chap. 27, and to serve as a rejoinder to it.

In the third speech, Elihu quotes Job once more (35:2–3). The quotation is either inexact or derived from a speech of Job no longer extant, because we cannot trace it to its source in the book of Job. However, Elihu's rejoinder in 35:6–7 is in the main a recasting of Eliphaz' words in 22:2–4, which in turn are a response to Job's speech in chap. 21. Elihu's third speech seems to fit that juncture (between 21 and 22) as well or better than any other. Or we may evade the problem by regarding chap. 35 as a continuation of the speech in chap. 34, and not as an independent unit requiring a separate position in the Dialogue.

In the fourth speech of Elihu, there are no explicit quotations from Job's speeches. It is a summary and recapitulation of Elihu's views, like a lawyer's closing argument in which the main positive arguments are repeated before the case goes to the jury. As such, it is intended to balance rather than refute Job's own closing argument in chaps. 29–31. When the first three speeches of Elihu have been removed to their several locations, the juxtaposition of the fourth speech with the final words of Job is seen to be appropriate. The close verbal similarities to passages in the Speech of Yahweh (chaps. 38–39) tend to confirm this judgment about the proper place of Elihu's fourth speech.

We can now fill out hypotheses concerning the Elihu speeches in somewhat more detail:

1. The first speech comes logically after Job's speech in chaps. 12–14, which closes the first cycle of the Dialogue.

2. The second speech fits best after chap. 27, which may have closed the third cycle of the Dialogue. Because of the disorder in the speeches of the third cycle, it is difficult to determine the proper position of this speech of Elihu, but its association with chap. 27 and the other speeches of the third cycle is clear.

3. There are alternative possibilities with regard to the third speech. If it is regarded simply as a continuation of the second speech (and it may be noted that the first and last speeches are about twice the length of the second and third speeches; if two and three were combined then there would be three speeches of approximately equal length. On the other hand, there is a break between chaps. 34 and 35, and structurally they appear to be parallel speeches rather than a single continuous one), then it would fall under No. 2. If it is to be treated as an independent unit, then it must be conceded that there is no certain link with any particular speech of Job. In general it seems to be associated in content and tone with the second and third cycles of the Dialogue, and may be placed to advantage after Job's speech in chap. 21, which concludes the second cycle. That would mean that Elihu's second and third speeches are in reverse order.

4. The fourth speech belongs where it is, after Job's final speech, and before the Voice from the Whirlwind, or in any case, the Epilogue.

In order to test the hypotheses, it is necessary to examine the Elihu speeches in some detail: to identify the direct and indirect correlations with the speeches of the Dialogue, and thus determine the probable intended setting of each speech. In such an inquiry it is the details which count. Direct quotations, both exact and approximate, are of the greatest value; more general parallels in content and tone are helpful, but less decisive because similar statements often turn up in a number of different places in the book. This latter circumstance must be borne in mind when testing the hypothesis.

Favorable data will consist of citations and correlations with speeches in the particular cycle to which the speech of Elihu is assigned. Occasional references to earlier cycles would be expected, since they precede the speech in question. The crucial problem concerns citations and allusions to later cycles. Thus the quotation from 27:2 is negatively decisive for the second Elihu speech; theoretically we might wish to assign it to the end of the second cycle and thus keep everything in order. But Job's speech in chap. 27 belongs to the third cycle, and there can be no question about the citation. However, more general correlations are not nearly so decisive, since their counterparts frequently occur in earlier cycles as well. Moreover, because of the repetition of themes and expressions throughout the Dialogue, the author of the Elihu speeches could be forgiven an occasional lapse in the citation of speeches and quote from a later cycle when he intended an earlier. But since that is precisely the point at issue, we will leave that decision to others. Our main concern is with the evidence we have, and the most viable hypothesis for explaining the phenomena.

Elihu's First Speech: In addition to the direct quotation already discussed, the following parallels, allusions, and correlations in general may be noted — 32:8–9 (cf. 12:12, 15:10). 32:21a (13:8). 33:3 (6:25). 33:5b (13:18, 23:4). 33:6 (10:9). 33:7 (9:34, 13:21). 33:12 (9:14–20, 30; 13:13–16). 33:13 (9:2–3, 19:7, 30:20). 33:15–18 (14:12–15). 33:15 (7:14); 15b (4:13b). 33:18a (9:31a). 33:19a (5:17). 33:23–24 (5:1, 9:33, 16:19–21, 19:25–27). 33:26 (22:27). 33:28 (3:16, 20). 33:30 (3:20).

The largest bloc of quotations and allusions derives from Job's speech at the close of the first cycle, chaps. 12–14, especially chap. 13. In addition the bulk of the correlations is with the first cycle of the Dialogue (chaps. 3–14). I count approximately twenty such allusions to speeches in the first cycle, and not more than half a dozen parallels from other passages in Job (most of these echo passages in the first cycle, which constitute the primary reference). We may conclude that the speech relates generally to the first cycle of the Dialogue, and specifically to Job's speech at the end of it, precisely as Elihu's quotation from chap. 13 implies. Certainly the logical place for this speech is after chapter 14, at the end of the first cycle.

Elihu's Second Speech: In addition to the direct quotation (cf. 27:2) discussed above, the following correlations may be noted — 34:3 (12:11 almost exact duplication). 34:6 (6:4). 34:7 (15:16). 34:8 (11:11, 22:15, 31:5). 34:9 (9:22–24, 30f., 10:3, 21:7–13). 34:10 (8:3). 34:11 (4:8, 8:4). 34:12 (8:3). 34:13 (9:12). 34:18 (12:17–21). 34:19c–20a (27:19–20). 34:20bc (19:21). 34:21a (24:23b, 31:4). 34:21b (14:16). 34:23f. (9:32f., 23:3f., 24:12). 34:27 (24:13). 34:29b (13:24, 23:9). 34:35 (38:2, 42:5). 34:36b (22:15).

While the references are scattered, there is a significant grouping of correlations with the speeches in the third cycle (I count eight, as against three for the second cycle; inevitably there are many relating to the first cycle, which is the most extensive, and where practically all the ideas are stated in their original form; significantly there are only two — both in a series of correlations from earlier cycles — from the final speech of Job). That is all the more remarkable in view of the disturbed and truncated state of the third cycle. The fact that there are reminiscences of the speeches in the first and second cycles does not affect the case, since Elihu can properly refer to earlier speeches according to our hypothesis. It is the latest correlations which determine the proper setting for the speech. Since, in addition to the direct quotation from 27:2, there are numerous other references to speeches in the third cycle, the conclusion is inescapable. The logical place for Elihu's second speech is after Job's remarks in chap. 27, at or toward the end of the third cycle of the Dialogue. The two correlations with Job 31:4 and 5 have earlier parallels (24:25b for 34:21a; and 22:15 for 34:8), both from the third cycle.

Elihu's Third Speech: As in the earlier speeches, Elihu quotes Job in order to refute him. As already mentioned, the quotation in 35:2–3 is not taken directly from any recorded speech of Job, so we lack the most important clue to the proper disposition of this speech of Elihu. Other correlations may be listed as follows — 35:5 (11:7–9, 22:12–13, cf. 9:8–11). 35:9–10 (24:12, cf. 22:8–9). 35:10–11 (10:8ff.). 35:14a (13:24, 23:8–9, 24:1b, 30:20); 14b (13:18, 23:4). 35:15 (21:7ff., 24:12).

The third speech shows affinities with both the second and third cycles of speeches. There may be some significance in the fact that besides the occasional allusions to Job's speech in chap. 21, there are extensive echoes of Eliphaz' speech in chap. 22. We have suggested that a feasible location for this speech is at the juncture between chaps. 21 and 22. Since the first and second speeches come logically at the end of the first and third cycles of the Dialogue, we might expect this speech of Elihu to come at the end of the second cycle (i.e., after chap. 21). The question, however, is complicated by the actual relation of the second and third speeches of Elihu. In addition there are a number of correlations between this speech and the third cycle.

Elihu's Fourth Speech: In addition to the remarks already made about the character of this speech, and its logical place in juxtaposition with Job's closing plea (chaps. 29–31), we may note here the numerous points of contact between this speech and the Voice from the Whirlwind, which also constitutes a rejoinder to Job's last speech. The correlations of this speech are as follows — 36:2 (21:22). 36:6a (21:7). 36:7bc (5:11). 36:8–11 (5:17, cf. 33:14–28). 36:8 (12:17–19). 36:13 (8:13, 30:20, 38:41). 36:15a (33:16–30); 15b (33:16a). 36:16 (7:11, 38:23, 18:7, 20:22, cf. 3:2, 7:2). 36:18 (27:23). 36:19 (13:18). 36:20 (13:22, 23:3–7). 36:22 (33:14ff., 34:32, 35:11). 36:23a (21:31); 23b (9:12, cf. 34:13). 36:24 (33:27, 35:10). 36:25 (26:14, 33:28). 36:27ff. (27:6, 10). 36:29b (30:22, 39:7). 37:5 (5:9, 9:10). 37:9a (38:22). 37:9–10 (38:29f., 21:18). 37:12 (38:35). 37:13 (21:9). 37:15–18 (chap. 38 passim). 37:15 (38:33, 39:1ff.). 37:18 (40:15; 38:37). 37:19b (13:18, 23:4; 32:14, 33:5). 37:23 (38:1); 23a (11:7, 23:8–9); 23bc (9:20–24). 37:24b (9:4).

In this speech, Elihu recapitulates earlier statements (especially chap. 33) and ranges over the whole preceding Dialogue for his materials. There are correlations with speeches from all three cycles, and from the friends as well as Job. But the most striking affinities are with the Speech of Yahweh from the Whirlwind, especially chap. 38. This speech is clearly Elihu's valedictory, and is appropriately placed at the end of the Dialogue between Job and his friends. Since it anticipates and overlaps with the Speech from the Whirlwind, while serving essentially the same purpose, namely to counterbalance Job's closing speech, one may wonder whether it may have been intended to displace the Speech of Yahweh, assuming that the latter had already been incorporated into the book. Alternatively we may suppose that Yahweh's Speech was intended to displace Elihu's closing speech.

In the light of our analysis of the Elihu speeches, the following conclusions may be offered:

1) It may reasonably be doubted that the four Elihu speeches were composed as a single address with only formal breaks in the sequence.

2) It is more likely that the speeches were intended to be placed separately at strategic points in the Dialogue. Thus: a) The first speech is clearly based upon and related to the first cycle of speeches. More specifically it is directly linked to Job's closing speech in the first cycle. b) The second speech is linked clearly with the speeches in the third cycle, and directly quotes Job's address in chap. 27, which belongs to if it does not close this cycle. The third speech is not so clearly related to any particular speech of Job, but has affinities primarily with the second and third cycles of speeches. It alone of the Elihu speeches may be a continuation of the preceding (second speech), and may therefore belong with the second speech to the third cycle. It is possible that our author devoted one speech to the second and third

cycles together (since they are each a good deal shorter than the first cycle, and together are about the same length). At the same time the third speech can be dealt with as a separate unit, and could then be assigned to the second cycle with some justice. c) The fourth speech clearly belongs at the end of the Dialogue, to serve as a counterweight to Job's closing speech; its function is essentially the same as the Voice from the Whirlwind, with which it has many affinities.

3) We believe that the author composed the four speeches as part of a general plan to reorganize the Book of Job, and that he intended to place each of the speeches at a turning point in the Dialogue, namely, at the end of each cycle of speeches, and in direct correspondence with Job's closing speech in that cycle. The fourth and last speech was to serve the same function in relation to Job's final address. The project was never carried through to completion, and seems to have been abandoned entirely, since no effort was made to link Elihu to the story in the Prologue or Epilogue, or with any of the characters except Job. It may be that the author failed to consider how extensive the revisions would have to be if Elihu and his remarks were to be made an integral part of the book, and not simply an intrusion. If the plan were to be carried out, it would be necessary to create transitions from Elihu's speeches to those of the friends, since Elihu's speeches would in effect break up the present continuity (maybe Elihu's speeches were intended to displace speeches by the friends, as, e.g., chap. 35, the third speech, and Eliphaz' speech in chap. 22). Furthermore, it would have been necessary to build Elihu into the story from the beginning, as well as at the end. Additional problems would have been posed by adding a fourth friend to the group; as it is, the three friends tend to overlap in their speeches, and we hear the same arguments over and over. It is already difficult enough for the reader to distinguish among the three: their dramatic impact, and the particular line of argument with which they are identified, are compromised as it is by the blending and blurring of the cycles of speeches. A fourth person who adds little and overlaps a lot would only make matters worse.

In addition, Elihu's final speech undercuts the speech of Yahweh from the Whirlwind. It is difficult to imagine that Elihu's speech was composed as a transition to or improvement upon the Speech from the Whirlwind. It is also difficult to imagine that the story of Dialogue ended with Job's final speech (chaps. 29–31). It may be that the Elihu "project," on the one hand, and the Speeches from the Whirlwind, on the other, were alternative proposals to deal with the problems both literary and theological posed by the Dialogue and especially Job's closing speech. Perhaps the author undertook the Elihu speeches first, and having written them, was dissatisfied with the results and abandoned the project. However, he used some of the material as a basis for the Speeches from the Whirlwind, which then provided a suitable conclusion to the Dialogue. They proved eminently effective, and required little or no restructuring of the text. The Elihu speeches were not finally lost, but found their way back into the book of Job through the industry of an editor who made a place for them at the end of the Dialogue between Job and his friends, and before the speech from the Whirlwind. If in fact the Elihu speeches provided the necessary stimulus for the composition of the Speeches from the Whirlwind, then they fulfilled an even more important function than the one conceived for them in the first place.

THE BROKEN CONSTRUCT CHAIN

Sporadic occurrences of the broken construct chain are listed in Gesenius-Kautzsch § 130; most of the cases involve prepositions (e.g., *hārē baggilbōăᶜ*, "the mountains of Gilboa" 2 Sam 1,21) or other particles. The list could be expanded considerably:[1] for example, there are a number of instances in which enclitic *mem* is attached to the construct in a chain. In Dt 33,11, we should read *motnē-m qāmāw*, "the loins of those who oppose him" for MT *motnayim qāmāw* (cf. Sam. *mtny qmyw*);[2] and in Ps 18,16, we suggest *ᵓăpīqē-m yām*, "the channels of the Sea" for MT *ᵓăpīqē mayim*, "channels of water" (cf. 2 Sam 22,16 *ᵓāpīqē yām*).[3] In Ez 39,11, the particle *šām* has been inserted between the construct and the absolute: *mĕqōm-šām qeber*, "a burial place there."[4]

A striking example of this phenomenon is to be found in Is 10,5,[5] which reads:

hōy ᵓAššūr šēbeṭ ᵓappī	Ho! Assyria, the rod of my anger
ūmaṭṭeh-hūᵓ bĕyādām zaᶜmī	and a staff is he in their hand my fury.

A literal rendering of the second line makes no sense, and the passage is widely regarded as corrupt. The RSV, in a drastic move, cuts out the troublesome *hwᵓ bydm* and reads: "The staff of my fury." Its merit lies in the recognition that *maṭṭeh . . . zaᶜmī* constitute a construct chain in parallel with *šēbeṭ appī*. There is no need to eliminate the phrase *hwᵓ bydm* which may be analyzed as follows: the independent pronoun, 3rd masc. sing., and the prepositional phrase *bĕyad*—or *bĕyādī*—with the enclitic *mem*. The meaning in either case would be "is he (i.e., Assyria) in my hand." The pronominal suffix is often omitted with parts of the body, and in any case the suffixes attached to *ᵓp* and *zᶜm* would serve to define *yd* as well. The verse may then be rendered: "Ho! Assyria is the rod of my anger / the staff of my fury is he in my hand." It is also possible, as proposed by Professor H. L. Ginsberg,[6] to read *bydm zᵓmy* as a construct chain (with enclitic *mem* between the construct and the absolute), and translate as follows: "and a staff is he (Assyria) in my angry hand." Such a reading is entirely plausible; however, it obscures the precise parallelism of *šbṭ ᵓpy* and *mṭh zᶜmy*, which is the most striking feature of the bicolon.

[1]Cf. M. Dahood, *Psalms III* (AB 17a; Garden City, NY, 1970) 381-383.

[2]Cf. F. M. Cross and D. N. Freedman, "The Blessing of Moses", *JBL* 67 (1948) 194 and 204, fn. 33.

[3]Cf. Cross and Freedman, "A Royal Song of Thanksgiving: II Samuel 22 = Psalm 18", *JBL* 72 (1953) 26, fn. 41.

[4]I owe this example to Professor Nahum Sarna.

[5]A similar instance occurs in Ps 140,10; cf. the discussion in Dahood, *Psalms III*, 303-304.

[6]In *JBL* 62 (1943) 115.

Another group of broken construct chains is to be found in Habakkuk 3. In vs. 8 we read:

kī tirkab ᶜal-sūsēkā	When you rode upon your horses
markĕbōtēkā yĕšūᶜāh	your chariots of victory.

The final phrase, *mrkbtyk yšwᶜh*, has every appearance of being a construct chain, except that the pronominal suffix is attached to the construct instead of the absolute.[7] The reason for this unusual but effective variation from the normal construction is probably to be found in the association of *mrkbtyk* and the preceding *swsyk*, as coordinate elements in the compound phrase introduced by *ᶜl* and controlled by *yšwᶜh*. The unit may then be rendered: "upon your victorious horse(-drawn) chariots." It is also possible to interpret *yšwᶜh* as an adverbial accusative, and render the clause as follows: ". . . when you rode victoriously (to victory) on your horses, your chariots."

In vs. 13ab we have the parallel expressions: *lĕyēšaᶜ ᶜammekā/lĕyēšaᶜ ᵓet-mĕšīḥekā*. The meaning must be: "for the salvation of your people / for the salvation of your anointed." Apparently the second phrase is a construct chain, like the first, except that the intrusive *ᵓt* has been inserted between the construct and the absolute. Exactly what the *ᵓt* is is difficult to say: it may be the emphasizing particle, normally used to identify the definite direct object of the verb (here of the action), or it may be the 2nd masc. sing. pronoun written defectively, used here to call attention to the pronominal suffix attached to the following noun.[8]

Turning to vs. 13c, we find the following difficult clause:

māḥaṣtā rōᵓš mibbēt rāšāᶜ	You smashed the head from the house of the wicked one.

It is possible to interpret *rᵓš* as "chieftain" or "leader"; but it is much more likely that *rᵓš* is to be taken literally in conjunction with the verb *mḥṣ*. We should then recognize that *rōᵓš . . . rāšāᶜ* form a construct chain; we can render the statement thus far: "You smashed the head . . . of the wicked one." The intrusive element in the construct chain, *mbyt* can be read as *mibbayit*, meaning "inwards, within."[9] We can then translate the line: "You crushed the head of the wicked one inwards." It makes an excellent parallel to vs. 13d: "You ripped him open from fundament to neck."

Another group of broken construct chains is drawn from the Book of Hosea. The distinctive feature of these is that a verb is placed between the construct and the absolute. In 14,3 we read:

qĕḥu ᶜimmākem dĕbārīm	Take words with you
wĕšūbū ᵓel-Yhwh	and turn to Yahweh.

[7]Cf. Genenius-Kautzsch § 131r.
[8]Cf. Gesenius-Kautzsch § 135.2: 1 Kgs 21,19; Prv 22,19; Gn 49,8; Zech 9,11.
[9]Cf. 2 Kgs 6,30.

ʾimrū ʾēlāw	Say to him,
kol-tiśśāʾ ʿāwōn	"Forgive all iniquity
wĕqaḥ-ṭōb	and accept (every) good (word);
ūnĕšallĕmāh	and we shall make restitution
pĕrī-m(i) śĕpātēnū	with the fruit of our lips."

In the clause *kl-tśʾ ʿwn*, the normal word order would be *kl-ʿwn tśʾ*; the translation would not be affected.[10] The reason for the unusual arrangement was doubtless a matter of emphasizing the term *kl*, which may also serve the same function in the next clause: (*kl*) *wqḥ ṭwb*, 'And accept (every) good."

In the final clause of the verse, the phrase *pārīm śĕpātēnū* "bulls, our lips," is admittedly difficult if not incomprehensible. It is commonly emended to *pĕrī śĕpātēnū* "the fruit of our lips."[11] This is unquestionably correct, but there is no need to alter the consonantal text. The *mem* in *prym* is to be recognized as the enclitic attached to the *nomen regens* in a construct chain.[12]

In 6,9 we read:

derek yĕraṣṣĕḥū-Šekmāh	They commit murder on the road to Shechem.

The normal order would be *derek Šekmāh* . . . (cf Gn 35,19 *drk ʾprth*, 38,14 *drk tmnth*).

In 8,2, we read:

ʾĕlōhay yĕdaʿănūkā Yiśrāʾēl	My God, we Israel know you.

The normal rendering has been questioned on a number of grounds, one of which is the awkward shift from first person singular ("my God") to plural ("we know"). As observed in BH[3] a more logical interpretation would associate *ʾlhy* and *yśrʾl* in a construct chain; the resultant translation would be: "O God of Israel, we know you." The normal order would be *ʾĕlōhē Yiśrāʾēl yĕdaʿănūkā*, but there is no need to alter the text as we have it in MT of Hosea. It is only a matter of recognizing the phenomenon of the broken construct chain.

[10]Cf. Gesenius-Kautzsch § 128e; also 2 Sam 9,1; Jb 27,3.

[11]While the exact expression does not occur elsewhere, we have an equivalent idiom in *pĕrī pī-ʾīš* "the fruit of a man's mouth," Prv 12,14; 13,2, and especially 18,20 where we read:

mippĕrī pī-ʾiš	By the fruit of a man's mouth
tiśbaʿ biṭnō	his stomach will be filled.
tĕbūʾat śĕpātāw	By the produce of his lips
yiśbāʿ	he will be satisfied.

We note the double-duty preposition *min*, which serves both *pry py-ʾyš* and *tbwʾt śptyw*.

[12]See above.

II SAMUEL 23:4

Having had the privilege of reading Professor H. N. Richardson's persuasive study of II Sam 23:1-7 in an earlier draft, I submitted a number of proposals to the author. He graciously adopted several of these, as noted in the printed version, while others were found wanting and considerately put aside. With more zeal than prudence, perhaps, I have revived one of these proposals, and the editor of the *Journal* has been kind enough to allot space for its presentation.

Not being entirely satisfied with Richardson's reconstruction of vs. 4, admittedly an obscure and difficult passage, I suggest a somewhat different analysis, arrangement, and interpretation:

And [he shall be] like the light on a morning at sunrise,	(4a)	וכאור בקר יזרח שמש
more brilliant than a morning without clouds,	(4b)	בקר לא עבות מנגה
[better] than rain [upon] the grass of the earth.	(4c)	ממטר דשא—מ ארץ

In this passage, the ruler (vs. 3) is compared in a two-fold simile with the brilliant light of a cloudless morning at sunrise, and also with the rain which nourishes the vegetation of the earth. For the latter figure, see Ps 72:6, where the king "comes down like the rain"; also Deut 32:2, where the terms *mṭr* and *dšʾ* both occur.

Noteworthy is the elaborate chiasm in vs. 5ab: *bqr yzrḥ šmš* (in which the clause *yzrḥ šmš* functions as a *nomen rectum* dependent on the construct *bqr*; I take *bqr* as equivalent to the common expression *bbqr*) is balanced by *bqr lʾ ʿbwt* (also a construct chain; literally, a "morning of no clouds"); *kʾwr* and *mngh* are a characteristic poetic pair, with *ʾwr* as the A-word, and *ngh* as the B-word. See Amos 5:20; Hab 3:11; Isa 60:3; cf. also Hab 3:4 and Prov 4:18 where the words occur together. The prepositions *kĕ* and *min* are also complementary, both introducing comparisons: *k* = like, as; *min* = more than. An attempt to bring out this nuance or shade of meaning has been made in the translation offered above. I might suggest, as a somewhat more daring alternative, that the preposition *kĕ* governs all three cola, and that the *mem* before *ngh* and *mṭr* is not the preposition *min* but a proclitic extending the preceding *k'*, i.e., *kĕmō—nōgah* and *kĕmō—māṭār*. The strange word order of vs. 4b is dictated by the chiastic structure. A similar drastic pattern is to be found in Amos 5:16, where the last bicolon reads:

wĕqārĕʾū ʾikkār ʾel-ʾēbel	And they summon the plowman to mourning,
ūmispēd ʾel-yōdĕʿē nehī	and lamentation to those skilled in wailing.

The chiasm is apparent: *ʾkr* is balanced by *ywdʿy nhy*, while *ʾbl* and *mspd* make a traditional pair. The preposition *ʾl* occupies the same relative position in each colon. The literal rendering offered above, however, makes the second colon seem unduly awkward. It would be possible to take both prepositions as serving double-duty, and interpret the verb as "calling to" both the persons and the mourning. It is both more drastic and more effective to read the second colon backwards: i.e., "those skilled in wailing to lamentation," an exact complement to "the plowman to mourning" of the first colon.

While the preposition *ᶜal* would be normal before *dšᵓ* (cf. Deut 32:2 *ᶜălē*), its omission is not to be regarded as a felonious assault on classic Hebrew grammar. An interesting example of omission is to be found in Amos 2:7, where we read:

wĕderek ᶜănāwîm yaṭṭū — And they push the humble out of the road.

(Cf. D. N. Freedman, *CBQ*, 30 [1968], p. 226, n. 3.) We also take the *mem* before *ᵓrṣ* as the enclitic between the construct and the absolute in a construct chain, a well-attested phenomenon in biblical poetry (cf. H. Hummel, *JBL*, 76 [1957], pp. 92-93, 97-99 for examples; also M. Dahood, *Psalms III* [Anchor Bible; Garden City, 1970], pp. 382-83).

ISAIAH 42,13

The translation of Isaiah 42,13 in the RSV may be taken as representative:

> The Lord goes forth like a mighty man,
>   like a man of war he stirs up his fury;
> he cries out, he shouts aloud,
>   he shows himself mighty against his foes.

By following the Masoretic punctuation, which divides the verse at *qinʾâ* 'fury,' the translators failed to preserve the basic poetic structure and metrical symmetry of the couplet, and thereby obscured the meaning and intention of the prophet. On the basis both of parallelism and meter, we hold that the word *qinʾâ* should be assigned to the third colon of the verse rather than the second where it is now placed. Such a shift would restore a proper balance between the first two cola: thus "Yahweh" serves as the subject of both verbs; *kaggibbōr* is paralleled by *kĕʾîš milḥāmôt* (ballast variant); the verbs *yēṣēʾ* and *yāʿîr* match nicely. Each colon consists of three stresses and exactly seven syllables.

Turning to the second pair of cola, we note first the internal parallelism between *qinʾâ yārîaʿ*, "with passion he shouts," and *ʾap yaṣrîaḥ*, "with rage he bellows." The term *qinʾâ* is used regularly with words for anger, fury, etc., and is found in parallel construction with *ʾap* in the Bible.[1] We might expect the preposition *bĕ* to be used with *qinʾâ* after verbs of speaking, as is the case in prose passages.[2] The omission of the preposition in poetry, however, is not uncommon.[3] Each colon consists of three stresses and seven syllables.[4]

[1]Dt 29,19; Ez 35,11. It also occurs with *ḥēmâ*, Ez 5,13; 16,38.42; 23,25; 36,6; and with *ʿebrâ*, Ez 38,19.

[2]Ez 5,13; 36,6 (cf. 35,11).

[3]An interesting example of such an omission is to be found in Am 2,7, where we read:

> *wĕderek ʿănāwîm yaṭṭû*
>   "and turn aside the way of the afflicted" (RSV).

The clause should be interpreted, however, in the light of Jb 24,4, where we read:

> *yaṭṭû ʾebyônîm middārek*
>   "they thrust the poor off the road" (RSV).

Note also Am 5,12 which reads:

Our rendering of the verse follows:

(7) Yahweh as a warrior goes forth,
(7) as a man of battle he stirs himself;[5]
(7) with passion he shouts; with rage
he bellows;
(7) over his enemies he prevails.

---

wĕʾebyônîm baššaʿar hiṭṭû
"they push the poor out (!) of the gate."

In the light of these passages, and the principle suggested above, we would render the passage in Am 2,7 as follows: "They push the humble out of the way."

[4]There is considerable leeway in counting stresses, and it would be possible to count four in the first colon, and two in the second. With regard to syllable-counting, we do not include the furtive *pataḥ* which is a late development in the history of the language, and a very slight sound at best.

[5]For the absolute use of *ʿwr* in the Hiphil, see Ps 35,23; Jb 8,6.

GOD ALMIGHTY IN PSALM 78,59

The Hebrew original, and the standard English version of Ps 78,59 are

šāmaᶜ ᵓĕlōhīm wayyitᶜabbār	When God heard, he was full of wrath
wayyimᵓas mĕᵓōd bĕyiśrāᵓēl	and he utterly rejected Israel. (RSV)

Although the text is clearly intact, and the rendering both reasonable and clear, I think it is possible to improve the latter, and on the basis of new insights and data, to come closer to the poet's intention. I propose a new rendering of the second colon for reasons that are both negative and positive:

1) Although the verb *mᵓs* occurs more than 70 times in the Hebrew Bible, it is never used with *mᵓd* elsewhere, or in fact with any other adverb. While the usage here is theoretically possible, and cannot be ruled out automatically, it is doubtful. If the poet had wished to express the idea, "he utterly rejected," the normal method of doing so was at hand in the infinitive absolute construction: cf. Jer 14,19, Lam 5,22.[1]

2) The divine epithet *mᵓd* "the Almighty," has been identified in the Hebrew Bible by M. Dahood, and supported by a number of compelling examples in the Psalter.[2] Another instance of this term, therefore, should occasion no surprise. In Ps 78,59, as also in Ps 46,2,[3] the word *mᵓd* is parallel to *ᵓlhym*, and provides us with a well-balanced bicolon:

God heard and was enraged
Then the Almighty rejected Israel.

[1]Incidentally, it is in Lam 5,22 that we find the only indirect connection between *mᵓs* and *mᵓd*. There we have the infinitive absolute construction, *māᵓōs mĕᵓastānū* "you have utterly rejected us," in parallel with *qāṣaptā ᶜālēnū ᶜad-mĕᵓōd* "you were excessively angry at us."

[2]Cf. M. Dahood, *Psalms III* in the Anchor Bible Series (Garden City, NY, 1970), Index, p. 473, under *māᵓēd* "Grand One." Since the root meaning of *mᵓd* is linked with "strength" in Hebrew, I prefer the rendering "Mighty One" or "the Almighty" when applied to the deity.

[3]See Dahood's discussion in *Psalms III*, p. xxvi.

INDEXES

SUBJECT INDEX

Boldface page numbers indicate a major entry—that is, a direct and substantial discussion. Minor entries are indicated by regular type; they are brief references without detailed discussion.

—*see* inversion
—*see* parallelism
—*see* personification
—*see* refrain
—*see* repetition
—time span (in victory odes) 147, 170
pottery 4
precative perfect 65, 68, 299
precentor 194, 195
preposition 251, 343, 344, 345
—omission of 345
priesthood **164-65**
promised land 145, 148
prophets 18, 19, 20, 21
—Former 6, 13, 34, 168
—oracles of 2
—poetry of 1, 13, 17, 23, 34, 45
Psalter 45, 102, 104, 108, 110, 188, 200, 208, 296-97, 315
pseudonymous writings 19
punctuation, Massoretic 27, 191
Punic 270

Qal and Hiphil 289
Qumran 4, 19, 63, 305
—1QIs[a] 39
—4QDt(32) 4, 100, 101, 123
—4QSam[a] 123, 251, 254, 255, 257, 258, 260
—4QSam[b] 266
—11QPs[a] 69, 303, 307
Quran 20

Rahab 139
Rameses II 132, 133, 142, 147, 177
Rameses III 135, 142, 162
reconstruction 2, 6, 8, 68, 109, 197, 198, 200, 201, 305, 320
refrain 33, 45-46, 179, 188-89, 191, 193, 194, 209, 213, 215, 216, 217, 222
reintroduction 330
relative pronoun (*ʾašer*) 2, 3-4, 199, 327
repetition 41, 46, 150, 151, 188-89, 206, 210, 215, 238, 246, 283, 305, 307, 309, 312
restoration, textual 3, 8, 45
rhyme 204, 236, 311
rhythm 7, 20, 26, 29, 30, 31, 32, 33, 34, 35, 36, 37, 41, 42, 43, 44, 53, 168, 187, 189, 192, 201, 204, 219, 306
—balancing 30, 32, 33, 35, 43, 44, 46
—echoing 30, 31, 33, 35
—falling 26, 42
—unbalanced 30, 42, 43, 44, 45
ritual 2, 16
rubric 329, 330

Samaritan Pentateuch 81, 86, 113, 200
Samson 156, 174, 177
Samuel 12, 33, 34, 97, 119,
Samuel, books of 18, 157, 166, 174, 178
Saul 79, 117, 155, 156, 157, 166, 173, 174, 177, 178
sea peoples 135, 142, 162
seers 18
segolates 192, 198, 245, 266, 279, 305, 313, 326
semantics 248
Septuagint (LXX) 28, 34, 41, 69, 81, 86, 89, 93, 100, 101, 113, 121, 198, 204, 207, 251, 254, 255, 256, 257, 260, 261, 266, 304, 305
seven 259
Shamgar 149
Shechem 84, 88, 156, 164, 172, 176
shepherd **275-302**
Shiloh 136, 141, 164, 166
Shittim 134
Sihon 15, 159, 163
Simeon 152, 153, 155, 156, 157, 164, 173, 174, 175, 176, 178
Sinai/Horeb 83, 88, 134, 136, 137, 138, 139, 140, 147, 148, 158, 160, 161, 165, 172, 174, 177, 178
—abode of Yahweh 135, 136, 137, 139, 158, 300
—location 138, 139
—proto-Canaanite inscriptions 88
Sisera 147, 158, 159, 160
Solomon 156, 157, 168, 174, 177, 178
Song of Deborah (Judges 5) 15, 16, 82, 105, 131, 132, 133, 143, **147-60**, **160-66**, 168, 172, 188, 194, 199, 226, 235, 258, 270, 310
—bibliography 147
—date 77, 78, 131, 132, 149, 160
—divine names **83-85**, 91, 104, 110, 165, 177, 300
—and Israel 14, 104, 110, 117, 152, 153, 153, 169, 172, 177
—tribes in 152, 153, 156, 157, 176, 177
Song of Hannah (2 Samuel 2:1-10) 5, 6, 9, 77, **93-94**, 109, 150, **243-61**
Song of Heshbon (Numbers 21:27-30) 159
Song of Moses (Deuteronomy 32) 14, 15, 77, **99-102**, 169
Song of the Sea (Exodus 15) 15, 16, 17, 44, **77-82**, 82, 83, 131, **132-46**, 160, 162, 168, 170, 171, **179-86**, **187-227**, 194, 235, 310
—composition 17

AUTHOR INDEX

SCRIPTURE INDEX

Joshua

Judges

Ruth

1 Samuel

Proverbs

Song of Songs

Isaiah

for Qumran references see Qumran in Subject Index

LANGUAGE INDEX